Cheers and Tears

A Marine's Story of Combat

In Peace and War

by

Lieutenant General Charles G. Cooper, U.S. Marine Corps (Retired)

with
Richard E. Goodspeed

Printed in Victoria, Canada

Co-published with:
Wesley Press
P.O. Box 33306, Reno, NV 89533
Phone (775) 322-6260
e-mail: wesleypress@charter.net

National Library of Canada Cataloguing in Publication Data

Cooper, Charles G., 1927-
 Cheers and tears : a marine's story of combat
in peace and war / Charles G. Cooper.
ISBN 1-55369-882-7
 I. Title.
VE25.C66A3 2002   359.9'6'092   C2002-903889-8

TRAFFORD

This book was published *on-demand* in cooperation with Trafford Publishing.
On-demand publishing is a unique process and service of making a book available for retail sale to the public taking advantage of on-demand manufacturing and Internet marketing.
On-demand publishing includes promotions, retail sales, manufacturing, order fulfilment, accounting and collecting royalties on behalf of the author.

Suite 6E, 2333 Government St., Victoria, B.C. V8T 4P4, CANADA
Phone   250-383-6864   Toll-free   1-888-232-4444 (Canada & US)
Fax   250-383-6804   E-mail   sales@trafford.com
Web site   www.trafford.com   TRAFFORD PUBLISHING IS A DIVISION OF TRAFFORD HOLDINGS LTD.
Trafford Catalogue #02-0695   www.trafford.com/robots/02-0695.html

10   9   8   7   6   5   4   3

Contents

Acknowledgments

I have enjoyed the benefits of working under, with and above many exceptional people in my 35+ years as an active Marine Officer. (Many of them appear in this book.) Although I owe them a great deal they are too numerous to mention individually here. Many others have earned my deepest gratitude: old friends, associates, and family, all of whom urged me on and helped me to move forward in producing this book of memories.

I dedicate this book to the fighting Marines of Baker Company, 1st Battalion, Fifth Marines, 1st Marine Division, with whom I shared my baptism of fire in the spring and summer of 1951. They were and still are, my "Band of Brothers," spurring me on to recall the events that form the book's foundation. Their selfless devotion and personal heroism are the basis for the creed I offer in this story as a role model for the entire Corps.

Others persisted in encouraging me to write down the "sea stories" they had heard. To Jim Carrington, a Navy football teammate; to Thomas "Tee" Luster, a boyhood friend and a high school teammate; to my own dear mother, Anna Cooper; to my mother-in-law, Vesta Edgerton; and to my wife, Carol, and children, Chip and Linda, all of whom have pressed me forward when I lagged behind, I extend my sincerest appreciation.

Two special friends and associates helped me immensely to focus my wandering thoughts and experiences. Initially, Major General Jarvis Lynch USMC (Ret.) assisted me in organizing the early portions of the story without detracting from its message. Later, a Naval Academy Classmate, Dick Goodspeed, offered his remarkable editorial skills to condense the text and give the entire book his magic touch. To both, I am especially indebted. The story is mine, but they helped me make it into *Cheers & Tears*.

Finally, to my wonderful wife of 51+ years (at the time of this writing), who read every page, red pen in hand, crying over some, and recommending rewrite on others, I send my love and deepest appreciation. She stayed with me to the end and often had a better memory than I. To my Carol: Thanks, My Love!

C.G. Cooper
Falls Church, Virginia
21 April 2002

"The Day It Became the Longest War " reprinted by permission of U.S. Naval Institute.

"Hill 907" reprinted by permission U.S. Naval Academy Alumni Association.

Preface

Organizations, at least the big ones, routinely identify the "nuggets," those having the potential to rise to the top, and put them on the fast track to positions at the upper levels.

The American post-World War II military uses such an organizational approach – but it is a little different than its civilian counterpart. The Military fast track is no guarantee of eventual elevation to high places. Yes, it does give relatively young officers access to power positions and those who occupy them. It also gives them repeated opportunities to command; but the military profession is less forgiving than those who are not part of it may think. For example, the officer of impeccable command credentials may be found wanting in a high-visibility Washington staff assignment and quietly taken off the track. Or the promising, polished and highly regarded staff officer may prove to be a bust in the field and eventually realize that the special attention he once enjoyed has evaporated. Or – and not to belabor the point – the meteor of the meteor-like career can burn out. Too many long nights or weekends at headquarters or aboard ship and too man family separations during long overseas employments can shake the strongest of constitutions and the most rock solid of marriages.

Then there's the biggest difference of all. Placed in harms way to prove themselves and climb another of the ladder's rungs, those of greatest promise can be and often are killed. In short, the military fast tracker is expected to take risks – even grave ones.

There is normally nothing formal about the decision to put an officer on the fast track. A senior somewhere decides that an officer may have extraordinarily high potential and throws him or her into the nearest available cauldron, hoping for the best. If the outcome is good, if all reasonable expectations are exceeded, the word gets around. The run on the fast track, a career of hard challenges and high rewards, is launched.

Charlie Cooper was one of those who were put on the fast track early – as a second lieutenant – and never got off. It almost killed him. But he survived, learned, led, taught, and rose to high command. The run on the track ended with retirement as a Lieutenant General of Marines

Jarvis D. Lynch
Major General, U.S. Marine Corps
(Retired)

Introduction

The Day It Became the Longest War
"The President will see you at two o'clock."

It was a beautiful fall day in November of 1965, early in the Vietnam War—too beautiful a day to be what many of us, anticipating it, had been calling "the day of reckoning." We didn't know how accurate that label would be.

The Pentagon is a busy place. Its workday starts early—especially if, as the expression goes, "there's a war on." By seven o'clock, the staff of Admiral David L. McDonald, the Navy's senior admiral and Chief of Naval Operations, had started to work. Shortly after seven, Admiral McDonald arrived and began making final preparations for a meeting with President Lyndon Baines Johnson.

The Vietnam War was in its first year, and its uncertain direction troubled Admiral McDonald and the other service chiefs. They'd had a number of disagreements with Secretary of Defense Robert S. McNamara about strategy, and had finally requested a private meeting with the Commander in Chief—a perfectly legitimate procedure. Now, after many delays, the Joint Chiefs were finally to have that meeting. They hoped it would determine whether the US military would continue its seemingly directionless buildup to fight a protracted ground war, or take bold measures that would bring the war to an early and victorious end. The bold measures they would propose were to apply massive air power to the head of the enemy, Hanoi, and to close North Vietnam's harbors by mining.

The situation was not a simple one, and for several reasons. The most important reason was that North Vietnam's neighbor to the north was communist China. Only 12 years had passed since the Korean War had ended in stalemate. The aggressors in that war had been the North Koreans. When the North Koreans' defeat had appeared to be inevitable, communist China had sent hundreds of thousands of its Peoples' Liberation Army "volunteers" to the rescue.

Now, in this new war, the North Vietnamese aggressor had the logistic support of the Soviet Union and, more to the point, of neighboring communist China. Although we had the air and naval forces with which to paralyze North Vietnam, we had to consider the possible reactions of the Chinese and the Russians.

Both China and the Soviet Union had pledged to support North Vietnam in the "war of national liberation" it was fighting to reunite the divided country, and both had the wherewithal to cause major problems. An important unknown was what the Russians would do if prevented from delivering goods to their communist protege in Hanoi. A more important question concerned communist China, next-door neighbor to North Vietnam. How would the Chinese react to a massive pummeling of their ally? More specifically, would they enter the war as they had done in North Korea? Or would they let the Vietnamese, for centuries a traditional enemy, fend for themselves? The service chiefs had considered these and similar questions, and had also asked the Central Intelligence Agency for answers and estimates.

The CIA was of little help, though it produced reams of text, executive summaries of the texts, and briefs of the executive summaries—all top secret, all extremely sensitive,

1

and all of little use. The principal conclusion was that it was impossible to predict with any accuracy what the Chinese or Russians might do.

Despite the lack of a clear-cut intelligence estimate, Admiral McDonald and the other Joint Chiefs did what they were paid to do and reached a conclusion. They decided unanimously that the risk of the Chinese or Soviets reacting to massive US measures taken in North Vietnam was acceptably low, but only if we acted without delay. Unfortunately, the Secretary of Defense and his coterie of civilian "whiz kids" did not agree with the Joint Chiefs, and McNamara and his people were the ones who were actually steering military strategy. In the view of the Joint Chiefs, the United States was piling on forces in Vietnam without understanding the consequences. In the view of McNamara and his civilian team, we were doing the right thing. This was the fundamental dispute that had caused the Chiefs to request the seldom-used private audience with the Commander in Chief in order to present their military recommendations directly to him. McNamara had finally granted their request.

The 1965 Joint Chiefs of Staff had ample combat experience. Each was serving in his third war. The Chairman was General Earle Wheeler, US Army, highly regarded by the other members.

General Harold Johnson was the Army Chief of Staff. A World War II prisoner of the Japanese, he was a soft-spoken, even-tempered, deeply religious man.

General John P. McConnell, Air Force Chief of Staff, was a native of Arkansas and a 1932 graduate of West Point.

The Commandant of the Marine Corps was General Wallace M. Greene, Jr., a slim, short, all-business Marine. General Greene was a Naval Academy graduate and a zealous protector of the Marine Corps concept of controlling its own air resources as part of an integrated air-ground team.

Last and by no means least was Admiral McDonald, a Georgia minister's son, also a Naval Academy graduate, and a naval aviator. While Admiral McDonald was a most capable leader, he was also a reluctant warrior. He did not like what he saw emerging as a national commitment. He did not really want the US to get involved with land warfare, believing as he did that the Navy could apply sea power against North Vietnam very effectively by mining, blockading, and assisting in a bombing campaign, and in this way help to bring the war to a swift and satisfactory conclusion.

The Joint Chiefs intended that the prime topics of the meeting with the President would be naval matters—the mining and blockading of the port of Haiphong and naval support of a bombing campaign aimed at Hanoi. For that reason, the Navy was to furnish a briefing map, and that became my responsibility. We mounted a suitable map on a large piece of plywood, then coated it with clear acetate so that the chiefs could mark on it with grease pencils during the discussion. The whole thing weighed about 30 pounds.

The Military Office at the White House agreed to set up an easel in the Oval Office to hold the map. I would accompany Admiral McDonald to the White House with the map, put the map in place when the meeting started, then get out. There would be no strap-hangers at the military summit meeting with Lyndon Johnson.

The map and I joined Admiral McDonald in his staff car for the short drive to the White House, a drive that was memorable only because of the silence. My admiral was totally preoccupied.

2

The chiefs' appointment with the President was for two o'clock, and Admiral McDonald and I arrived about 20 minutes early. The chiefs were ushered into a fairly large room across the hall from the Oval Office. I propped the map board on the arms of a fancy chair where all could view it, left two of the grease pencils in the tray attached to the bottom of the board, and stepped out into the corridor. One of the chiefs shut the door, and they conferred in private until someone on the White House staff interrupted them about fifteen minutes later. As they came out, I retrieved the map, then joined them in the corridor outside the President's office.

Precisely at two o'clock President Johnson emerged from the Oval Office and greeted the chiefs. He was all charm. He was also big: at three or more inches over six feet tall and something on the order of 250 pounds, he was bigger than any of the chiefs. He personally ushered them into his office, all the while delivering gracious and solicitous comments with a Texas accent far more pronounced than the one that came through when he spoke on television. Holding the map board as the chiefs entered, I peered between them, trying to find the easel. There was none. The President looked at me, grasped the situation at once, and invited me in, adding, "You can stand right over here." I had become an easel—one with eyes and ears.

To the right of the door, not far inside the office, large windows framed evergreen bushes growing in a nearby garden. The President's desk and several chairs were farther in, diagonally across the room from the windows. The President positioned me near the windows, then arranged the chiefs in a semicircle in front of the map and its human easel. He did not offer them seats: they stood, with those who were to speak—Wheeler, McDonald, and McConnell—standing nearest the President. Paradoxically, the two whose services were most affected by a continuation of the ground buildup in Vietnam—Generals Johnson and Greene—stood farthest from the President. President Johnson stood nearest the door, about five feet from the map.

In retrospect, the setup—the failure to have an easel in place, the positioning of the chiefs on the outer fringe of the office, the lack of seating—did not augur well. The chiefs had expected the meeting to be a short one, and it met that expectation. They also expected it to be of momentous import, and it met that expectation, too. Unfortunately, it also proved to be a meeting that was critical to the proper pursuit of what was to become the longest, most divisive, and least conclusive war in our nation's history—a war that almost tore the nation apart.

As General Wheeler started talking, President Johnson peered at the map. In five minutes or so, the general summarized our entry into Vietnam, the current status of forces, and the purpose of the meeting. Then he thanked the President for having given his senior military advisers the opportunity to present their opinions and recommendations. Finally, he noted that although Secretary McNamara did not subscribe to their views, he did agree that a presidential-level decision was required. President Johnson, arms crossed, seemed to be listening carefully.

The essence of General Wheeler's presentation was that we had come to an early moment of truth in our ever-increasing Vietnam involvement. We had to start using our principal strengths—air and naval power—to punish the North Vietnamese, or we would risk becoming involved in another protracted Asian ground war with no prospects of a satisfactory solution. Speaking for the chiefs, General Wheeler offered a bold course of action that would avoid protracted land warfare. He proposed that we isolate the major port of Haiphong through naval mining, blockade the rest of the North Vietnamese coastline, and simultaneously start bombing Hanoi with B-52's.

General Wheeler then asked Admiral McDonald to describe how the Navy and Air Force would combine forces to mine the waters off Haiphong and establish a naval blockade. When Admiral McDonald finished, General McConnell added that speed of execution would be essential, and that we would have to make the North Vietnamese believe that we would increase the level of punishment if they did not sue for peace.

Normally, time dims our memories—but it hasn't dimmed this one. My memory of Lyndon Johnson on that day remains crystal clear. While General Wheeler, Admiral McDonald, and General McConnell spoke, he seemed to be listening closely, communicating only with an occasional nod. When General McConnell finished, General Wheeler asked the President if he had any questions. Johnson waited a moment or so, then turned to Generals Johnson and Greene, who had remained silent during the briefing, and asked, "Do you fully support these ideas?" He followed with the thought that it was they who were providing the ground troops, in effect acknowledging that the Army and the Marines were the services that had most to gain or lose as a result of this discussion. Both generals indicated their agreement with the proposal. Seemingly deep in thought, President Johnson turned his back on them for a minute or so, then suddenly discarding the calm, patient demeanor he had maintained throughout the meeting, whirled to face them and exploded.

I almost dropped the map. He screamed obscenities, he cursed them personally, he ridiculed them for coming to his office with their "military advice." Noting that it was he who was carrying the weight of the free world on his shoulders, he called them filthy names—shitheads, dumb shits, pompous assholes—and used "the F-word" as an adjective more freely than a Marine in boot camp would use it. He then accused them of trying to pass the buck for World War III to him. It was unnerving, degrading.

After the tantrum, he resumed the calm, relaxed manner he had displayed earlier and again folded his arms. It was as though he had punished them, cowed them, and would now control them. Using soft-spoken profanities, he said something to the effect that they all knew now that he did not care about their military advice. After disparaging their abilities, he added that he did expect their help.

He suggested that each one of them change places with him and assume that five incompetents had just made these "military recommendations." He told them that he was going to let them go through what he had to go through when idiots gave him stupid advice, adding that he had the whole damn world to worry about, and it was time to "see what kind of guts you have." He paused, as if to let it sink in. The silence was like a palpable solid, the tension like that in a drumhead. After thirty or forty seconds of this, he turned to General Wheeler and demanded that Wheeler say what he would do if he were the President of the United States.

General Wheeler took a deep breath before answering. He was not an easy man to shake: his calm response set the tone for the others. He had known coming in, as had the others, that Lyndon Johnson was an exceptionally strong personality, and a venal and vindictive man as well. He had known that the stakes were high, and now realized that McNamara had prepared Johnson carefully for this meeting, which had been a charade.

4

Looking President Johnson squarely in the eye, General Wheeler told him that he understood the tremendous pressure and sense of responsibility Johnson felt. He added that probably no other President in history had had to make a decision of this importance, and further cushioned his remarks by saying that no matter how much about the presidency he did understand, there were many things about it that only one human being could ever understand. General Wheeler closed his remarks by saying something very close to this: "You, Mr. President, are that one human being. I cannot take your place, think your thoughts, know all you know, and tell you what I would do if I were you. I can't do it, Mr. President. No man can honestly do it. Respectfully, sir, it is your decision and yours alone."

Apparently unmoved, Johnson asked each of the other Chiefs the same question. One at a time, they supported General Wheeler and his rationale. By now, my arms felt as though they were about to break. The map seemed to weigh a ton, but the end appeared to be near. General Greene was the last to speak.

When General Greene finished, President Johnson, who was nothing if not a skilled actor, looked sad for a moment, then suddenly erupted again, yelling and cursing, again using language that even a Marine seldom hears. He told them he was disgusted with their naive approach, and that he was not going to let some military idiots talk him into World War III. He ended the conference by shouting "Get the hell out of my office!"

The Joint Chiefs of Staff had done their duty. They knew that the nation was making a strategic military error, and despite the rebuffs of their civilian masters in the Pentagon, they had insisted on presenting the problem as they saw it to the highest authority and recommending solutions. They had done so, and they had been rebuffed. That authority had not only rejected their solutions, but had also insulted and demeaned them. As Admiral McDonald and I drove back to the Pentagon, he turned to me and said that he had known tough days in his life, and sad ones as well, but ". . . this has got to have been the worst experience I could ever imagine."

The US involvement in Vietnam lasted another ten years. The irony is that it began to end only when President Richard Nixon, after some backstage maneuvering on the international scene, did precisely what the Joint Chiefs of Staff had recommended to President Johnson in 1965. Why had Johnson not only dismissed their recommendations, but also ridiculed them? It must have been that Johnson had lacked something. Maybe it was foresight or boldness. Maybe it was the sophistication and understanding it took to deal with complex international issues. Or, since he was clearly a bully, maybe what he lacked was courage. We will never know. But had General Wheeler and the others received a fair hearing, and had their recommendations received serious study, the United States may well have saved the lives of most of its more than 55,000 sons who died in a war that its major architect, Robert Strange McNamara, now considers to have been a tragic mistake.

5

Chapter 1

Clarksdale, Mississippi
"I'd Rather Be a Bullfrog . . ."

The Mississippi delta town of Clarksdale was not a bad place to grow up during the Great Depression of the 1930's. In fact, it was one of the best. Times were tough—but people took care of each other. Those who could afford to do so hired people to do make-work jobs, but the numbers of unemployed never seemed to stop growing. I cannot recall Mother turning away anyone who came to our back door to ask for food. They came and they came. Black and white. Singles and families. We knew nothing about "welfare": there just wasn't any. Everyone who had anything shared it with someone less fortunate. Health permitting, those receiving help worked at some chore to pay for the meal or meals. Those who weren't well enough or strong enough to do chores still received the help.

Clarksdale was a plantation town of 10,000 or so in the heart of the deep South's cotton country. It was largely a credit community—the farmers settled their debts "when the crops came in." The town's population was about evenly divided between whites and blacks: the surrounding Coahoma County's population was primarily black. We also had a growing number of immigrants from Italy and Syria, mostly truck farmers attracted to the fertile black delta soil. Surprisingly enough, we also had a small Chinese business community scattered across the county.

Clarksdale was a microcosm of the Bible Belt. All races emphasized family and church. And all, even the new immigrants, lived the southern traditions, especially those related to the military. Service in the nation's armed forces was a point of great personal and family pride. Most of the middle-aged men, including my father, were World War I veterans. Our "40 and 8" chapter of the American Legion (named for the World War I French railroad cars that carried 40 men or 8 horses) was highly respected and a positive influence in the community.

My father had spent more time in France than most of the other veterans. In 1915 many of his friends went through flight training and then joined the Lafayette Escadrille, a squadron of American volunteers who fought for the French before America entered the war. Dad, having lost an eye in a childhood accident, was not qualified to fly. He was more than qualified to help, however, by raising enough money from a wealthy uncle and others to recruit and equip a volunteer ambulance company. He became a sergeant in the US Red Cross Medical Auxiliary and went to France with his company to support the British Expeditionary Force. When America entered the war in 1917, the US Army, overlooking the eye problem, commissioned him in the Army Medical Service and promoted him to the grade of captain. His ambulance company and field hospital supported the Marines in 1918, and he remained in France after the war with US Army units that were later deployed to Russia.

During my childhood, Dad often showed me his World War I photo album and its snapshots of him with the Royal Air Force or with the Fifth Marine Regiment of the US Army's Second Division. He often spoke of the time his field hospital supported the US Marines during the 1918 battle of Belleau Wood, about 50 kilometers northeast of Paris. It was there that the Marines, in a bloody struggle, stopped the lead elements of Germany's last offensive of the war. The album also contained numerous pictures of a lovely French lady—whom I was to meet years later.

Other fathers in town must have been showing similar albums, with or without photos of pretty French ladies, because at one time little Clarksdale had four of its sons attending Annapolis, two at West Point, and many more in the ROTC units of civilian colleges. While those numbers say much about the southern attitude toward service to country, they say even more about the strength of the local school system.

As positive an influence as Dad was, the fact remains that he lost both his business and his health during the Great Depression. Mother was the rock upon which I and my younger sister and brother relied. She worked almost full time at a variety of jobs, and in the mid-30's ran Dad's resurrected business for months when he had a series of major illnesses. Mom was also one of those who helped make the school system a superior one. She augmented the family income by working as a substitute teacher, and at one point became the fulltime teacher in a one-room schoolhouse outside town. Her students' parents were immigrant farmers who could not afford to send their children to the city schools. The county found a schoolhouse and recruited Mom to run the school. "Miss Anna," as she was respectfully and affectionately called, trained the older children to teach the younger ones, a practical and effective way to reach the hodgepodge of ages and abilities in her classroom. I was three years old: I went to school with her, sat with the little guys up front, and became one of the pupils.

A large part of the teaching in those days was oral recitation, a particularly important way of learning for those pupils whose parents spoke little or no English. Miss Anna encouraged communication skills in every conceivable way: I can still hear her admonition to "always speak up, look your audience in the eye, and have your subject matter organized." She gave her all for wages paid largely in the form of farm produce and promised labor. She also ensured that her son was getting a solid educational foundation.

The city fathers had wisely insisted on a first class school system and enacted tax laws to ensure that it would be staffed with the best talent available. In the 1920's they brought in a tough, dedicated, uncompromising young German-American educator, Harvey Heidelberg, to establish the system. He exceeded all expectations. Clarksdale city schools led the state in caliber of teachers, level of teachers' pay, requirements for student promotion and graduation, and excellence of curriculum. Those going beyond high school studied college-level courses during their senior year. As a result, our graduates attended major universities throughout the country and always excelled. Our system even produced a Rhodes Scholar. We also had an excellent extra-curricular program that featured a band and orchestra as well as athletic teams that received the fervent support of the small student body and the town. Even Heidelberg, the normally humorless Superintendent of Schools, got carried away at a football pep rally before a game with archrival Greenwood, declaring in his thick German accent that he "would rather be a bullfrog living on the banks of the Sunflower River in Clarksdale than a millionaire in Greenwood." The bullfrog symbol caught on—so much so that the local chamber of commerce still encourages those raised in Clarksdale to return after retirement and "be a big frog in a little pond."

Despite the financial struggles of the Great Depression, Dad's health problems, and the anxieties brought on by World War II, my childhood was full of adventure and fun. While

I was having fun, my loving parents and others were making certain that I was well prepared for adulthood.

The summer of 1945 ended my permanent association with Clarksdale. Now it was time to "get on with it." The first stop was the University of Mississippi, where I spent three busy semesters in one year as an engineering student on athletic scholarship----a blur of classes, labs, and football practices. I was a starting left tackle for the Ole Miss Rebels, as major colleges manned their teams with youngsters while awaiting the return of veterans. Ole Miss was like a big, friendly southern family—an ideal college life. Yet I was experiencing a growing desire to attend Annapolis as the reality of military service demanded a decision. Rip Miller, the Naval Academy's line coach and recruiter, wrote me repeatedly, encouraging me to apply for entrance in 1946. With the full support of my parents I left the pleasant environment of Ole Miss for the more rigidly structured life of the Naval Academy.

My decision to attend Annapolis opened the route to what would become a 35-year career as a United States Marine, a career of challenges, opportunities, rewards, and association with some of the finest people the nation has ever produced. It was a decision I never regretted and, next to the decision to marry my Carol, the best one I ever made.

Chapter 2

The Apprenticeship
"Midshipmen and Third Lieutenants"

The Naval Academy of 1946 may have differed little from the academy of previous decades, but the Class of 1950, the first of the post-World-War-II classes, was far different from its predecessors and, for that matter, from those that followed. We started with 915 Midshipmen, which was not unusual. What was unusual was the fact that roughly 70% of them had had previous military experience. Several hundred had attended the Naval Academy Preparatory School at Bainbridge, Maryland, as enlisted sailors or Marines. A dozen or more had been commissioned officers, and several of them wore Navy or Army Air Corps pilot's wings. Several hundred more had attended college as members of World War II officer programs, the best known of which was probably the Navy's V-12 program. And finally, there were those in my category—younger than most, with no military experience, but with a year or two of college under our belts. It was the oldest Class ever to enter the Academy, it had the most military experience, and it also had, in aggregate, more academic preparation than any Class before it or, probably, after it.

Four years later, on 2 June 1950, 691 of us graduated. The attrition rate of about 24% is probably about average for Naval Academy Classes and, as usual, was mainly a result of the stresses of Plebe (freshman) Year (initially) and academics (eventually).

Plebe year was designed to test our mettle and adaptability, and to weed out those men who did not have a strong desire to become Navy or Marine officers. A big part of the weeding-out process was hazing, with its physical exercises, harassment, drills—any number of things that made a Plebe's life miserable. There was, however, no physical "laying on of hands." Many of the combat-experienced veterans saw no need for this harassment, often delivered by upperclassmen who were younger than they, and left during the summer or first semester. Most who left, however, did so after the first-semester exams.

The curriculum was much the same as it had been for decades—with history courses changing when current events became history, and engineering, ordnance, and aviation courses changing as the technology advanced. With the exception of foreign languages, there were no electives. The Midshipman studied a foreign language during his first two years, and he supposedly had a choice of language. However, the Academy urged him to "elect" a language he had studied before or one that his family had spoken at home.

There was usually a daily quiz in every class session, a quiz which, on good days, came right after the instructor had gone over the day's lesson. On bad days, the class took the quiz before receiving the explanation—an approach designed to encourage the student to prepare the assigned lesson. It was a fast track, made all the faster by the college experience already resident in the class. Had it not been for my three semesters at Ole Miss, I would have been lost. Many of the textbooks we used were the same ones civilian colleges used, so some of us had seen them before. But the speed at which we covered the material far exceeded the pace in the colleges and universities we attended.

The underlying regimen throughout the four years was one of discipline and institutional socialization. For example, we marched to all classes: quite often, an officer or senior Midshipman inspected us after we had formed up to march off to the academic buildings.

9

We also marched to meals, giving the powers that be another opportunity to inspect us before we marched off. It was possible for any one of us to undergo as many as seven uniform inspections during a full academic day.

Socially, our four years at the Academy amounted to a deliberate leveling process. My Classmates included the sons of wealthy, worldly families, along with those whose last names ended in a vowel, those whose fathers were coal miners, and those who were of the first generation born in America. Many of the latter received mail from home written in a foreign language, but otherwise the differences between us—among us—were unidentifiable. We were not allowed to have automobiles: those who had money had little or no free time away from the Academy to spend it. Perhaps to emphasize the point that life in the military was not the road to riches, we received cash allowances of $4, $7, $15, and $21 per month, respectively, in the years from our Plebe to First Class (senior) years.

Athletics were the primary means of letting off steam: everyone played a sport, whether he needed it or not. Despite the stern atmosphere, the lack of freedom, the discipline, and the unremitting academic pressure, there were good times to be had, rewards to be enjoyed, and solid lessons to be learned.

The first of my major lessons occurred during exam week at the end of Plebe Year's first semester. As good as Superintendent Heidelberg's school system had been back in Clarksdale, it had never put a foreign language into my curriculum. That's probably why the Academy had me study Spanish, considered to be the easiest of foreign languages to learn. I was concerned about the Spanish final exam, but fear is a great motivator and for that reason, if for no other, I was well prepared. Prepared, that is, until the bell rang in the large room used for exams and almost a thousand of us turned over the examination papers to begin work. Mine was marked at the top *Tercero Clase*. Even at that stage of Spanish experience, I knew that the paper was an examination for the Third Class (sophomores), knowledge that I confirmed when, upon examining the paper, I found that the major requirement was to write a 500-word theme on the World War II "Evacuation of Dunkirk." Sweating bullets, I raised my hand, seeking help.

A nearby exam proctor, an all-too-obvious master of the impatient frown, came to my desk. Despite my earnest efforts, he managed to neither pay attention to what I was saying nor look at the *tercero clase* examination. His only reaction was to comment to the effect that, "Nobody else is complaining, mister. Get to work."

I tried, but to little avail. After one hour, the room began to empty as my Classmates wrapped up their exams: at the final bell some two and one half hours later, I was the only one left. My thoroughly impatient Spanish section was waiting outside to march back to our company area in Bancroft Hall, our huge dormitory. Back in our room, my roommates were all laughing about the exam. One said it was the easiest he had ever taken. When I asked what they had said about the evacuation of Dunkirk, they went silent for a moment, then asked what I was talking about. Their exam, they said, had involved writing about a picnic in the country!

Filled with the confidence of those who believe that though the system may be hard, it is also fair, I quickly went to the Department of Foreign Languages and asked to speak with the department head, a Navy captain. He was astounded that I had been issued the *tercero clase* exam and more than annoyed that the proctor had done nothing to correct the situation. Directing me to look through the glass partition separating his office from the instructors' "bullpen," he asked if I could see the proctor. After I pointed him out, the captain departed at about 60 knots, cornered the professor and verified what I had reported.

The aftermath was short and sweet. It was also instructive. With a cup of coffee provided by the captain, I took the proper exam sitting at his desk and finished it in about 40 minutes. The captain personally graded the paper and in short order I was on my way back to Bancroft Hall with an excellent grade. Before departing, however, I gave the captain my word of honor that I would not discuss the earlier exam with any members of the third class, since they were scheduled to take that same exam on the following day. The captain had listened, done the right things, and, most important, put great trust in a young man's word of honor.

The company areas in Bancroft Hall were close-knit societies, so it did not take long for the Third Classmen in my company to learn that I had seen their final exam in Spanish. On my return, several of them were standing in the hallway outside my room, waiting for me. Marching in the center of the corridor as Plebes were required to do, I had just "squared" the corner to enter my room when I was ordered to halt. They asked what had happened. I told them the story, adding that I had given my word to not discuss the *tercero clase* exam. They understood and went back to their studies. No more was said.

Our summer cruises took us away from the academic world and immersed us in the practical aspects of the Navy. The 1947 cruise was the first major fleet deployment to European waters since World War II. Our task force comprised two battleships, an aircraft carrier, several cruisers, and even more destroyers. A large percentage of the regular enlisted crews had been given leave, not only to make space for us, but also to ensure that there would be plenty of seaman's work available. We, so very recently promoted to Midshipman Third Class, gained an appreciation for what the sailors do by doing what they did: holystoning wooden decks, chipping paint, standing engine-room watches, and manning gun mounts during general quarters. The newly promoted First Classmen performed the duties of junior officers or senior petty officers.

There were few if any hardships associated with the cruises, and life was particularly good in 1947, when we visited such places as Scotland, Norway, Sweden, and England. In England I was able to reestablish contact with my grandfather's family, contacts that we cherish to this day.

It was the cruise of 1948 that taught me how small the world can be for those involved in the naval or military professions. Our first European port of call was Lisbon, Portugal. While we were there, I received a small package from Dad. It contained several photos of a lovely French girl, Evelyn Chauvenet, the girl in many of the pictures in his World War I photo album. It also contained her last known address in Cannes, France, and a letter of explanation. Dad knew that Cannes was our next scheduled port. In the letter, he explained that he and Evelyn had been engaged to be married after World War I. However, since he had not seen his mother for five years, he felt that he should return home to visit her before marrying Evelyn. His mother disapproved of the wedding plans, and Dad never returned to France. He hoped that I would be able to find her.

The Cannes of 1948 was a dream come true for young American sailors, Marines, and Midshipmen. Prices were low and the beautiful beaches were occupied by slim, curvaceous young women covered with sun tan lotion and little else. By late morning of our first day in port, I was ashore, French-English dictionary in hand, strolling down the beach with two buddies whose heads were on swivels—much more interested in the available scenery than helping me search for Dad's old flame. An older gentleman reading in his beach cabana looked up curiously as we passed, and I decided to start the search with him, broken French or not. As I turned toward the cabana, my two "wingmen" veered beachward, hoping to do their bit for American-European relations.

When I reached the gentleman, he introduced himself as Captain Bob Blick, Indian Army, retired, and asked, "May I be of service?" I described my "mission" and found that fate had guided me to the perfect person to hear the story. When he retired from the Indian Army, Captain Blick had taken up residence in Cannes—and knew Evelyn Chauvenet. Indeed, he could hardly avoid knowing her. Evelyn, her English dentist husband, and their daughter, also Evelyn, were his neighbors. He reached for his telephone, spoke briefly in French and then shifted to English, saying something on the order of, "Evelyn, Bob Blick here. You can't possibly believe who I have on the beach with me—a husky Yank Midshipman named Cooper who says his father was hoping he could locate you and pay a call. He's from Mississippi in the States. Would you like to speak to him?" She did and the result was a wonderful week. We met for dinner that evening, and I spent most of the rest of my free time with her and her family. Her attractive twenty-year-old daughter and I had a brief reprise of my father's experience a number of years before.

At the end of the cruise, we had a thirty-day leave. I headed for home, flying into the Memphis airport, some 80 miles from Clarksdale. Usually, both parents met me, but this time it was just Dad. I had written him about the stay in Cannes, and he wanted to spend the drive back to Clarksdale alone with me to hear about it first hand. Dad and I had never been closer.

Our time together that summer became all the more special because he suffered a massive stroke and passed away the following December, just before Christmas. My uncle took on the task of selling the business property and many trucks while I tackled the chore of collecting money that many of the wealthier families in the county owed my father. The two efforts yielded a considerable sum, but once again, "Miss Anna," with a daughter in college and the youngest son at home, would be put to the test. As always, she would meet the challenge. Operating out of a shop added to our garage, she established a successful florist business. She needed the money: Dad left no insurance.

My roommates and I generally fit the Class of 1950's statistical mold. Four of us started in 1946. One, Bob "Rufe" Hunter, from LaGrange, Tennessee, had been in the Navy before coming to Annapolis. He had been an aerial gunner, then got into the NROTC program at "Ole Miss." He was a natural distance runner, but struggled with academics and could not take time from his studies to be a varsity performer. However, he did run the mile in intramural meets, and was undefeated in four years. When we graduated, he and I joined the 47 others who were commissioned in the Marine Corps.

Gene "Chip" Chipman, a tall, bright, and athletic former University of Michigan student, rowed for America's Olympic crew team of 1948 and captained Navy's crew in 1950. After graduation, Chip became a naval aviator, and later left the Navy to become an attorney.

During the four years, we lost only Bob Peterson, an All-Big-Eight basketball guard who resigned in the spring of Plebe Year and returned to Iowa State.

Academically, I ranked somewhere between Chip and Rufe. The ability to do better may have been there, but varsity football took too much of my time.

In those days, Navy routinely played one of the toughest schedules in the country. During the 1947 season, we took on eight of the nation's top ten teams, including, as usual, number-one-ranked Notre Dame. We lost more than we won—many more than we won—but through all the disappointments and losses, we had good times worth remembering. One of them was the Army-Navy game of 1948.

Army's coach was the legendary Red Blaik, and in 1948 he had one of his best teams ever. Quarterback Arnold Galiffa made most of the All-America teams that year. He was a superb passer and had a number of fast receivers. Army played a sophisticated, stunting defense that lined up a yard off the ball and wore down opposing teams through the liberal use of manpower. Their offense used every "mind game" in the world to confuse defenses with multiple formations and men in motion.

On the other hand, we had just experienced our worst season in Navy's history. But at game time, we were healthier than we had been at any time during the year. Our co-captain and fastest back, "Pistol Pete" Williams, had returned to form after a serious knee injury. He, our big fullback, Bill Hawkins, and the arm of our senior quarterback, Reaves Baysinger, were our big threats. It was our last chance to salvage something of the season. We worked hard in practice, impressing nobody. Army was a 33-point favorite!

Navy coach George Sauer came up with a good game plan, but we would have to execute as never before. Gone were the complicated blocking schemes that had not helped, anyway. We would block straight ahead and let the backs find the hole, and we would use simple plays with an occasional reverse tossed in to keep them honest. We would limit our passing to short first-down passes, and we would strive to control the ball and keep their offense off the field. Defensively, we planned to penetrate and interrupt their lateral movement in the backfield. We had the best approach possible, but Army would play 44 or more cadets, while we would probably use not more than 20 or so players. The talent was not there.

Navy's leadership came from the lettermen and our co-captains, Scott Emerson and Pete Williams. We had a meeting the night before the game after the usual movie ended. At that meeting we decided to clear the locker room 20 minutes before it was time to go on the field. We would tell the coaches, academy officials, admirals, trainers, and anybody else to leave. We would have a team meeting right there, and give each letterman a chance to say something.

We did just that—and there were some impassioned, even surprising words. The thought evolved that the game was not about Navy pride; the fleet; former players, the heroes who had preceded us; the Brigade of Midshipmen; or any thing else in the world except the 43 of us in that locker room. We can win . . . we can hit until they know they are beaten . . . we can, we can . . . we will, we will . . . and so it went. We dedicated the game to ourselves and the love, respect, and comradeship we felt for each other. Mass hysteria reigned. When we opened the door and ran up the ramp to the field, we almost trampled each other getting there. We were ready!

Today it would be called "smash mouth football." Nobody asked for mercy and nobody gave any. The grass field in that old Philadelphia stadium soaked up a lot of blood from both sides. Offensively, we made our plan work. Running the ball consistently, we broke some long gainers: but mostly, we just kept the chains moving for first downs. Defensively, we could not stop Galiffa and the Army passing attack as they repeatedly victimized one of our defensive backs. They scored just before the end of the first half to

13

take a 14–7 lead, but we still felt that we owned the line of scrimmage. The second half was a repeat of the first. Late in the fourth quarter we led 21–14, but they had too much talent and their passing game was too good. They scored one last time and made the extra point. The 33-point underdog had fought mighty Army to a 21-21 standstill.

Army's team captain, Bill Yeomans, met our co-captains at midfield, where the referee flipped a coin to see who would take the game ball home. Yeomans called "heads," and heads it was. They took the ball, but every Army player stayed on the field to shake hands with every Navy player. Some might say that the tie in such a hard-fought game was poetic justice. I can't agree. We gave it every last ounce of courage we had and deserved to win.

1949 Navy football team, the author is number 63

The following Tuesday evening, the team was told to report to Smoke Hall, a Midshipmen's recreation room, after evening meal. When we had gathered, Pete Williams moved to the front, carrying a box. He announced that it had arrived by special courier that afternoon and that inside were the game ball and a short handwritten note from Army Captain Bill Yeomans. The note said that they had held a meeting after the game and decided that, regardless of the score, we had kicked them all over the field and that they were lucky as hell to have tied a "great football team." The note concluded with the sentence, "This ball should be in your trophy case, not ours." It is still there today. A rare bit of sportsmanship, indeed.

In mid-twentieth-century America, one of the most positive, exhilarating, and purely joyful experiences had to have been graduation from one of the service academies. Four years of rigid schedules, exams, challenges, regulations, and discipline culminated in a week of parades, ceremonies, awards, social events, and finally, what it was all about in the first place, commissioning. There was the anticipation associated with moving on to the first assignment as a new officer, but the real excitement was in the newly won freedom. Most important to me, however, was the fact that through the insistence of my dear sister, I met for the first time and dated a young lady from Fletcher, NC, who was to move center stage in my life. Miss Carol Edgerton, a Southern beauty in every sense of the word, became the total focus of my affection and attention through that fast moving summer after graduation. In a word, I was "smitten."

In 1950 as well as now, the thrill of graduation did not mark the end of the apprenticeship for most of us. There were schools to be tackled before we could be entrusted with responsibilities for ships, aircraft, and, most important of all, the lives of sailors or Marines. For the newly commissioned Marines, it meant a period of "graduation leave," followed by reporting to the Basic School at Quantico, Virginia. There we would attend the almost-eleven-month-long program designed to produce young officers who had a basic understanding of the Marine Corps and how it does what it does best, fight wars.

One of the joys of graduation leave was that of attending Classmates' weddings. Chip Chipman, my roommate who had captained Navy's crew, took the plunge in Norfolk on the 25th of June. Naturally, I was a groomsman, and just as naturally, it was late before the reception finally ground to a halt. The place for any young traveling officer to stay was and probably still is the nearest bachelor officers' quarters. As I returned to the BOQ at the Naval Air Station, the Marine sentry at the gate stopped me and told me to report immediately to the Officer of the Day. When asked why, the Marine told me that we were now at war and that I had to inform the Commandant of my whereabouts—in the event, he added, that the Commandant needed me. In those days, all written correspondence or messages electronically transmitted to Headquarters, U.S. Marine Corps were referred to as being mailed or sent "to the Commandant." It was as though the Commandant read and acted upon everything. (Many Marines believed that he did.) Feeling very much a part of the brotherhood of warriors, I joined a large group of sleepy-eyed junior officers who were filling out a form message addressed to the Commandant of the Marine Corps, or the Chief of Naval Operations for our Navy counterparts. The North Koreans had attacked south, and the world, at least the world of Marines, was about to change. Dramatically.

The reply to the form message came within 24 hours. It told me that there would be no change in my leave status, and that I was to report to the Seventh Basic Class, convening at Quantico, Virginia, on 1 August 1950. The message also advised that the course was being greatly reduced in length, and then added a stipulation that is burned in my memory: "Do not, repeat do not anticipate future leave during an accelerated wartime course." The message concluded with "Enjoy your leave." The Commandant's staff was trying to tell us that this would be the last leave we'd probably get for quite some time.

On 25 June 1950, the Marine Corps was not quite 70,000 strong, and despite its more-than-significant contribution to the World War II victory was again fighting for organizational survival. By the end of the year, the Marine Corps Reserve was fully mobilized and the Corps roster had swollen to more than 250,000. Also by the end of the year, Marines were again proving the value of the Marine Corps by their outstanding performance in combat, putting at least a temporary halt to the talk of either eliminating the Marine Corps or reducing its strength to that of a corporal's guard. But the lieutenants of the Seventh Basic Class were not quite ready to make their contribution to the Marine Corps and its combat reputation.

15

The Basic School does a number of important things, not the least of which is serving as a melting pot for new officers who have come from a variety of sources. The Seventh Basic Class had 48 Naval Academy graduates, almost as many meritorious non-commissioned officers, and even greater numbers from the various commissioning programs available to students at civilian colleges. Whether you graduated from Notre Dame, Tufts, or the Naval Academy—or were a former sergeant—was irrelevant. The Seventh Basic Class became our Marine Corps class, and what we did there was what counted to the Marine Corps. To reinforce that mindset, our instructors frequently stressed that we would be "third lieutenants" until we had completed the Basic School course.

In 1950, the third lieutenant concept was reinforced by the resource-poor Marine Corps' lack of facilities for housing its student officers. The school billeted us in World-War-II-era wooden barracks with communal "heads" (lavatories). Each of us had a bunk, two footlockers, and a wall locker. It was the standard fare for enlisted Marines at that time. We kept any spare clothing or equipment in the trunks of our cars or in the barracks' suitcase room. Adding to the no-nonsense, spartan atmosphere was the Richmond, Fredericksburg and Potomac Rail Road, a railroad that had linked Richmond and Washington since before the Civil War. Its tracks were no more than five paces from the barracks, and at least two trains rumbled past every night, vibrating bunks out of alignment and waking up even the heaviest of sleepers. In spite of all the other reminders of our third-lieutenant status, our training was professional. It had to be. It was obvious that we would soon use it in battle.

Colonel David M. Shoup, the Commanding Officer of the Basic School, had won the Congressional Medal of Honor as a regimental commander during the extremely bloody and difficult amphibious assault at Tarawa in the Gilbert Islands during World War II. Eventually, when Shoup was a major general, President Eisenhower would reach past several of the senior Marine Corps generals, select him for four-star rank, and appoint him Commandant of the Marine Corps. A skillful poker player who wrote articles about the game and got them published, he combined the physical toughness of a bulldog with an unusual intellect and an amazing talent for writing poetry about one subject: combat.

His primary task, and one he took very seriously, was that of preparing us to become combat infantry leaders. A rather humorless man, he seemed perpetually annoyed by his third lieutenants' occasional lighthearted approach to his school and to life in general. We—all but a handful of us—worked hard to learn as much as possible, but we also believed that a little fun now and then was not a bad thing. This persuaded Colonel Shoup that we were not serious enough about the fact that most of us would soon be in combat. He was determined to motivate us, and the vehicle he chose for this was his combat poetry.

Periodically, he would order our two student companies to assemble in a classroom after we'd finished the week's training. It didn't take us long to learn that the order meant we were about to be treated to new and frequently macabre poems about combat scenes. There were never any prefacing remarks. He would have his notes attached to an old piece of cardboard. After tossing it onto the floor where he could see it, he would start talking. To this day, there are classmates of mine who can recite some of his more vivid lines. All of the poems he read dealt with Tarawa, where he had led an assault that,

16

because of him, succeeded—and without him, or someone like him, would probably have failed.

There was a poem entitled "Bill" that told of a young Marine whose head was blown off while he was talking to Colonel Shoup in the landing craft as it approached the island. And there was a long poem about how he used his entrenching tool or, as he insisted on calling it, his "spade" to motivate others. He had lost all of his equipment and his weapon in Tarawa's lagoon when his landing craft sank. Wading ashore, he picked up an abandoned "spade" and used it to rally the disorganized troops hugging the beach. He approached one individual who had a pistol and was cringing in the sand. Because of the pistol, the colonel assumed that the young man was an officer. Swatting him on the rear end with the spade, he ordered the startled man to gather a platoon and assault an enemy bunker on their left. The colonel added that, once the bunker was silenced, the young man was to report back to him on the beach for further instructions. The young man, stirred to action, collected about 30 Marines and, running low, moved out toward the bunker. The colonel presented all this in poetic meter and vivid language.

The poem went on to tell us that within 15 minutes a series of explosions erupted on the left and the flanking fire from the bunker ceased. A few minutes later, a Navy corpsman slid into the shell crater the colonel was using for a command post and, gasping for breath, reported that the bunker was destroyed. He wanted to know if the colonel had any other orders, since a number of his troops had been wounded and he had to go back and treat them. The "young officer" that Colonel Shoup's spade had motivated was an 18-year-old Navy corpsman. And the corpsman, in turn, had saved the landing forces from some serious trouble by his heroic action.

After hearing that particular poetry reading, we young officers referred to Colonel Shoup irreverently as "Colonel Spade," or simply "Spade."

On September 23, the summer's romance blossomed into a wedding when my fiancee, Carol Edgerton of Fletcher, North Carolina, became my beautiful wife in ceremonies at the U.S. Naval Academy chapel. Considering that I was expecting to receive a combat assignment very soon, getting married was probably not the smartest thing we could have done—and to top it off, we had no honeymoon. However, I now see our decision to get married then as unquestionably the best judgment of my entire life. We were married on a Saturday evening, with our families, my Basic School platoon, and an almost equal number of Mary Washington College lovelies in attendance.

One of the phenomena of the post-World-War-II military was "varsity sports." All of the services had them and every major post or station was, in some respects, a sports franchise. Quantico was no exception. In truth, because of its large population of third lieutenants, many of whom were former college athletes, Quantico was a leader in the world of military varsity athletics. A neck injury I'd incurred playing football at Navy prevented me from playing on the Quantico football team, but not from helping to coach it. Added to my duties as a Basic School student, then, were those of line coach and scout. The former entailed doing what any line coach would do, while the latter involved being flown to opponents' games in the back seat of a World War II dive bomber, a few of which still operated from Quantico's air station.

Early in the season, we developed a highly proficient squad—a squad, in fact, that went on to win the Armed Forces Championship. But I was meeting myself coming and going. In particular, what I was doing was not learning enough about how to be a rifle platoon leader in combat. After the third game, it was obvious that something had to change. I approached the head coach, a World War II fighter pilot who was not only an excellent coach but also an outstanding Marine leader. I explained the problem and asked to be relieved of my football duties so that I could concentrate on preparing for combat. I was surprised to learn then that the head coach lacked the authority to do this. "Management" was the "team owner," and the owner was the commanding general, Lieutenant General Franklin "Jock" Hart. Only he could get me off the football coaching hook and for that I would have to go to "request mast."

Quantico football team's all Naval Academy coaching staff, Charlie Cooper '50,
Bill Chip '43, Hal Harwood '42, Joe Donahoe '43, J.T. Hill '42

When I reported to the general, he eyed me up and down for a moment and then asked what was the "crap" he had heard about my wanting to quit the team, adding that "Marines don't quit anything." After I gave my reasons, he swiveled around in his chair and gazed out the window for several minutes. Finally, he swiveled back and got to his feet. He extended his hand and said that he would never deny a Marine officer the right to prepare himself to lead troops in combat. The "owner" had accepted my resignation. Once again the system had worked, just as it had with the third class Spanish exam.

The hard training continued, but even old Spade got easy and gave the class two days off for Christmas. Then we froze in winter field exercises. The Marine Corps was still using pre-World-War-II packs and canvas leggings with ankle-high field shoes called "boondockers." During the seriously cold weather we were issued large galoshes to wear over the boondockers. There were no sleeping bags available: we did our best with two wool blankets and a camouflaged canvas poncho. As cold as it was, we couldn't complain. The Marines in Korea were going through the Chosin Reservoir battles and their aftermath with more heroism than anybody had a right to expect of those fighting in that frozen hell. On our side of the world, we were still playing war games and firing blank rounds.

Finally, on February 28, 1951, we graduated. Maybe Colonel Spade was as glad to see us gone as we were to go. Or maybe—and more likely—he was concerned that he and we had not done enough. It made no difference. Life as third lieutenants was over, and the apprenticeship—nearly five years of it—had ended.

18

Chapter 3

The Lieutenant's Road to War
"For duty beyond the seas . . ."

The wording was a bit elegant, reminiscent of 19th century Union or Confederate military documents. Not many years later, the era of computers and cryptic messages would arrive, introducing such terms as "WESTPAC GROUND" or "WESTPAC AIR" to Marines being ordered to Vietnam for duty. But in the early 1950's, the Corps used the full force of the English language: lieutenants at the Basic School; formations of recruits at Marine Corps Recruit Depot, Parris Island or its counterpart, Marine Corps Recruit Depot, San Diego; and thousands of Marines elsewhere were ordered, "For duty beyond the seas with the 1st Marine Division, wherever it may be." And in 1951, the First Marine Division was in Korea, heavily engaged in combat with the armies of North Korea and communist China. There was not a chance in the world that it could have moved "wherever" else before those reporting for "duty beyond the seas" arrived.

The initial stop on the journey to the First Marine Division was the Replacement Regiment at Camp Pendleton, California. On April 1, 1951, I said goodbye to my pregnant wife and met three of my Basic School classmates in Memphis for a "speed run" across the country in Bob Whitesell's 1950 Pontiac. Our plan was simple: we shared expenses, driving duty, and, where possible, relatives or friends who fed and even, on occasion, bedded us.

When the four of us arrived at Camp Pendleton, we were issued field equipment, including cold-weather gear, and given our first real troop-leading responsibilities. Assigned to companies of young Marines who had recently completed reeruit training and a short advanced infantry training course, we took them to a cold-weather training camp at a ski resort called Idylwild, overlooking Palm Springs. It was more physical test than cold-weather training, but we learned something about survival in a subfreezing climate. When we returned to Pendleton, we were given one night of liberty before joining our units of the Eighth Replacement Draft. The journey "beyond the seas" was about to really begin.

The night before we were to report to the Eighth Replacement Draft, I met my company commander. He was also a second lieutenant, but one who was two years senior to me. He informed me that I was to be his executive officer, second in command, a decision that could not have been difficult for him to make, since we were the only two officers in the company. Noting that he had an urgent personal matter to attend to before we left for the Orient, he told me to take charge of things, adding that he would see me two days hence when the company boarded ship at San Diego. His cavalier attitude toward the company seemed strange. It became even stranger when he mentioned, in an off-hand manner, that it was a newly constituted "composite company." I had no idea what he meant and didn't ask. I should have. Some second lieutenants have been around longer than others.

A long-established Marine Corps custom with respect to wartime replacements had eluded me up to this point. In those days, whenever there was an acute personnel shortage and all other sources of personnel had been drained, the one remaining source—the bottom of the barrel—was the military brig or prison. This was the source of the composite company, a conglomerate of "critical" or hard-to-find occupational specialties.

A prisoner who had one of the sought-after skills and was serving a sentence for a non-violent crime was offered a conditional pardon. The condition, of course, was that he serve an honorable tour in combat. If he did so, the condition would be removed and the offense expunged from the Marine's record. All of the brigs on the west coast had been combed for the needed occupational specialties: the men this process had found formed the Eighth Replacement Draft's Composite Company for transportation to Korea and assignment to combat duty.

This particular company contained radio operators, cryptologists, surveyors, aviation metalsmiths, legal clerks, artillery fire controllers, armorers, and many other hard-to-find specialties. They had been gathered together the previous day, formed into platoons, issued equipment, and assigned spaces in the barracks. Unfortunately, they had also been paid $50 each and given access to the enlisted Marines' club adjacent to their barracks. There was no doubt that they had enjoyed themselves for either $50 worth or the evening, whichever ran out first. The result of all this fun and frolic was mine at 10:30 the next morning.

As I approached the barracks, I saw more than 200 Marines on the grass plot out front, sitting or lying in ranks with rifles and packs at their sides. Some were asleep. Others appeared to be unconscious. The odor of secondhand beer was overpowering. The odor got worse when it was joined by that of recently emptied stomachs. All I could think was, "My God, this is the Marine Corps?" As I was taking in all this carnage, a tall, lean master sergeant stepped out of the barracks, saw me, saluted, and walked over to introduce himself. He was the company first sergeant: at six feet, four inches he was an impressive-looking individual. He reported that he had cleared out the barracks and that his four platoon sergeants would join us shortly. Looking around, he smiled and said something to the effect that, "I thought you might want to inspect the company, sir. It's not in very good shape." He was right . . . more than right. And this ragtag collection of misfits was scheduled to board ship the next day.

We hadn't studied anything like this at Annapolis, and Colonel Shoup's finishing school for third lieutenants had featured combat training, not training in the art of shepherding drunks. Nevertheless, it was obvious that something had to be done and done quickly. The first sergeant's suggestion that I inspect the company was an excellent start. He was a true professional: although our association with the replacement draft was to be relatively brief, I came to rely on his judgment and, in a very real way, his tutelage. We discussed possible courses of action while waiting for the platoon sergeants to join us. We made some quick decisions and, when the platoon sergeants arrived, issued the orders.

There was no specific authority for us to do what we did. It made sense to the sergeants, and it seemed like the right thing to do at the time. Besides, as long as what is contemplated is not illegal, it is usually better to ask for forgiveness rather than permission. First, the platoon sergeants forcefully aroused the troops, getting them all on their feet, at the position of attention, some more so than others, and prepared the company for inspection. The first sergeant told the troops that I would inspect each man and that when I halted in front of them, each was to state his name, rank, and military specialty. Since they were all privates, the rank business was not really necessary. It did, however, remind them of their status in the eyes of the Marine Corps. Besides beginning the process of pulling these less-than-sober yardbirds back to the paths of righteousness, the inspection gave me the all-important opportunity to size up the platoon sergeants. If they could not carry the load, we were in trouble.

The plan was to march the company with packs and rifles until they were sober, take a short break and then march them up and down the hills until they looked and acted like Marines, even if it took all night. There is no shortage of hills at Camp Pendleton, and the next one is always steeper than the last. At best, we were facing a long day. The inspection went fairly well, although several of the men, unaccustomed to the heavy intake of alcohol, fainted from the effort of standing at attention.

After the inspection, I stood them "at ease" and talked to them about their status. Reminding them that they were on probation with the Marine Corps, I informed them that they had to get ready for duty as Marines. If they could not get ready today, we would ship them back to the brigs whence they had come. When they boarded ship in the morning, they were not only going to look like Marines, they were going to *be* Marines—proud Marines. Then I did something that I ought not to have done. I told them that, for now, they were the "Asshole of the Marine Corps" and that I had no intention of being known as an "asshole company commander." It was crude, but every one of them knew what I was talking about. It was a challenge and one, I am glad to say, that worked.

We marched and we marched. The first break came after about three hours. There was no lunch—just one short break and a great deal of sweat. During the break, I walked back along the column, patting a few on their packs: they were sober. Some were even smiling. We refilled canteens and started again, following a route calculated to get us to the messhall for the evening meal, but after most of the other troops had eaten and gone. The first sergeant strode along at the rear of the column, "motivating" the stragglers to get moving and rejoin their platoons. Every hour we stopped for a brief break and to move the last platoon to the head of the column. Late in the afternoon, after one of the short breaks, I told the first sergeant to call cadence so that we could march in step. It worked. The men picked up the beat. The first sergeant then started using the old cadence chants and they responded loudly as we moved in the late afternoon dusk toward the messhall, the sound bouncing back from the nearby hills. They were marching like Marines. When we reached the messhall and before I turned the formation back over to the first sergeant, I told the troops that they were still what I had said they were but that they were beginning to look like Marines; that they were restricted to the barracks that night; that they would be prepared to move out early the next morning; and last, that the Marine Corps needed them, but most important of all, they needed the Marine Corps.

The next morning dawned bright and clear and cool enough to call for field jackets. Civilian dignitaries, high-ranking military officers, and just plain American citizens crowded the pier and occupied surrounding vantage points. "A" Company, marching under the weight of field transport packs, the heaviest of the heavy, led the replacement draft onto the pier. The troops looked good and as we swung past the crowds, a Navy band struck up the "Marines' Hymn." It was like something out of a movie. We halted at the aft gangway of *USS Menard*, an amphibious troop transport ("APA" in the Navy's bottomless well of abbreviations) recently awakened from her post-World-War-II slumber in a backwater somewhere, taken out of mothballs, and returned to commission. My platoon sergeants marched their platoons aboard—platoons that were now indistinguishable from the others waiting to board ship.

21

The Eighth Replacement Draft was principally an aviation draft, comprising mostly Marines from Marine Corps Reserve F4U "Corsair" Squadrons. The pilots, mostly WW II vets, were a salty bunch. The bonding between aviation and ground officers that took place aboard *Menard* was to pay important dividends later.

As we were clearing Point Loma, the first sergeant sought me out to tell me that the troops wanted to retain their title as "Asshole Company." Marines like to be different and this certainly met that criterion. To their credit, in our time at sea, in port in Japan, and enroute to Korea, we had not one disciplinary incident. They had regained their pride in themselves.

The ship had a major navigational problem: the navigator. He was a newly recalled Reserve officer—a lawyer by trade and a pleasant individual, but one who knew only how to use LORAN, a radio navigation system that was useless once a ship got out of the transmitters' range. In 1951, most of the Pacific Ocean was out of LORAN range. The navigator knew nothing about the sextant, the book of tables that goes with it, and the computations it took to combine sextant sights, the tables, and charts to determine the ship's position at sea. In other words, he was just not qualified to be doing what he had been assigned to do—a vitally important function in any seagoing ship. As a First Class Midshipman (Naval Academy senior) on the 1949 summer cruise, I had acted as an assistant navigator aboard *USS Leyte*, an aircraft carrier, and that sealed my underway fate in *Menard*. In a move to help the undermanned crew, our Commanding Officer of Troops agreed with the ship's captain to seek qualified Marine officers to voluntarily stand shipboard watches. As a result of this Marine augmentation program, I became *USS Menard*'s assistant navigator, and had to shelve, for the time being, my work with A Company.

The ship did have a quartermaster, a chief petty officer Reservist from the merchant marine, who knew how to use the navigational tables once a navigator gave him the information he obtained by "shooting" stars, planets, and the sun with the sextant. The quartermaster and I quite naturally became fast friends. After a few days of cautious relearning, we developed our system. In the meantime, the ship's official navigator was learning everything he could from us about the old-fashioned way of navigating. Thirteen days later, when we hove to at the mouth of Kobe Bay to take aboard the Japanese pilot, the ship's captain officially relieved me of my navigator's duties. Unfortunately, Lieutenant Colonel Kelly, our Commanding Officer of Troops, was there to remind me that A Company would be the duty company and that I would be the Officer of the Deck during our first—and only—night in the Japanese port.

One of the things I had learned during three Midshipman summer cruises was that Marines and sailors who had been drinking (too much) often attempted to smuggle liquor back aboard ship. It was illegal, and the alcohol was always confiscated. Equally commonplace and having nothing to do with alcohol is the tendency of even the best of troops to seize on rumor or myth and convert it to gospel. This gospel, usually devoid of any basis in fact, is persistent and hard to combat. One of the common gospels of the day held that alcohol taken from those attempting to bring it aboard ship was stored in the officers' wardroom and consumed by the officers at their leisure.

I addressed the subject of confiscating liquor being brought aboard when I briefed the quarterdeck guard detail. We quickly agreed that, with more than a thousand Marines

22

ashore on liberty, we were going to have a big booze seizure problem. I detailed the senior non-commissioned duty officer to supervise the collection of a large number of boxes from the galley and sick bay. On the spur of the moment, I asked him to get several rolls of adhesive tape and a few pens. We would tell each Marine whose bottle we seized that it would be returned to him in the morning. We'd write his name, organization, and compartment number on a piece of adhesive tape and stick it on the bottle. Then we would store the bottles in the boxes.

Several hours later, we had a busy time at the Marine gangway. While most of the troops returned in varying degrees of "instability" and without contraband, we did collect several hundred bottles. The owners seemed both surprised and pleased when told that their treasures would be returned in the morning.

Late in the evening, a mellow Lieutenant Colonel Kelly came aboard and mentioned in passing that the ship would remain in Kobe an additional day. A Company and I would have the chance to go ashore, after all. The company had probably been given the duty during what was expected to be the only night in port in order to keep its brig alumni on board and out of trouble. Now the alumni would have a make-or-break chance.

The next morning we read the "booze roster" over the ship's PA system. All of the men named were directed to report to the ship's fantail, where they were formed in ranks. As they reported, each received his own bottle or bottles. When all of the "hootch" had been distributed, each rank, in turn, was ordered to march a certain number of paces forward and on command, drop its bottles over the side. My final word was, "You know I don't have it and I know you don't have it. Dismissed." At least a small segment of the Marine Corps had come to understand that alcohol was not confiscated for the officers' benefit.

That night, A Company and most of the rest of the replacement draft went ashore for the last liberty any of them would enjoy for some time. The Marines of A Company caused no problems and all were back aboard ship at the appointed time. Not bad for troops who had been "conditionally" released from the brig to go to war.

Early the next morning, while the more enthusiastic students of Kobe's night life were sleeping it off, *Menard* backed gingerly away from the pier and entered the channel. With the help of a Japanese tug, she turned until her bow pointed seaward, and then slowly got underway for the port of Pusan, on the southeast corner of the Korean peninsula.

Menard arrived off Pusan on a dismal morning. Low visibility and a raw wind blowing offshore would have been depressing enough. The cold rain showers that walked across the sea to *Menard* mocked those standing on deck looking for their first glimpse of Korea—for generations a harsh land of tragedy. We didn't have to see land to know that we were getting close. We could smell it five miles out. The World War II veterans said that the odor was that of "night soil," human excrement used for fertilizer. Welcome to Korea. Welcome to the war.

Chapter 4

The Lieutenants' War

"We few . . .we happy few...we band of brothers"

It was mid-morning before the sailors snaked *Menard's* lines over the side to moor her to the pier at Pusan. A feeble sun was still trying to work its way through the overcast, but the late-April day continued to be cool, rainy, and altogether miserable. No sunshine, no bands, no welcoming dignitaries, and aside from the dock workers, no onlookers. Nothing but a light steady rain, waiting trucks, and enough war to go around. Laden with packs and weapons, Marines of the Eighth Replacement Draft picked their way carefully down the aft gangway and slowly boarded the waiting mud-coated green Marine Corps tractor-trailer rigs. The trailers had wooden benches inside, and their sides, from about mid-height upward, were covered with wooden slats that were separated to let the air flow through. They looked very much like something designed to transport animals, and for that reason Marines at Quantico—and wherever else the trailers moved troops in large numbers—called them "cattle cars." They seemed oddly out of place in Korea.

The cattle cars, each carrying about fifty Marines, cleared the port area and turned onto a narrow two-lane concrete highway. It reminded me of those laid down in the States during the 1920's and early 30's, but this one had no shoulders. The highway stayed on the outskirts of Pusan, winding past rice paddies and villages. While most of us tried to absorb our first impressions of Korea, the peasants along the way ignored our passing. They were too busy trying to scratch out a living here in a land that had known little but hard times since the Japanese had occupied it decades before.

After going about five miles, the driver slowed, down-shifted, and turned off the highway. We were now on a two-lane dirt road . . . or, more accurately, a two-lane mud road. As the truck fought its way forward, we got a good look at our destination, the staging area. Housing American soldiers and Marines as well as troops from Canada, Great Britain, France, and Turkey, the camp was a sea of thick, ankle-deep mud. For those unfortunates who had to navigate the "goo," the technique was to lift each foot free without allowing the heavy mud to suck the boot off of it. The saving graces were the duckboard sidewalks between the tents and the wooden flooring of the tents themselves.

Braking with great care, each of the arriving cattle cars slid to a halt in the mud in front of the U.S. Marine area. After going through the gyrations it took to get field transport packs shouldered and in place, then retrieving their rifles, the troops left the trailers and began filing into a series of office tents. Here, personnel assignment officers, supported by what seemed to be a battalion of clerks manning ancient field typewriters, divided the troop draft into detachments. They then issued those detachments written orders assigning them to various units of either the First Marine Division or the Third Marine Aircraft Wing. The Eighth Replacement Draft and its A Company were no more.

Most of our aviator bunkmates from *Menard* went to squadrons based on CVE's (small aircraft carriers) operating off the Korean peninsula's east coast. Not long afterward, those former bunkmates appeared overhead when we most needed them and made their presence known with rockets, bombs, bullets, and napalm. They were good men and wonderful brother Marines. Sad to say, too many of them never made it home.

When my turn for assignment finally arrived, I asked for orders to the Fifth Marine Regiment. When the personnel officer asked why, I told him that my father and his hospital company had supported the Fifth Marines during World War I. He gave an understanding nod, then honored my request. It was a pretty small favor, but it showed that the system had a heart.

By the time we were finished it was nightfall, and we had missed whatever hot chow had been served in the Marine mess hall. I was the only Marine officer going to the Fifth Marines, so they put me in charge of the regiment's detachment, showed me our tent area for the night, and told me where to draw C-rations for the evening meal. The detachment had only one non-commissioned officer, a tough-looking corporal who was a machine gunner by profession. It also had a Navy doctor, Lieutenant St. Mary, and 92 enlisted Marines, all of whom were soon fed and ready to bed down for the night. Cleaning the mud off my war-surplus-store paratrooper boots was the only chore left.

The Marine Corps had done a wise thing for us during our instruction at Quantico. When certain lieutenants who had led Marine rifle platoons early in the Korean War had acquired combat experience, the Corps transferred them back to the Basic School as instructors. There they taught us the lessons they'd learned the hard way. They had begun arriving not long before we graduated, and quickly let us know that the war was a "lieutenants' war." Maybe lieutenants always consider a war to be a lieutenants' war, but in this case, our instructors were probably more right than wrong. Terrain has much to do with how a war is fought. The Korean terrain, coupled with the enemy's great numerical superiority, dictated a liberal use of reinforced-platoon-level activities both on offense and defense. The radio nets could provide mortar, artillery, air, or naval gunfire support and maybe even good advice, but most often the lieutenant was in effect an independent operator.

The practical advice we had received at Quantico even included suggestions about footwear. The standard footwear issue for the Marine Corps was the World War II "boondocker," a low boot worn with canvas leggings. The enemy had first encountered U.S. Marines during the hot summer of 1950 in the deadly fighting on the Pusan Perimeter. Summer's dust had turned the khaki leggings a yellowish color, prompting the North Koreans to call the Marines "yellow legs." For a variety of reasons, including our gull-winged aircraft, the North Koreans disliked tangling with the "yellow legs": the boondocker-legging combination had given the Marines a psychological edge. Nevertheless, it was a cumbersome rig, and newly returned instructors recommended that we buy Army paratrooper boots. A brand new pair was more than my wallet could bear, but I was able to find a less expensive pair in an Asheville, NC war surplus store. This pair had received the level of attention usually reserved for first-born babies, and I heard a lot of envious, sometimes snide comments whenever I wore them. Even the aviators noticed. Sad to say, despite all the loving care I gave them, they didn't last very long.

By the time my boots were clean, the others had turned in for what proved to be a fitful sleep. The night was punctuated with yelling and loud screams. I suppose that one of the national contingents had been issued an alcohol ration: whatever its cause, the noise, combined with rapidly building levels of nervous energy, prevented real rest. Then just before dawn, I snapped to full alertness: I could smell frying bacon. I roused the corporal: we dressed hurriedly and left the tent to track down that tantalizing smell. The source was a Canadian messhall that was actually nothing more than a tent fly rigged over a small galley. The cook, a huge Canadian sergeant, was frying bacon and eggs. Slicing small loaves of bread on the long axis, he would butter one half and then pile on a layer of bacon followed by a layer of two or three eggs before closing the sandwich. Great grease! It was heaven. He didn't bat an eye when we asked if he could feed our detachment of Fifth Marines. Bring 'em over, he said, and bring 'em over we did. After breakfast, we squared away the tents, shouldered our packs, and moved along the duckboards to the cattle car pick-up point. The trucks soon arrived and wasted no time starting their struggle through the mud to a nearby Marine airstrip and the aircraft that would take us north to the Fifth Marines.

The airfield was an expeditionary one—tents, mud, and the heavy metal matting that engineers had laid down to make usable runways out of plain old ground quickly. To the north, the Chinese spring offensive had started, and most of the First Marine Division units were accessible only by air. The Fifth Marines were one of those units. Three venerable R4D's, the twin-engined Douglas transport known as a DC-3 in the civilian world, were waiting to move us. As we began to dismount from the trailers, the pilots broke from their chatting groups and climbed into the aircraft. They were all enlisted Marines, mostly master sergeants. More than one looked old enough to be my father.

The rest of the field was full of activity. Corsairs, one after another, were landing, refueling, rearming, and immediately taking off again—like a pit stop at Indianapolis, no wasted motion. It was much quicker for them to operate from this expeditionary field than to fly out to the CVE's and go through the same evolutions on cramped flight or hangar decks. I was impressed. They apparently had a lot of targets out there.

Before we divided up into three aircraft loads, we did one more thing: we drew rifle ammunition and a case of hand grenades, all for us to use after we landed "up north." Our destination landing strip was fairly far from the Fifth Marines command post: trucks would meet us and take us the rest of the way. Making life interesting was the fact that the area the trucks would take us through was infested with roving bands of North Korean soldiers operating as guerrillas. Trouble, we were told, was always just around the next bend. We were to waste no time getting clear of the aircraft at our destination. They would not remain on the ground any longer than it took to unload us and then load lightly wounded Marines and those lucky souls whose Korean War tours of duty had ended. As we boarded, two Red Cross ladies handed out cups of hot coffee and doughnuts. It was a nice touch. It was also lunch.

Our flight north lasted about an hour. As we circled to land, I looked out the window and saw the "wind sock," a red rag tied to a small bush. I could also see the "runway," a narrow dirt road that curved as it headed north into a valley. A number of vehicles and a small body of troops waited in an open area near the improvised landing strip.

After we touched down, the pilot kept the plane on the curving road as it rolled to a stop. Then he gunned one engine to pivot the aircraft around and taxied quickly back down the road to the waiting trucks and troops. He had to unload, load, and launch before the next aircraft could land and go through the same cycle. The pilot throttled the engines back to idle, and we jumped out and came face to face with the departing Marines. They were good-looking troops. Some had bushy mustaches, but all were clean and otherwise freshly shaven. Their uniforms were tattered, but recently hand washed. Most of the men were carrying an assortment of souvenirs: "burp guns," rifles, Chinese bugles and knives. A tired-looking first lieutenant was obviously in charge of them.

I walked over to him and asked something like, "How is everything up at the front?" It was not the brightest question to ask, but he understood, responding that it was not a bad war if I didn't mind eating C-rations. Then as he started for the aircraft, he said something that I've never forgotten: "Good luck, Marine, watch your six." He was referring to the numerically superior enemy's ability to flow around our isolated outposts like water, then attack from any direction, including the rear, or "six o'clock." When all the walking wounded and homeward-bound Marines had climbed aboard, the door slammed shut and the old R4D headed down the road on its takeoff run.

A gunnery sergeant of the Fifth Marines was the "honcho" of the airstrip and replacement operation. He explained that we were some 30 miles from the Fifth Marines command post, and the truck drivers knew the route well. He added that we would have the unpleasant experience of driving through "massacre valley," the scene of a major U.S. Army defeat earlier in the war, and warned that we could encounter one or more North Korean guerilla bands. To help deal with that problem, each open-bed truck had a .50 caliber machine gun mounted behind its cab. After I had explained to the troops what we would do if any North Koreans decided to take us on, we boarded the trucks.

There were more than enough trucks, and we made certain that each was only lightly loaded. The fewer the Marines in a truck, the faster they could dismount in an emergency. By the same token, if one of the trucks was lost along with its occupants, the number of casualties would be minimized. Putting Dr. St. Mary in the cab of the lead truck, I manned its machine gun. The corporal assigned gunners for each of the other trucks and then climbed on the last truck to man its gun. When he was ready, he signaled and I told the driver to move out.

Without the huts and rice paddies, the terrain that surrounded us as we started out could have passed for western North Carolina. Farther north, the terrain would become more forbidding and rugged. We soon entered "massacre valley." We were not mentally prepared for the sight. It was sickening. Rusting and rotting burned-out tanks, trucks, and tracked vehicles were everywhere, as were destroyed artillery pieces. We could sense the chaos and terror. It was obvious that the Americans had not won. I don't know who they were, but it had been a big unit. It looked as though they had been ambushed after they had gotten well inside the valley, probably because they tried moving on the valley floor without controlling the high ground on either side. Establishing and maintaining security by controlling that high ground would seem to make common sense—and it does. But all too often, common sense fails, a failure not confined to the Korean War.

During the first hour of our trip, we received sporadic long-range machine gun fire. It kept everybody's adrenaline flowing but was otherwise ineffective. Our return fire silenced the enemy, and the trucks continued their careful northward movement without halting. The pattern—brief enemy activity followed by our return fire—was interrupted when two men suddenly broke from cover and darted across the road a few hundred yards ahead of us. I snapped off a short burst but missed them. My burst did bring heavy fire from automatic weapons in return. This was more accurate: it flattened one of the truck's front tires and hit the radiator. This time they were going to stand and fight—at least for a while.

27

The troops did exactly what they had been briefed to do: they leaped off the truck, sprinted off the road, and found good firing positions. Once there, they began placing a methodical stream of well-aimed rifle rounds into the area of the enemy position. Meanwhile, the next two trucks in line moved forward. Their machine guns would add weight to mine, and their riflemen would add to the base of fire being laid down by the Marines of the lead truck.

In the rear of the column, the corporal quickly assembled an assault element and started climbing up the valley wall to our right. When his group reached a position roughly 50 yards above us, he turned in the direction of the enemy. In a half crouch and well spread out, he and his men sprinted parallel to our covering fires until they reached a position above the North Koreans. Once there, the corporal gave a signal and they began the assault. We ceased fire but remained tense and alert. The tension broke when two of the enemy attempted to flee. Maybe they were the same two whose clumsy actions had triggered the ambush prematurely. In any case, it made no difference. Fires from either the corporal's assaulting element or our supporting force quickly bowled them over. We found three others dead in the ambush position.

As the troops changed the truck tire and plugged the radiator with a sharpened stick, I examined the dead. They were filthy, wore torn uniforms, and were obviously North Koreans. We removed documents and a map from their pockets and took off their rank insignia, all to be given to the regimental intelligence officer (the S-2) when we arrived. I could not believe how well our simple plan had worked. It was my baptism of fire and my first look at Marines going after an enemy. These Marines, just arriving in the combat zone, not really knowing each other, hadn't hesitated for a second to move out without wasting talk or motion. Discipline, solid leadership from the corporal, and sound training in the fundamentals had all come together and paid off.

We continued our cautious journey northward on the dirt road without further interruption. The driver was obviously mulling over the action, because at one point, he turned in his seat, glanced at me, and remarked that the replacements had looked good in action. It was a sound assessment. I agreed with him and we continued in watchful silence. Eventually, we turned off the road and bounced along a dry stream bed for about a mile. Then we saw tents among the bushes and in the near-by draws. Everything was camouflaged, the expended "brass" on the ground showed that the command post's defenders had been in some recent firefights. A quick look upward was reassuring. The hills above were outposted. We had finally reached Headquarters, Fifth Marine Regiment, First Marine Division.

When I turned the troop roster over to the adjutant, he told me that the regimental commander, Colonel Hayward, wanted to talk to all of the replacements. That news was more than welcome. We were strangers: new, apprehensive, and somewhat disoriented. We needed reassurance. Our introduction to combat had indeed gone well, but we all knew that it had been little more than a pre-game warm up. We needed the stability and confidence we would find in being part of a permanent organization.

Colonel Dick Hayward had been around long enough to know exactly how we felt, and he also knew what to say to bring us into the fold. He had been a parachute Marine during World War II and still acted like one. He wore his jump wings on his cap above the large eagle denoting his rank, and he had seen enough war to know that our most intense loyalties would go to small units—squads, platoons, maybe even companies, but nothing higher—and what he gave us was the umbrella of the Fifth Marines. A short man, he stood on the sandbags surrounding a mortar pit. We could see him and he could make eye contact with any one of us.

His words made an indelible impression on me: although I can't quote him, I can certainly paraphrase what he said. He began by welcoming us to what he called the "Family of the Fifth Marine Regiment, the Band of Brothers." My education had not included enough Shakespeare to have ever heard the term "band of brothers." It turned out to be a term I'd never forget. As could be expected, the colonel told us that we were joining the best fighting organization in the Marine Corps. He also told us that we would make it even better, and at the same time it would make us better. Then he laid down some very special, practical rules for us to understand. First, we never left our dead or our wounded. Never! We would never, under any circumstances, surrender. If we ran low on rations or water, we would share with each other. If we ran low on ammunition, we would redistribute what we had; we would share it. If we ran out of ammunition, we would fix bayonets and attack. We are our nation's finest and its toughest. The Fifth Marines have never been defeated and never will be defeated. If you are hurt, we will take care of you. We will never leave you, but you have some big shoes to fill. Welcome aboard! There are one helluva lot of "gooks" out there looking for us. Go get 'em.

His talk, the words of a commander who understood his troops, hit the mark. This was the commander's philosophy, explained in short, pithy terms that we all understood. Afterward, we got some hot "B-rations," a level of meal between fresh food ("A-rations") and the ubiquitous C-rations, or "C's." It was beans and something. It tasted good.

During our overnight stay at the regimental command post, I met an old Naval Academy acquaintance, Second Lieutenant "Red" Peterson. Red had graduated a year ahead of me and, in defiance of all the odds, had completed, unscratched, ten months of service with a rifle company, a tour that included the entire Chosin Reservoir campaign. When we met, Red was in command of the headquarters security troops. It was an assignment intended to keep him out of harm's way while he finished the last few weeks of his Korean tour— but Red wasn't cooperating fully. Every day, he took a sniper rifle and a few Marines into the hills, looking for North Korean guerrillas. We talked at length that evening, and he passed on much useful information, life and death stuff. I listened to every word.

The next morning, in a pouring rain, I said good-bye and good luck to the corporal and boarded a truck waiting to take several of us to the nearby First Battalion, Fifth Marines. Colonel Hayward waved as we departed. Dr. St. Mary remained at the regimental command post, becoming the new regimental surgeon.

After reporting to the battalion personnel officer, I met the battalion commander: tall, lanky Lieutenant Colonel John Hopkins. After making a short pep talk, he assigned me to B Company or, in the phonetic alphabet of the day, Baker Company. I was the replacement for Second Lieutenant John Abel, a platoon leader who had been killed several days before. Accompanied by four of the Marines who had been with me since Pusan, I left the battalion command post on foot and started the steep climb up a nearby hill to join Baker Company. As we left, I overheard someone refer to the company as "the bandits."

As the five of us labored up the hill under the weight of reconfigured but still heavy packs, I did some serious thinking. Things had been moving rapidly, and the pace had left

29

me unsettled. I knew that the Marine Corps had given me as much preparation as possible: there could always be more, but there comes a time in warfare when the talking stops and the doing starts. I wondered if I was ready to make the inevitable split-second decisions correctly and wisely. I thought also of the troops. Those who had been with me when we hit the North Korean guerrillas had been an example. They had shown impressive levels of discipline and confidence during that brief encounter: in that regard, they were the same as any other group of Marines. The corporal had shown how the young Marine non-commissioned officer responds to such a situation: lead, follow, or do whatever might be required.

As we climbed slowly upward, the doubts began to evaporate—as did any preoccupation with personal danger or, even worse, fear of failure. The physical exertion beside these four Marines had been a tonic. I was ready to get on with it. As we neared the top, the rain eased: just up the slope I saw fighting holes and "hootches," the common term for sleeping shelters. The skipper of Baker Company, First Lieutenant Jim Cronin, greeted us. We chatted for a few minutes and then he introduced me to the company's other officers. Afterward, he took me to the third platoon and introduced me to the small command group as its new platoon leader. It had been a long trip but I was finally "home." This platoon of Marines and its two Navy corpsmen were to become my "band of brothers."

Chapter 5

The Baker Bandits
"Watch Your Six . . ."

B Company had been "closing with" the enemy for many months. Part of the original yellow legs, the company had entered the war in Korea as part of the First Provisional Marine Brigade at the Pusan Perimeter during the late summer of 1950. The brigade, built around a Fifth Marine Regiment that was at roughly two-thirds strength (two rifle companies in each of the three battalions), had done yeoman service by counter-attacking to plug holes as they developed in the perimeter defenses at Pusan. The company then withdrew and embarked in amphibious assault ships, along with the rest of the Fifth Marines. After being beefed up with replacements, they landed at Inchon, drove northward, then redeployed with the entire 1st Division to the east coast. There they landed at Wonsan and took part in the Chosin Reservoir campaign.

The company had seen a lot of combat in less than a year. It was all the more costly and brutal because of such realities as the tremendous contrasts between the hilly terrain and smothering humidity around Pusan and the frozen, sub-zero Arctic temperatures in the rugged mountains in the Chosin area; or the jarring psychological blow that came when the foe, a fleeing, beaten, demoralized North Korean army, was suddenly transformed into the surrounding, outnumbering hordes of fresh, aggressive Chinese "volunteers" that had materialized without warning out of the snow and night, undetected by higher levels of command that ought to have known. They had seen it all, and they had persevered.

I was fortunate to have been assigned to B Company. It was a company with a history of success that stemmed in large part from leadership it received from a series of professionally solid company commanders. Among these was Captain "Ike" Fenton, whose tired features had graced a *Life Magazine* cover late in 1950. First Lieutenant Jim Cronin, the company commander when I arrived late in April of 1951, followed in the tradition of his predecessors. He had been the company executive officer until the company's highly respected "skipper," First Lieutenant John R. Hancock, had been killed by a sniper just weeks earlier. Lieutenant Cronin had most recently led the Baker Bandits through bitter fighting at the Hwachon Reservoir. When I joined the Bandits, they were in regimental reserve, licking their wounds while patrolling the regimental front.

Unlike the lack of mobilization for Vietnam, the Korean War had prompted total recall of all Marine Corps Reserve units and individual Reservists. As a result, Baker Company was about evenly divided between Regulars and Reservists. Many of the Regulars, including most of the company's senior non-commissioned officers, had come from Marine Barracks throughout the Pacific. Many were WW II veterans. They formed a solid base of professionals.

The educational level of the Reservists was remarkably high. Many of them were either college students or recent graduates, and most had served a brief tour of active duty after World War II. A few of the Reservists had had combat experience in one of the other services during World War II and for whatever reason had joined a Marine Reserve unit after the war. The company supply sergeant was one of these. He had been a master sergeant in the Army Air Corps, where he'd accrued an impressive number of bombing missions over Germany. After the war, he accepted a reduction in rank to sergeant in order to join the Marine Corps Reserve unit in Kansas City. His reason was pure Americana. He wanted to play on the unit's championship softball team.

As is the case in all wars, combat caused a constant turnover in the rifle companies, yet the bonding among the troops was as real as life itself. New arrivals were more likely to become casualties than those who had been around for a while. The Marines were candid in talking about the fact that if a newcomer made it through the first few weeks, his chances of completing a tour of combat duty were pretty good. It was the age-old advantage of being "battlewise," along with not doing anything stupid. Unfortunately, sheer bad luck and the skill of the enemy could break this general rule, and often did.

A Baker Bandit, Don Roush with his captured Burp-gun

If the troops watched each newcomer with care, and they did, they watched their new lieutenant with even greater interest. A new platoon leader could get them killed. The platoon sergeant, Staff Sergeant Reiman, was the first to express the platoon's concerns when he told me something like, "I hope you can read a map, Lieutenant. Mister Abel was a good officer but he never knew where he was." Use of the term "mister" when addressing lieutenants was part of the Marine Corps lexicon in the 1950s. That has since changed, but the troops' concern for whether or not an officer can read a map has not and never will.

They didn't give the new lieutenant any time to hang around the company area and get lazy. Within a day of my arrival, I was told to return to the battalion command post, find the S-2 (intelligence officer), and get briefed for my first patrol. I was told that the patrol would be a combat patrol—a patrol out looking for trouble—and that the prime reason for the patrol was to determine how long and by which route the entire battalion could move north to occupy a specific area. The walk back up the mountain was no easier than it had been the first time.

This patrol became a huge confidence builder. The platoon was reinforced with a section of light machine guns from First Lieutenant Stu Wright's machine gun platoon and a squad of anti-tank rocketmen from Second Lieutenant Eddie Fisher's rocket and mortar platoon. The platoon command group included our two Navy medical corpsmen, two radio operators, the platoon guide (whose primary duties dealt with supplies), and Staff Sergeant Reiman. Rounding out the command group was a bright and pleasant young Korean college student who spoke excellent English and passable Chinese. He wore a Marine uniform and made himself very useful as an interpreter, particularly when it came to getting information from Korean civilians or enemy prisoners. Counting the command group and various reinforcements, the platoon numbered somewhere between 65 and 70 men—enough to give anyone serious trouble, at least for a while.

When briefing the patrol, I started a precedent that was to continue: they would be kept well informed, both before and after any action. Having impressed them with that particular approach to leadership, I then annoyed them with another, equally important one. Every group should be inspected before going out on patrol, and despite the fact that we were not carrying much and were scheduled to return before nightfall, this group would be no exception. What's more, having just assumed responsibility for their performance and well-being, I had to know what equipment they had available, or more to the point, did not have available, for future patrols and actions. The platoon sergeant supervised them as they arranged their gear on the ground for inspection. As I checked their equipment, I could sense in their looks and bearing the general thought that they had been saddled with some sort of regulation-happy zealot. Some were hauling around a few souvenirs—and that was their business. The essential fact was that they all had what they needed, including hand grenade pouches, extra magazines for the automatic rifles, and three canteens, an absolute necessity because we were seldom resupplied with water. Even with three canteens apiece, a group could get into trouble.

(On a later patrol, we once continued to move for three days after the last canteen had been drained. We could not find water in the hills and, for whatever reason, could not be resupplied. The troops were beginning to talk about the need to recycle what little urine they were passing when we were saved by the first mountain stream we had seen in days.)

When the inspection was completed, the patrol formed up just inside the company positions. At my signal, the lead squad leader motioned to the point fire team to move out. The patrol moved in a column formation because the intended patrol route would take us along the tops of narrow ridge lines. As each man got underway, the one behind let him take three or four paces before starting after him, and then maintained that distance whenever we were moving. The column stretched out more than two hundred yards as we steadily but carefully traversed terrain that resembled that of the Great Smoky Mountains.

33

Riflemen and automatic riflemen moved with their weapons cradled across their bodies or secured in the crook of one arm, much as many of them had done when hunting back home. The assistant machine gunners, perennial beasts of burden, moved with their guns high on their backs, balanced across their shoulders. Each gunner had the gun's tripod slung on one shoulder and carried at least one can of ammunition. If they changed loads, they changed duties. The others in the machine gun squads labored under the weight of at least two ammo cans per man.

Alternate Marines in the column watched the area to either the right or left, and all watched for any sign of movement in the draws and valleys below. The radio operators, the interpreter, and I moved just behind the lead squad. Staff Sergeant Reiman and the rest of the command group moved with the rearmost squad.

We had moved for a few hours without incident when suddenly the point halted and, crouching low, began taking up firing positions. They had sighted a group of men several hundred yards north and slightly east of our intended track. After watching for a while, we moved carefully toward them. Eventually, they saw us and started shooting at us. Something was strange. It was hard to tell what they were doing, but they were not moving and reacting like a North Korean or Chinese unit that had just sighted a Marine patrol. The sharply spoken command "guns up" brought the machine guns forward, where their crews emplaced them and made ready to fire. The rest of the patrol hit the deck and took up good fighting positions.

We made preparations but did not return the group's fire. Then we used the radio to report the situation to Lieutenant Cronin, along with the opinion that the ones we had sighted might be friendlies. He had no way of knowing, but checked by radio with battalion headquarters. After several minutes, his voice crackled over the company radio net to tell us that our instincts were right. The group was an Army patrol that had gotten lost and strayed into an uncharted mine field. He gave us their radio frequency and we contacted them, identifying ourselves and offering to help. The Third Platoon had encountered that same minefield on previous patrols and knew its general size and layout. As a result, steering the soldiers around the minefield and out of danger was not too difficult. There were no casualties from either the mines or the small arms fire.

Our close brush with an "intramural" firefight was the last excitement of the day. We continued the patrol but had no further sightings. Having covered ten miles of rugged terrain in six and a half hours, we returned on schedule by an alternate route. I was relieved to have completed my first mission with the platoon. The responsiveness of the men was impressive. They knew what they were doing. Since we had not gotten lost, maybe they were beginning to think that their lieutenant knew what he was doing, too. It had been a mutual confidence builder. Once we got settled after our return, I wrote a short patrol report to the battalion S-2. It was delivered within an hour and told him what he needed to know. All of us, including him, knew that the peaceful terrain we had just covered could be crawling with enemy soldiers within a few hours.

Our regimental reserve status came to an end shortly after that patrol. B Company was put on the alert, and ordered to reinforce the Second Battalion, Fifth Marines immediately. The Chinese spring offensive was exploding and we had to fill a gap in the Second Battalion's lines. It was not at all unusual for a company of one battalion to be attached to another battalion for an operation. Under certain circumstances, the change in battalions could make a real difference, though it wasn't noticeable at the platoon level. Given the nature of the war in Korea at the time, I doubt that even the company commander noticed any real change, other than that he was talking on the radio to a different battalion headquarters. There were no "front lines" anywhere, just strong points on key terrain. Fire covered the gaps.

Late one afternoon we were notified that a company of the U.S. Army's Seventh Division would relieve us the next day. They began pouring in about mid-morning, and it was obvious that discipline wasn't their thing. They were a mixed lot of regulars, reservists, national guardsmen, and even some South Korean troops. When we tried to brief their officers on our positions and mine fields, they half-ignored what we were saying. I heard one of their senior non-commissioned officers ask our company gunnery sergeant for the location of the "bug-out route" for them to use if they were attacked. I began to develop a real concern about what would happen to them if they got hit hard. Two days after we left, we learned that they indeed had been hit hard. The Chinese had overrun them and destroyed them. Jim Cronin commented that the Chinese had been probing to learn the position but had deliberately waited until we left before trying to take it.

After the Army company replaced us, we started a long march southward, back to our parent First Battalion. The pace was an easy one, intended to eat up the miles but not wear us out. It was a good way to go, but it didn't last very long. Within a few hours, we received word that a Republic of Korea (ROK) corps had folded under the pressure of the Chinese offensive, exposing the entire rear and flank of the U.S. Army's Second Division. We received orders to reverse course and move north into blocking positions intended to contain enemy penetrations of the UN lines. The rest of the First Battalion was already on the move and would join us as soon as possible.

Shortly after we turned north, a light rain started. Soon it got heavier and began making its contribution to what would become an agonizing forced march. Halting briefly, we struggled into our gray ponchos. We were already wet and the ponchos didn't help us much, but they kept the weapons and ammunition relatively dry.

I've forgotten how far we marched—if I ever knew—but even after the cold, wet day slipped into night, we plodded on. Without taking time to eat or rest, we stayed on the march, straining to move northward as rapidly as possible. It was a nightmare. The pounding rain made the hilltop trails we were using slick: in the darkness, many of the heavily loaded troops slipped and fell. Some of them, rocketing down the steep trails at uncontrollable speeds, hit other Marines, who crumpled under the force of the collision. The impact was always bone-jarring: occasionally it was bone-breaking. Some of the injured had to be carried. The loads of the injured who could walk with assistance had to be redistributed to the uninjured. We stopped only to pick up the pieces and care for the injured.

At last the column slowed and turned off the ridgeline we had been following. Carefully carrying or helping the injured, we slowly picked our way down a steep hillside, finally reaching bottom and suddenly splashing into a cold, knee-deep stream. We struggled against its current as we once again turned north. Walking in the stream wasn't easy, but it was better than sliding around on the muddy slopes above. I don't know why, but we waded in the stream for a long time. Perhaps there was no road nearby, or perhaps on a clear day the stream bed was the road. Each Marine following the Marine ahead, fighting the stream and fatigue, we moved north.

The march ended the next morning when we began moving into positions that dominated a broad valley. B Company had been assigned a huge area, making it physically impossible to tie the platoons into a company position like the one we had turned over to the Army company the day before. The rest of the battalion with all its firepower had caught up with us: it gave the Third Platoon reinforcements in the form of a section of two water-cooled heavy machine guns, a section of two 75 millimeter recoilless anti-tank rifles, and a squad of anti-tank rockets. The company's other two rifle platoons, the First under Lieutenant Harvey Nolan and the Second under Lieutenant Pat McGahn, received similar reinforcements. Each of us, now heavily reinforced, was ordered to occupy an independent strong point. We prepared our position as quickly and thoroughly as possible, but it was not as strong as I would have liked. We could not follow our usual external security procedures and rig booby traps or warning devices, because we had been told to expect friendly stragglers entering our lines for the next several hours. I was nervous, afraid that we might either shoot some friendlies or not shoot some unfriendlies.

As the day wore on, American and South Korean stragglers began arriving in increasing numbers and filtering through to the rear. Many had no weapons and most had the zombie-like stare that often follows in the aftermath of a bloody fight. During the night, the rains came again, the stragglers tapered off, and the enemy never showed.

All night we listened to the thunder of artillery all around us and the ominous sound of somebody's tanks on the move, maybe ours, maybe Chinese. We reported what we heard, especially the tanks. Early the next morning we were issued rations and told to attack northward up the valley.

Shortly after we had inhaled a can of cold C-rations, we started up the valley in a column of platoons, Third Platoon in the lead. The valley was several miles wide, so the lead squad was deployed in a wedge formation covering a broad front. It wasn't long before we started to see increasing evidence of a terrific struggle. There were crumpled bodies; burning trucks, tanks, and half-tracks; destroyed artillery pieces; abandoned equipment; and other wreckage of war, including smoking houses between the road and the flanking hills. Chinese army units were just ahead of us to the north, but their main body kept its distance. All we hit were their rear guard units as they slowly and deliberately withdrew, fighting a skillful delaying action that included continuous sniper fire from the low-lying hills on either side of the road.

I had orders to push the rear guard without stopping to treat any wounded we might find—just report them and keep moving. Units following would care for them and get them evacuated. As we continued, American soldiers emerged from every conceivable location; draws, stream beds, hilltops, and even a few houses. In places, the major stream bed was piled high with bodies, both American and Chinese. It was a horrible sight. Many bleary-eyed walking wounded came wandering in, most describing a massive attack from the rear. Somebody had forgotten about "6 o'clock."

We moved as rapidly as possible through the battle area, keeping one eye on the enemy rear guard and using the other to search huts, hillside caves, and other likely hiding places for the enemy or for friendly survivors. While we were involved in one of these searches, word came back from the point squad leader that there were people moving toward us on the road. He added that they seemed to be carrying a flag. After moving to a good vantage point and focusing field glasses on the area that the squad

36

leader had indicated, I saw an amazing sight. Some 25 to 30 soldiers were walking down the road in a double file, led by an individual carrying what appeared to be battalion or regimental colors on a staff. Stuffing the field glasses back into the case, I collected the point squad and began moving toward the strange procession. In the meantime, my company radio operator reported the sighting to Lieutenant Cronin. Unlike most of the stragglers we had previously met, these men were still armed. As we approached them, the Marines began waving to attract their attention. Within moments, they responded. As the distance between us narrowed, I could see that the soldier carrying the colors was a captain. Contrary to the way Marine officers usually wore their rank insignia hidden under the collar, if they bothered wearing them at all, his large captain's bars were clearly displayed. His eyes were buried deep in their sockets: he was obviously totally exhausted.

That valley floor was not the best place in the world to exchange salutes, but I saluted him. Whoever they were, they had done their best. They had also kept their pride and self-respect even though they had certainly suffered at the hands of the Chinese. It was an emotional moment for all of us. As he returned my salute, I recognized him: I had known him since boyhood! The leader of this bent but unbroken band of soldiers was Captain Albert Metts, a Clarksdale native and West Point graduate. His younger brother and I had grown up together. I called him by name and after studying my face for a moment, he remembered me. We shook hands and then embraced. With tears running down his cheeks he told me that he was carrying the regimental colors of the 23rd Infantry Regiment, adding that he and his men were the survivors of the regiment's M Company. He also thought that he was the senior surviving officer of the regiment. Having seen what we had seen, I thought that he might have been the regiment's *only* surviving officer. We had a brief conversation that ended when a speeding jeep carrying Lieutenant Cronin and the battalion operations officer (S-3), Captain Jack Jones, slid to a halt a few yards away. As the two gently took Albert Metts in tow, we exchanged goodbyes and good lucks. Higher headquarters wanted to talk to him and he had much to tell. As the jeep swung around and started south, the Third Platoon "saddled up" and resumed the attack up the valley.

This time, we stopped early enough to dig in properly for the night and prepare for what we were certain would be a tough counterattack. It never came. Instead, we received accurate 120mm mortar fire during the evening and scattered small arms fire from the front and rear throughout the night. The enemy was all around us but not quite ready to slug it out. At times, night almost turned to day as artillery illumination rounds or flares dropped by the aircraft circling overhead swung from their parachutes during their descent. Enemy units caught in their glare were pummeled by Marine artillery or our aviators circling above and waiting to be called in on a mission.

Early the next morning we resumed the attack, but had not gotten far before surrendering Chinese began to pour in. They were hungry; many were wounded; some had typhus; and all had had enough. Looking at them, the platoon guide said something like "These Chinese farm boys seem to have just run out of gas." He was right. Their offensive had lost momentum. That day, we escorted more than two hundred of them to the rear of the company column, where MP's were waiting to move them farther south.

As the valley narrowed and the surrounding hills closed in, the Third Platoon was ordered to guard the battalion's flank on the high ground that dominated the right flank of our advance. We had brief firefights throughout the day, but the enemy, apparently spent, continued to withdraw. Our main problem was keeping up with the battalion column on the valley floor as we climbed and descended the steep hills on the flank. It was exhausting, back-breaking work, but it had to be done. It was absolutely critical that we show no weakness. The enemy could not be allowed to get the idea that he could gain control of the high ground dominating the route of advance.

Days were now becoming steamy and hot, and it quickly became obvious that this flank security business was going to get even tougher. Secure in the belief that the really cold weather had ended, I made a classic error in judgment. If we got rid of the winter sleeping bags we were carrying, the load would be much lighter and our grueling work on the flanking ridgeline would be much easier. I had been told that we would be issued summer sleeping bags any day, information that made decision making even easier. It all made sense, especially since some of the troops were starting to straggle. Straggling was one thing that could not be allowed under any circumstances. Something had to be done, and we certainly could not discard precious ammunition to lighten the load.

During a short rest break I told the platoon that I was going to get rid of my winter sleeping bag liner but save the lightweight shell. I said that those who wanted to do so could wrap up in a poncho inside the shell. That and the issue flannel shirts they were wearing would keep them warm at night. The troops had the option of either keeping or discarding the liner. Everyone knew that a decision to discard was a calculated risk. Within five minutes after I tossed mine over a cliff, every liner in the platoon was floating into the valley below. We resumed the march greatly relieved. Temporarily.

That night we dug in at the top of the small mountain we had been straddling for the past few days. It got cold. Real cold. So cold that the water in our canteens started to freeze. The troops began to grumble. Their grumbling grew louder as dawn approached. They said nothing directly to me, but mumbling in tones loud enough for me to hear, they talked at length about their goddam new lieutenant and his bright ideas. Ten or more days later, we got the summer-weight sleeping bags. I'd made a major mistake. I shouldn't have gotten fancy. We could have pushed the stragglers for a few more days. By then, we would have been replaced on the flank, anyway.

The nightly freeze was not their goddam new lieutenant's only problem. My impressive paratrooper boots were giving new meaning to the expression "coming apart at the seams." The boots had been wet since the day I joined the Bandits, and the stitching that held the soles to the boots was rotting. Maybe they had been on the shelf in Asheville for too long or maybe they had been a cheap imitation of the real thing. It made no difference. What did make a difference was the fact that one sole flapped in the breeze with every step and the other was beginning to come loose. Fortunately, ammunition clips for the M-1 rifles came in cloth bandoleers, and I was able to use one to tie the flapping boot sole to my foot. However, the thick bandoleer made for cumbersome walking. I felt like something out of Robert E. Lee's Army of Northern Viriginia.

Within a day or two, Lieutenant Cronn radioed to tell me that we were to be relieved of the flank security mission. He added that we should move to the highest peak in the chain of hills we had been following. There, a patrol working its way up from the valley floor would meet us. Buoyed by that good news, we moved out and arrived at the rendezvous well ahead of our climbing relief. As we neared the peak, the point fire team suddenly froze. None of them were reacting the way they did when they sighted enemy troops, but something was wrong. I moved forward rapidly, and in seconds saw why they had stopped. Several yards ahead, at the top of the crest, were some 40 zippered winter sleeping bags, arranged in the random pattern of fatigued men seeking any good place to sleep. Torn pieces of cloth and down lining flapped or gently swayed in a macabre dance of death in the mountain breezes. There was no sound. We just looked. The bags had been riddled with bullets and viciously torn open by slashing bayonets. Occupying each was a grinning skeleton.

The identification tags were still fastened to their chains and remained in place around each bony neck. These had been American soldiers: their platoon-sized unit unquestionably had been annihilated while they slept. We carefully removed all of the dog tags and radioed the exact location of the remains. It was gruesome work. It was also a reminder of what can happen if cold and fatigue are allowed to take over. Forty or so MIA's were now confirmed KIA's.

After we had collected the tags and made our report, we had nothing to do except rest and wait for the relief patrol. I was contemplating my footwear and the need to get another bandoleer to tie the second sole when the platoon guide walked over and said that he had a solution to the boot problem. Checking boot sizes of the skeletons, he had found a serviceable pair that matched mine. We removed the boots, carefully emptied the foot bones and returned them to the sleeping bag, and cleaned the boots of dried flesh as best we could. The boots fit well and I wore them for the rest of my tour in Korea. They had belonged to the Army lieutenant who had led the massacred unit. His boots went back to war—and served as an everpresent reminder to me never to get careless.

There are no words that can describe the fatigue we felt as we kept pressure on the retreating enemy. For several days there was no time to heat a can of rations: we ate them cold on the march or in the fighting holes at night while listening as Chinese soldiers poked around, looking for a vulnerable place to attack. The Navy corpsmen, our "docs," advised me that several of my troops had pneumonia or pleurisy: more and more, they had to be prodded to dig in properly. There were usually two Marines to each fighting hole, one of whom was always awake. Enemy units were all around us in what we thought were small groups. But then again, that's what the Army Regimental Combat Team in the broad valley had thought just before the human tidal wave hit their six o'clock and roared over them. Memories of what we had seen in that valley and the sight of the sleeping skeletons were enough to keep us going. But only barely.

Operating on foot in that rugged terrain meant that we had to carry everything we needed to survive. Ammunition was critical, and strict fire discipline was essential. Reinforced platoons or, at most, reinforced companies occupied defensive positions at night. In order to save ammunition, we routinely rigged American or Chinese hand grenades as booby traps. Putting the grenades out in front of the lines in the dark, remembering where they were, and retrieving them the next morning, were duties that no one wanted. It was dangerous and we had men killed or wounded doing it. Salvation came in the form of "Jonah."

One afternoon we arrived at our objective area early and had time to cook rations and take a breather before digging in for the night. Staff Sergeant Reiman came to me and said that the platoon had a "Jonah," a misfit who had to go. The Marine in question was a corporal in the first squad. I did not need the headache, but the problem was in the open and had to be addressed. I sent for the corporal.

Initially, he did not welcome the attention and was reluctant to speak freely. Once convinced that he was going nowhere until we got to the bottom of his problem, he started talking. It was unbelievably simple. He was inwardly seething at the fact that, as a reenlistment incentive, he had been trained as a combat engineer, but because the Marine Corps needed infantrymen more than it needed engineers, he had been assigned to B Company. In the parlance of the '90's, he had an "attitude." No one liked him, and to make things even, he didn't like anyone, either.

We struck pay dirt when I asked him what skills he had learned as an engineer. His enthusiasm grew as he talked about using demolition charges and installing or breaching minefields. He also confessed to having better than passable skills in the realm of using grenades or explosives to rig booby traps. The corporal was a walking, talking gold mine. His talents and training had never been used because nobody had ever asked and he had not volunteered. That night, the corporal, a Portuguese fisherman's son from San Diego, joined my platoon's small command group. He became one of our most valuable and respected men, proudly accepting the dirtiest and least desirable job in the platoon. Each night, he took charge of our external security—the mines and booby traps—and unfailingly made a neat sketch of where each was installed so that if he was killed or wounded we would be able to find them and remove them. Before I left, he received a meritorious promotion to sergeant.

In the late spring of 1951, the war was being fought largely on the platoon or company level. We hit the enemy aggressively by day and he countered at night when our fire support was not as effective. The terrain usually dictated that we move and attack in column formation, with one platoon in the lead. Most of the enemy we faced had pulled back into the mountains and operated out of well-dug-in areas. His camouflaging skill made it extremely hard for us to locate his positions until we were almost on top of them. To be fair to all, I constantly rotated my squads and fireteams so that as much as possible, each unit took its turn in the dangerous point position. Everyone knew that if a man walked point every day, he was not going home alive. On the other hand, as long as the rotation system was fair, then the units would take their turns in the exposed position without a murmur.

B Company was blessed with solid, courageous, and reliable officers. We learned from each engagement: when time permitted, Lieutenant Cronin assembled the platoon leaders to critique our performance. This was a valuable step, because as the Chinese offensive forces increasingly lost their punch, the enemy moved the North Korean Tenth Division in and used it as a rear guard to cover the Chinese redeployment. None of us ever took any North Korean prisoners. The World War II veterans compared them to the Rikusentai—the Japanese naval infantry—the emperor's general equivalent to the U.S. Marines. The North Koreans fought with a ferocity bordering on the inhuman until they were killed. We learned that many of their senior officers had indeed been Rikusentai, trained to fight to the death.

Late in May, B Company was moving through wooded mountains looking for trouble. We had been on the move since shortly after sunrise, but the Third Platoon, leading the company, had sighted nothing until about mid-morning, when the point fire team signaled that it saw enemy ahead. We hit the deck and I moved up carefully. The team leader pointed out several men using axes to cut trees near a half-completed bunker. No other enemy were in sight. Remaining concealed, I signaled a section of machine guns forward to cover the enemy position. The gunners came forward quietly, double-timing but crouched as low as possible. As they reached the selected firing positions, they silently went through the gun drill practiced so often by machine gunners everywhere: gunner putting the tripod in place to his front as he falls to the prone position; assistant gunner placing the gun on the tripod and sliding into the prone position next to the gunner, ready to load as the gunner raises the cover group; both loading the gun and then awaiting the order to commence fire.

Machine gunners move rapidly when going into action. They have no choice. Once the enemy realizes the gun is there, he gives it plenty of attention. Our gunners had been quiet, but their movement probably alerted the enemy. Just as the guns got in place, one of the enemy soldiers yelled and pointed in our direction. The tree cutters started running toward the bunker. We opened fire and brought them down, but the firing created a much larger problem in the form of heavy return fire. We deployed off the trail and brought a rocket squad forward: we would move to the enemy's flank. The enemy saw our move: there was another accurate burst of enemy fire, and two Marines went down wounded.

I radioed Lieutenant Cronin to ask for another section of machine guns as I spread the platoon out farther to the right and left. We had to protect our flanks against possible attack by another enemy unit. It was a confusing picture. We were pinned down and could not locate the source of the enemy fire. The two sections of machine guns (four guns) were using precious ammunition at an unaffordable rate, trying to give us fire superiority. I was stumped. Frontal assaults are usually idiotic. Here, one would have been suicidal. There had to be a better way.

As enemy rounds snapped through the underbrush above me, my brain moved into overdrive, trying to develop a sound scheme of maneuver. Nothing. I was starting to get a feeling of despair, when I was startled by a tap on the shoulder. I looked around just as Captain Jack Jones, the battalion operations officer, slid forward along my side. He had a reputation for showing up wherever there was action.

Lying next to me, he shoved a small, dirty bag of jelly beans toward me. I declined, but he insisted and I took a handful. Putting his head close to mine, he started talking over the noise of the firefight in a calm, almost fatherly way. What did I think they had up there? How many automatic weapons? Where were their flanks? Had I checked them out? Had I given the company commander the location of the enemy positions so he could zero in the mortars? Had I thought about using "Willie Peter" (white phosphorous) mortar rounds to blind the enemy? As he talked on, he gave me enough time and ideas for me to form a plan.

He offered more jelly beans as I told him what we were about to do. Nodding in agreement, he told me not to worry about the mortars. He would make those arrangements when he rejoined Lieutenant Cronin. He added that the mortarmen had only a dozen Willie Peter rounds and warned me not to waste them. Then, worming his

41

way backward until it was safe to crouch, he was gone. Within twenty minutes, the first squad had maneuvered to our right flank, undetected behind a cloud of white Willie Peter smoke, six machine guns were now hosing down the enemy, and high explosive (HE) mortar rounds were beginning to fall on the objective area some 100 yards to my front. As the last mortar round of the fire mission landed, Sergeant Gibson, the first squad leader, gave a signal and quickly moved into the objective area from the enemy's left flank. The machine guns shifted their fire, beating down the area in front of his squad as they moved from our right to our left. They found 12 dead enemy in the position, an unfinished bunker without overhead cover. Our mortars had done most of the damage. These were North Koreans, so there were no prisoners, but their leader left us his diary. He had been a second lieutenant and was a recent graduate of their military academy in Pyongyang.

The corpsmen treated our wounded and we carried them to the rear. The company command group would see to their evacuation while we resumed our duties as the lead platoon. As we moved out, my thoughts turned briefly to a never-ending concern. Water.

All of the streams and rivers were considered to be polluted, so water was a "company problem." Translation: find your own. All except the Navy corpsmen had three canteens. The "docs" had a fourth one for their patients' use. Three canteens were not much, especially considering the fact that a platoon or company could spend several days on a mountain without access to water. Men could and did lose their heads and suffer acute dehydration and emotional breakdowns. Sending water parties down to lower ground was a risky solution. A canteen-laden water party was not much of a fighting force. Moreover, they were frequently fired upon and always risked being ambushed.

We were supposed to use halizone tablets in all of the water to make it safe for drinking. Officers were specifically charged with enforcing this impossible mandate. We tried, but who could resist the temptation? The Marines knew that they would soon be climbing one of Korea's innumerable mountains, and that the next water resupply might be a long time coming. They filled their canteens at some stream and dutifully dropped the proper number of pills—pills that took 20 minutes to become effective—in each. The question then was whether or not to have a long, refreshing, canteen-saving drink before leaving the stream. The answer was always "yes." The platoon guide put it all together one day when he observed that the doctors can cure worms, but "if you die of thirst, there ain't nothing left to cure."

Those were the days when the official line held that, with proper water discipline, men could survive on minimal amounts of the life-sustaining fluid. How did we survive and defeat a tough enemy when we had little water and plenty of worms, dysentery, pleurisy, pneumonia, and infected, unreported wounds? This is a question worth asking. The answer is a rugged blend of discipline, training, pride in being Marines, and a deep, unshakable faith in each other. We were a band of brothers and we watched our brothers' "six."

Chapter 6

Operation Mouse Trap
". . . Now squeeze."

When the Chinese offensive ground to a halt and as their severely battered units attempted to regroup, the pace of our operations increased. The underlying philosophy was as basic as it was brutal: never give a beaten enemy the opportunity to do anything except surrender, run, or die. We were applying unrelenting pressure to the badly mauled but still dangerous Chinese masses. Given enough time, they could reorganize, resupply, refit, and return with a vengeance.

An estimated 5000 Chinese soldiers were in front of our 1000-man battalion, sullenly withdrawing as we pushed them northward through a broad valley. On the skyline of flanking hills we could see Chinese cavalry mounted on Mongolian ponies. They were performing the traditional cavalry reconnaissance mission: avoiding contact while observing and reporting on our movements.

Battalion made several attempts to get rid of them. Battalion called for artillery fire missions, but it was difficult to put the first rounds right on target. When the first rounds exploded with their characteristic crack-crumph, the horsemen would scatter, leaving no worthwhile targets for additional rounds. Battalion also tried Marine air, but as soon as the cavalrymen decided that the man flying the circling airplane was interested in horses and horsemen, they would bolt from the ridgeline into the trees and bushes partway down the slopes. Again, no target. After the artillery fire ceased or the aircraft had departed, the cavalrymen would reassemble on the ridgeline and resume their watching, seemingly mocking our inability to do anything about them.

Studying the map of the territory north of us, Captain Jack Jones finally devised a way to get rid of the shadowing cavalry. If the map was accurate (often a big if), the horsemen were using a ridgeline that ended at a cliff or drop-off far too steep for the horses to negotiate safely. Betting on the mapmakers and taking advantage of available concealment including darkness, A Company worked its way to the top of the ridgeline south of the cavalry and began to herd the horsemen along. Cantering northward and keeping a wary eye on the trailing Marines, the horsemen continued to perform their mission. They obviously saw no cause for serious concern. Infantrymen had never overtaken horses before and there was no reason to think that they would now.

The cavalry leader made two mistakes. If he had a map, he failed to study it. Worse, he failed to use some of his troops to learn more about the ground ahead. Pushed along by A Company, the horsemen finally reached the point where they could go no farther. The map makers were right. The ridgeline ended in a drop too steep for the horses. The stunned cavalrymen wheeled to attack. It was too late. Horse cavalry never had much luck against machine guns: A Company quickly cut most of them down. The rest surrendered. The company led their prisoners and rode ten captured Mongolian ponies back to the battalion command post. They were turned over to the battalion's 81mm mortar platoon for use as sorely needed pack animals.

Shortly after the Mongolian cavalry incident, we received a warning order for an attack. Company commanders and platoon leaders, and especially the latter, are seldom cut in on the "big picture." In many respects, that's just as well, since the chances of their falling into enemy hands are reasonably high. This time, what we did

43

know was that the warning order concerned our role in Operation Mouse Trap, part of the counteroffensive called "Operation Killer" ordered by a first class soldier, the Eighth Army Commander, General Matthew B. Ridgway, U.S. Army.

Mouse Trap started sometime during May of 1951 and ended in June. The operation became possible when the Seventh Marines and the U.S. Army's 187th Airborne Regimental Combat Team got behind an entire Chinese Army corps and cut it off. The Fifth Marines, with the help of the Korean Marine Corps, were to complete the encirclement by attacking right into the heart of the Chinese positions. Much better disciplined than their Republic of Korea Army counterparts, the Korean Marines were tough men who had been with our First Marine Division during the Inchon landings of the previous September. It was good to know that we would have their help. It was also good to know that, for a change, we would ride to the war. What was not good to know was that, once we arrived and started our attack, less than ten thousand Marines and soldiers would have thirty-five to forty thousand Chinese soldiers "surrounded."

The morning after we received the warning order, we boarded amphibious trucks. This vehicle, a boat hull built around a truck frame with a propeller in the rear and all four tires showing, was a World War II innovation. Officially designated "DUKW's," the trucks were, naturally, always called "ducks." As the company commanders, platoon leaders, and forward observers for the various supporting arms waited to climb into their assigned ducks, each received four new maps. The amphibious vehicles told us that we were going to cross a river or two. The four map sheets told us that we would be moving about 20 miles due north—near the 38th parallel, where this Chinese Army Corps was about to be surrounded and pummeled with every weapon we had.

There is usually a noticeable air of tension among the troops before an attack. This time it was different. That they were riding instead of walking probably had more to do with it than anything, but whatever the cause, an atmosphere of lighthearted excitement masked the tension. As the convoy of DUKW's began to move, the two Marines seated next to me were laughing at a badly worn paperback book they had been sharing. Ribbing each other, they turned the pages of Bill Mauldin's *Up Front*, the book about Willie and Joe, the caricatures of World War II Army infantrymen. The two Marines saw and felt the humor in Mauldin's cartoons about the life of foot soldiers in a different war. Neither seemed to realize that they would have made the perfect Korean War version of Mauldin's characters. Unlike Willie and Joe, whose escapades were largely rear area adventures, these two had to face the realities of combat and the coming counter-offensive. Within a week, one would be killed and the other severely wounded.

The trip north was a real show. As the trucks bumped along, we saw thousands of troops: Frenchmen, Brits, Turks, and, of course, soldiers of the U.S. Army. The route was lined with artillery positions: in many of them, the tubes were almost vertical, indicating targets at near-minimum range. One artillery battalion, its hustling cannoneers serving their 75mm pack howitzers, was an excellent example of Marine Corps frugality and ingenuity. The "pack 75" was not in the Marine Corps inventory, yet the gunners were clearly Marines. We later learned that units of the First Marine Division had captured large numbers of Chinese artillery pieces complete with ammunition. It had all been part of war material supplied to Chiang Kai-Shek during World War II and later captured by the communists. It was all in mint condition. Unable to resist the temptation, the 11th Marines, our artillery regiment, had used its

44

cooks, bakers, clerks, supply troops, and whomever else they could get their hands on to form an extra battalion equipped with the "free" pack howitzers.

Overhead, the nearly cloudless sky buzzed with Marine Corsairs orbiting like birds of prey waiting for an unlucky rodent to show itself—but these birds were waiting to be vectored to any Chinese target foolish enough to make its presence known in broad daylight. When a two-aircraft section received a target assignment, the planes would break out of the circling pack and proceed as directed by the forward air controller. When the pilots had located the target, they would nose their Corsairs over into the characteristic whistling dive that meant rockets and napalm were on the way. They were working over the hillsides on both our flanks, and if smoke and fires were any indication of effectiveness, theirs was another virtuoso performance.

Heavy traffic delayed us at two road junctions, where we had to make a slow crossing of a rain-swollen river. During late afternoon, the support units lining the roadside began thinning out, and by dark there were none. We had reached the place where the infantry of both sides had set up for business. Our day of being tourists watching the war machine in action had ended.

The convoy halted shortly after dark. Moving quickly and quietly, the Marines dismounted and struggled into their packs. On the hills above and in front of us, our machine guns hammered, sending streams of tracers streaking across the valley into nearby hills. Not to be outdone, Chinese machine gunners on the hills opposite returned the favor, sending their own streams of tracers slamming into the Marine positions and ricocheting off into the night. This was no place for thin-skinned vehicles: the column of empty DUKW's quickly turned and roared south, back down the valley.

As the DUKW's left, we gave quiet orders. "Saddling up" their weapons, mortar base plates, and ammunition loads, B Company's Marines and corpsmen began climbing a winding trail to the top of the nearest ridgeline. Occasionally, one of the more heavily laden troops would slip and fall. A quiet string of obscenities would follow as the Marine, helped by others, struggled to his feet, retrieved dropped equipment, and continued the climb. When we were near the top, the column halted and the platoon leaders went forward to be assigned platoon defensive areas. With no wasted motion and few words, the troops started digging in, their efforts accompanied by the chattering of machine guns, the shifting shadowy light of artillery and mortar flares, and the sound of an occasional artillery duel when the cannoneers decided to get personal.

B Company was an experienced, well-disciplined rifle company that knew exactly what had to be done. Even so, it took almost four hours of hard work to get us properly entrenched and ready for any Chinese counterattack. We were lucky. It took the enemy that long to find us.

We had just finished digging when the Chinese started working us over. At first they tried to get us with a high-velocity, direct-fire weapon, probably the 76mm anti-tank gun. The first volley made a nasty, screeching whistle as it passed over our positions on the ridgeline and exploded harmlessly somewhere to the rear. The next volley hit on the hill below us, doing no damage. We were bracketed. There was no question about what was coming next. The weapons were in the hills well in front of us, but the Chinese obviously had a forward observer much closer to us, adjusting the fire. The next rounds would be "on target." Everyone flattened, hugging the bottom of his fighting hole. Even so, we started taking casualties with the next rounds. After 15 minutes, the direct fire ceased and we began absorbing punishment from their 120mm mortars. The mortar fire was quite accurate, but it too ceased after about 15 minutes. The Chinese were obviously short of ammunition. We weren't, and our counterbattery fire continued throughout the night.

At first light the next morning, we left the hillside positions and, retracing our steps of the previous night, moved back down to the road. Yesterday's northward movement would continue, but now we would move on foot in our familiar company column. My Third Platoon would start in the lead.

The stench of death was all around us. There were bodies or parts of bodies everywhere. A nearby river might as well have been called "the river of death." Countless bodies in various stages of dismemberment and decay dotted its surface, erasing all thoughts of filling canteens. Once again we found ourselves starting a day of heavy exertion with half-filled canteens.

Shortly after the column started moving warily up the valley, a jeep carrying two Associated Press reporters caught up with us and began moving past the machine gunners who were following the lead riflemen. The brakes screeched as the jeep came to a reluctant stop. The reporters wanted to continue northward: we could not convince them that their going ahead of us would be stupid, with enemy all around us. The column continued moving past the jeep as the reporters photographed the passing Marines while discussing what to do. A burst of machine gun fire from a hill about 500 yards ahead of us ended the debate. Passing between two Marines, the slugs punched holes in the jeep, spoiling our chance for media fame. Skidding in a wide arc, the jeep pointed its radiator southward and left in the proverbial cloud of dust, its occupants clinging to the sides for support.

It was a long day. As we moved off the road into the foothills to the east, another platoon took the Third Platoon's place on the point. Safety is a relative thing, but moving from the point to the rear of a company column is almost like taking a vacation on the French Riviera.

As the company snaked its way up the hill, the smooth pace gave way to an erratic pattern of moving then halting. We would move a short distance, stop when we heard firing and explosions up ahead, and then move again once the firefight ended. Before long, we encountered Marines carrying dead and wounded down the hill in ponchos. They were working hard to get their brother Marines to the valley floor and ambulances waiting on the road. Those carrying the dead and wounded were as careful as they could be, but sometimes it made no difference. One or more of the carriers would slip and dump the wounded or dead Marine on the rocky ground, then make the great effort it took to retrieve him. Soon the word was passed back that these dead and wounded were from the Seventh Marines.

The hillside was steep: all hillsides in Korea are steep, and they never seem to have a down slope. It was always up, up, up. As we climbed, the angry sounds of the firefights got closer. It wouldn't be long before we took our turn in the barrel. Finally, after an almost impossible climb, we found ourselves halted in position next to a company of the Seventh Marines. Our own C Company of the Fifth Marines was also somewhere in the area. The enemy was defending a strongpoint 150 yards up the ridge from the Seventh Marines company. They had tried all day to take the position from

46

the front and were now working on an envelopment. It was their dead and wounded we had seen earlier.

Taking advantage of the halt to learn whatever I could about the situation, I ran over to the nearest unit of the Seventh Marines company and asked one of the Marines where his platoon leader was. Moving in the direction in which he pointed, I soon found the platoon leader, Earl Roth, a Basic School classmate and former University of Maryland halfback. He was one tired-looking man. Earl had two cans of hot beer in his pack and offered me one as he filled me in on their unsuccessful attacks. The beer was wet and over it we had a quick conversation that ended when his radio cackled, telling him that his platoon was to move out. As I left him, I recalled that he had been a corporal during the brutal World War II fight for Okinawa. Now he was about to attack another enemy position in another war.

Earl made it through his second war, but our paths never crossed again. And as fate would have it, he was not moving out to attack the position. We were. It takes time for word to filter down to the platoon level.

Advising the company commander that there were no enemy troops on the southern end of the ridgeline we had just climbed, battalion ordered us to move there and envelop the enemy position from that direction. It was late in the day when the order came out, and moving to the southern end of the ridgeline was obviously going to take a lot of time and energy. We were to get as far as we could during daylight and then be prepared to launch the attack the next morning.

When we started pulling back, C Company, Fifth Marines covered us with streams of machine gun fire aimed at the strongpoint. The Chinese kept their heads down. With little delay and no wasted motion, the company column re-formed and we were soon on our way back down the hill. Once on the valley floor, we would cross behind C Company, find the next finger to the south that led back to the top, and start the climb all over again. The Third Platoon was still at the rear of the company column. Jim Cronin and his radio operators moved with the lead platoon, directing the way.

Getting to the valley floor was easy and we had no problem either crossing behind C Company or finding the finger that would take us up to the southern end of the ridgeline. As we struggled upward, it was clear that the path we were following had been much used. It doesn't always work, but more often than not, people stay alive in combat because they think. What got my brain waves going in hyperactive mode was the much-worn condition of the trail we were climbing. Could the area to which it led be unoccupied? Not likely!

But the position we were going to attack had to have been important to the Chinese. It had held out against two days of determined attacks by the Seventh Marines: it was probably going to be a hard nut to crack. The Chinese were not dummies about security, and the information given us by battalion was, at best, suspect. Darkness set in and the big question became how much farther we would get before running into enemy outposts or major positions.

Muscles screaming from the exertion of the steep climb gradually began returning to normal and the lungs that had been working so hard to get more oxygen started to demand less, sure signs that the trail was beginning to flatten. We were nearing the top of the climb. Soon the column halted, every man grateful for the rest. We had come to a fork in the trail; Lieutenant Cronin told me to cover both flanks while he decided what to do. It was pitch black. Without being told, the troops kept their five-yard intervals and alternately faced right and left, weapons at the ready. Field glasses are helpful at night: as I started looking up the slope through mine, the sound of a rifle bolt clicking home, or what could have been a rifle bolt clicking home, seemed to come from that direction. The area was heavily wooded, with low brush between the trees. After making a careful, deliberate sweep of the area, I saw the corner of something man-made come into focus. There was a log bunker about 40 yards up the slope. There were also more clicks of rifle bolts going home. Somebody was chambering rounds and about to fire.

The platoon radio operator was a few yards from me. Moving to him, I reached for the radio and quietly called the company commander. He answered immediately. The message was short: we were in the middle of an enemy position, about to be fired on, and we would assault up the hill immediately. His answer was shorter. "Do it." I yelled to the platoon something about facing left and assaulting to the top, now! Whatever it was, they understood and we started in a series of squad rushes, the troops screaming and firing as they moved. The Chinese reacted and all hell broke loose. Return fire came from at least a half dozen locations, but we were among them too fast and the sound of our grenades started overpowering the sounds of rifles and machine guns. Some of the enemy soldiers broke out of their positions and started running for safety at the top of the ridgeline. We cut them down. Repeated cries of "corpsman" made it evident that the Chinese were not the only ones paying a price.

It was a dark, confused melee punctuated by grenade explosions, rifles firing, the chattering of machine guns, and the almost inhuman screams of men whipped by frenzy, fear, or both. Saving us was the fact that we were the ones causing most of the confusion. A spontaneous assault was not what the enemy had expected, and his reactions were slow. For all that, we were in the middle of a well-developed strong point and could still be in a world of trouble.

I was moving with the first squad and talking on the radio to Jim Cronin when something exploded near me. I felt myself being turned over in the air, then falling and rolling downhill. I was numb. My ears seemed to have been blown out and there was a dull buzzing sound. As the world began to come back into focus, I realized that Staff Sergeant Reiman was shaking me and yelling something. I nodded to let him know that I was all right and reached for help to get up. Jim Cronin had arrived and was waiting for me to come around. We had to make a quick decision. Reiman pointed to the bunker that had dropped the grenade on me and slid his forefinger across his throat to tell me that it had been knocked out. He knew that I couldn't hear him.

After considering the possibilities, Cronin decided to pull back, regroup, and try again in daylight. The truth is that we should not have been sent to that hill that late in the day without a reconnaissance. In any event, Cronin made himself understood to me and we began to organize to move several miles back to the battalion area. We were in a precarious position, but walking out was not going to be easy, either. We had three wounded, one seriously, and none killed. As usual, our corpsmen had done a superb job on the wounded, and one could walk. The other two would have to be carried.

We had killed at least a dozen of the enemy and wounded many more in the surprise engagement. It could have been tragic, but if we could get back to friendly territory safely, we could call it a good day's work. We could not have had a cooler head or more competent leader taking us down that treacherous path. We all worried about our skipper. He had only a few days to go before this Korean tour of duty ended, and we'd all heard the old story about the guy who had only a few days to go when he got killed.

We made it down safely. I carried our senior corpsman all the way. He never whimpered despite having had a slug pass cleanly through his knee. When we were halfway down the hill, the Army turned on its "artificial moonlight"—the beams of huge searchlights bouncing off the low-lying clouds. The result was like instant daylight, and we felt completely exposed. We need not have worried. The Chinese must have felt the same, because they did nothing.

After a long walk, we reached the battalion area. Battalion was alert. Too alert. The skipper had radioed ahead to tell them that we were coming in, but it had done no good. We knew we were getting close when a light machine gun starting groping in the night for our column, sending rounds snapping overhead. It was soon joined by another. After our lead elements yelled an unprofessional but totally impressive string of obscene observations concerning those who serve in rear echelon battalion areas, the firing stopped and we were able to enter the battalion command post perimeter without further incident.

The wounded went directly to the battalion aid station. Then we were assigned an area and began digging in. Within minutes, we were issued rations and real, honest- to-God water. We had been on the move for 36 hours and had had no food for the last eighteen. I wondered how much more the troops could take.

When everyone was settled, I went to sick bay to find out what damage the explosion on the hill had done to me. Other than a lost left eardrum, it wasn't bad. The doctor and corpsmen removed a few pieces of metal and bandaged other minor wounds. Apparently the weapon had been a concussion grenade, designed for use in a confined space. For whatever reason, the Chinese had used this one in the open. One of the few pieces of metal in the grenade was the two-inch-long detonator spring. It had entered my back and evidently made one of the minor wounds that the corpsmen bandaged, without realizing what was inside. It would surface almost twenty years later.

After the corpsmen had treated the effects of the concussion grenade, one of them gave me a cheese sandwich and a paper cup filled with warm tomato juice. Those and two hours of uninterrupted sleep did wonders. By early morning, we were ready to go. The troops about whom I had worried so much a few hours before were in great spirits as we moved out, headed back toward the hill we had left the night before. It was May 29, 1951: I had not yet been with the company for two months. Time flies when you're having fun.

C Company, commanded by First Lieutenant Spike Schenning, had been ordered to attack the position we had tangled with the previous night. As we passed the area, we witnessed their assault, led by Second Lieutenant Pete McCloskey. With some help from early morning fog, C Company quickly overran the enemy positions and the firefight turned into hand-to-hand combat. The surviving enemy raced out of their fighting positions and tried to take on the Marines with fists, rifles used as clubs, grenades at a range close enough to get anybody, and any other weapon they could use. Schenning's Marines met the Chinamen with a fury of their own: in a matter of seconds, it was obvious who was going to win.

Pete McCloskey, a reserve officer from Stanford University, had an enviable reputation in the battalion for courage. He added to it that morning as he jumped on top of an enemy bunker and started screaming to his Marines, "We've got 'em by the balls! Now squeeze!" It was over quickly, but the victory celebration was short-lived. The enemy had 120mm mortars zeroed in exactly on the position: as the officers and staff non-commissioned officers of C Company were reorganizing their jubilant troops, 120mm mortar rounds started raining on them. They suffered several critical casualties, one of which was the company commander.

The battalion talked about the guts and heroism of that hand-to-hand fight-to-the-death for weeks, and at reunions for decades. Pete McCloskey was a real fighter who later became Congressman McCloskey, a Republican member of the U. S. House of Representatives from California. His words screamed from atop that bunker were typical of the fighting spirit of our battalion.

The Marine rifle companies could not have survived without Marine aviation. Whenever the weather allowed it, F4U Corsairs, our "flying artillery," were overhead waiting for the rifle companies to call them in on attack missions. It also was not unusual for us to get additional support from Navy pilots flying Douglas ADs, dive bombers with an exceptional ability to carry a very heavy load and stay on station for hours. On rare occasions, we got help from Air Force F-80's. They couldn't stay on station as long as the prop planes, but these jet fighters could get to us very quickly in an emergency.

Each Marine had a brightly colored "air panel" in his pack. During ground action, our lead elements would mark our forward positions for the pilots either by displaying the panels on their backs or by setting them out on the ground. Our pilots, particularly the Marines, were so skilled at delivering close air support that we never hesitated to ask them to attack enemy units that were 40 to 50 yards from our positions or, in emergencies, even closer.

When we were on the attack, we often asked the pilots to alternate live and simulated bombing runs. Our units would advance under cover of the dummy runs while the enemy tried to make himself as small as possible before the bombs exploded. We were able to perfect the technique because we talked directly to the aircraft section leader, whom we often knew by name. This close coordination and skilled support was unique to the Marine Corps. We bragged that our pilots were Marines first and Aviators second. They took good care of their ground buddies.

Day after day and night after night, Marines of B Company—and, for that matter, those of the other rifle companies—would cheer like schoolboys when the Corsairs arrived overhead. After most of their attacks, when we reported the damage to them, they would give us a "victory roll" and a wave on their way back home. The aviators who had been aboard *USS Menard* had kept track of "their" infantry types and knew where we had gone. At the end of a mission they would frequently fly over us low and slow so that one of the pilots could open his canopy and toss out a small parachute. As the chute floated down, we knew we were in for a treat: a loaf of bread stuffed with cheese, maybe some sardines, and usually one or two miniature bottles of bourbon. There was always a note of encouragement, reminding us that we had plenty of support. It seems like my old friend from the troopship, 1st Lt. Pete Keeling, was more often than not the source of that parachuted loaf of bread: addressed to 2nd Lt. Charlie Cooper.

Near the end of May, First Lieutenant Bill Kerrigan transferred to us from C Company to replace Jim Cronin when his tour of duty ended. As we moved out the day after C Company's hand-to-hand fight, the Third Platoon, accompanied by the soon-to-be new company commander, was at the end of the column. Moving up a broad mountain trail behind so many other Marines, we had that feeling of safety and security. It didn't last. Mortar fire suddenly rained down on the column, and even though we scattered like rabbits, the First Platoon, immediately ahead of us, took casualties. Two men were killed outright and a third died shortly after. Several others were wounded.

This was mountain warfare and, since we had no medical evacuation helicopters, we had to carry our wounded until we reached an accessible road. Since the Third Platoon was in the rear of the column, we made litters from ponchos and tree saplings in which to carry the wounded and dead back down the hill. There jeep ambulances would meet them and transport them back to the battalion aid station. Fortunately, this time the hill was not far from the road.

Later in the day, the Third Platoon moved to the head of the company column. The Chinese, now surrounded, were pulling back as the Fifth Marines drove into their positions. However, they were trying to keep us off balance and slow the pursuit by periodically standing and fighting, then withdrawing when the pressure got too great. As we climbed, the platoon's point Marines picked up a blood trail. It led to what appeared to be an unoccupied major bunker complex. Or maybe that was what we were supposed to think. Making an occupied bunker complex look unoccupied until it was too late for the attacking force was one of the enemy's favorite stunts. We had seen it before.

With the rest of the platoon covering them from good positions, one fire team carefully worked its way to the rear of the complex and began checking out individual bunkers, using the convenient method of shoving white phosphorous grenades through the apertures. At first, nothing happened. Then a grenade exploding in one of the larger bunkers flushed out several Chinese like a covey of quail. Bolting into the open, some with their clothing carrying burning white phosphorous, the panic-stricken soldiers started running up the hill, seeking safety. They never made it.

A few more of the bunkers also contained enemy soldiers, hiding quietly in ambush, waiting for us to make a mistake. We didn't make any, and the drama of the first occupied bunker was replayed until the area was cleared. Behind the bunker complex were four 82mm mortars, each with a few rounds still neatly stacked beside it. A glance back down the hill showed clearly that these were the mortars that caused us so much trouble on the trail earlier in the day.

The next day, Jim Cronin was promoted to captain and detached from the battalion. We were sorry to see him go, but all of us were relieved that he had made it through safely and was on his way home. Bill Kerrigan, our new skipper, was an entirely different personality. A soft-spoken reserve officer who had a large family at home, Lieutenant Kerrigan was a professional who knew and understood the basics of combat leadership. Exceptionally wise in the use of supporting arms and a tactical genius when it came to preparing defensive positions, he taught us a great deal in our short time together. We would not have survived a few nights later had it not been for his cool leadership and defensive savvy.

The routine with the Chinese had become clear. Every day, we attacked, using our superior supporting arms to our advantage. At night, there was a role reversal: we defended and the Chinese attacked. Some of their attacks were hard to imagine. One night several hundred of them hit our company position. The first waves were

51

composed of three-man teams, two men carrying a wicker basket filled with grenades, the third running behind, picking grenades out of the basket and throwing them into our positions. If they were expendable, and they were, they were also ineffective. Their purpose was to draw fire so that others waiting in the darkness could locate and plot our positions. Our well-disciplined company never responded with rifles or machine guns. We used artillery, mortars, and when the enemy got close enough, our own hand grenades to break up these initial probes. When they were able to penetrate into our main battle positions, everyone stayed in the fighting holes and used rifles and machine guns to cut them down. They didn't penetrate that far very often, but if the Chinese commander was willing to expend enough men, they could do it. Temporarily.

Sending out these basket grenadiers was not the only method the Chinese used to try to destroy the Marine rifle companies that were tightening the vise. They would broadcast to us on our tactical radio frequencies: the Chinese-accented "Hello, Marines, this is Captain China calling" would precede less-than-flattering comments about our lineage, fighting abilities, or whatever else they thought might get a response. Their intent was to get us talking so that their radio direction finders could locate our command posts and call in mortar or artillery fire. We never responded to the various Captain Chinas, but once in a while one would talk too much for his own good and our radio direction finders would send our artillery or mortars his way.

Another aid for the Chinese enemy was the radio antenna. Radios don't work without antennas: ever since the tactical radio arrived on the scene, the antenna has been a necessary evil. The antenna indicates that an officer in command or control of something is somewhere in the vicinity. We had several excellent snipers who spent most of every day looking for even loose groupings of radio operators or antennas. When they found one, they would go to work searching out the enemy officer. Unfortunately, the enemy also had good field glasses, sniper scopes, and snipers.

Maybe it was the antennas or maybe it was something else, but about this time, the war got to be too much for the company's artillery forward observer, a first lieutenant whose task it was to control our supporting artillery fire. In the France that my dad knew during World War I, the lieutenant's problem would have been called "cat fever." Later, it was called "battle fatigue." But whatever we call the malady, it made him scared to death of death—so much so that he had to be medically evacuated. His replacement was to be Second Lieutenant Holcomb "Hawk" Thomas, a Basic School classmate. Hawk arrived at the foot of our long hill early one morning. I was looking at him through my field glasses, thinking about things to tell him, watching as he left the jeep that brought him and started up the hill on foot. He took a few steps and disappeared from view in the flame and smoke of an explosion. He'd stepped on an enemy anti-personnel mine. Hawk's war was quickly over, but he did survive and regain full use of the foot the doctors at first thought he would lose. The rest of us had to take up the artillery forward observer's duties, duties that gave us another antenna to worry about.

As the Fifth Marines continued to exert pressure, the Chinese night counterattacks became noticeably larger and more determined. The Chinese soldiers were at home in the dark and seemed oblivious to the casualties we inflicted. Our new skipper responded to the increasing Chinese pressure by wisely allowing more time each day for preparation of our defensive positions. Fire discipline was paramount. We had to conserve ammunition because emergency resupply was largely restricted to air drops, a method that was weather-dependent and most times inaccurate. In addition to rigging booby traps outside our lines, we used pre-planned artillery and mortar fire to avoid wasting precious ammunition and divulging details of our defensive positions.

Bill Kerrigan went a few steps farther. He had us prepare back-up fighting holes not only for us to sleep in when off duty but also to give additional depth to our perimeter. We had accumulated a large supply of our own and captured Chinese hand grenades. Someone had to carry this heavy stock all day, every day, but there was a payoff at night when each two-man fighting hole had 15 or 20 grenades laid on the parapet, ready for action. If time permitted, we also scraped out dummy positions outside of our lines. These were booby trapped shallow holes filled with brush rigged to look like men. The extra digging and other extensive preparations added to the burden of exhausted troops but it all had to be done.

The increasing intensity of the night attacks signaled an impending major Chinese effort. All of us were convinced that a disciplined company of Marines, properly supported, could hold off the whole Chinese Army if necessary. That confidence was soon to be tested.

On the night of the "big attack," we had completed the most thorough defensive preparations we'd made since I joined the Baker Bandits. We never knew whether Lieutenant Kerrigan had received intelligence information indicating a major Chinese effort or if he was following his own instincts and good judgment. This evening, all was quiet until about eleven o'clock, when Chinese bugle calls broke the silence on three sides of the company perimeter. The calls were followed by the sounds of their reconnaissance units moving into our defensive belt of booby traps and non-lethal devices designed to make noise when disturbed. It was time to unlimber the fire support system. We called for illumination rounds. We also called for some of the pre-planned artillery and mortar fire missions to be ready for action when the lights came on. The illumination rounds popped up overhead: as the cannisters that had contained them whirred and spun their way to the ground, the large flares swung from their parachutes in slow descent. Night turned to day for 20 or 30 seconds. Large groups of Chinese were everywhere, huddling together, apparently waiting for orders to charge. The artillery and mortar fire missions were moved to the known targets while the skipper spoke quickly but calmly into the radio handset, asking for air support. There was no question: tonight we would need the whole support bag.

The Third Platoon's first squad began the infantry fight. With cries of "fire in the hole," a warning to nearby Marines, they began throwing grenades. The Chinese had already crept that close. I talked to the company commander on our wire line, informing him that there was a large number of enemy directly to our front. He responded that there were large numbers on three sides and that he was walking 4.2-inch mortar fires closer to our lines.

The intense exchange of hand grenades continued as the Chinese tried to batter their way into our position while we did our best to destroy them before they generated any momentum. The numbers of grenade explosions increased steadily, their sounds reaching a lasting fortissimo, a sign that their infantry was following in the assault. Then we heard the staccato sounds of their burp guns, and the deep chugging sound of their heavy machine guns. The burp guns were the mainstay of the North Korean and Chinese armies. Resembling our old Thompson submachine gun, the burp gun had a cyclic rate of fire of 550 rounds per minute. If they had been accurate, or if the soldiers using them had had even average marksmanship training, the Chinese assault would probably have proven too much. But they were poor marksmen and used a large volume of fire to compensate. Even so, there were cries of "corpsman." The enemy's grenades, mortar fire, and machine gun fire were beginning to take a toll. The night became a fury of incoming grenades and mortar fire followed by the deafening staccato of hundreds of enemy assault weapons closing in, while our grenades and mortar and artillery fire broke up the repeated assaults.

Each time that they could no longer take the punishment, the Chinese would turn and flee. There would be an eerie calm and then it would start all over. At last, we heard the sounds of aircraft engines overhead. The Chinese were attacking everywhere: the Marine Corsairs had been busy helping others. Now it was our turn. While we used mortar and artillery white phosphorous rounds to mark target areas, Whistling Death began making dummy runs, getting familiar with our positions. When they were ready, they roared in on a napalm run as Baker Company's Marines cheered.

The napalm didn't stop the Chinamen. Not that night. It cut down some of them and started fires on two sides of the perimeter, helping to light the area, but the Chinese came back again and again. Their last effort almost succeeded. Several of them actually got inside our lines, but then, confused, stopped for a moment to get oriented. For the first time that night, they felt the lash of well-aimed rifle fire and machine guns. In seconds, there were no survivors. The Chinese survivors outside the perimeter sullenly withdrew, heaving parting grenades and firing poorly aimed bursts from their burp guns. We didn't know it then, but it was over for the night. We had suffered only a few killed but had a large number of wounded. It had been close, the hardest fight yet for B Company. But what was bad for us was worse for the Chinese. Their dead covered the entire area for a hundred yards.

The attrition of almost constant battle was shrinking our company. Lieutenant Pat McGahn of the Second Platoon was seriously wounded and evacuated. Others were killed or wounded, and we had numerous cases of broken spirits—battle fatigue. It was not uncommon to pass a young Marine on a trail during a break and see that he was quietly sobbing. Maybe he had just lost his best friend, maybe he was ill with fever or pneumonia, or maybe he had reached his limit. Whatever the cause, he had to be sent to the rear. These incidents increased in frequency. Officers and non-commissioned officers were not immune, either. Usually, the men would strongly protest being evacuated. They did not want to leave their "family" or let the unit down, but their effectiveness was largely gone.

Our senior corpsman was a key man in this evacuation process. His coded write-up on the medical evacuation tag described the problem and recommended a treatment. Sometimes, it took only a few days. Sent to the rear to a battalion headquarters or a medical company with its field hospital, the men could shower, get clean uniforms, eat hot chow, and, more important than anything, sleep without fear. Most of the time, the recovery rate was miraculous.

Word of the company's dwindling numbers reached the rear area aid stations and hospitals, producing results that were both positive and predictable. Many of the recovering troops were used as medical orderlies once they became ambulatory. It was good therapy and helped save skilled corpsmen for more demanding work. When they heard of the company's plight, these temporary medical orderlies took matters into their own hands—they deserted. It was the opposite of deserting from battle. They were deserting *to* battle, back to B Company, their Band of Brothers.

They arrived in all sorts of ways, and without much notice, at least initially. There was the former automatic rifleman who showed up with a carbine, a weapon normally used only by platoon leaders. Then there was the corpsman who'd had to be evacuated a week earlier, after the big night battle. And there were others filtering back—so many that, at one point, the company had to go on reduced rations to feed everybody. It had become a replacement draft of healing, brave, and loyal members of a fighting unit who had deserted their posts in the rear in order to help their family at the front. Similar things happened to other rifle companies. It was not a reaction confined to the Korean War, either. I saw it time and again later in Vietnam, under very different circumstances. The strength and impact of Marine bonding is miraculous to behold.

The fighting slackened somewhat for the next few days. Both sides had pushed themselves to exhaustion and both needed a respite. The respite, such as it was, ended for the Third Platoon when the battalion commander alerted B Company to the fact that the enemy had been sending heavy mortar units into the valley on our right flank to conduct nightly shellings of the rear area command posts. Additionally, prisoner interrogations had revealed that the Chinese were conducting a build-up for a push south through that same wide valley. Colonel Hopkins directed B Company to form a task force to seek out enemy forces in the valley. In particular, the task force was to locate and destroy the mortars and prevent any buildup of forces. He added that the task force, built around B Company's Third Platoon, would be reinforced by a tank platoon and one section each of 75mm recoilless rifles and heavy machine guns. He called back later to add that, on the previous day, our aircraft had spotted an unknown number of Chinese tanks hiding in the valley. Great news!

We owned the dominating high ground, but the broad valley into which we were to move was not occupied by any friendly forces. On the valley floor were several small hills that dominated the terrain around them. The hills were divided into two groups and designated as our objectives one and two.

The next morning, my heavily reinforced platoon of more than 125 Marines and corpsmen, carrying two days' rations and all the ammunition they could, started the long, easy downhill walk into the valley. In addition to incorporating the other reinforcements specified by the battalion commander, we took along one 60mm mortar with white phosphorous and illumination rounds only. We would meet the M-48 tanks at a checkpoint in the valley. Our combat sage, the platoon guide, could not help but observe that tanks were nice to have around if you ran into other tanks, but that they tended to "draw fire."

The troops were in high spirits, having had a reasonably calm night and a breakfast of fresh bread, hard-boiled eggs, and canned fruit juice, all brought forward on the backs of the Korean Service Corps "chiggy bearers" the previous afternoon. It was a beautiful day, and for a while things went as planned. We met the tanks as scheduled, and their platoon leader, a first lieutenant, asked for a squad of troops to give him close-in protection. There was a fairly good two-lane gravel road on the left flank, and it paralleled our direction of advance toward an area where the valley narrowed considerably. The narrow portion of the valley was where the enemy tanks had been sighted. We agreed that his tanks and my squad would move on the road on the left flank as we started across the open area toward our first objective.

As we approached the first hill, I studied it carefully through field glasses. It was covered with trenchlines and bunkers. There were no troops visible. There didn't have to be: one of the enemy soldiers had left his laundry drying in the sun to show us that the bunkers were occupied. Without delay, we had the tanks lay in five or six rounds of 90mm main gun ammunition, just to test the reaction. At Quantico, our instructors called it a "reconnaissance by fire." Whatever they called it, it worked. We received long-range machine gun fire in return and immediately deployed to take the hill.

The attack was a classic infantry assault by fire and maneuver. Using tank fire, artillery support, and heavy mortars firing smoke and white phosphorous for concealment, the platoon moved to the base of the hill. Sergeant Gibson and his squad then moved to the right flank and when ready assaulted under the cover of machine guns and the remainder of the platoon. There were two grenade explosions, and shortly afterward Sergeant Gibson appeared on the top of a bunker and waved us up. There were 25 or more enemy dead, all Chinese. Most of them still had their ration rolls of rice looped over their shoulders. They were either just arriving or getting ready to leave when we started the attack. The troops rolled all of them into a large bunker that had collapsed and shoveled dirt over the impromptu grave. The hillside position was extensive and beautifully dug in. It would make a good patrol base. The tanks moved abreast of us as the last of the platoon climbed the objective and got in place. We would operate from here, possibly riding the tanks up the valley. So far, so good.

About two hundred yards to our north, there was a small hamlet of huts with straw roofs and without signs of life. The huts were next to a stream, but otherwise had no appreciable cover or concealment anywhere near them. The number of Chinese troops that had occupied our newly won patrol base probably meant that there were more nearby, and the only place they could be was in the huts, long since abandoned by the farmers who once tilled the adjacent and now vacant fields.

It was time for another reconnaissance by fire, this time with machine guns firing incendiary rounds to ignite the straw roofs. It didn't take long. The roofs burst into flame and men began to scramble from the huts, running in all directions. They were armed and trying to escape. The tanks and machine gunners went to work and within a matter of minutes, all of the enemy were on the ground, one of them holding a white cloth aloft on a stick. There had been about 60 of them, and we captured all 35 of the survivors, many of them wounded.

A quick search of the huts yielded maps, radios, wire lines, telephones, and several large bags of rice. The complex had been a headquarters of some sort. We learned later that one of our prisoners was the lieutenant colonel who commanded the mortar unit that had caused so many problems for our rear areas. The commanding officer had no rank insignia, and half his left buttock was shot off, but the deference shown him by the other prisoners made it obvious that he was important. The corpsmen examined him and were surprised that the open wound was not infected. All of the muscles were exposed, and the wound was several days old.

The intelligence non-commissioned officer sent along by battalion was helpful in trying to extract information from the prisoners, but the interrogation was the least of my worries. I wanted more than anything for someone to get them off our hands. Overnight responsibility for 35 prisoners seemed too much for a small, isolated task force. Our radioed report that we had captured what appeared to be a command group, perhaps including senior officers, was intended to stimulate higher headquarters' interest in retrieving the prisoners.

Now the Chinese decided to move on us with tanks. Four Soviet-built T-34's emerged from the narrow portion of the valley, about a mile to the north. Apparently they had not seen the Marine tanks. Our tankers radioed that they saw enemy tanks and wanted to go after them. That Fort Knox Armored School aggressiveness was showing as the tank commander visualized a once-in-a-lifetime tank-on-tank battle. He received orders to deploy where he was and engage the T-34's if they closed.

The intent was to attack them with aircraft first. There were Corsairs in the area, but not under our control. That changed quickly, once the report of enemy tanks in sight reached battalion. From our hill observation post, we could see four distinct shapes rolling toward us in staggered column formation. Our tanks, hiding in a nearby stream bed, held a hull defilade position, with only their turrets and guns exposed. The tension was rising fast when I remembered the Chinese prisoners and told the platoon sergeant to find a safe place to stash them.

A section of two Corsairs checked in on the radio, reporting an ordnance load of rockets and 1000-pound bombs. The pilots were as excited as any of us: seldom, if ever, would any of us see one, much less four, Chinese tanks out of hiding during daylight hours. The enemy tankers must have been moving with the turret hatches open, because they soon saw the orbiting birds of prey. They knew who was the prey, but beyond that seemed confused. They stopped about a half-mile from our front.

The pilots had been briefed to start from the back of the column and work forward. Our tankers, waiting less than patiently, were instructed to take on the Chinese from front to rear. As the first Corsair rolled into its dive, our tank guns barked and the first rounds screamed downrange at the trapped T-34's. Two runs of the aircraft and it was all over. The Corsairs destroyed three of the T-34's and the tankers got the fourth. During all this excitement, battalion radioed with the less-than-good news that the prisoners would be our responsibility until some time the following day.

The prisoners were not the problem I had thought they would be. Staff Sergeant Reiman had formed them into a working party and issued each an entrenching tool. He first had them remove their dead comrades from the impromptu bunker grave and bury them in shallow graves at the foot of our hill. He then took the prisoners back to the collapsed bunker and had them widen it and dig another five feet straight down. When the work was done, he ordered them into the large pit. When I arrived, they were all squatting on their haunches, looking up at me, waiting to hear their fate. The interpreter explained to them that if they caused any trouble, we would throw grenades into the pit. If, on the other hand, they remained quiet and did as ordered, they would be taken to our rear area in the morning. He stressed the point that their war was over and that they would receive medical care, food, and water in the rear, but none at this time. They nodded in understanding and never became a problem, even during the harrowing night that followed.

Taking a leaf from the Kerrigan book of defensive tactics, we spent the afternoon organizing the hill as a defensive position and operating base. There are times in combat when there is an ominous feel about things and the air smells of disaster. This was one of them. Only the foolish or suicidal ignore them. We were a long way from friendlies, and the valley north of us apparently sheltered large numbers of Chinese troops.

Because a tank is more a target than a help in a reinforced platoon's night defensive perimeter, we sent the tanks to the rear. We could not spare the infantry to protect them. The tank platoon commander and I agreed that they would return early the next morning. We would then resume our move northward in the valley.

For the most part, the slopes of our hill were steep and almost impossible to negotiate at night, but there were three clearly defined avenues of approach leading up to our positions. We covered these very thoroughly with the 60 mm mortar and machine guns. Topping it off we had the work of our engineer corporal, who handled all of our external security work and had gotten ever more sophisticated with his booby traps. Among other things, he had installed several illumination grenades forward of our lines. They could be used to light up a sizable area when and if the Chinese attacked.

As night closed in, we set up the platoon command post in one end of the largest surviving bunker. The docs moved into the other end, to use it for an emergency aid station. The last thing we did before we settled in for the night was to register artillery and mortar fire on all four sides of the hill. We could shift their aim rapidly from one of these reference points to another to cover our entire perimeter with their fire. By nightfall we had done all that we could have done to get ready. After dark, we sat back and waited, ears straining to pick up the slightest unusual sound.

When it happened, it was not what we had expected. Rather than the scrabbling sounds of someone slowly crawling, or the muffled rattle of a carelessly secured rifle sling or bayonet, what broke the silence was the "thunk, thunk" sound of heavy mortars starting a fire mission. The sound was coming from our right rear, no more than half a mile away. At first we thought we were the target, but flashes followed by the crumping sound of distant explosions well to the south indicated that they were after bigger game. There were eight mortar tubes firing rapidly. These were the 120mm mortars that had been creating problems in our rear areas. Destroying them was part of our mission. The fact that we worried them so little that they ignored us as they continued their nightly routine did not bode well for us. Apparently, someone else would deal with us.

When we reported the location of the mortars to battalion, we got the initial response that they were under fire and would contact us later. A few expletives later, we got the point across. Within minutes, we were adjusting an artillery fire mission on the still active 120's. After two corrections for range, the artillery batteries swept the entire area with a huge barrage. The portion of our mission involving eliminating the Chinese 120's had been completed. It had been easy. Too easy. The control that we exerted over the valley now had to be obvious to everybody. Trouble was just around the corner.

We returned to watching and waiting: individual Marines nervously fiddling with their grenades, making certain that all were in place, ready for trouble. The quiet of the moonless night was broken only by the sounds of distant explosions. Somebody else was fighting for life. With a sudden "pop," one of the corporal's illumination trip flares exploded, lighting its immediate vicinity for ten or twenty seconds. It showed us hundreds of the enemy huddled at the foot of the hill. The cries of "fire in the hole" rang out as the Marines started tossing grenades down the hill to explode among the waiting Chinamen. We were about to have a battle royal and it wasn't going to be one-sided. The basket grenadiers were all around the hill and their throws were entirely too accurate. We had problems all over the hill, and casualties were filling our aid station.

58

We radioed for the first of the protective barrages that were to continue throughout the night. Mortar illumination rounds and the corporal's illumination grenades showed enemy right up to the edge of our lines. These all appeared to be dead or seriously wounded. Farther away we could vaguely see large groups of 50 or more milling around, apparently reorganizing for another try. An artillery concentration caught one of these milling groups dead center, filling the night with the cries and screams of their wounded. Two of our machine guns had been knocked out, but backup gunners had returned one to action.

The Chinese tried hard that night, maybe harder than they had ever tried before. They made three major assaults, the first two of which were followed by regrouping and probes. Between attacks, we could hear an officer screaming at the Chinese soldiers. Our interpreter said that he was threatening them with death if they failed to take the hill. By midnight, all of our grenades and 60mm mortar ammunition were gone and we had taken a big bite out of the machine gun and rifle ammunition. Things were getting desperate and I radioed battalion, asking for an air strike and an emergency air drop of ammunition. There was a long pause, followed by the rather disheartening word that they would get back to us. They did, however, and soon.

In short order, the aircraft arrived overhead, one of them a transport kicking out parachute flares that lit up the surrounding countryside like daylight. The Corsairs rolled in, getting oriented and practicing their attack runs. They reported that the enemy was moving away from the hill, but for some strange reason the Chinese soldiers were still moving in large, vulnerable groups. As the flare plane continued to circle and light the area, the Corsairs tore into the Chinese with napalm, bombs, and machine guns. As the Corsairs finished their runs, a new voice called us on the tactical air net we had been using to control the Corsairs. The voice said that the ammo resupply was on the way and advised us to "hang in there, jarheads." It was my old aviator buddy from *Menard*, 1st Lt. Pete Keeling. I literally wept.

With the entire area lit up from aviation flares, the air drop worked, even though half of it fell outside our lines: ammunition, precious water, and radio batteries—more than enough to carry us through the night. After the aircraft left, we received continuous fire support around our hill: artillery to the east and west, 4.2-inch mortars to the north and south. Considering the magnitude of the Chinese effort, we had gotten off lightly. Two of our wounded died during the night, leaving 12 others wounded, most of whom could walk. There were huge piles of Chinese bodies all around our perimeter on the hill, and many others farther out. We didn't try to count them: the numbers didn't matter. They had made a major effort to destroy us and failed.

The next morning, higher headquarters decided that we had done enough and directed us to return. As we started out, the tank platoon returned, this time escorting ambulances for the dead and wounded. The prisoners marched with us. During a break in the march, they got water from a stream and ate some of our extra rations. After eating, they all promptly vomited: the food was probably too rich, but the platoon guide observed "They can't stand that crap, either."

When we got farther south, we turned the prisoners over to military police. The weapons crews that had been attached to us peeled off to rejoin their parent units. Our work on the valley floor was done. We headed back to the hills.

Chapter 7

Hill 907

"For he today that sheds his blood with me
Shall be my brother . . ."

We never knew when Operation Mousetrap ended and another counter-offensive, Operation Killer, began. Not that it mattered. The real issue was how much longer we could go on doing the things that had to be done. The Chinese continued to attack, but in smaller units, and they continued to surrender, but in larger numbers. The North Koreans remained unchanged. They fought until they died.

We received new battle maps imprinted with a symbol of hope called the "Kansas Line." The line followed commanding terrain features across our front from southeast to northwest. The dominant mountain peak in our area, named for its height in meters, was Hill 907. Nearly 3000 feet high, it looked to us like a smaller version of Mount Fuji.

In late May and early June of 1951, most of the enemy long-range anti-tank and mortar fire came from Hill 907. Our forces believed that Hill 907 housed the command post of the 10th North Korean division serving as the rear guard of the Chinese Corps.

Early in June, Lieutenant Kerrigan let us in on the general campaign plan. We would continue to attack until we reached the Kansas Line; then we would stop. Hill 907, dominating the surrounding area, would be the Fifth Marines' regimental objective.

Our battalion commander, Lieutenant Colonel Hopkins, was anxious to reach the Kansas Line. He was scheduled to be relieved of command, but wanted to conduct the attack on Hill 907 before he left. He was running out of time. To make matters worse, he had lost his operations officer, Captain Jack Jones, who had suffered severe wounds from a booby trap. Jones was no longer available to control our operations or to give calm, professional advice to the battalion commander.

Several days before the actual attack on Hill 907, we heard that the Fifth Marines would be launching a coordinated two-battalion assault when the time came. Since the hill mass had at least half a dozen large finger ridges leading to its summit, and because a determined enemy who knew how to use terrain was there in strength, a coordinated assault by several companies seemed essential. We expected the Third Battalion, because of its location, to conduct a flanking attack down the ridgeline from west to east. Either we or the Second Battalion would have to carry out a frontal assault, because we couldn't get to a flanking position from where we were. Except for the six or so fingers leading down from the summit, the sides of the hill descended almost vertically into the valley.

The soldiers of the American Civil War called battle casualty lists "the butcher's bill," and that's as good a term as any. Everyone from the newest rifleman on up knew that the butcher's bill to be paid for taking Hill 907 was going to be big. The only real question was which names would be on it.

Early in June of 1951, the Fifth Regiment was attacking northward just west of the Soyang-gang River. The Third Battalion was on the regiment's left, and our First Battalion was on the right, with its right flank stretched out to the river bank. The Second Battalion, following in the tracks of the other two, was in regimental reserve. B Company was more than busy. Before he was wounded, Captain Jones had identified fourteen intermediate objectives leading to Hill 907, the regimental objective. Of the fourteen, ten had been assigned to our Baker Bandits.

The company had been attacking cross-compartment—from one ridgeline straight across to the next. Just the climbing itself would have been exhausting, but that paled by comparison with the fighting. Each of the objectives was stoutly defended. The Baker Bandits had ten heated firefights and conducted ten casualty-producing assaults before reaching the base of Hill 907. As we had done for weeks, we attacked during daylight hours and defended ourselves at night against the waves of Chinese soldiers sent to destroy us. Baker Company was wearing out.

On June 6 we received two lieutenants and several enlisted Marines as replacements. This infusion of new blood helped. First Lieutenant Dave Gally was assigned to lead the First Platoon, and Second Lieutenant Ray Fagan was assigned the Second Platoon. Typical of the company's trials was the June 16 death of Lieutenant Ed Fisher, the mortar section leader. Ed and several others were killed by mortar fire just as we reached the base of Hill 907.

Our arrival at the foot of the 907 fortress was to have ended the daily routine of attacking into the teeth of well-prepared enemy positions. We expected A Company to relieve us and allow us to get at least a brief rest. As planned, A Company joined us on June 16 and took over our defensive positions of the previous night. We moved to a nearby place and established new positions. That night, A Company took a heavy attack and had one of its platoons overrun. It was a close thing, but they held on and finally ejected the enemy force. In the process, the company took many casualties and lost a light machine gun. B Company was not called on to assist, but after it was over, the air around the company was heavy with foreboding. We could all feel it. A Company had been hit hard. It had fought most of the night and in the process had lost something. We were no longer certain that A Company was going to replace the Bandits and take over our assault duties. Hill 907 loomed even larger in the foreground, both geographically and psychologically.

Sometime during mid-morning of June 17, battalion ordered Lieutenant Kerrigan to conduct a company-level patrol to Hill 578. This hill, a prominent knob, was the gateway to the maze of climbing ridgelines that culminated in Hill 907. Hoping to lighten our load, or perhaps trying to get a better feel for our future, the skipper sought battalion's permission to leave our packs behind, since we would be returning once we were relieved by A Company. The response came quickly—an ominous "negative" that was a strong clue to future possibilities. With Dave Gally and the First Platoon in the lead, B Company moved to Hill 578 and climbed it without incident. Reporting no enemy in sight, we took up tactical positions and waited for A Company to appear and relieve us.

The wait gave us an opportunity to look over Hill 907, above. A wide, well-used path led up the nearest finger. Large trees along the path formed a canopy that filtered or screened out entirely a bright sun that beat down with increasing intensity as it climbed the midday sky. The enemy had cut most of the underbrush away, a sign that it had cleared fields of fire for defensive positions somewhere on the slope. Using binoculars, I finally picked out at least ten of them—well-camouflaged bunkers some two hundred yards up the hill. It looked like a Gibraltar!

Unlike the previous several days, this day was quiet, almost peaceful—so much so that the troops relaxed and began to doze in the hot sun. Fighting the temptation to do the same, the officers studied what they could, silently examining the terrain and defenses in front of us. Shortly after noon, a stirring around the company command post showed that the battalion radio was demanding attention. It was the battalion commander and he wanted to speak to Lieutenant Kerrigan. The conversation was brief, its message unwelcome but in some ways not unexpected. Lieutenant Colonel Hopkins told the skipper that the Fifth Marines had given the First Battalion permission to seize Hill 907. He ordered B Company alone to go and do it. All thought of a coordinated, carefully planned, and heavily supported two-battalion, multi-company attack floated away into space—to the never-never land of tactical plans that should have been executed, not discarded. None of us ever learned why.

It was late in the day to start an attack of this magnitude without either planning or advance preparation, but that is exactly what the battalion commander was demanding. To make matters worse, he preempted the company commander by specifying that "Charlie Cooper's Third Platoon will lead the attack."

The terrain held by the enemy dominated the area, and there was no doubt that, having observed our climb to Hill 578, the enemy knew our strength and the nature of our weapons. Soon they would know our intentions as well. We, on the other hand, would be moving directly into the enemy's main battle position with no more information than what we had gleaned from our limited view up the hill. The Third Platoon, followed by the rest of the Bandits, would have to attack on a narrow front with no planned fire support, with both flanks exposed, and with no reinforcements: just move out and attack. The concept was almost overwhelming, but there was no alternative. It was time to remember that for a Marine officer, the one thing worse than dying is failing his troops in battle.

When confronted with an operational problem in combat, an officer must suppress personal fears and concentrate on the professional things that can and should be done. The problem was simple enough to describe: in many respects, our situation and mission bordered on the suicidal. What we had to remember was that there were positive aspects as well. First and foremost, we were Marines, a point that may seem trite or even juvenile to the outsider, but one that meant much to us—and of at least equal importance, it also meant much to the enemy. The Marines of this platoon had been through a great deal together: they were experienced, they knew what they were doing, and they were like brothers. They had never failed me or the company, and they understood the meaning of "orders" just as well as I did.

If those factors were not enough, and they might not have been, we also had a potential hole card. Marines have a penchant for taking combat souvenirs: as a result, we had our own stock of captured enemy ammunition and weapons. We had brand new, mint-condition burp guns, not especially accurate at a distance, as the enemy had so often proved, but handy for close-in fighting. The troops had been intrigued by these sparkling new weapons ever since we had captured them, and although we had turned in most of them (too much to carry), we had managed to hang onto a dozen, along with sizable amounts of ammunition. It was time to do something different. We might confuse the enemy by using his own weapons against him. If we did, we would be saving our own limited ammunition. More important, our using his weapons against him would give our platoon a psychological boost.

Agreeing with that rationale, Bill Kerrigan approved the idea of arming the two lead squads with burp guns. He also said that battalion had just confirmed that 907's defenders were North Koreans, and probably our old enemy, the Tenth Division. We knew what to expect. There would be no surrendering, and there would be a lot of dying—all of the North Koreans and maybe most of us.

There was little time to make a reconnaissance. Staff Sergeant Reiman, the platoon guide, the machine gun section leader, three squad leaders, and I moved forward to a large boulder to learn what we could. It wasn't much, but it helped. The cut undergrowth had left the area open, but there were boulders and folds in the ground that we could use to mask our movements. We developed the plan, then explained it to our men. Hiding behind the terrain folds and boulders, the two lead squads would work their way around the bunkers and take them from the rear. In a procedure unlike that used in most other attacks, the machine guns would move with the assaulting squads, constantly changing position and always furnishing support. The plan may not have been the best way to deal with what appeared to be mutually supporting bunkers, but it was the best we could come up with.

In my final conversation with Bill Kerrigan, I expressed confidence that we would be able to penetrate a number of the bunkers. The problem was that each penetration would leave us more vulnerable to enemy fire from both flanks. It was clear that our frontage and maneuver room would narrow as we moved upward. If the assault went as planned, we were going to need impressive quantities of accurate fire support on both flanks.

We finished making preparations. We had issued the orders, and everyone understood them, down to the newest rifleman. Glancing up the hill as they listened to squad or fire team leaders explaining how we would operate, the troops steeled themselves for what they knew would be, at best, a long afternoon. At worst, it could be the last afternoon. We issued burp guns and ammo to the two lead squads, an action that had helped divert their attention from the coming ordeal. To lighten the load, the men had removed their packs and put them in squad stacks for retrieval after the attack. We carried canteens and ammunition. It was time to go.

Once I informed Bill Kerrigan that we were moving out, the lead troops started forward in a series of fire team rushes that produced early successes. In the first half hour we took four bunkers from the rear and destroyed them without meeting any enemy resistance. Then the North Koreans began reacting. They had us pinpointed. Scattered rifle fire gave way to persistent and accurate firing. Suddenly, when we were halfway up the hill and fully deployed, a murderous fire erupted on three sides: from directly ahead and the two flanks. We were in real trouble. Only the rear was secure. We called in air strikes and artillery fire without letup. We used everything that was available, and there was plenty. No one else was fighting that day, so we had it all.

In spite of the continuous curtain of supporting fire to our front and on the flanks, we were taking casualties. The North Korean machine guns were relentless. My platoon radio operator took a round through the neck, and appeared to have died instantly. A Marine sprang forward, removed the radio from its dead operator, started moving toward me, and was killed before he could get to cover.

Inexplicably, Lieutenant Colonel Hopkins's voice suddenly came over the company radio net, screaming obscenities at the enemy. He knew they were listening. Maybe he was trying to rattle them. Whatever his intent, he was clearly getting out of control and his tirade was having no visible effect. The well-concealed North Korean machine guns chattered the language of death, and Marines were dropping in increasing numbers when Hopkins decided that he wanted to talk to me. It was a short conversation. We had to have him call in additional air support on the crest and more heavy artillery fire on the flanks if we were to continue to move. I hastily gave the proper map coordinates for both.

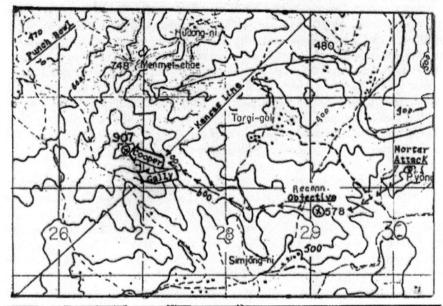

The ground shook under our feet and red hot machine gun shell casings dropped on and around us as strafing aircraft swooped in overhead, hosing down the area to our front. But each of the platoon's successes in the tortured progress upward brought more difficulties. As we moved deeper into the North Korean defenses, our location and tactics became more obvious, and our maneuver room shrank to almost nothing.

We had used confusion, maneuver, envelopment from the rear of their bunkers, and the shock effect of massive supporting arms. I remained with the two assaulting squads and kept the two machine guns close, because a counterattack could come at any time. With all we had done, the volume of enemy fire did not reach its maximum until the ground began to level. We were nearing the top, but could move no farther—and Marines were dying. The noise, smoke, confusion, killing, and increasingly fanatical enemy resistance were almost overpowering. The issue was in doubt.

During our move up the hill, the skipper had sent Lieutenant Dave Gally's First Platoon up an adjacent finger on our left flank with orders to suppress enemy flanking fires that were hurting us badly. About the time we assaulted, the First Platoon uncovered and destroyed an enemy outpost that was causing our problems. In turn, they began receiving fire from slightly ahead on both flanks, losing one killed and three seriously wounded in the initial exchange. They returned fire, and received orders to hold their ground. Sooner rather than later, they and their casualties would have to be removed from that exposed position.

While this was going on, Lieutenant Ray Fagan's Second Platoon had been sent forward to assist in moving our dead and wounded. Ray became one of the assisted when he went down with a hit from a machine gun burst that eventually resulted in the loss of a leg.

64

About 4:30 we seemed to be on the military crest, just short of a final assault position. There weren't many troops left, but we still had the machine guns and we couldn't stay where we were. If we stopped, the North Koreans would pick us all off in short order. There was no turning back. It was move forward or die. I asked for one more air strike. Hopkins radioed that two Air Force F-80's armed with napalm tanks were orbiting overhead. Eavesdropping on our tactical air support radio net, they had checked in to offer help. We agreed that I would mark the target area with my last white phosphorous grenade. The cloud of white smoke would rise through the trees, the pilots would see it easily, and all they had to do was drop on the smoke. The pilots "rogered" the instructions and reported themselves ready to turn for the "hot" run to the target. I signaled what was left of the platoon—12 to 15 Marines—to move forward with me, then pulled the pin on the grenade. We were moving forward, screaming madly: "Gung Ho, you bastards, we're Marines"! The volume of fire swelled when I heaved the grenade as far as I could.

The grenade had flown some thirty yards between the trees when a massive blow on my left side flattened me. It was like being hit with an ax. A large ax. It spun me completely around. The senior corpsman, Doc Roderick, moved like a flash, trying to plug the hole in my left side. I looked up to see enemy troops forming a line beyond where the grenade had exploded and apparently confused them. They seemed to be milling around in the grenade's smoke. Considering the F-80's on their inbound run with the napalm, from our viewpoint there was no better place for North Korean confusion. My platoon, or what was left of it, was on the ground, firing at the line of North Koreans. The machine gun section added its weight and I was able to continue firing my carbine. The North Koreans were feeling the punishment.

As the smoke rose, the shadowy figures of the enemy became more visible. It was a long line of North Korean soldiers, dressed in camouflaged uniforms, each with leaves and twigs added for additional effect. They looked much like clumps of bushes. Armed with burp guns, they were firing from the hip: had they been more accurate, they would have killed us all. We took them under fire with everything we could muster and couldn't miss at that range, particularly with machine guns. It was the North Koreans' turn to fall like bowling pins. But they kept on coming. The yells, the screams, and the noise of chattering automatic weapons, all hemmed in by the trees, shut off outside sounds.

We couldn't kill them fast enough and, heavily outnumbered, were about to take on the North Korean counter-attack in hand-to-hand combat. As they started moving, my carbine was hit on the stock and literally blown out of my hands. Conscious but unable to move my legs, I drew my fighting knife. It would be the last resort. There was nothing else left.

We never heard it coming. Hell exploded through the trees. The napalm bombs burst in the branches directly over the North Korean troops, not thirty yards away. Fire and flames were everywhere. The heat was unbelievable. We had burns and almost suffocated, but the North Korean counter-attack had been incinerated, en masse. It was no more. Hanging by our fingernails some 100 yards from the peak of Hill 907, we were no longer an effective fighting force. Our courageous machine gunners and that lucky, perfectly timed napalm drop had saved what was left of the Third Platoon. We could go no farther.

"Doc" Roderick had violated all medical protocol by stuffing a kidney back into the large hole in my lower left side and doing everything possible to plug it up. He asked me what time it was. (Corpsmen were trained to ask their patients the time as a means of getting their minds off their wounds and avoiding combat shock, which was often as fatal as the wounds.) I told him it was 1700, and that I was not going into shock. He told me not to worry about it: he wouldn't let that happen, but he had to get me out of there before I bled to death—which he then did. I wasn't the only one he saved. He was the miracle man of the day, saving lives by the dozen as men dropped all around him. Hospitalman Stanley Roderick should have received the Medal of Honor for his courage and his selfless devotion to duty that afternoon.

The next day, June 18, other elements of the Fifth Marines approached Hill 907 from the left flank and occupied the regimental objective without firing a shot. The enemy had pulled out, having apparently held at all costs until the headquarters of the Tenth North Korean Division could move out. Ironically, our assault was the last action undertaken by United Nations forces in Korea during the summer of 1951. A three-month ceasefire followed almost immediately.

Two days later, on June 20, the Tenth Corps Commander recognized what B Company and the rest of the Fifth Marines had accomplished since early June. There were other forms of recognition as well, but General Almond lent special meaning to the sacrifices of so many when he sent the following message:

Please express my appreciation and high commendation to the officers and men of the Fifth Regiment, U.S. Marines, and its supporting units, for their valor, persistence, and combat effectiveness in the fighting of the past ten days. Today I made an aerial reconnaissance of the near impossible mountain peaks east of Taem-san captured by the Fifth Regiment. I have nothing but admiration for the dauntless men who scaled those peaks and now remain on their assigned objectives.

But late on that afternoon of Father's Day, June 17, the occupation of Hill 907 by the Fifth Marines and General Almond's message were yet to come. There was still work to be done on the forward slope of Hill 907.

The dead and wounded of what was left of the Third Platoon had to be evacuated. The battalion commander had dispatched a single rifle platoon from A Company to reinforce B Company. That force might have helped somewhere, but the meager reinforcement reached the Bandits only after Lieutenant Kerrigan had moved the company halfway back down the mountain.

It was time for me to go back down the hill. As they half carried, half dragged me to a safer place, the machine gun section leader ran forward to the spot where I'd been hit. Risking sniper fire, he retrieved my helmet and returned it to me. He knew that it held a picture of my wife.

Earlier in the day, we'd cut saplings in an attempt to clear firing lanes for the company's 60mm mortars. The 60's were never able to make a real contribution, but the saplings now came in handy. Our men used them and ponchos to rig improvised stretchers that took the dead and wounded to the bottom of the mountain, where the jeep ambulances waited. As carefully as possible, the sad procession started slowly downhill. It was a trip that we had seen so many others make. Now it was our turn. For most of us, the war was over. For many of us, a different sort of a battle was about to begin.

Chapter 8

The Long Road Back
"I'm going to prove you wrong!"

The enemy had mined the ford across the river: the first jeep that tried to cross to get us blew up. One available helicopter was shuttling the wounded across the river two at a time to the waiting ambulances. I was drifting in and out of consciousness, but I remember the night's pitch blackness. I remember lying on the ground in a stretcher, waiting to be carried across the river on the skids of that small Bell helicopter—one of those with the big bubble canopy.

Like in a dream, I recall overhearing Colonel Hayward, CO Fifth Marines, and LtCol Hopkins discussing my case with a senior corpsman. "What a great job that young lad and his platoon did today," said one of the officers. "He's a damn good Marine, one of our best, and it's a shame. The doc says he's lost so much blood that there's no chance he can make it." Hearing this, I swore to myself that I'd live to confront both of them, somewhere, someday.

I remember having my stretcher lashed on that helicopter's landing skid and being flown quickly across the mined river. Several jeep ambulances were lined up: the medics put me in the last one. One of the corpsmen said, "He's lost a lot of blood, so Doc said not to waste any time getting him back to the regimental aid station." They had some sort of IV in my arm, and attached it to a bag hanging from the overhead as a corpsman hopped in beside me. I learned later they were pumping blood plasma into me as they rushed me to a place where I could get what I really needed: whole blood. We were driving without lights down a rocky stream bed. Although morphine had made me mostly numb all over, I felt excruciating pain in my left hip and figured that's where the bullet must have lodged. Then I blacked out again.

I came to in a brightly lighted tent. I knew it was the regimental aid station, because standing over me was Dr. St. Mary, the replacement doctor that had reported in with me two months earlier. He saw my eyes open and said something I couldn't understand. For some strange reason I held up my right index finger, one from which he had removed a wart when we were coming over in the ship, and said, "Doc, the damn finger never has healed and is still infected!" He calmed me down and said they were just going to clean up my wound a bit, get some whole blood into me, and send me on back to "Charlie Med," the Division's field hospital. I learned later that the whole blood, collected just minutes before from an O-positive Marine or sailor, probably saved my life. Later I awoke in a much larger field ambulance, being transported with several other patients down a much smoother road that led to more surgery that same evening.

"Charlie Med" was a very busy place that night, courtesy of the Baker Bandits. I vaguely remember being wheeled into an operating room and looking up to see an X-ray machine over me. Then they gave me something that put me out. It was daylight when I came to in a tent ward where the stretchers were set on wooden horses. The sides of the tent were rolled up on this very hot day, June 18, 1951. I was still numb all over, and I had an overwhelming thirst. It must have been nearly a day since I'd had a drink of water. About that time one of my old troopers appeared. He had been wounded about two weeks earlier and was serving as an orderly while recuperating.

He had realized that I was conscious and come over to see what he could do for me. I told him I would sell my soul for some cold fruit juice. He immediately went and got a quart of ice cold tomato juice and a small paper cup. God bless him, he pulled up a camp stool and poured that juice for me until I had consumed the entire quart. Lord, but it tasted good, but the pleasure wasn't to last. My well-intentioned trooper didn't know that I wasn't supposed to have anything to drink. In short order, I almost went into convulsions from pains in my abdomen. My plumbing wasn't working. In fact, a lot of things weren't working, I was to find out. The emergency action was to use a catheter to siphon out my bladder. Relief was immediate, and I didn't drink much after that.

As soon as this procedure was completed, I pulled my battle map and a pencil out of my tattered utility shirt, marked on the map the spot where I'd been hit, and wrote a brief note to my sweet wife on the back. It's in my hand as I write this. The battle map delineates clearly all of the bitter fighting leading up to that final battle. Someone found me an envelope and the letter went out later that day.

At that time I still thought the slug was in my left hip because of the sharp pain there that wouldn't quit. Later a surgeon came back to tell me briefly what they had learned the night before. He wasn't too specific, but he said the missile, which was still in me, had caused considerable trauma. It had fractured one vertebra and shattered the spinal process on two others and done some damage to my spinal cord. He added that it was not unusual to lose both bowel and urinary functions, temporarily, after such trauma. They had pumped quite a bit of blood into me, and he was pleased that I was looking much better than I had been the night before. They were about to move me to a nearby Army hospital train. It would take me to Pusan: he expected that I would end up in *USS Repose*, the Navy hospital ship.

That all happened within the next 24 hours, in a well-orchestrated blur of medical care and efficiency. Sitting at the dock in smelly Pusan Harbor was the prettiest, whitest, cleanest looking ship I had ever seen. And they took me aboard.

Once I'd moved into the immaculate, sterile, air conditioned world that was a floating Navy hospital, I started to feel better fast. The place looked "squared away," and there were women all over the place. They smelled so good. After the corpsmen had eased me gently into a low-lying bunk in a large ward, I was confronted by the tall, white-garbed figure of a woman who had the three wide stripes of a full commander on her cap. She too smelled good. (I seemed acutely sensitive to the new, pleasant smells.) She acted like she was in charge. And she was, being the senior nurse of the large main ward. She welcomed me aboard with a big smile and added, "You smell like a billy goat, Lieutenant." I grinned and said that keeping clean wasn't something we'd had much time for in the last month or so—that we'd been kinda busy. She put her hands on her hips and said, "Don't you worry about it, Lieutenant. We're going to clean you up if it takes all day, and I'm going to start on those feet myself!" Two male corpsmen joined her and they improved the morale, comfort, and most importantly, the smell of this disreputable and totally helpless fighting Marine officer.

I still felt like hell, but that full-court-press scrubdown was an experience I have cherished to this day. They even shaved me and washed my crummy hair. Somehow, I knew from that point that I was going to make it. Nobody was shooting at me any more, and I was in good hands. The Navy medics would take care of me. God bless 'em all.

Later that day, a doctor examined me. He had a copy of the X-ray that had been forwarded with me and informed me the slug wasn't in my hip, where I had thought it was. He rolled me over onto my stomach most carefully and began to probe an area in my lower back. I could feel the pressure but not his touch until suddenly he pressed on a spot in my right lower back. It caused an immediate, massive spasm of cramping in my lower back. The pain was so intense that I screamed. He quickly injected me with something that knocked me out. I came to in the X-ray room, where they were taking more pictures. They scheduled me for surgery early the next morning: there appeared to be some urgency in getting the slug removed from wherever it was.

For the surgery they gave me a spinal, so I was awake and talked with the surgeons during the operation. It lasted for more than two hours. They had some difficulty getting to and removing the bullet, and wound up making an incision that was almost as large as the entry point of the bullet, but they did get it out. It had slipped into my abdominal cavity, where it caused some problems for the doctors. I couldn't tell much difference, except that the severe pain in my left hip had mostly subsided.

Since being wounded I had been receiving massive injections of penicillin every three hours. The day after surgery I had a violent reaction to the early morning injection. My entire body immediately ballooned up so much that I couldn't speak and could hardly breathe. A massive dose of an antidote saved the day. It was the last of the penicillin for me, but they gave me other antibiotics that were almost as effective.

The surgeons had decided to leave both of my rather large "holes" open, to allow me to heal from within. They were afraid the wounds might become infected deep inside if they were sealed up. It would be a long time before they closed, and the constant drainage required frequent bandage changes.

My favorite nurse explained to me that they wanted to "stabilize" me so that I could survive a move back to the US Naval Hospital in Yokosuka, Japan. All of my nourishment was still from IV's and the little bit of fluid I was allowed to sip each day. I had no feeling from my chest down, except for a continuous dull ache in my back where the bullet had entered. Every injection in the buttocks reminded me that there was no feeling there. (It would be more than five years before feeling returned.) I spent my days napping fitfully, learning to shave myself and brush my teeth while prone, and seeing a stream of visitors—other Baker Bandit patients who were ambulatory.

We were still a Band of Brothers. My old troops seemed to come out of the woodwork as they limped into my ward to visit me. Wearing the ill-fitting blue pajamas, paper slippers, and seersucker bathrobes, they would shuffle in to "see how the Lieutenant was doing." It was wonderful therapy and a great relief for me to see how many of them were recovering well from life-threatening wounds.

The first to come by was my radio operator, who had been shot through the neck on Hill 907. How could he have survived, I wondered? We all thought he was dead. He walked in with a large bandage around his neck and reported that the bullet had passed through cleanly and hadn't hit anything vital. He was going home within the week, because he had had more than enough time in combat.

The second was the BAR man who had deserted from "Charlie Med" in order to return to the company during our period of heavy fighting. He had been evacuated with pneumonia and acute exhaustion and had returned to the company armed with an officer's carbine. He fought like a tiger during the several days before we attacked Hill

907, and had reportedly been one of the few in my platoon not to be wounded on that fateful Sunday. These "illegal replacements" were still among us for the big battle.

As this man limped into the ward and approached me, I greeted him and said that we had heard he made it through the battle unharmed. What had happened? He looked sheepish and smiled. After we had stopped the enemy counterattack, the corpsmen put him in charge of a detail to get the dead and wounded down the hill and to a safe area. He told me the names and conditions of the men from our platoon that he had moved during that recovery period. He told of the jeep ambulance that hit a mine and blew up in the middle of the river and of the arrival of the helicopter to ferry the wounded. Then he described how I'd been evacuated with the last of the dead and wounded late that night. Finally he said, "Lieutenant, after we got everybody cared for and the colonels had cleared the area, I was about to collapse on my feet. I sat down on a dead tree to take a breather and damn near killed myself. Some jarhead had left a rifle with a bayonet attached leaning against that log and I sat square down on it. I cut me a new one, sir. They took about 20 stitches in my rear end!"

I had to laugh—couldn't help it. He laughed too. He had survived hell on earth and then had almost disemboweled himself on a razor sharp bayonet left by one of our wounded evacuees. He would recover, but he was embarrassed. He deserved a medal, as they all did, for his bravery and the lives he saved. Unfortunately, all too few received medals: most of the key witnesses were dead, or wounded and evacuated.

My stay of almost two weeks in the good ship *Repose* was about to come to an end. On July third they told me that a Navy hospital flight would take me and five other "basket cases" to the large Navy hospital in Yokosuka, Japan. The specially configured twin-engined R4D (DC-3 in the civilian world) would have on board a doctor, two nurses, and two hospital corpsmen, in addition to the normal aircraft crew. All of the patients were on IV's and listed as critical. I was impressed with the briefing they gave me, and I looked forward to moving one step closer to a return to duty. I refused to acknowledge any possibility that I wouldn't be able to return to my beloved Baker Bandits after a reasonable period of hospitalization. It was a state of mind inspired by the most powerful bonding in the world, the overwhelming sense of loyalty a combat Marine feels for his small-unit comrades.

Pusan is in the southeastern corner of Korea. Yokosuka is in central Honshu, south of Tokyo. We were to fly into an airfield at Atsugi and go by ambulance to the former Japanese Imperial Naval Hospital. It looked like a long day of uncomfortable but uneventful travel: by air across the Korean strait and up the Japanese islands, and then by ambulance on a fairly long ride from the airport to the hospital.

We took off and headed for Japan. After what seemed to be a very short time in the air, one of our engines began to backfire and lose power. The pilot announced that he was trying to return the sick engine to health, and that if he couldn't he would be forced to make an emergency landing on Kyushu, Japan's southernmost island and the closest point of land. So here was a plane full of combat casualties, barely alive at best. Were we about to take the final count after we had defied the odds in combat? Damn, damn, damn! Then I started to pray. Our pilot must have been praying too. As we lost altitude, the nurse holding onto my stretcher said, "We are over land again. The pilot is looking for a place to put us down." About that time the sick engine stopped and left us flying on one engine and rapidly losing altitude.

The pilot pulled off a bit of a miracle. He set the plane down on a Japanese highway near the coastline of Kyushu. There were wires, of course—telephone lines or power lines. We hit several of them, but even though they spun us around and almost sheared off one wing, we remained upright and came to a halt on the road with wires and cables wrapped around the two propellers. The impact knocked all but two of the litters off their supports. Mine was one of the two that weren't dumped on the deck, and my IV was still intact. None of the medics or crew were seriously injured: I don't know how much damage the forced landing did to those poor troops who were jarred out of their litters. But we were down and alive, and there was no fire. Very soon, I heard the wail of sirens. There was help on the way, and from the most unexpected of sources.

We had almost miraculously landed about half a mile from a US Army General Hospital near Tagawa, Kyushu, Japan. In just a few moments we had US Army medics and Japanese civilians helping us out of the airplane and into ambulances. Accompanied by our own medics and our hastily retrieved medical records, we soon arrived at the emergency room of this huge hospital. It was the Fourth of July, 1951.

Within an hour we had all received quick examinations and been checked into the hospital. Then a pair of medics pushed my gurney to my new ward, where my fellow patients would be 60 or 70 US Army paratroopers from the 187th Airborne Regiment, our old comrades from Operation Mousetrap. They too had seen very heavy fighting. As the medics pushed me through the ward's swinging doors, the Marine in me took over. I started barking like a dog to announce the presence of a US Marine, "Doggies" being the Marine name for all soldiers! I got a response, you can bet on that, but the airborne troops and Marines respected each other as fighters. You might even say we look down on the rest of the world.

I now had a new home: I'd survived again. In a few days we would be on our way, but a nurse cautioned me that we all had to be "stabilized" before continuing our journey. They stabilized me by immediately lashing me to a padded board to totally immobilize my fractured back.

The next day I was able to call my wife at her parents' home in Fletcher, N.C. I used a portable ham radio telephone that they brought into the ward for me. This was entertainment for the kibitzing "doggies," who mimicked everything I said to my bride. The call wasn't very efficient or satisfactory, but she knew I was in Japan and that I loved her. And she loved me, and the baby she was expecting in mid-month had not yet arrived. All of this was accompanied by a chorus of 65 soldiers yelling "We love you, Carol!" Before I left a few days later, I asked to be wheeled past their beds to shake hands with each of them. Almost to the man, they responded with a "Semper Fi, Marine. Good luck!"

Unlike the military ambulances I'd been riding since being wounded, the ambulance that met us at the airfield in Atsugi was a commercial type that helped cushion those Japanese potholes and bumps on the long drive to the hospital. When we arrived at the former Japanese Imperial Naval Hospital, we found it to be a sprawling affair, all on one level, with dozens of wings and long connecting corridors. In the summer of 1951 it was filled to capacity and then some. They had some beds in the hallways.

After I'd gone through the usual check-in procedures, they wheeled me into a room with two Corsair pilots, one Marine and one Navy. Major "Pop" Evans had been forced to bail out at a very low altitude and had landed before his chute had fully deployed. He had a broken back, broken hip, and two broken legs. His first question

71

was "Do you play chess?" His personal courage and physical toughness were to be inspirational for me. Our Navy roommate, Jim (I forget his last name), a lieutenant, was totally encased in bandages, with his arms and legs suspended—the treatment for burns in those days. Enemy fire had hit one of the napalm bombs he was carrying as he made a run and the bomb exploded. He was on fire when he bailed out. Both men had been saved from capture in heroic rescues by the tiny Bell helicopters in use at the time. I never saw Jim's face, although his bandages were changed daily. Years later, Pop Evans, then a colonel back on full duty, told me that Jim had recovered but had been medically discharged from the Navy.

Wearing a body cast, the author is awarded a Purple Heart
by CO USNH Yokosuka. Japan 1951

A team of doctors descended on me. Including many specialists, it gave me a thorough examination, literally from head to toe. They ordered more X-rays, they tickled my feet, they stuck pins in me, they scratched me with cotton swabs. At first I tried to claim that I could feel them doing things to me, but when they told me that they hadn't even touched me yet, I had to admit that all of my lower extremities were numb. Their early judgment came the second day. First, they were amazed that I was alive. I had a fractured vertebra, the spinous process on two vertebrae had been shattered, and there was extensive but as yet undetermined nerve damage. They weren't sure how bad the main spinal cord had been damaged: it appeared to have been nicked but not severed. They would continue to immobilize my back, but take it a step farther. They put me in traction and cranked the bed up in the middle. Weights on my feet and shoulders pulled the pieces of the fractured vertebra together, theoretically, when my back was in this arched position. It was a beginning. The goal was the eventual fusion of the two reduced vertebrae, as well as the mending of the fractured vertebra.

They terminated the IV's and increased my oral intake of fluids. The goal here was to concentrate on getting my plumbing and bowels to function. My weight had fallen to about 130 pounds (one doctor's estimate: it wasn't feasible or necessary to weigh me). My spirits were on the low side, but I'd be damned if I'd admit it. After I'd been there a day or so, we had established a routine. Once a day my very delightful nurse would roll me over to change the bandages on my "holes" and give me a wonderful back massage that was designed to head off bed sores, help circulation, and improve my dwindling morale. Her fiancé was a Navy flier I had known at the Academy. As long as I talked about our associations, she would continue the massage. I'm sure she

72

knew some of my stories were contrived, but I was not above spinning a few yarns to prolong those wonderful massages.

Before being put back into my harnesses, I would be helped to a regular toilet to try again, and again, and again. Then one day it happened, bringing about a remarkable physical rejuvenation. The locked dam was broken. No more catheters, and the promise of real food! I never dreamed that jello and beef bullion could be so delicious. If all went well, I could look forward to scrambled eggs with milk toast. Hallelujah!

The doctors continued to measure, sample, and test me in every possible way. Now that the bowels were beginning to function, the doctors told me I had worms! They didn't have to tell me that I also had dysentery. That had started long before I was wounded. My half-hearted joke was that I had gone from one extreme to the other: dysentery, then the shut-down of the bowels, and now dysentery again. My dysentery was of the amoebic variety, but the drugs now seemed to have it under control.

A day or two after I'd entered this hospital, a radiologist and an orthopedic surgeon came in with a bundle of X-rays and asked when I had broken my neck. I told them that I never had, as far as I knew, but I'd sure had a lot of trouble with my neck when I was playing football in 1948 and 1949. They wanted to know about it, and also about the times that I had lost memory from concussions. They then held up a film of my neck and showed me two distinct fractures, in two different vertebrae. I couldn't believe it. No wonder my last year at the Academy had been such a nightmare, but thank God the vertebrae had healed and were not involved in my present problems.

I had lots of visitors. Naval Academy and Marine Basic School classmates came to see me, as did fellow patients from other parts of the hospital. Several of my naval officer Classmates were in ships home-ported in Yokosuka; many of the Marines were still being treated, others were getting ready to go home. They all cheered me up, brought me good books to read, and helped me to remain positive despite my somewhat dubious prognosis.

I soon graduated to small amounts of oatmeal and crushed fruit, and the remnants of my legendary appetite were stirring, demanding more food. Then what I later called "The Committee" paid me a visit: five doctors, two of them captains and heads of the departments of orthopedics and neurosurgery. Another captain entered with them, but stood in the doorway, apart from the group. The two captains did the talking, and as I listened my world seemed to crumble around me.

They told me that I should realize that not one person in a thousand could have survived the type of wound I experienced. They all admired my courage and determination to return to duty, but it just wasn't to be. Their collective judgment was that I had sustained permanent damage to the spinal cord and would most likely never again have full or even partial use of my legs. The surprisingly quick return of my bodily functions had been encouraging, but it was too early to conclude that my innards were going to handle that consistently. The words went on and on. I wanted to scream back, "No, no, no! You don't understand. I'm going to get well, damn it!" But I didn't do any screaming. Their goal was to help me gather strength so I could start some limited physical therapy and be able to fly back to the States for additional therapy preceding medical retirement. A medical retirement! Second Lieutenant, USMC (Retired)! Before they left, they all came over to shake my hand: it must have been difficult for them. I told them quite calmly, "I don't know how I'm going to do it, but I'm going to prove you wrong. Thank you for telling me straight out what your best judgment is."

As they walked out, the captain in the doorway came over to my bed and introduced himself. He was a reserve officer, recalled to active duty for 90 days as a special consultant. He was Dean of the California Medical School at Berkeley, an orthopedic surgeon, and a nerve specialist. He didn't call me lieutenant, he called me son. He had studied my case from top to bottom, knew of my athletic background and combat experiences, and had read a special write-up a psychologist had prepared on me. (I didn't remember talking to any such person.) His message was short, but it gave me new life. He said, "Son, don't ever give up, never. You Marines have a special gift that the Good Lord endows you with. I've seen very few, but I have seen some people with injuries as traumatic as yours actually regenerate their nerves, grow them back. We don't understand how it happens or why, but it has happened and in my mind you are the type of person that might make it work, with God's help. Another thing, don't let anyone try to 'fix' you with surgery; this has to be you, therapy, and time. If I were a betting man, I'd bet that you just might pull this off: it's a long, long shot, though." How do I remember words like that for 44 years? How could I ever forget them? That night I had a profound, totally exhilarating, personal religious experience.

I fumbled through my liquid, pureed supper and got halfway through a chess game with Pop Evans, but had to beg off finally. The corpsman pushed my bed back to its usual corner and I cut out my reading light. It was time for me to face up to life as it really was, not as I wanted it to be, and I sorely needed some very strong help. I had grown up in the Methodist Church, had been an active participant my entire life, and had a deep belief in God, but no one that knew me would have called me "religious." My God was a private one. I always tended to ask God for more than I probably deserved as a child, but I also felt totally comfortable pouring my heart out to him when things weren't going well. In Baker Company, most of us freely admitted that we prayed all day long on the tough days, when we had time. Never in my life had I made a promise to God and asked him for one in return, but I did that night.

It's difficult, even now, to share that evening and its special moments of prayer. I do so here because of the profound and unexplainable things that came out of my desperate plea to the all-powerful Being, the one being to whom I could turn for help in dealing with the news I had received. I decided that night to turn my life over to God and ask him to help me "grow back" for a totally unselfish reason. What God first heard from me was thanks for the opportunity to be associated with the men in Baker Company and learn from their sacrifices and unexplainable courage, and for the strength he gave me to serve as an effective leader for this special breed of men. I told the Lord that if he would help me beat the odds and get my strength and spirit back, I would spend the rest of my life giving those young 18-to-21-year-old miracles, those U.S. Marines, the kind of dedicated leadership they needed and deserved. It was a solemn promise, a commitment, a pledge. Now, in addition to rejoining my own loving family, soon to increase by one, I was asking to rejoin my larger family, my *Band of Brothers*.

I don't believe I slept that night. It doesn't matter. Maybe it was all a dream. Whatever I experienced, it lasted a long time and produced a certain calm and confidence I still find difficult to explain. It reinvigorated me with what I had used so effectively as a combat leader, a sense of calculated recklessness, not foolishness; of

74

being unafraid to try; of being willing to face up to anything, no matter what. Now I believed that things were going to get better. Now I felt more strongly than ever that I had to get back to the troops, my family. Now there was a new sense of purpose.

Adding to that new sense of purpose was the impending advent of fatherhood. Carol and I had decided in advance what our new child would be named, regardless of gender. If we had a boy, he would be Charles Grafton Cooper III, but we didn't want any more Charleses, Chucks, or Charlies around. We were going to call him "Trip" from day one. If we were blessed with a daughter, she would be named Linda Carol Cooper, after a dear friend and the baby's mother. A blond-headed, blue-eyed boy entered our world on July 15, 1951 in Asheville, N.C. My wife's father, Tracy, a truly delightful second father to me, sent a telegram that arrived in Japan on July 16. It read "TRIP ARRIVED SAFELY. CAROL FINE. SIGNED, TRACY." I truly believe that my body chemistry started changing that day.

New dads are supposed to tell the world the good news and hand out cigars. I couldn't really do that until I solved a few small problems. One problem was that I had no money. My pay records had been lost and had not as yet been reconstructed or received whatever treatment it took to get me some funds. Another problem was that of getting out of the room to go visiting and spreading the earth-shaking news up and down the halls of "Boys' Town," as they called the officers' wing.

First, the money. I buzzed for the ward corpsman who had delivered the telegram and asked him to get me a disbursing officer, any disbursing officer. I had to talk personally with one of the people in the pay office who maintained the records. He left—and returned in about 30 minutes with a Navy warrant officer carrying a briefcase and wearing a .45 caliber pistol. I guessed that he probably had money in that case. We negotiated what is called a "special money requisition," and he promised to open up a skeleton pay record for me so that I could have what was called "Health and Comfort Money." My SMR was a whopping $20.00—enough to get me a large box of good cigars from the hospital's post exchange and leave $16.00 change. A good start!

Now how could I hand out those Havanas up and down the ward? By this time I was going to the toilet daily in a wheelchair, but was always dependent on and carefully assisted by a corpsman. I didn't want to have someone push me around the ward in a wheelchair when I was announcing the arrival of my new son. The alternative was unthinkable, but it came to mind. *I had to get out of my harness and walk out there.* Maybe I could find a chair in the hall to hold onto. Pop Evans became my father confessor and Jim joined in the conversation. They both put their heads to work on figuring how I could do what they knew I couldn't or shouldn't do. Since they were both totally helpless, the idea that I even considered this after what the doctors had told me was sort of like striking a blow for freedom *for them*, or something. We discussed it for a long time, how to pull up, slide off the bed, lock the knees, steady myself on the bedstead, reach out for the nearby door handle, pull along the wall to the door, carry the cigars in my bathrobe pockets, and work my way around the ward, *ad infinitum.* I decided to sleep on it. Merely discussing it had exhausted me, but now all of us were excited. Tomorrow we'd have a "test flight," going as far as the door and then back into the bed. I still had zero feeling in my lower body, but something big was going to happen!

The next morning you would have thought it was D-day. Both of my roommates asked if I had slept well. It was like grooming an athlete for the big game. Jim suggested that I have two cups of coffee with breakfast: that caffeine might help. Pop suggested that we ask our corpsman to leave a wheelchair in the room in case I needed a quick run to the head. In other words, I could use it as a walker, or at least something to hold onto.

Breakfast came and went. I'd had three cups of coffee—but the wheelchairs were all in use. No soap there. After about an hour of thinking about it, I managed to crank the bed down to its lowest point and gradually ease my way out of the harnesses. It took a long, long time and completely exhausted me. Coach Evans called me "Harry Houdini." I felt like a criminal in the middle of a jail break. Suppose someone caught me? What the hell!

I started loading the cigars, then was able to swing my dead legs around and use the headboard to pull myself up to a sitting position. Next I worked my feet down to the floor. Coach Evans was giving me advice at each turn. Now to stand—and stand I did. After damn near fainting I sat down again. I was amazed: how had I done that? Enough with resting: back to work. Up again. Slide past the headposts against the wall. Golly, I had moved three feet. I grabbed the door handle and pulled a little more. Now I had the door handle and the door facing. I was standing in the door, but getting faint. It couldn't last much longer. I yelled down the hall, "Hey, you jarheads, Charlie Cooper has a brand new baby boy and here are some cigars!" I threw a handful out into the hall and passed out.

When I came to, there were a lot of people hanging over my bed. They seemed to be shaking their heads. I gradually got my senses back, with the help of some ammonia capsules. My "orthopedic" captain said, "How in the living hell did you get out in the hall?" No one had bothered to ask my coach, Pop Evans, who had watched the whole thing. I began to realize that maybe I was in trouble; maybe I had done some real harm to myself. I said, "My wife just blessed me with a baby son and I had to get up and tell somebody about it!"

The doctors checked me over and made no attempt to put the harnesses back on or ask me how I slipped them off. Instead, they went out in the hall for a long conference. They finally returned to announce that they were absolutely dumbfounded. One junior doctor volunteered that it was almost like a miracle. Later in the day they had me fitted for a hip-to-armpit body cast, with two holes in the back through which to change my dressings, and a large hole in the front through which my stomach would be able to expand. They were going to change my diet and feed me four times a day to put some meat on my bones. The summary: "Lieutenant Cooper, you taught us all something today, but the battle isn't over, you know." I simply nodded. My biggest battle had been that first step, and it was behind me.

One of my visitors was another Marine second lieutenant, Bill Long, who had been one of my best friends on the 1948 midshipmen's summer cruise. At that time he was an NROTC midshipman from Tulane University. Bill had taken an enemy shell fragment in his chest, and it lodged so close to his heart that they were afraid to operate to remove it. He was ambulatory and allowed to take liberty out in the "ville," as Marines called the city of Yokosuka. He came in one day and asked if he could get anything for me from the hospital PX. I asked him if they had any Marine officers' swords. He replied that they did and that some were on sale at this very moment for a ridiculously low price, one fifth of what they would cost at home.

I thought this would be a great way to demonstrate my determination to return to full duty: buy myself the officers' sword we were all required to have within two years of having been commissioned. And I now had some funds available from my skeleton pay record. We would do it. Another SMR from the Navy pay officer gave me the funds, and I passed them on to Bill. He bought the sword for me, and our corpsman found a nail on which to hang it on the wall over my bed.

All of these maneuvers had a spectator: the small, stooped Japanese janitor that cleaned and mopped our deck every day and whom we called "Mac" for some unknown reason. He always bowed deferentially—and now he kept his eye on that sword like a child looking in the window of a candy store.

One day after he'd done his chores in our room, he put his broom and mop aside and approached me. After bowing, he pointed to the sword and asked in what seemed to be broken English if he could hold it in his hands. At first I didn't understand what he was asking, but Pop Evans explained that the Malemuke sword carried by Marine officers intrigued Mac, and he wanted to examine it.

He always shuffled along, humped over, bowing to everyone. My nodded permission transformed him. He stepped quickly up onto my bed and lovingly removed the sword from the wall and pulled it from its scabbard. After examining it carefully, he returned the sword to its scabbard and thrust the scabbard into the sash he wore in lieu of a belt. He then moved to the center of the room, faced all three of us, snapped to attention, and drew the sword, handling it like a Marine on dress parade. Then he executed a perfect sword salute and said in perfect English, "Sir, I report myself and salute you. Commissioned Warrant Officer Hiato Kurishashi, 42 years' service, Japanese Imperial Navy!" We were dumbfounded, but a little relieved when he returned the sword, ceremonially, to its scabbard, then removed the scabbard from his sash and put it back on the wall.

He never attempted any special familiarity after this incident, but he did stop using broken English when speaking with us. He told us he had been serving on the Imperial Navy's gigantic battleship *Nagato*, the largest ship in the world, that late in the war came out from its base here in Yokosuka to do battle. It had no escorts or air cover, so U.S. Navy carrier planes quickly sank it with enormous loss of life. We had an "old pro," as Jim called him, cleaning our deck. We didn't call him "Mac" anymore. The Japanese name I've used is not correct, but we chose to call him "Gunner," a Marine nickname for our warrant officers. He liked that!

After a few days of excitement over my new body cast, my improved menu, and the start of work with the physical therapist, my mind and body started to run out of steam again. I recognized that my short struggle to reach the hall had revealed great possibilities, but the rest of the journey was uncertain at best. It was going to be a long, hard battle. Could I really make it? The late summer days in Yokosuka were hot and humid: my heavy cast increased my discomfort, and I started asking myself whether or not a full recovery was possible. My burst of confidence after that evening of prayer and reflection had left me with the simple premise that no matter how bad things are, you have the power, with God's help, to make them better. Now, once again, my inherited urge to *do something* when you're in a slump or losing ground saved me. As my inner search for an answer continued, I reasoned that I must take a decisive, positive course of action. It should be creative and useful, and should reflect my deep-seated, emotional feelings about combat with the "Bandits."

I realized then that I had a sort of legacy to leave the fighting Marine Corps if my return to active duty didn't materialize. My legacy would be the story that I had to tell. All I had to do was get it down on paper. I asked the Red Cross visitor that day if I could have several of her lined paper pads and a few pencils. The reflecting and writing commenced, and I soon became totally preoccupied and unaware of any physical discomforts. There weren't enough hours in the day. What I was trying to capture then is largely what has appeared in this book up to this point. I had been a Marine for 15 months and was 23 years old, but as we say in the Corps, "It's not the age; it's the mileage." I did have a story to tell, the miracle of my Marines.

The format I chose was an easy one. I would write a long letter to my baby son. At first it was like pouring my soul out onto a blotter. For a number of days I continued the process of recalling the day-by-day events and explaining them to a young child. Then my thoughts began to shift somewhat. Although I continued the narrative, I started inserting a brief principle or tenet at the top of the page when I finished a portion. What was forming in my mind was some sort of creed for a fighting man, one that could be taught during peacetime training and that would be reflected in battle. I was like a chemist trying to fathom the formula for the glue that holds Marine Corps units together in battle, even against the most overwhelming odds. Colonel Hayward's words about family and the *Band of Brothers* kept coming back to me.

What I finally composed and salted away was to become the seed for what would be my Marine Corps philosophy of command for the next 34 years. It eventually became a set of eleven principles that defined relationships between individuals and stressed an unselfish pursuit of excellence by each Marine. I've rewritten it now and then, rewording it somewhat, and published it in many different formats and different places, but its idealism and practicality have remained constant. In 1951, taking this first step toward a creed was good medicine for me. It was a convincing reminder that no matter what happened to me in the immediate future, I had a part of me to leave to the Marine Corps. It was very important to me that the essence of my two unforgettable months as a Baker Bandit not be lost. If I was fortunate enough to recover completely, these concepts would guide my own approach to leadership. If that was not to be, they would be meaningful standards to pass along to future Baker Bandits.

The doctors asked me if I was writing a book. My response was, "Not really. It started as a letter to my baby son, but seems to be growing into something else." I had to put it away in order to concentrate more heavily on therapy and make the small number of steps I could take grow each day. I had to get well enough to go home, and do it quickly.

They had to give me a new body cast almost every week as I grew out of the old one. Oh, how I lived to get a cast removed, to scratch a little, and to air out my skin and get it clean again!

The medical evacuation chain from the Korean war zone did not end in Japan: it stretched thousands of miles across the Pacific Ocean and branched out to all sections of the US. It could carry long-term patients like me to hospitals near our homes of record, if those hospitals had adequate facilities and medical skills. The airplanes it used were primitive compared to the long-range pressurized jet hospital planes used during the Vietnam conflict, but those four-engined propeller-driven transports moved thousands of men wounded in Korea back to their home areas.

Before the medics would let us undergo the rigors of long-distance travel, we had to have recovered to the point where we could walk aboard the airplane. The "primitive" aircraft had to make several refueling stops en route, and everyone had to get off the plane while ground crews filled its tanks with high-octane fuel. The repeated getting off and getting on would prevent the most critical patients from making one of these homeward-bound trips.

That is why I was concentrating so hard on therapy. There were various interpretations of "walk aboard," but I aimed to get myself into such a condition that I could do it, no matter what interpretation I was being judged by. My immediate goal was to get started on the homeward-bound journey.

My destination would be the hospital at the Naval Air Station in Memphis, Tennessee. The travel legs were short by today's standards. Hawaii would be the first stop, and it was routine for patients to enter Tripler Army Hospital temporarily for stabilization when they got there. Then there were other stops and visits to other hospitals on the way to the destination hospital. Although the stops were very frustrating, the one constant was the dedicated and professional care we received from the medics of all the military services.

By late August I could walk slowly out into the hall and down to the communal toilet we shared in "Boys' Town." A hospital corpsman always accompanied me to make sure I didn't have any problems. My maximum marathon distance was about 20 yards, done very slowly and carefully. There was no way that I could remain in an aircraft seat for an extended flight. The heavy cast was too restrictive and awkward; nevertheless, I tried to sell the idea I could go to the aircraft in a wheelchair, stand up and walk aboard (with a little help), then stretch out on a litter for most of the journey. I could move about the aircraft, feed myself, and visit the small toilet alone. That was my pitch, and finally the doctors gave the okay for me to be on the next week's flight to Hawaii, en route to the West Coast. I spent most of my last day in "Boys' Town" telling all the residents good-bye, getting a haircut, and putting all of my notes and letters into two small overnight bags. I would hand-carry my new officers' sword.

My two roommates were also making progress. Pop Evans was looking forward to getting his cast off and starting therapy. Jim said the doctors were talking about removing his bandages permanently within a week or so. The commanding officer of the hospital came to bid me farewell and to present me with a Purple Heart medal.

We touched down at Hickam Air Force Base long after midnight. The fresh, clean smell of Hawaii was quite a contrast to the smell of the Orient we had left behind. The sweet odor of plumeria blossoms, the gentle night breezes, and an efficient reception crew all helped to perk up six otherwise travel-weary Marines. There were others on the flight with us, but the Marines took care of each other and stayed together. I was the only officer and the puniest. Three of the men were Baker Bandits and two others were also from our battalion. Our bus took us up the hill to Tripler Army Hospital; aides escorted us to a room where we could all stay together. It had six beds and a private head. The first order of business was to use the head, clean up a bit, and get into some clean pajamas. The night nurse promised us anything within reason to eat if we were hungry. We all were.

One of the most beloved leaders in the entire history of the Marine Corps was the Commanding General, Fleet Marine Force, Pacific at the time of our arrival in Hawaii. Lt. General Lemuel C. Shepherd, later to become Commandant of the Marine Corps, had his headquarters at Pearl Harbor on the island of Oahu. A legendary hero from World War I and World War II, and a driving force in the successful Inchon amphibious landing in 1950, he was the image of a warrior/gentlemen, with his cultured manners and Virginia accent. All Marines knew who he was.

About 3:00 AM I was sitting on the bed clad only in my pajama bottoms and my newest body cast with the large stomach hole. Something made me look over toward the door of the room. Standing there alone in the doorway was a three-star Marine general. We all tried to stand up, but he waved us down immediately. This wonderful, caring leader had come down to visit with us, talk about our outfits and our battle experiences, and tell us how proud he was of us. He told me he had been wounded as a platoon commander in the Fifth Marines during the battle for Belleau Woods in 1918. He asked each of us when and where we'd been wounded and checked a list he had to verify our names. He pinned a second Purple Heart on my pajamas that night, and stayed with us while we had an early breakfast of fresh scrambled eggs and sausage. When he left, one of the troops summed up our mutual feelings: "Old Lem Shepherd, he really cares about his troops, doesn't he?"

We left late the next day on an overnight flight to Travis Air Force Base, spent the night there, and then were bused out to the naval hospital on Mare Island, a naval base near San Francisco. Mare Island Naval Hospital mostly handled any patient overload from several of the larger Army and Navy hospitals in the Bay Area. We went to Mare Island principally for maintenance treatment while we waited for transportation to other destinations. We didn't stay there long, but those days seemed to drag as we waited for news about when we would continue our journey. My "holes" were still draining, but didn't call for attention as frequently as they had in the past.

There was no TV available in those days, but we gathered in the lounge after dinner to listen to the radio. One show that we all enjoyed originated every night at the "Top of the Mark," the garden restaurant on the roof of the Mark Hopkins Hotel. The announcer would interview patrons of the restaurant, and always featured returning Korean War veterans, usually patients from one of the area hospitals.

After two especially boring days, a few of us gathered in the "Boys' Town" lounge to listen to the show. That night the roving master of ceremonies interviewed two soldiers. They were especially braggadocio and infuriated all of us with their war commentary, quite inaccurate from *our* point of view. Here we were, a bunch of young, mending, but still seriously ill troopers. None of us were fit to leave the hospital on our own. Most of us were either on the critical or at least serious list. No one among us could appear on that show and tell the unvarnished *Marine* truth about the war. I was the only one who could even walk, and my range was all of 25 yards. Golly, somebody has to do something about all the garbage being broadcast! But who? Then a plot began to develop.

A salty captain in a wheelchair with his heavy leg cast sticking straight out made a comment that led to an evening of unbelievable plotting and planning. He looked at me and said, "Cooper, do you have any uniforms in your sea bag?" The half dozen or so junior officers turned to me for my answer. Our ward hospital corpsman was with us in the lounge at the time. I laughed and said that I hadn't looked in that sea bag since we were in Kobe, Japan, en route to war, but I did have a set of enlisted kersey greens, a jacket and trousers, that officers were allowed to wear. I reminded him that the uniform was cut for a 210- pound body, and I had no shoes, ribbons, cap, shirt, tie, socks, or even underwear.

The discussion went on as if we were plotting to escape from Alcatraz. I didn't think anyone was serious at first, but soon learned otherwise—when our self-appointed leader, the captain, asked the corpsman if he would go down to the basement storage area and get my sea bag out so we could see what was in it.

Our good-natured corpsman was getting caught up in the plot, but I'm sure he didn't think he was going to become a party to an escape attempt. At any rate, he returned shortly with my sea bag. After a few moments of deep concentration, I recalled the combination that opened its lock. Out came the crumpled greens. Also in the bag were a field scarf (tie) and a green piss-cutter (garrison cap). What came next was to take the matter out of my hands. They all helped me put on the trousers and jacket on over my huge body cast. They fit like a tailor-made suit: I looked like a barrel-chested wrestler. Even the waist of the trousers fit perfectly around the cast. Talk about having lost a lot of weight! Someone then said what we'd all been thinking: "My God, with a little more planning and some sharing of gear, we could probably sneak you out of here for liberty in San Francisco. That new ensign nurse doesn't know diddly. Hell, once we got you dressed, you could walk right up to her desk and just sign out for overnight liberty."

This wily group of plotters had an exciting mission in mind for someone, and Charlie Cooper was their only plausible candidate. Logistics problems? They were there to be overcome. Our cooperative corpsman returned with sea bags belonging to all the officers present, and we sorted through the gear to find me a complete and "correct" uniform, including service ribbons. I insisted on wearing my two Purple Heart medals. Since we had all received Purple Hearts, we merely had to rearrange someone's ribbons to accommodate the addition of mine.

I got caught up in this dressing of the mannequin for a moment, but then I stopped them all. I told those liberty hounds that I had two somewhat smelly open wounds in my back, I was still was running low fever, I had zero stamina, and I couldn't dress or undress myself. I couldn't reach my feet to tie my shoes, or do any of the things one had to do to operate out in the "real world." Suppose I just passed out in downtown San Francisco. My arguments didn't even slow them down.

Their answers were immediate and convincing. First, tomorrow was Sunday. That made it easier to dodge the reduced staff and get out. I would have my bandages changed tomorrow morning. They would dress me after that. The entire group could kick in some $125.00, which would be more than enough to pay for bus fare to San Francisco and back, a hotel room in the Mark Hopkins, food, and some cab fares. The ward corpsman was now a full participant in this wild scheme. He volunteered that the bus stop was only about a hundred yards from the front door of the hospital, and there was a bench halfway to it where I could stop and rest. We war-gamed every step. They finally convinced me that I had to represent the entire group at the Top of the Mark and tell the true story of our battlefield accomplishments in Korea. Sunday night was the big night for them to listen on the radio. Ludicrous, ridiculous, mad, completely irrational? Yes, all of those. What a caper!

Initially, we pulled it off. I walked up to the nurse's desk about eleven o'clock Sunday morning and asked for the liberty log. She was reading the paper and hardly

81

looked up, but she asked, "When are you coming back?" I told her I'd probably be back later tonight, but maybe Monday morning. She didn't even comment.

From then on, our plan clicked at every turn. To the rest bench, then the bus stop, and then the bus, and I was off to the city. A cab to the Mark Hopkins, a room, room service lunch, and a long nap with clothes on. God, I was almost totally wiped out! My next move was to go up to the roof restaurant about six o'clock to have dinner and meet the radio personality. Now the witching hour was approaching. I felt strangely alone and weary. It occurred to me that this had to be one of the dumbest things I had done in my entire life, but now that I'd come this far, I had to get through it. My buddies were waiting to hear me on the air.

Then the problems began. I got on the elevator that said "Top of the Mark" with about ten people. Half of them were in uniform and all looked as puny as I felt. One Army major was on crutches and wearing a uniform that swallowed his body. The high-speed elevator took off for the roof, but we never made it. About halfway up we lurched to a sudden halt and people flew around the elevator like bowling pins. I fell on top of the major. We finally picked ourselves up and took stock. One woman started crying. Later, I thought she had good reason. We were trapped in that blasted elevator car for at least 30 minutes. The puny major fainted once, but we revived him. I finally had to tell everyone that I was in a body cast and just couldn't stand up any longer. We all adjusted so some of us could take turns sitting down. The major remained prone with his feet up in my lap. Damn, what had I gotten myself into?

Finally, a workman crawled down through a trap door in our ceiling, talked to someone on a telephone he had brought with him and in short order we moved up a bit to the nearest floor. I announced to the management people that helped us out of the car that I was heading up to the restaurant for the radio show. One of them said, "We don't have a show on Sunday night. The restaurant is closed, but you can go up and see the view." Damn, damn, damn! After a hamburger in the hotel grill, I retired to my room. It had been a long day.

After taking my jacket and shirt off, I realized that that was as far as I could go. Calling room service, I asked for a bellman. This young lad was shocked when he saw me standing there in my body cast, trousers, and shoes. He helped me get them off and allowed as how this was the first time he had seen any vets on liberty wearing a body cast. I slept the sleep of the dead, had a room service breakfast, and was assisted by another bellboy as I attempted to put my clothes back on. The cabby taking me to the bus station would not accept any money for his fare, saying he had been a WWII soldier and he appreciated what we had done for our country. It wasn't an unusual gesture in the San Francisco of 1951—in its better days, I think.

My return was exhausting, if uneventful, but it was as if I'd set off a burglar alarm when I walked through the door of our ward. There were at least four doctors, two nurses, and several corpsmen there, and the hospital CO was among them. They were truly concerned about me and even more amazed than my doctors in Yokosuka had been earlier in the summer. They checked me over more carefully than ever before. My temperature was normal for the first time since I had been wounded. I announced that I was wiped out, but felt pretty good, otherwise.

Then I asked the dumb question: "How did you find out I was missing?" The CO, looking relieved but definitely put out with me responded, "We never would have known, Lieutenant, but your wife called to talk with you and the nurse told her you were on liberty. She told the nurse that that was impossible, and the search was on!" My heart sank. My sweet wife thought I was half dead and here I was out on liberty!

The doctors told me the next day how dumb I had been, but added that there was no need for any more "stabilization" before I continued my journey homeward. I would be put on the next available flight heading east. I called Carol and tried to explain some of this, but she wasn't too sure what was going on. I did promise to explain it all when we were back together, and we both hoped that would be soon.

The next leg of the journey home was a shorter one. Along with four enlisted Marines also heading for the hospital in Millington, Tennessee, I departed from Travis Air Force Base. Our plane landed at Lackland Air Force Base, Texas, where we went to the sprawling base hospital to await further transportation. This was in late summer, deep in the heart of Texas, and the single-story wooden hospital, a relic of World War II days, was hot as Hades. The many pedestal fans the medics installed to ease our discomfort didn't help much. I took to using a coat hanger as an improvised back scratcher to relieve the itch that flourished under my cast. We were stuck there for several days, until finally a desperate phone call to base operations reached a friendly ear. A sympathetic lieutenant colonel scheduled a plane to take us on our final leg to the Naval Air Station, just outside of Memphis, 75 miles north of the "Golden Buckle on the Cotton Belt," my hometown of Clarksdale, Mississippi.

My wife and wee son were still with her parents in Fletcher, North Carolina, but would drive with her mother, Vesta, to meet me soon after I arrived at the hospital. That wonderful day was drawing closer. With no therapy and with little desire to move about in that heat, I had not gained any stamina, but the two back wounds were finally closed. No more drainage and, I hoped, no more antibiotics or fever.

We departed Lackland in an Air Force medevac plane. It was fully equipped for any emergency, but we didn't give those thoughtful medics any problems on the short flight to the Naval Air Station, Millington. I had bummed aircraft rides from here back to Washington, D.C. in my Midshipman days when returning to the Academy from summer leave, but the station took on an entirely new look as our bus drove past the base operations building toward what I hoped would be my last hospital. This was the eleventh medical facility that had treated or processed me since June 17, 1951. Memphis was hot, but nothing like Texas!

Chapter 9

The Homecoming
"Back to the Corps"

The hospital in Memphis wasn't a backwater by any means, but it was not a major medical facility. Most of the Marines and sailors who had returned from Korea earlier had been victims of frostbite and gunshot wounds. They didn't need physical therapy, so the Memphis hospital's excellent physical therapy department had been a bit underused before I put it to work and started to enjoy its benefits.

Immediately after I checked in, the senior orthopedic surgeon paid me a visit, accompanied by the hospital's cheerful physical therapist, Miss James. The doctor didn't take time to pour through my lengthy medical history. Instead, he took notes as I walked him through my rather amazing recovery up to this point. He was intrigued by my comment on "the regeneration of some nerves" and the continuing numbness over most of my back and lower extremities. During our discussion I mentioned that my doctors in Japan had said the cast could come off when I returned to the states if X-rays supported that action and my doctors thought it was time to commence therapy in earnest.

In retrospect, I think I may have implied that the cast was *supposed to come off* when I reached Millington. At any rate, the doctor said, "Let's get some X-rays now. If they check out, we'll take that cast off right away." To my surprise, the X-rays did pan out, and the cast would come off the next morning.

I was on the phone to Fletcher, North Carolina in about 15 minutes, "a collect call for Mrs. Carol Cooper from Lt. Cooper in Memphis." She told me that all three of them would drive over the mountains and across the full length of Tennessee to see me the next day. Carol's mother would fly back to Asheville after a short visit with us and my mother in Clarksdale.

At eight o'clock the following morning they escorted me down to the "body shop," where they installed and removed casts. I told them ahead of time that I wanted to save this cast as a souvenir. It came off in just a moment as the vibrating saw sliced through the plaster. What a relief! I had forgotten how good it felt to have air bathing that skin. They stood me in front of the full length mirror, and we all cocked our heads. I was canted about 15 degrees. I had healed "off center." The doctor shook his head and said, "Not to worry: this isn't a major problem. Your spinal column can be adjusted. Just a little more work for the therapist. Miss James will have you standing at attention in no time at all."

That day I had the first bath and shower combination I'd had since leaving home for war. Then while I was dressing in clean pajamas, a corpsman said, "Lieutenant, that blue 1950 Pontiac just pulled into the parking lot. Do you want a wheel chair?" I said, "No thanks, Doc. I'm going to walk out and meet my wife, my mother-in-law, and my new son," and I did just that.

One of the first things I learned after that wonderful reunion was that my son's name had changed. The little bundle I'd been thinking of as Trip had become Chip. One of my wife's best friends had visited her in the hospital in Asheville the day after the baby arrived. Upon seeing the child in Carol's arms, she said, "He sure is a chip off the old block. He's every bit his father's son." It had stuck, and I sure wasn't going to say a word about his new moniker. Come to think of it, Chip was better than Trip anyway.

The details of the therapy aren't important. Miss James took me on as a major project. I relished my sessions in the large Hubbard tank, where I floated in a mass of swirling waters and therapeutic bubbles. This loosening up, twice each day, led to dumbbell work and stretching exercises to help me bend over. I now had two fused vertebrae: I couldn't even *lean* over at first, but the flexibility slowly improved. I still had a "starboard list," but Miss James promised me we would start working on that with hanging exercises. When they took the cast off, I was a whopping 145 pounds—and that was a lot heavier than I'd been when the first cast went on.

The best news was that I could get weekend liberty after the first week, and would be able to drive to Clarksdale and be with my whole family. They could visit me regularly— but it was good to get home. My mother relieved Carol's mom as the nanny while we enjoyed our second honeymoon, almost a dream come true.

Late that fall, while on convalescent leave in Fletcher, North Carolina, I had some sort of negative reaction to my exercises and general level of activity. One morning I felt as if the bottom had fallen out from underneath me. I was floored for about three days, and everyone was getting concerned. It may have been some kind of a bug: bed rest and about 15 hours of sleep each day brought me back around. My lack of stamina was still a problem, and I continued to have a nap almost every day.

When I returned from that leave, my thoughts turned immediately to how and when I could get out of the medical system for good. I didn't report any of the problems I'd had while on leave to my doctor.

Then I learned that a former patient, a recovering Marine staff sergeant, was manning the patient affairs office at the hospital. I paid him a visit. He explained that the Marine Corps sent anyone with two Purple Hearts to non-field duty at one of the several Marine barracks on the East Coast. He also told me about a Marine Corps practice that I decided immediately to try to avoid.

The hospital routinely convened a board of medical survey that examined every seriously injured patient before he could be discharged. This board, which consisted of five doctors, evaluated the patient's physical ability to perform the duties of his rank and specialty. When appropriate, the board recommended that patients be put in a limited duty status or be medically retired with a disability pension. This news reawakened a fear I'd had ever since the "committee" visited me in Yokosuka and announced my impending retirement. That board was something I would do my best to avoid.

During my last few weeks of hospitalization, I was allowed to live at home and commute to the hospital three times a week for treatments and therapy. It wasn't a long trip, and someone always chauffeured me back and forth. Toward the end I began to drive part of the way.

All this while, I was pressing my doctor to let me return to duty. His response was that any return would have to be for "limited duty" for my own protection. When I asked the staff sergeant in patient affairs about orders, I told him that the doctor had said I would be on "limited duty" but could return to duty shortly. The staff sergeant had to send a message to Headquarters, Marine Corps, informing them of my availability and requesting orders. Someone had to authorize him to send this message, and I didn't ask who.

When my doctor was transferred late that fall, I visited my friend in patient affairs and asked him to request orders for me. He had me fill out a request form with my choices of duty stations, which could be any Marine Barracks on the East Coast, if there was a vacancy. I opted for Charleston, South Carolina; Pensacola, Florida; and Norfolk, Virginia, in that order. Somehow, the request was released and I received a copy of the message. It was from the commanding officer of the hospital, so someone in the CO's office had to have released it. Within a few days, I had a set of orders, but not to any of the stations I had requested. It was to Marine Barracks, Camp Lejeune, N.C., the Corps' largest base on the East Coast. (In 1951, the term Marine Barracks represented what later was to be called Marine Corps Base, the non-Fleet-Marine-Force supporting structure, a large organization during our wartime mobilization.) The orders did specify that I was in a "limited duty" status.

There had to be some administrative adjustments on the date of departure and the date I had to report, but no one at the hospital questioned the validity of the orders. I didn't either, and in early December I checked out of the hospital for good. Looking back, I realize that I wasn't fit even for limited duty—but what the hell, the urge to return to the real world was overwhelming. I was sure it would all work out, but it wasn't my duty to question the orders or say anything about a board of medical survey. My staff sergeant friend understood my feelings and had apparently given me a little help with the orders. Sloppy administration had enabled me to escape!

Miss James, my dedicated therapist, gave me a huge hug before I left. She cautioned me that I could expect months and even years of cramping and spasms as my aggressive nerves attempted to grow back and force their way through muscle tissue. She was right. It lasted for years, but the feeling did return, however gradually.

For now, the small Cooper family left Clarksdale in that 1950 Pontiac, headed back to the Corps. We arrived at Camp Lejeune shortly before Christmas.

Chapter 10

Military Police and Stateside Marines

When we arrived at Camp Lejeune just a few days before Christmas, we were fortunate to find off-base rental housing available immediately. The summer cottage on the banks of Bogue Sound seemed idyllic to a new family such as ours. All of our neighbors were Marine officers who commuted to either Camp Lejeune or Cherry Point.

I was assigned to the Barracks Military Police Company as its executive officer. My tour with the MP's was short, but several interesting things happened to me. First, I was defense counsel on dozens of special court martial cases, mostly those of Marines who had been absent without proper authority (AWOL), but also a few more serious cases. A new military justice system, the Uniform Code of Military Justice, had gone into effect in June of 1951, and I got a crash course in its many complexities.

Second, the provost marshal was short one officer in his CID (Criminal Investigation Division) office. After my efforts as a defense counsel had resulted in a large number of acquittals, the PM had me removed from the courtroom and assigned to full-time work in CID. The talent working in MP Company was impressive. They all were Marine Reservists who had been recalled. Our senior night desk sergeant, a black master sergeant, was a PhD and president of a black university in West Virginia. The head of CID had been chief of detectives in the Chicago Police Department. And so on.

One day soon after I'd joined CID, Major Cruise, our provost marshal, called me into his office. He had just received a phone call from an anonymous member of the Jacksonville Police Department telling him that he ought to send someone to the city jail. A Marine officer was locked up there, and he was in bad shape. The provost marshal didn't have the sort of relationship with the Jacksonville Police Department that would allow him to make a direct phone call to the chief of police about a matter like this, so he sent me out to pay a surprise visit. He wanted a return phone call ASAP.

I walked into the jail unannounced, accompanied by a large gunnery sergeant, a former Virginia highway patrolman. I told the jailer that I had come to see the officer they had in custody, right now! He mumbled something, and my "gunny" stood face to face with him and said, "Where is he?" He escorted us to the officer's cell. The officer was a Reserve major who had been charged with driving under the influence and resisting arrest, but someone had beaten him into a bloody pulp. We could hardly distinguish the features of his face, and he had not had any medical treatment. I turned and strode back to the desk, picked up the phone, and called Major Cruise. He told me to stay where I was: he was on the way.

The officer's story, later verified by others, was that he indeed had been intoxicated. He had run a red light and the local police pulled him over. When he had reached for his driver's license, the two policemen threw him against his car and beat him senseless. Most of his front teeth were gone, his nose was flattened, and he had cuts over both eyes and on his jaw. We immediately demanded custody of him and delivered him to the naval hospital on base.

After the major had been treated and sewn up, he gave us a complete statement of his travails. With his statement in hand, Major Cruise and I proceeded to the office of the Commanding General, Major General Ray Robinson, USMC. There I learned that this wasn't the first incident of this type: there had been all too many. General Robinson had made calls on the mayor, warning him, and had threatened to take unusual and drastic action if the authorities failed to get the rogue police under control. They had failed to do so. This was the "straw," apparently. While we were still in his office, he summoned his staff judge advocate and told him, "I've had enough of this crap. Let's do it. Declare the city of Jacksonville off limits to all military personnel and their dependents. We'll make those bastards crawl!"

The restriction lasted just eight days and served its purpose—in spades. The merchants went ballistic and applied the proper pressure. Before the order was lifted, the chief of police and a third of his officers had been fired. The county sheriff fired three senior deputies, and the attorney general of the state paid a visit to Camp Lejeune, dispatched by the governor to help us in our conflict with the local authorities. The governor wanted to put a quick lid on this tempest. He and his attorney general did just that. They proved most helpful.

Lt Cooper is awarded the Silver Star

One day I found on my desk a document with many attached endorsements. It was from the Secretary of the Navy and contained a battlefield citation: "For conspicuous gallantry and intrepidity in action against enemy aggressor forces." It presented me with the Silver Star medal for my "heroic actions on 17 June 1951." It had followed me halfway around the world. I felt greatly honored for what that award represented, and still do to this day. Two days later at a battalion awards ceremony, Colonel John White, our commanding officer, pinned the medal on this still skinny but now rigidly erect second lieutenant. My 15-degree tilt was gone, but the medics weren't through with me.

88

In March I learned that I would be promoted to first lieutenant on the first of April. As I was reading the message about the promotion, I received a call from a Navy Medical Service Corps Officer in "sick bay" (the base dispensary). He asked point blank, "What in the devil are you doing on active duty?" Thrown suddenly into a mild state of shock, I managed to ask why he should pose such a question. Several months ago I had received orders and been discharged from the hospital in Memphis. It was all in my health record. He pointed out that there was something missing from that health record. Had I been examined by a board of medical survey? I gave him a straight answer: No, I had not been before a board. He asked me to come over to see him in his office next door. It was now late March: I felt much better than I had four months earlier, but it hadn't been easy for me to maintain a full work schedule six days a week.

Our visit was cordial. He was simply trying to get some order in the medical jumble that many of the health records had become. I was honest and frank with him, telling him of the "committee" in Japan and my fear of medical retirement. What I wanted most in life was to return to full duty as soon as I possibly could. He was very supportive.

A formal board was convened the following week. He had encouraged me to bare my soul to the members, all of whom had served recently as combat medics. After my session before the board, its members met briefly in private and then returned to announce their findings. I was to remain on limited duty until December of 1952, when I was to report back for a full physical to determine my fitness. They also pronounced me fit to be advanced to the grade of first lieutenant when eligible. After reading the formal statement, the head of the board, a Navy captain, remarked that my medical history was indeed unusual. He added that I had a great deal to be thankful for, and the Marine Corps was fortunate to have officers like me. Frankly, I almost lost it, but thankfully I didn't.

Late in March, a new battalion commander arrived to relieve Colonel White, who moved up to become the general's chief of staff. The new commander had just been promoted to colonel; he was a Reserve officer who had been selected for augmentation as a Regular. His name was Hamilton Hoyler, and he was to have a major influence on my life. A Harvard Law School graduate, he had been a very successful civilian attorney. In WWII he had commanded two different infantry battalions in the South Pacific. He had every personal decoration for heroism except the Congressional Medal of Honor, and he was simply a great human being. Shortly after he assumed command, I was ordered to report to his office.

We had not met before and this meeting was probably a "look over" for me. This astute, smooth, and totally professional CO impressed me from the moment I stepped into his office. The situation he laid out for me was this: he was facing a massive personnel turnover in his large, unwieldy Headquarters and Service Battalion, and was figuring out what talent was available to help him tighten up some loose ends. He said that he had heard good things about my brief stay in the battalion. He talked about one of his largest headaches, Casual Company #1, a processing center, disciplinary holding barracks, and court martial legal center. It had five officers, all Reserves who would be leaving shortly. Two of them were lawyers. The CO's billet called for a major, a legal officer. He was going to make me the CO and give me an administrative officer to help me until we could get around to reorganizing this impossible combination of functions. He added that one of my jobs would be to recommend how to restructure the unit. It was the most unusual and frustrating job I ever had, but what I learned in the next nine months made it all worth while.

One positive thing I recognized at once was the unique quality of the officer who was to replace the four that were leaving, Commissioned Warrant Officer-4 Cecil M. Dietz, USMC. "Gunner" Dietz was one of a kind. He had more than 38 years of service, was a sergeant major when he had been captured in Shanghai in 1941, survived four years as a Japanese POW, and knew everything there was to know about the Marine Corps. He was all of 5ft. 2in. tall. A model of the "Old Corps," he had joined the Corps when he was 16 and served in Haiti for 15 years. The day I took command, he brought in a pot of coffee and pulled up a chair for a long talk. When we had finished, the pot was empty and I knew then that with Dietz at my right hand and Hoyler up above, we were going to make this outfit run the way it should.

The Marine Corps was in the middle of a massive turnover in 1952. We were still fighting a war in Korea, but all Reserves were being released to return home. The Corps was forced to accept large numbers of draftees to maintain its strength. This created real quality problems. The consequences were concentrated in my new company. This small unit was the mouth of the East Coast funnel through which all criminals, misfits, and undesirables were sifted out of the Marine Corps. It did other things, but that was its principal mission.

There were some 50 "permanent personnel" on my rolls. All others were transients: the number varied from day to day, but averaged more than 800, 450 of whom were in the two base brigs, either serving sentence or awaiting trial. Most of these were absence offenders, but a handful were hardened criminals. Among our "customers" were many draftees who couldn't read, speak coherently, or meet minimal physical standards. These men hadn't done anything wrong, but they were not fit for military service and were transferred to us for processing and discharge. We were also a collection point for homosexuals slated for discharge. (In 1952, they were given the option of court martial for sodomy or an undesirable discharge. Only one ever opted for trial. He was acquitted and requested a return to duty.)

At times I felt that my unit was the toilet bowl of the Marine Corps, and I expressed it that way one day to my patient colonel. It had been an exasperating day, and I stormed into Colonel Hoyler's office to tell him the Corps was going down the tubes, it was absolutely a disgrace, and this battalion was a sewer. He sat me down and calmly shared his wisdom with me. Today we would call it counseling. His words became mine in the years to come as I dealt with aggressive, idealistic junior officers who tended to take the mantle of the Commandant of the Marine Corps on their own shoulders.

As I recall it, he said, "You're absolutely right. I know it, the General knows it, and the Commandant knows it. These are tough times, but the Marine Corps isn't going under. On the other hand we won't solve our problems by complaining. There is a solution, Charlie, and you can be a very important part of it. What I have to say is not a gimmick. I'm going to give you an imaginary candle to put in your pocket. Take it back to Casual Company and think about it. What I want you to do is light that candle, hold it up high over your head so that your piece of the Corps is there for all to see. Make it shine so brightly you cast the light of your excellence on other companies in this battalion. I know you will, that's why I sent you down there. Looking ahead, as you grow in rank and responsibility, I'll expect you to expand that light over larger pieces of the Corps. For now, today, help me with this command: make your part of it the best you possibly can. Sure, we have problems, but if we light enough candles, things are going to improve. Can I count on you?" He hit the nail on the head. Bingo! I went back to work.

The headaches at the office didn't diminish, but my home life became more pleasant. We were able to move into new family quarters in late spring—into a new development just outside the base called Tarawa Terrace. It put us in closer contact with friends and base facilities, and was much less expensive than our civilian rental cottage. Here our son Chip celebrated his first birthday by burying his face in a chocolate cake placed before him at his party. Someone observed that he was a "chow hound" like his old man.

About this time, Major Cruise, the provost marshal, asked me to speak to the entire MP company about my Korean war experiences. (None of them had served in Korea.) It was the first time anyone had asked me to give such a speech. I would give it during the two-hour period set aside every Saturday morning for non-commissioned officers' school. I took my preparation seriously, and broke out the notes I'd made in Yokosuka, including those that covered the "Band of Brothers" principles. My "students" seemed to take a sincere interest in what I had to say. At the end of the first hour, I uncovered a blackboard with my eleven "Band of Brothers" principles on it. I told how they originated and concluded by giving each man an imaginary candle to use in lighting the way for his own "Band of Brothers."

It was an emotional presentation. When it was over, most of the men came up to thank me and ask for a copy of the principles. I offered to have them typed up and reproduced. It was the beginning of what years later a Marine in the First Division called "The 11 commandments according to General Cooper." The document I passed out to those Marines that day started with a prologue and then listed the principles. It went something like this:

> The term "Band of Brothers" aptly describes the close comradeship and mutual respect there was among combat Marines during the most difficult early days of the Korean War: a military brotherhood in which every man is the same, never lets a comrade down, and would give his life to protect and save a fellow Marine, if necessary. This all-for-one-and-one-for-all approach has made us unique among the world's military services.
>
> We have survived the many battles in our history because we consistently produced a cohesive fighting team, one whose members are completely unselfish in their approach to duty. I have personally experienced the effect of this brotherhood in battle—and am alive today only because my men took care of one of their own. Several Marines died rescuing a severely wounded Lieutenant Cooper in 1951. I can never forget it.
>
> I consider it to be my fundamental mission to foster this spirit of closeness, pride in organization, and mutual respect that leads to success in battle. We must show the entire Marine Corps that if there is a better way for all Marines to live and work and, if needed, fight side by side, we can develop it as a Band of Brothers. I offer it to you.
>
> /s/ C. G. Cooper, 1st Lt.,
> USMC

1. All Marines are entitled to dignity and respect as individuals, but must abide by common standards established by proper authority.
2. A Marine should never lie, cheat, or steal from a fellow Marine or fail to come to his aid in time of need.
3. All Marines should contribute 100% of their abilities to the unit's mission. Any lesser effort passes the buck to someone else.
4. A unit, regardless of size, is a disciplined family structure, with relationships based on mutual respect among members.
5. It is essential that issues and problems that tend to lessen a unit's effectiveness be addressed and resolved.
6. A blending of separate cultures, various educational levels, and different social backgrounds is possible in an unselfish atmosphere of common goals and aspirations and mutual understanding.
7. Being the best requires mutual effort, hard work, and teamwork. Nothing worthwhile comes easy.
8. Every Marine deserves job satisfaction, equal consideration, and recognition of his achievements.
9. Knowing your fellow Marine well enables you to learn to look at things "through his eyes," as well as through your own.
10. Issues that detract from the efficiency and sense of well-being of an individual should be brought out into the open and evaluated for their effect on the unit as a whole.
11. The brotherhood concept depends on all members "belonging": being fully accepted by all others in the unit.

The concept was idealistic to a fault, but it lasted, passed a lot of tests, and pulled the best out of the people that subscribed to it.

Early in September my family moved into quarters on the base that were only blocks from my barracks. The huge turnover in officers had made these small units, affectionately called "the crackerboxes," available. As we were enjoying a Marine Corps Birthday celebration with friends at the officers' club on November 10, another company commander stopped by our table to tell me that he had heard from a friend in Headquarters, Marine Corps. The Corps was "reactivating" its Reserve, nationwide, and I was one of the 50 ground officers to be sent out to start the ball rolling. I'd be going to Columbia, S.C.: the orders would be effective after January 1. Carol had just gotten the curtains up in our new home, but what the heck, it sounded interesting.

My December evaluation physical went well, and I was restored to full duty status. One of the doctors examining me suggested that I have my "football nose" operated on while I was in Washington. He prepared a referral to allow surgery at the Bethesda Naval Hospital after I finished my orientation week. It was a good Christmas in the crackerbox. We were detached in early January after less than 13 months at Camp Lejeune.

Chapter 11

Rebuilding the Reserves

General Lemuel Shepherd was now Commandant of the Marine Corps—a changing, much expanded, Marine Corps. By the end of 1952, the Reserves who had been recalled to active duty for the Korean War had all been released and returned home. Early in 1953, the Commandant started to reconstitute the Marine Corps Reserve. He would do this with the help of 50 inspector-instructors, regular officers chosen to activate old units and start up new units all over the country.

General Shepherd well knew the sacrifices our Reserves had made when they were called to active duty for the Korean War. They had given up their families, businesses, schooling, and in many cases their lives. He expected that old Reservists would show some initial reluctance to reaffiliate. He thought it might help to overcome that reluctance to choose the organizers—the inspector-instructors—carefully. He specified that each inspector-instructor must not only have served in Korea, but also have been awarded a personal decoration for heroism and "at least" one Purple Heart. I was the only first lieutenant assigned to this duty, but my instructors in Washington told me I would become a captain in 1953. The Marine Corps was setting me up in business, independent duty.

My unit was to be the 89th Special Infantry Company in Columbia, South Carolina, a guard and security unit trained to relieve regular Marines at a Marine Barracks or Navy base in time of war. It was to operate out of a Naval Reserve Training Center until we could build our own facilities. I was also bonded and designated an "accountable officer" to manage the supply account, given additional duties recruiting officer candidates statewide, and charged with recruiting reservists to serve on my own staff.

The Marine Corps gave me a staff sergeant major, a Navy hospital corpsman, a supply chief, and a clerk to help me launch this balloon. First we had to recruit reservists to round out my staff. Once the staff was assembled, we were to start recruiting men to form the unit. Our task was like giving birth under Marine Corps auspices. We were a tiny base in a civilian world—encouraged to become good citizens and join in all kinds of community activities.

This tour of duty lasted a bit longer than it should have, some 42 months, but it got my creative juices flowing. My family and I became very much a part of this southern state capital and university town—and I did make captain late in 1953.

Carol and I hocked everything we owned, took a second mortgage, and bought a home for the first time. It was a small three-bedroom cottage on the outskirts of town. We added a sweet little daughter, Linda Carol, to our family in September of 1953.

My new Marine Reserve unit got involved in all kinds of activities. It had its own athletic teams, some of which were city champs a number of times. Our unit's annual "Toys for Tots" campaign got national recognition. After a few ups and downs, the unit grew to full strength, won honors in summer training, and finally moved into its own new facilities next to the Navy Training Center. The new Commandant, General Randolph Pate, a native of South Carolina, accepted my invitation to speak at the dedication ceremony for our new building.

Toward the end of my lengthy tour I began to feel as if the Marine Corps had forgotten all about me. At the same time, my wife and I faced a crushing bit of news. A joint Navy-

93

civilian board of doctors had diagnosed our son as having muscular dystrophy. The doctors had given him only three to five years to live. If I was to be ordered overseas without dependents, as most Marines were, it would leave my wife to deal with this tragedy alone. As we approached the three-year mark with no word of orders, I sat down at my typewriter and wrote a letter to the Commandant, via the chain of command. I explained the medical situation and asked that I be assigned overseas as soon as possible so that I could return and be there to comfort my family when it needed me most.

An Inspector General team visited our unit two weeks later. I welcomed these annual inspections because we had few such opportunities to show off our unit and its successes. The colonel that led the team was a breath of fresh air for me. He knew all about my letter, and was concerned that after three years I had not received any word on what my new assignment would be or when I'd be leaving for it. He was much impressed with the unit and my staff. He gave us top marks for the work we had done and praised our professionalism. He also promised to drop me a note about my orders.

Late in the spring of 1956, I received a copy of orders sent to my relief, a Captain J. W. Duncan, who would be coming in July. That was the first good news. The next day I received a note from Colonel Steiner, the IG, that gave me the best news of all. The Marine Corps was moving a brigade of troops from the Third Division in Japan and Okinawa to Hawaii. The First Provisional Air-Ground Brigade was forming at the Marine Corps Air Station, Kaneohe, Hawaii. I was to join this brigade in August, and "P.S. Bring your family with you." A Marine overseas with dependents: it was revolutionary! We sold our little house, paid cash for a slightly used car, and started across country. Wonderful times were ahead. I was going back to the troops, to the Fleet Marine Force in Hawaii, and Carol, Chip, and Lindy were all going with me.

Chapter 12

Back to the Troops

After being starved for troop duty, I was now heading overseas to join the "China Marines," the Fourth Marine Regiment. Weight training, running, and three busy years had rounded out my physical recovery. The muscles had returned, and I now weighed the same 212 pounds that I weighed the day I was commissioned.

We flew out of Alameda on the Mars, a huge Navy flying boat reputed to be the largest airplane in the world. We arrived late in the evening, weary but elated as those warm, sweet-smelling breezes blew through the windows of the bus taking us across the "Pali" to Kaneohe Bay. We were billeted in a motel near the base called the "Thailiana." It was rumored that the owner/manager was one of the principal characters in James Jones's book, *From Here to Eternity*. Carol thought she was the madame of the whorehouse. I thought she was the whore that befriended Pruitt, the bugler. Either way, she was very nice to us.

The next day I reported in to the First Marine Brigade. They sent me down to the Fourth Regiment. The executive officer, Lieutenant Colonel Frank Garretson, wouldn't be able to approve my assignment until he returned from a conditioning hike. I listed my three preferences for duty: 1. rifle company, 2. rifle company, 3. rifle company. I added a note saying that my independent duty had lasted 42 1/2 months.

When Colonel Garretson called me into his office, he said, "I gather you're kinda hungry to get back with the troops, right?" I smiled and said, "Colonel, you'll never know how hungry I am!" He responded that there was a rifle company from the Third Battalion in the field at Bellows Beach, an old Air Force base now used for small-unit training. If I wanted to take command of G Company, his jeep and driver, sitting out front, would take me there. "Their CO, Jim Stemple, knows you're on the way." And there they were, a real, live Marine Rifle Company, putting up their shelters in the sand on Bellows Beach as their new CO arrived. Master Sergeant Pyles, the first sergeant, greeted me. Hallelujah, I was back!

The Fourth Marine Regiment was well stocked with combat-experienced company-grade officers. My tour was for two years, but those after me were to stay for three. We had no overseas deployments or commitments. It was peacetime, so we could concentrate on quality training and combat readiness. Intramural and varsity sports were large parts of our high-octane training program. It was a situation that fostered professionalism at its best—good, solid soldiering at every level. The brigade, both the air and ground portions of it, was in every sense a peacetime Band of Brothers.

The regiment was completing a tough training cycle, preparing to make an amphibious landing and then spend a month on the "Big Island" of Hawaii. The troops, after weeks of forced marches, were at a high level of fitness when I joined them. Although keeping up with them was a bit demanding at first, my problem was not conditioning, it was my feet. I relished the physical demands, but there were no hard callouses inside those boots of mine. The high-speed marches, frequently on hard surfaces, gave me all sorts of blisters and caused bleeding. My hospital corpsmen helped pull me through with pads, tape, tincture of benzoin, and some horrible looking purple solution that I soaked in nightly. The first sergeant would shake his head when he looked at my raw, bloody feet, but I swore him to secrecy and we weathered the sore foot storm.

My predecessor was a well-regarded professional officer, and the company reflected his priorities. I didn't attempt any immediate adjustments. My priorities were short and sweet: to prepare myself as their commander and to establish a relationship with the troops before we went aboard ship. My short message to them: "Looking good isn't enough. We're going to train the way we fight, no short cuts. I'll never ask you to do anything I couldn't or wouldn't do myself, and there's a 72-hour pass for any man that beats me in the physical fitness test. I'm proud to command G Company and I want each of you to be proud that you're in it."

Sergeant Pyles, "the Top," as the troops called him, was on their case from dawn to dusk—and they loved him for it. At home he had a close-knit family with seven daughters, but his wife told him he had 225 sons. He did. I've known countless competent, loyal, professional senior non-commissioned officers in my 35+ years as a Marine, but this one deserves a special tribute. He was the best. This Band of Brothers, this company was his extended family.

Pyles's office counseling sessions were legendary. He hadn't had one of his Marines "go over the hill" since the company had been in Hawaii, and we were the only company that could make that boast. But two nights before we were to load out, "The Chief" turned up missing. The Chief was a full-blooded Apache Indian, a "buck sergeant" who epitomized everything about being a Marine—everything except one. He couldn't handle alcohol. It turned him into an animal. He knew this and regularly abstained, but apparently he'd had one of his infrequent falls off the wagon. If we didn't find him right away, he would be declared a deserter when we sailed.

Pyles's plan was to take four younger NCO's and personally conduct a search of the fleshpots of Honolulu. He needed my blessing for this recovery effort. I could see how distressed he was. The Hawaiian Armed Services Police (HASP) were tough on belligerent drunks, and that's what Pyles said the Chief tended to be. Well, "Task Force Pyles" launched and recovered within hours. A very much "hung over" Chief appeared before me at Office Hours the next day, swore he'd never do it again, and returned to duty in time for the exercise. I put him on six months probation. He was the best squad leader we had, and his men would follow him to hell and back. Our Band of Brothers was alive, taking care of its own.

Our battalion didn't have far to go for our amphibious landing exercise: it was on the neighboring island of Kauai. We boarded ships at Pearl Harbor and spent two days at sea simulating all of the usual pre-D-day activities. My company was on an LST: we were to lead the beach assault in amphibious tractors. We were opposed by aggressor forces, and umpires accompanied all of the attacking forces. Our landing proved to be quite realistic.

After the exercise, we took a lunch break while the umpires prepared their critique. It pleased me greatly that G Company was cited and praised frequently. As we trudged down the mountain to head back to the ships, I overheard a typical Marine lament. "It's always great to get off those rust buckets, but after a few days of mud, dirt, and C-rats, it's sorta nice to get clean and eat a hot meal again." Some things never change!

We disembarked at Hilo, Hawaii, and trucks carried us up the mountain to a military tent camp named "Pohakuloa." It was in the saddle between the two volcanic

96

mountains, Mauna Loa and Mauna Kea, at an elevation of 8500 feet. Our training missions would take us even higher. The weather was stimulating, warm but not hot during the day; cool but not extremely cold at night. We lived in strong-back tents with wooden decks. We worked long and hard, but the food was great. We had two hot meals a day and C-rats for lunch. Officers and troops each had beer tents where they could go for relaxation in the evening, but taps came early because the days were long and exhausting.

Although there were some trees and scrub brush on the hillsides, most of the area was black lava rock. Because of this, each of us had brought along two pairs of boots. Every three or four days of training, we turned in one pair to be resoled by the service support unit. This cycle recurred so often that the regiment had to fly in a large stock of new boots from Kaneohe.

For me, it was a long-awaited experience. I knew Company G had improved a great deal tactically in those two weeks. We'd been able to improve our marksmanship by firing all of our weapons in the wide open lava beds. As the company tests approached, I sensed that the company was going to be a contender. We had never been tested before.

The formal critiques of the company tactical tests were conducted by the regimental staff. The briefers were circumspect and avoided overly critical remarks, but the truth surfaced in the grades. Each company was graded in three areas: tactical proficiency, live firing proficiency with all weapons, and leadership at all levels. When all was said and done, each battalion had one company surface as clearly superior. It was Captain John Cobb's B Company in the First Battalion, Captain Jim Harrell's F Company in the Second, and Captain Charlie Cooper's G Company in the Third. I was relieved and elated to be singled out in our report with the highest marks for any company tested. The battalion tests were to follow and we would be first.

Our battalion commander, Lieutenant Colonel Ernie Freeman, was not an experienced infantry officer. His primary field had been intelligence. He was a thoughtful, personable man and had been blessed with a seasoned staff, but this exercise worried him. He knew it was going to put him under close personal scrutiny—under the immediate, watchful eye of our tall, imposing regimental commander, Colonel Bryght D. Godbold, and his staff of umpires.

The problem commenced atop a huge cinder cone hill. The regimental commander pointed out the distant objectives, similar cinder cones, and gave an oral attack order to Colonel Freeman. He had 15 minutes to analyze the situation, call some of his staff forward to consult, and then issue his attack order to the companies. The scenario wasn't too realistic, but it did put him under pressure. What followed may not have been a textbook solution, but it proved interesting.

Colonel Freeman called his battalion operations officer forward. After a brief discussion, he called the company commanders up to the observation point. Major Pates, the S-3, pointed out the objectives, outlined a proposed scheme of maneuver, and turned things over to Colonel Freeman. About 20 umpires were taking notes and listening to every word he said. Ernie Freeman was clearly on the hot seat. He noted that the objective was about three miles away and the terrain was impassable lava except for a narrow road and adjacent shoulders. He was going to put H Company in the lead, followed by I Company. G Company would be in reserve and follow I Company. At first glance, it looked like a conditioning march rather than an attack, but

I didn't say anything until he turned to me and said, "Charlie, do you have any questions or maybe a comment on how to use G Company?"

My response was slow in coming. Perhaps we could take a few minutes for me to make a visual reconnaissance and see if there was some alternative. We had all operated over this "impassable lava bed forest" the previous week: maybe we could find a way to get across it in order to swing out wide, completely hidden, and envelop the objective from the rear. My XO and I both used our binoculars to make a quick study of the route. We could lighten up the company, leave the heavy weapons behind, get machetes for each man in the lead platoon, and cut our way through that terrain. No one could see us once we entered this maze of brush and rock. If we pulled it off we could attack from the rear and end the damn war.

Colonel Freeman heard my plan, and quickly approved it. He called the main attack a "feint," which is what it would be. We finalized visual signals to use if the radios were masked, and moved out with 150 men, leaving the remainder to follow in track on the road, as originally proposed. I took the three rifle platoons and a section of machine guns. We managed to collect 20 machetes to help with the brush and thorn bushes.

What had been a routine test, largely using check-off sheets to grade troop-leading steps, had become an immensely challenging physical feat. Fortunately, the tattered and torn troops of G Company succeeded in making their way unheard and unseen across that hellish terrain to a position some 150 yards behind the final objective. The aggressor force was absorbed in watching for action in the opposite direction, so we were able to climb up the rear of the steep objective, take up firing positions, and tell them the war was over with a few bursts of blank machine gun fire.

They stood up, raised hands, and stacked their weapons as we searched them. We had captured 200 "shock troops" from the Brigade Drum and Bugle Corps and Headquarters Company. The exercise was over. Colonel Ernie Freeman was a regimental hero that day.

Colonel Freeman had a soft spot in his heart for G Company thereafter. Our prowess in the tactical tests and our overall performance on the Big Island followed us when we returned to our barracks at Kaneohe. We became the lead company in a number of exciting and challenging new training opportunities. (See note page 106)

Colonel Godbold, a Wake Island POW and an "Old Corps" Marine, insisted on high-quality formal staff work, which translated into much paper and a plethora of formal orders. It was his personal priority to make a tour in his regiment the staff equivalent of a tour at Marine Corps schools. He insisted on written orders, technically correct and complete, for every conceivable project. While it seemed to be overkill at the time, it turned out to be a marvelous training vehicle-one that helped me immensely.

Our first op order I had to write was for a 24-hour amphibious raid to be launched from an LST and landed in amphibious tractors under cover of darkness, to secure an objective by day, and to withdraw the next evening. It would have been a good drill for a battalion staff or a tough workout for the regimental staff. it was one extraordinary challenge to a young captain who had never written a formal five-paragraph order. The raid itself was a great learning experience. G Company again acquitted itself admirably.

The positive chemistry and the troops contagious enthusiasm made this the best year I ever had in the Corps. Colonel Godbold sent a number of problem Marines, officer and enlisted, to G Company. His instructions were simple: motivate them, counsel them, help them to achieve their potential, or recommend them for discharge. We had five such cases, two officer and three enlisted. I'm happy to say we salvaged them all.

Late in April, Colonel Godbold called Lieutenant Colonel Ernie Freeman to say that he planned to move me up to regiment as the assistant operations officer. My CO commented that he had thought the Colonel's policy was to keep company commanders in a command billet for a full year. No one ever protested anything very strongly to Colonel B. D. Godbold, and I received orders effective early in May. I was sorry to leave the battalion, but it had been a truly memorable tour, just a bit more than a month short of one year.

My XO, Norm Cote, was to assume command. He was a senior lieutenant and good with the troops. I told Top Pyles we would exchange the company guidon in the parking lot and I wanted to say a few words to the troops after the brief ceremony. I also reminded him of my policy of absolutely no gifts.

After a brief ceremony outside, they all gathered in the end of one of the squad bays where we held company school. It was crammed with benches, my old blackboard, and a large map of the Hawaiian Islands. My short remarks were obviously emotional as I thanked them for the 110% they had always given me. I reminded them that they were now charged with continuing to form their own Band of Brothers wherever they went in the future. For the first time I gave each of them an imaginary inspirational candle and encouraged them to light it. My final words were: "The greatest reward I could ever receive, throughout the rest of my life, is that whenever we meet in the future, when we salute and greet one another, would be for you to say to me, 'Captain, my candle is still lit!'" There was a momentary pause, then they exploded. It just about wiped me out, until "Top" Pyles came forward and really did me in.

The Top acted a little embarrassed, but made one of the finest short speeches I've ever heard. "Skipper, troops go through their lives living from one CO to another. CO's come and go, but the troops just stay on. Some CO's are better than others. Some aren't worth a damn, but the troops just have to keep doing their thing, trying to be good Marines. Every once in a while, maybe just once in a lifetime, a CO comes along that makes all the pain, hard work, mud, rain, inspections, and low pay seem worthwhile. This CO gives a man pride, a reason to do his best, a purpose in his life, a sense of belonging to something better than he is. Yes Sir, he teaches them about a family called the Band of Brothers. What he does when he leaves is to give them pride, faith, and hope for the future. They tell themselves that someday they'll have a CO come along that will be like you, Captain." I thought I was going to break down, but before I did he changed his tone.

He said he knew that I told him not to allow any gifts, but the troops, entirely on their own, took up a little collection. They didn't know how to thank you so they asked me to get something you needed. "Sir, I've tried to read your writing for almost a year and I'm going blind, but I've seen you late at night banging away on the company typewriter. Here's a portable typewriter from your troops, your Band of Brothers. God Bless you, Captain! Please take it to remind you of G Company." What more could a Marine ask for in all this world than troops like that? Words can't quite capture the emotional attachment I held with this group of men, my second Band of Brothers.

99

My tour on the Fourth Marines staff wasn't to last very long, but it was like a year's staff training at Marine Corps schools. The officer I was to replace was a smart, some said brilliant, officer. Captain Dick Crowley, class of 1948A, U.S. Naval Academy, had been the mastermind behind the Big Island training evolution, including tactical tests for every unit in the regiment. He had carved out a very large niche on the staff because of his imagination and his writing skills. On the first day of our two-day turnover he built two-foot-high stacks of Landing Force Manuals, doctrinal papers, and staff manuals. His comment, terse as always, was "You should be intimately familiar with all of this material." He also noted that we had a Brigade Landing Exercise coming up, the largest training evolution ever conducted in the islands. Dick had been Marine Corps school trained; I was not. The references were there, however, so off to work I went. Much midnight oil was expended in the Cooper house on Kulauli Street, but I relished every minute of it.

The Brigade Landing Exercise took place on Kauai's Barking Sands Beach. This beautiful stretch of white sand was impressive enough to be used as the site for the movie version of *South Pacific*, starring Mitzi Gaynor and Enzio Pinza. As a matter of fact, the producer, Joshua Logan, had asked to have 800 Marines serve as extras for three days after we finished our exercise. He was also to spend thousands of dollars creating a battle environment on the beach: palm trees that appeared to have been shredded by naval gunfire, shell craters, barbed wire, etc. It made our landing very realistic.

My workdays grew longer—and I still did long hours of homework. Master Sergeant Final, our operations chief, was my strong right arm as we struggled through the many changes to the landing plan and the regimental order. Our young embarkation officer, Lieutenant Pete Wilson, had just completed his embarkation training. He waded right in to coordinate the loading of the ships with our scheme for deploying units. Pete and I later had a reunion when he was mayor of San Diego between 1979 and 1981, and I was the new Commanding General of the Marine Corps Recruit Depot. I remembered him as a smart, responsive young man. He remembered me as looking like a linebacker and being very mission oriented. I guess we were both right! Pete later served as U.S. Senator and later as the Governor of California.

The exercise went like gangbusters. During its last day, the umpires "killed" my boss, Major Angus McDonald, the S-3, and Colonel Godbold, the CO. The XO, Lieutenant Colonel Picardi, and I had the opportunity to run the show. This was 1957: many of our tactics took into consideration the threat of tactical nuclear weapons. As a matter of fact, the movie battalion was phased out of the exercise after being "nuked," and we had to carry out a mass evacuation that was horrifying even to contemplate. Removing 900 men that had been (simulated) killed or seriously wounded proved to be an almost impossible task. We ended the exercise on that somber note. Thank God I never had to deal with such casualties, but in 1957 no one knew what the future might bring.

General Edwin A. Pollock was the Commanding General, Fleet Marine Force, Pacific in 1957. His headquarters were across the island of Oahu at Camp Smith, a former WW II naval hospital. A South Carolinian and a Citadel man, he was another of the patrician warrior gentlemen the Corps was blessed with in its higher commands. He was a veteran of Guadalcanal, had fought across the Pacific in WWII, commanded the First Marine Division in Korea, and was now at the zenith of his career as the senior

100

field commander of the Corps. He knew me from my days in Columbia, S.C. He, like General Franklin Hart at Quantico, was an avid sports enthusiast. The only person I ever knew that was more enthusiastic about sports was his chief of staff and right-hand man, Colonel Henry W. Buse. They had both arrived at their present assignments a year earlier. Marine sports in Hawaii and the entire Pacific had gone into high gear.

In early August, the pace of my operations had slowed considerably. A call came from FMF PAC. It was Colonel Buse, and he had a short message: the Hawaii Marines football team would start its preseason practice the following Monday at Marine Barracks, Pearl Harbor. He and the general had finished choosing the coaching staff, and I was to be the line coach and assistant head coach. A Major Marvin "Hoss" Hewlitt was to be the head coach. He and his family were flying in today from Parris Island. Colonel Buse would look forward to seeing me at practice on Monday afternoon. Major Hewlitt would call me after he arrived tomorrow. I was not surprised.

General Pollock and Colonel Buse had talked to me about coaching at Parris Island while they were there. At that time I had just received orders to Hawaii. Little did I know that they were both to arrive in Hawaii when I did. General Pollock had a winning football team in 1956, and did not pull me out of my much-needed command tour to coach. Apparently this year was different. After the call from Colonel Buse, I headed directly for Colonel Godbold's office.

I told him of the call and flatly stated that I didn't want to coach or leave the regiment. I specifically asked him to call General Pollock and "explain the situation." He told me to take a seat, then looked up at the ceiling for a few seconds before speaking. Again that sour-mash drawl emerged. "Cholly, if you think I'm going to call up that three-star general over at FMF PAC and tell him I can't spare a captain that he needs to help him with his football team for three months, you've got another think coming. You're doing just fine over here, but you go on over there and help General Pollock with his team. He'll send you back in December and we'll have some decent job waiting for you when you come back. You understand?" Apparently, the regiment would survive without me. What a shock!

That night I went back to my foot locker to dig out the Navy playbook from 1949, a book on winning football by Bud Wilkerson, and several others that had languished there since my Quantico days. Coach Cooper had been activated and would report on Monday, as ordered.

The team's home base was at the Marine Barracks, Pearl Harbor, which meant that I had to commute across the island and back each day. We weren't deep on the coaching staff. Initially, Hoss Hewlitt served as head and backfield coach, I was the line and assistant head coach, and Lieutenant Colonel Hal Lindfelt, the area auditor, served as end coach and worked part time at his regular job. Hewlitt was a WWII vet who'd been recalled for Korea and decided to remain in the Corps. He had played and later coached at Auburn University during some of its good years. He understood the game, and had been head coach at Parris Island before he came to Hawaii. He was married, had a bevy of pretty little daughters, and called everyone "Hoss," hence his nickname.

Our trainer was Chief Petty Officer Lou Legarie, the best hospital corpsman to ever wear a Marine uniform. He knew sports and sports medicine, was a decorated combat veteran of two wars, and a fine athlete in his own right. He is still one of my best and most loyal friends. Lou was also our unofficial chaplain. Any players with problems they didn't want to bring to a coach would see "Doc" Legarie. They got straight talk and good advice. He gave me my nickname of "03," pronounced "Oh-three," a code for the infantry specialty number. This reflected my daily reminder to the troops that they were not just "jocks," but still needed to look and act like Marines, on and off the field.

We had our ups and downs that fall—mostly ups, I suppose. General Pollock and Colonel Buse made every practice, like the franchise owners they were. Their enthusiasm was contagious, although perhaps a bit overly expectant, as we moved through the early preseason drills. Hewlitt was at his best on the conditioning and drilling aspects of coaching. Today he would be a good defensive coach, but in 1957 football was a two-way game. Players had to play offense and defense, and his offensive approach was Auburn's "three yards and a cloud of dust." We had two excellent passing quarterbacks, both lieutenants, one from Rice and the other from Holy Cross, but our emphasis was entirely on the running game. We struggled early in the year, showing little offense. What we had was too predictable, and Hewlitt wasn't making adjustments at halftime. We were going to have to change, to perk things up. He was responsive to my ideas.

What I recommended was that we put in some misdirection, counterplays, and play-action passes. The 1949 Navy playbook had what the doctor ordered, and Hoss agreed to give it a try. We also let the quarterbacks alternate, each playing a quarter at a time, until one became dominant. That worked too. In our second game with the Hawaiian Rams, a semi-pro team of former college and high school stars, we beat them 38–0. (We had frittered away our first game, a 14–7 loss.)

Our biggest game of the season was against the University of Hawaii in Honolulu's Aloha Stadium. We had improved and they were undefeated. They had a huge line and a stable of fast running backs. They were favored by several touchdowns, but we were geared for an upset. During our usual heavy scrimmage on the Wednesday before the game a young corporal who played guard and served as our middle linebacker broke his leg. We weren't deep in that position and his loss was a real blow. Hoss and I discussed our options after practice. There were some adjustments we could make.

General Pollock was waiting impatiently in the coaches' office as I stepped out of the shower. He walked into the locker room with Hoss Hewlett as I was putting on my shoes. His comments went something like this. "Charlie, you're in damn good shape! Looks like you've fully recovered from that old back wound. I watched you out there knocking heads with the linemen before the scrimmage. Hell, you're the best lineman we've got! Didn't you play linebacker at the Academy?" I could see it coming. He wasn't subtle.

Sure I was in great shape. I led the calisthenics each day, I ran the sprints with the line, and I put on a helmet and shoulder pads to teach blocking and defensive moves to my troops. We worked on the weights and the chinning bar together. I loved to hit in our line drills, but with two broken necks and a broken back to remind me, I limited my coaching work very carefully. That didn't matter: what General Pollock saw was a 29-year-old captain, 215 pounds, six feet one and a half inches tall, and a middle linebacker to plug the holes against Hawaii. He asked me if I had considered "putting the pads back on"? My response was guarded. I told him every former athlete dreams of taking one more shot at the game, too often with poor results. I told him I'd have to think about it. My wife was the key and we would discuss it that evening. The good general probably went home thinking he had solved his problem for Saturday in Aloha

102

Stadium. Hoss Hewlitt didn't add any pressure. He knew my medical history and had seen those two large scars on my back.

My sweet, wonderful wife, a 26-year-old mother of two small children and the wife of a "mission oriented" Marine captain, has always been known as a low-key, thoughtful, considerate person. She is always even-tempered and soft-spoken to boot. That night when I broached the subject of playing Saturday, Carol Cooper turned into a tiger! She stomped her foot and let me have it. "I've been nursing you back to life since 1951 and now you pull this on me! You've finally regained your health, your strength, and your stamina. You've had three fractures and every nerve problem in the book: you're a walking medical miracle right now! If you're dumb enough to throw all of that away and risk destroying yourself just to please some three-star Marine general, I'm going to take these two kids and get on an airplane, and you'll never see any of us again! Do you understand what I'm saying to you?" I did, and I didn't play on Saturday.

We tied Hawaii in a good, tight game. We used an overshifted line and it worked rather well. Thanks, Sweet Carol!

The team's West Coast swing home-based us at the Marine Corps Recruit Depot in San Diego. We played a good San Diego State team and beat them 20–0. Their coach was Paul Governali, a former Columbia All-American. He talked to me after the game about some of our enlisted Marines who were college material. Four of our backs later received full college scholarships; two of them eventually made it big in the pros.

Our final game was with the Recruit Depot squad, against which we had lost a 21–20 squeaker in Hawaii earlier in the season. We played in front of the entire boot camp population, and I later learned that most of my liberty-loving linemen had been lured out into the "ville" by a number of young ladies sympathetic to their local Marines. We folded in the fourth quarter after an otherwise well played game. What was it Captain Tom Hamilton, my coach at the Naval Academy, had said? "Foo-foo and football don't mix!" Our men had proven it once again.

Our team banquet back in Honolulu was a royal affair. General Pollock gave us all a Hawaiian lamp/clock combination with a football statuette and two weeks leave before our return to duty. It was my first time off since I'd arrived in Hawaii in 1956. We took a family vacation at the Kilauea Military Camp, a recreational area near the active volcano on the Big Island. It was a grand adventure—exactly what the doctor ordered for the Coopers. Before Christmas I reported back to Kaneohe to see what the fates had in store.

While I was gone, the Fourth Regiment had restructured under a new Table of Organization. Each infantry battalion now had four instead of three rifle companies, albeit each somewhat smaller. The old weapons company was now part of headquarters company, and the reconnaissance platoon had grown into a full company. Also, the anti-tank platoon had grown into a reinforced company and was to be equipped with an entirely new weapon system. It was called the "Ontos" which is supposed to be Greek for "the thing".

My new assignment was as commanding officer of Company B (Reinforced), Third Anti-Tank Battalion. We would be starting from scratch: new people and the Ontos, and no one had ever seen the new vehicle. It arrived, looking like a miniature tank: a tracked vehicle mounting six 106mm recoilless rifles, three on each side of its tiny turret. It took a crew of three men. Our company would have fifteen of these vehicles:

three weapons platoons of five vehicles each. We were to join new personnel from all over the regiment, receive new weapons, and figure out how to use everything. It was like building a house without plans, but it was to be an interesting six months.

This was an infantry unit, but it had tracked vehicles and was fully motorized. We would all ride into battle. We rated fewer people than a rifle company, but they would include weapons armorers, truck mechanics, tracked vehicle mechanics, turret repairmen, communicators, and more administrative clerks. And we had to obtain all of these skills from units within the brigade. One thing I learned right away was that no one gives up his best people to a personnel draft.

We received people from quotas levied on their units: these were average at best. Some volunteered, looking for new opportunity or an escape from old assignments: these were largely productive. Others were transferred from the old anti-tank platoon that we were replacing: these were good solid men who knew the recoilless-weapon system. My challenge was to establish goals and create a focused team. As the men moved into our new barracks and we awaited the arrival of our new Ontos "machines," my new XO, First Lieutenant James Webb, and I worked up a series of goals and objectives. We aimed high—that in six months (my time of departure) we would be technically proficient in all our systems, able to mount out all of our equipment on 24-hour notice, and have established ourselves as the best all around company in the Fourth Marine Regiment.

We needed another Top Pyles, a first sergeant that was tuned in to my Band of Brothers concept. What I found was not a Top but a Gunny. Gunnery Sergeant Herberich proved to be a man for all seasons in this new company. He hadn't had the experience of Pyles, but he was energetic, dedicated, smart, and unflappable. He did the work of two men from the day he arrived. I would have to include him in my all time Marine Hall of Fame. He became my strong right arm. Another unforgettable Marine was Staff Sergeant, later Gunnery Sergeant, Baumgardner. He had anti-tank experience and was so good that I just couldn't put an officer over him. A muscular former drill instructor, he became my best platoon leader. His platoon radio call-sign was "Squads Right" because of the way he used to drill his buttoned-up vehicles by radio. His men loved him and they set high standards for the entire company. Their bright candles did, indeed, light the way for B Company.

Early in 1958 we received a new regimental commander. John Hillary Masters was a gifted leader, a charming man, and a fighting Marine. His older brother Jim had brought the regiment to Hawaii from Japan and was now a brigadier general. He was a South Carolinian by birth, had graduated from the Naval Academy, and had spent WWII with the OSS behind the lines in China, leading guerrilla forces against the Japanese. After the war he had been treated for tuberculosis contracted in China: he now had only one lung. He was commanding in manner, but he had the common touch—quite a contrast to staid Colonel Godbold. Both were exceptionally effective as leaders, but "Bud" Masters was without peer; he had God's gift as a leader of men. Some have it, some don't.

He created a "provisional battalion" out of his three separate companies—headquarters, reconnaissance, and anti-tank—and designated me its battalion commander. The title was applicable for sports competitions, parades, promotion boards, and inspections. He included me in his weekly battalion commanders' conference with the lieutenant colonels. I was indeed honored and fortunate to work for him.

He loved to use us for VIP demonstrations. Marines like to show their wares, and we had something to show. The Shah of Iran visited early in the spring of 1958. They told us he was thinking of buying some of the Ontos vehicles for his armed forces and wanted to see a firepower demonstration. All of the senior officers on the island, Navy, Army, Air Force, and Marine, were also there. We lined up the 15 vehicles, had them execute close order drill with their hatches closed, wheeled them up on the beach, and opened fire in a ripple on painted barrels we had anchored some 1200 yards out to sea. It was an impressive display of the firepower these small vehicles could project. Bud Masters gave the company a 72-hour pass as a token of his appreciation—a nice touch, as always.

B Company won the quarterly regimental reenlistment award and by way of reward enjoyed a memorable luau at Bellows Beach. There were a number of Hawaiian Marines in the company, and their families collaborated to give us a wonderful afternoon of entertainment. Our "Island Marines," as we called them, were also the heart and soul of our successful sports squad. The Marine Corps Inspector General put the icing on our cake, however.

Major General Homer Litzenberg was the craggy-faced "IG." His feats as CO of the Seventh Marine Regiment in Korea were widely known. He was a respected leader and supposedly a tough inspector. One of the items on his inspection agenda was to take a hard look at the new anti-tank company of the Fourth Marines. In that sense, he deviated from the normal inspection routine of drill, personnel, clothing, equipment, and administration. He wanted me personally to show him how we could perform. It was an unexpected requirement, but it made our day. I took him for a ride, let him shoot our 106's, and had Staff Sergeant Baumgardner "drill" the Ontos by radio. The IG walked through our shops and the motor pool and talked to the troops. He departed two days later after an oral critique in which he gave us high accolades.

As time neared for the Coopers to head for home, Captain John Fox reported aboard as my relief. He had been serving as regimental motor transport officer and was well qualified to deal with our assorted maintenance headaches. I had scheduled a one o'clock guidon exchange in the parking lot, no big ceremony, and was going to tell the troops good-bye at that time. Gunny Herberick suggested that it might be nice for all the officers and Captain Fox to have a lunch with me in the mess hall.

I hated to leave this little outfit. Telling them good-bye wasn't something I looked forward to. As we were having a cup of coffee before heading back to the company area, my driver dashed into the mess hall. He was wearing full field gear, had his helmet on, and seemed excited. He blurted out "Captain, the Gunny told me he had to see you right away! It's really important that you come right now! I've got jeeps for all the officers outside, Sir!" We all departed on the double, John Fox and I in the lead jeep. My young driver looked like the proverbial cat that had just eaten the canary.

We didn't stop at the barracks, but continued on to the nearby field where we usually conducted our inspections. I couldn't believe my eyes! Displayed in line on the field was every piece of rolling stock in my company, some 42 vehicles, including four that had been out of commission for weeks. The regimental reviewing stands had been set up facing the vehicles, and some 300 people were assembled, including the brigade commanding general, Brigadier General Avery Kier, Colonel Masters and his staff, and

105

dependents from the whole company. I also saw Carol and our two kids. The drum and bugle corps started playing as we drove up. The Gunny was CO of troops! Not an officer in B Company had a clue, nor had they been involved in any way. This was to be my change of command, and the Gunny had mounted out the entire company. They had every stick of our gear in those trucks.

They'd set up a public address system, and my driver served as the announcer. This was a combat review in honor of the departing company commander. Every piece of equipment and all weapons assigned to B Company were on display. If Captains Cooper and Fox would please mount the jeep, they would "troop the line." Then the company would pass in review before the reviewing area. As we drove down the line of troops, standing in the general's ceremonial jeep, I caught the eye of every man in the company. We then returned to the reviewing stand and dismounted to take the review. It was professional, perfectly executed, and all without rehearsal. The Ontos commanders were standing, goggles on, and saluting as they passed the reviewing stand. My Gunny and his NCO's had pulled off a wonderful and unforgettable surprise. This Band of Brothers proved once again what happens when the troops feel like they have a "piece of the rock."

My remarks were very brief. I believe they amounted to "Thanks, troops, for everything. I'll never forget you. You showed me you're ready. Semper Fi." This ended our two years with the China Marines. After a few very pleasant days in a hotel on Waikiki waiting for a ship, we sailed back "to the land of the great PX," as the troops say. I was headed to Quantico, Virginia, for duty at the Officers' Basic School, where it all had started.

---

* While we were on the Big Island, my son, Chip, had a severe attack of tonsillitis. He'd had these for years but this one was worse than he'd ever had before. Carol took him and his entire medical record to Tripler Army Hospital for a consultation and they admitted him for immediate surgery. From that day forward, the symptoms that had led to his earlier diagnosis of muscular dystrophy began to disappear. As time went on this five-year-old became more energetic and stronger. We have thanked the good Lord a thousand times for the almost-miracle that Army doctors, Hawaiian sunshine and the determination of that small child brought about.

106

Chapter 13

Teaching "Third Lieutenants"

The Officers' Basic School was at Camp Barrett, in the rolling countryside at Quantico, Virginia. The Commanding Officer was Colonel Lowell English, one of the Marine officers who had been stationed at the Naval Academy during my student days there. That barrel-chested former Nebraska fullback welcomed me warmly and assigned me to instructor duties in the Tactics Section. It was like throwing Brer Rabbit into the briar patch: I was delighted. The students, all newly commissioned 2nd Lieutenants who where there to receive their basic officer skills education, were referred to by the staff officers as "third lieutenants" until they had successfully completed the course of instruction.

The section was headed by the officer who had been my boss when I coached the Quantico Marines, Lieutenant Colonel Joe "Bigfoot" Donahoe. I was to be a principal instructor in offensive tactics under Major "Bull" Fisher and a backup instructor in defensive tactics. It was a busy, challenging, and rewarding assignment. Normally, new instructors went to Instructors Orientation Course (IOC), but we were short-handed, so they postponed my formal schooling indefinitely. Not to worry. "Tactics" was my middle name, and my enthusiasm carried over to the students.

That was fine, but all was not well on the home scene: our household goods had not arrived in Quantico. Although it usually takes as much as a month for ocean-transported household goods to get where they're going, ours still hadn't arrived almost two months after we had. They seemed to have disappeared. We could hardly get settled without them, and we had to get Carol and the kids moved in before school started.

The Corps put us temporarily in a small two-bedroom apartment in a base housing unit called Thomason Park. The kids were still young and could room together for a while, and I borrowed some basic government furniture. We expected to be there about four months.

Carol, Chip, and little Linda, whom I had left with Carol's folks in Fletcher, NC, arrived at the Alexandria, Virginia, train station at eight a.m. on Labor Day. The train had been packed: my wife and children had been sitting on their suitcases all night. As we drove to our new home, I told them that I'd heard nothing new about our household goods, but I'd bought some cheap kitchenware and stocked the small fridge in the apartment.

We had wonderful, caring, supportive neighbors in "Courtney Court." They ranged from lieutenants to lieutenant colonels, and many became lifelong friends of ours. We were all in the same boat: we all referred affectionately to our housing development as "the Slums." We were to remain there for two years before moving into larger accommodations on the main base.

I was into my second month at the Basic School when we learned that our household shipment had turned up in a Norfolk warehouse. It arrived in Quantico the following weekend. A total disaster. Half of it was missing. The moving van's driver was drunk and his locally hired assistant had quit, so I had to help him unload the shipment. All of it was in pieces. It had obviously been packed improperly, damaged, and pilfered for items of value. We hadn't had very much to start with, but now it was like starting from scratch. I felt like tossing in the towel at first: Carol had a good cry, and we were both about as low as we had ever been. Three things saved us: good neighbors, the Marine Corps household goods claims section, and the United Services Automobile Association, our insurance company. After three months of massive paper work, photos, letters, and countless manhours of paperwork, we finally received full reimbursement for our losses. I rebuilt some of the furniture, but we had to replace most of it.

Thank God for the Fallons, Marge and Doc, next-door neighbors who came to our rescue that first night. (Doc was a lawyer, a major.) The two of them insisted that we join them for dinner. While our youngsters were eating, Doc produced a pitcher of martinis. A bit older and wiser, the Fallons reminded us that the worst was over. Things would get better. After two of Doc's dry martinis, I had to agree! The Band of Brothers worked in all sorts of ways.

A tour of duty at the Basic School involved an interesting variety of duties and functions. My basic job as an instructor was to teach all aspects of offensive tactics. Most of our students were recent college graduates; a small percentage of them were former NCO's who had completed Officer Candidate School. As a teacher, leader, and counselor, I had the opportunity and responsibility to instill in these men positive values that would last a lifetime and could save peoples' lives. We were training the Corps' future leaders, but they were a lively crew and still performing college hi-jinks that frequently tested both our sense of humor and our patience.

One of my additional duties was to serve as a narrator for a weapons and tactics demonstration we called "Jay Cocks," a pronounceable version of "JCOC." This is an abbreviation for the "Joint Civilian Orientation Conference," a tour the Department of Defense sponsored for business, educational, and civic leaders from all over the country. Once a year, each of the four services hosted this group of some 200 citizens for a full day, showing them our military capabilities. In the late 1950's, the Marine Corps hosted its portion at Quantico, where we put on a small but quite realistic mock war and simulated the use of all of our weapons in a small area known as E-6 Pond, an artificial lake. The "VIP battle" had troops arriving by both helicopter and amphibious tractors.

Our school tactics staff ran this complicated demonstration, since it had experience in putting on simulated battles. We used various types of explosives to create realistic effects, and had a large team of skilled demolitionists to install all the charges and set them off on cue. The narrator, Captain Vic Ohanesian, described the battle scene from a tower behind the grandstand. Lieutenant Colonel Joe Donahoe directed the exercise from this same perch.

I was the narrator for the introductory presentation, which came before the battle portion. I stood immediately in front of the audience and introduced it to the heart of the Corps, the Marine rifle squad: 13 men organized into three fire teams, augmented with rocket and flame-thrower teams. My men came forward from a lower slope and fell in behind me as I explained their functions. The description of these men and their weapons and tactics took exactly 21 minutes. Then followed a five-minute narrated attack on a nearby pillbox that we destroyed before the visitors' eyes. Although I had memorized my talk, I delivered it conversationally, as if it were just off the top of my head. I can still remember most of it: "Wars, large or small, can be won only by closing with the enemy and destroying him. This is the role of the Marine Infantryman, the rifleman you will meet here today . . . "

The demonstrations were exciting to watch, and the rehearsals usually were well attended by groups other than our VIPs. An early dress rehearsal for one of these shows was more exciting than any actual demonstration had ever been. Thunder showers were in the area, and the powers that be were deciding whether to scrub or go. There were only a few spectators this day. Two of them were my in-laws, Tracy and Vesta Edgerton, sitting with my wife, Carol, in the almost-empty stands before me. We started the demonstration in spite of the threatening weather.

I was concluding my "squad narration" when a lighting bolt struck nearby. It was as if someone had set off a nuclear explosion! There was a deafening roar. A huge cloud of smoke covered the area. One of the safety officers, a young captain, standing behind the stands with a field telephone to his ear was thrown 15 feet when the telephone literally exploded. The lightning had set off every demolition charge in the entire exercise loop: more than three thousand pounds of explosives. Everyone listening on the safety net was injured and in shock, and we didn't know who or where the rest of the injured were. Very quickly the backup radios came on, and people went into action to deal with the problem.

The squadron of helicopters that had been airborne just out of sight behind some trees was sent to evacuate the injured. It was a skillful reaction. In just minutes, the helicopters were transporting about 90 people to the Base Naval Hospital for examination and treatment. Colonel Joe Donahoe was orchestrating all of this activity by radio from his tower. My demonstration troops acted as stretcher bearers to collect and load the injured in our immediate area.

When the last helicopter had departed and we met in front of the stands, Joe Donahoe walked up to shake hands with Carol's parents. Tracy Edgerton told him, "I know this wasn't exactly the way you planned it, but now that I've survived by not having a heart attack, that was the most realistic damn bit of combat I've ever seen, WWI included. At first, I thought it was for real, but Carol explained that God had taken a hand in the game with the lightning." He had indeed!

The good news is that none of the injured suffered any permanent damage. Most were admitted to the hospital for overnight observation. Some were in a state of shock, and many had had their ear drums perforated. From then on, the exhibition team took measures that would allow them to disarm the entire demolition circuit with one switch in the event of sudden weather changes.

An important part of the basic course was a "five-day war" that we conducted for each student company. These tested the students physically and tactically over a five-day period. The students rotated through the various command billets, from a four-man fire team up to company level. The exercise used enlisted troops as "aggressors" to oppose the students and add realism by acting as prisoners. The instructors and company officers observed and graded the performances. They also served as umpires to keep matters from getting out of hand. Critiques followed the exercises. We reminded the students that the real "fog of battle" wasn't much different from what seemed like organized chaos in some phases of these five-day wars.

During a winter five-day war, we decided after three difficult days of subfreezing weather to take an administrative break, during which we would serve some hot food, check feet for possible frost bite, and rest our charges a bit. They were exhausted from wading about in 18 inches of snow. A large cheer went up when I announced our decision to go "nontactical" for a few hours. The students marched into an area normally used for summer picnics and dropped their packs. The first order of business was to build a fire while waiting for the hot-food truck to arrive. The industrious and innovative officers

109

removed vines from several nearby trees to get dry tinder for some of the damp wood they had collected. In no time at all, we had a roaring fire going.

There were woods downwind from the fire, and many of the students and some of the instructors proceeded to the woods' edge to relieve themselves. We were all heavily clothed and wearing face masks and gloves or mittens as we lined up abreast to do what we had to do. The smoke smelled good as it wafted our way. However, within twenty-four hours we had a major epidemic of poison ivy among about 50 students and one staff officer—me. We all had genitalia covered with the assorted miseries that wonderful Virginia poison ivy vine can inflict, even in the dead of winter! The hike back on Friday was miserable. A large number of us were walking like cowboys that had ridden too many bucking broncs.

Colonel Louis H. Wilson relieved Colonel English as our commanding officer. A native of Mississippi, he had won the Medal of Honor on Guam in WW II. He was a tall, lean, athletic officer who had definite ideas on every subject and set about making a few changes in the way we did business at Camp Barrett. Nicknamed "the blue eyed cobra," Big Lou could zap you quicker than a snake, but he was also a thoughtful and positive leader. He was later to become Commandant of the Marine Corps during a crucial and difficult period. He emerged as one of the Corps' all-time great leaders. He gave me a number of important assignments that were very meaningful to me. One of them was to take command of a student company, normally a major's responsibility, while I was still a captain.

My company was an Officer Candidate Course Company. All of its students had come from that one source: they weren't balanced by a mix of NROTC, PLC, or US Naval Academy officers. These graduates of the OCC had not had leave between a rugged 12-week screening course and their reporting to us. They had arrived at Basic School in top physical condition, but after a few weeks of training they had become difficult to control. All of them had made late decisions to join the Marine Corps, and many of them had anticipated that they'd have an easy time once they had received their commissions. Such was not the case. From two years experience with two similar companies, I knew that they would stick together in a group, and the group's actions and reactions would almost be predictable. They were all happy, sad, or ready for hijinks at the same time. It was like tides and the moon. The solution with an OCC company was to use a "tight rein" when the mount started to feel its head. After about two months with me, B Company TBS 1-60 was getting close to that magic moment.

Normally student officers controlled and marched the company en route to and from training. One day we were returning from a full day of live-fire exercises that we had finished a bit early. All day long the unit had not been responsive or efficient in its execution of the various firing courses. There'd been a lot of horsing around, and I wasn't happy. We finished training early and the buses weren't due for an hour. We were only three miles from Camp Barrett, so I decided to cancel the buses and walk them home. I reminded them that they weren't a bunch of school boys, and they had not pleased me today! We headed out at a good clip with me leading the march.

As we neared Camp Barrett there was still some horseplay going on in the ranks. As we reached the edge of Camp, I halted them, dressed them, and gave them "Double-time march." We ran right past their barracks and continued on twice around the block. They were about shot, but they knew why they were running. When we finally halted in the parking lot, I gave them "At ease" and told them that I had seen them at their worst today. They were unsatisfactory and I wasn't going to see my company act like a bunch of rag-tailed draftees. I said a few other things and then dismissed them. As I turned around to go to my office I saw Colonel "Big Lou" Wilson standing in the doorway.

"Charlie, how long since you've been on leave?" I had to think a moment. "Sir, it's been almost 18 months." Colonel Wilson allowed as how I needed to get away for a few days and relax. He was very pleased with the job I was doing with this OCC company but "it almost looks like you've gotten to the point where you hate lieutenants." I didn't hate them, but he was right. I needed to back away a bit. He ordered me to turn the company over to my XO, take off for 96 hours, and get out of town somewhere.

Two days later, Carol and I, visiting old friends at Virginia Beach, were dressed in shorts and having a beer at a jazz concert on the beach. My lieutenants could have been a million miles away. Suddenly Carol said, "Charlie, there are some men across the room waving at us. Do you know them?" Did I know them! They were my lieutenants! Six of them, off for the weekend, were spending it at Virginia Beach. They had picked up an assortment of ladies and wanted to come over and say hello. I waved them over and they came over carrying pitchers of beer and smiling from ear to ear. God, I loved them. My Third Lieutenant Band of Brothers!

Carol found time to be an active participant in the post's equestrian program, both as a competitive rider and as a children's riding instructor. Our children signed up, of course, and proved to be excellent young riders. Even I qualified and enjoyed riding with the family.

Colonel Lou Wilson's emphasis on sports led to the formation of a semi-organized group of teams, aptly called the "noon league." The all-staff-officer league sponsored touch football, basketball, and volleyball. Big Lou had his own volleyball and basketball teams and selected me to play on both. We worked well together in volleyball. In basketball, I was an enthusiastic football player, but we usually won. (I still blocked well.) We played without officials and used the Marine version of "jungle rules": anything you can get away with is okay. Sick bay (the camp dispensary) was on special alert during the noon hour. It got a lot of business.

One day I was late returning from a morning tactics exercise. As I crossed the parking lot where the volleyball teams were forming up, I told Colonel Wilson I would return as soon as I changed clothes. He said to forget changing. He needed me right now, and I could just play in my combat boots. I took off my jacket and the game began. It was going well. I would set him for a spike and then he would set me. We were both good at blocking on the net (sometimes over it). As we started our third and final game of the match, he and I were abreast on the net. The other team set the ball on the other side and we both went up to block it. I came down on his instep with all of my weight on one boot. He yelled and sat down. Someone called the ambulance, and off he went. Sick bay sent word that they were applying a cast to the CO's foot. I had fractured not one, but two of its bones. He'd be on crutches for a number of weeks. To his ever-living credit, Colonel Lou Wilson never said a word about this except to ask who won the game. He could dish it out, and he could take it, too.

The next week his basketball team played without him. Team-mate Fred McLean and I collided head-on going after a loose ball. Fred had a big cut on his head and was unconscious. I had a gusher cut over my right eye. Our teammates tended to us and flagged down a truck to take us to sick bay. I held a balled-up sweatshirt over my gushing eye cut. A young doctor and his duty corpsman greeted us. I told him to get everything ready because when I removed the shirt blood was going to start squirting out of my eye. He and the medic calmly made arrangements and took me into a treatment room while someone was tending to Fred. I asked him if he was ready and he replied "Yes, take off the shirt." I removed the shirt, blood gushed directly into the doctor's face, and he fainted. I put the shirt back on my eye and waited until they had revived him. To his credit, he bounced back, sniffed a few ammonia capsules, and expertly applied 22 stitches, 11 to close the cut and 11 to replace the eyebrow. It grew into a neat scar. Such were the fortunes of war in the noon league under our athletic leader, Colonel Big Lou Wilson.*

My three years at Camp Barrett generated many lasting memories. Because of my anti-tank experience I not only taught this subject for three years, but also drafted the doctrinal publication that prescribed the use of the Ontos company in the Marine Corps. One of my classmates, Pat McMillan, headed up the leadership section. Colonel Wilson directed that the two of us prepare a two-hour package of instruction called "Men in Battle." We gave it to each company late in the course, and it was in some respects the highlight of the entire curriculum. The first hour was a "Huntley-Brinkley" two-person narrative that used film clips, slides, and recordings. Its sole purpose was to describe a battlefield situation and show how in the battle for the city of Seoul one Marine lieutenant actually saved the day and turned the tide of battle at a crucial point.

The second hour was a question-and-answer period during which I was on stage to respond to the questions the first hour had raised. They ran the gamut. "How do you cope with your imminent death?" "What keeps you going in the face of almost certain death?" I was brutally honest: I had personal experience to fall back on. Just before they left the room, I presented my thought-provoking conclusion: "Not many of you will face this ultimate, direct threat to your life, but we never know how, when, or if it will occur. There are many ways to die or be injured in battle, but I leave you with this undying principle for an officer of Marines. There is one thing worse than dying, one thing worse than losing your own life: that is to fail your troops in battle. Remember that, and they'll never fail you." The message of "Men in Battle".

After almost three years, I emptied my wall locker and packed my bags. It was finally time for me to become a student at the Amphibious Warfare School.

---

* The shirt was an old Navy Athletic Assn. one belonging to Capt. Wes Hammond, a year behind me at the Academy. It was his third tour at TBS and he used to admonish the lieutenants, "Pay attention the first time or they'll keep sending you back!" Both Fred and Wes commanded infantry battalions along the DMZ in Vietnam in 1967. The "Band of Brothers" in the Marine Corps is *ubique.*

Chapter 14

The Young Professionals

The officers attending the 1961–62 Amphibious Warfare School (Junior Course) had between 9 and 13 years of commissioned service. Some 200 in number, all had seen service in the Korean War. A few had served in WWII. The class also included a small group of "allied officers" from Israel, Venezuela, Colombia, Republic of China (Taiwan), Canada, and one or two other nations. The group of American Marines in the course was a cross-section of all the military specialties in the Corps.

On our first day we listed those areas in which we had the most and the least experience. We also took a broad inventory exam to establish a baseline of our general knowledge. (It was truly amazing to see how much we'd improved when we retook the same exam nine months later.) This school was a long-awaited, eagerly anticipated opportunity for me—a serious undertaking—and I intended to make the most of it.

A year in school doesn't make for a lot of interesting stories, but this one gave me a look at some interesting personalities. One was Lieutenant Colonel Emil Shaked, an Israeli Army paratrooper. He was 30 years old and had been fighting since he was 15. Blond and blue-eyed, he was a Sabra, a native-born Israeli, but his family had come from northern Italy. He used to laugh, point to his blond hair, and remind us of the Huns' frequent invasions of Italy. He was married and had a small daughter. I wasn't his sponsor, but Carol and I took it upon ourselves to show them a bit of Americana. Besides having them in for dinner in our home, we also invited them to join us for a Navy football game at Annapolis, complete with tailgate picnic, fried chicken, potato salad, and biscuits.

Navy had a good team that year, and the stadium was packed for a game with Georgia Tech. The Shakeds took in every aspect of the game and asked dozens of questions. Their daughter was about our Linda's age, so those two carried on a lively exchange. We left the stadium after the Midshipmen had sung "Navy Blue and Gold," the alma mater, as they do after every football game. As we got into our car, we could see quite clearly that the traffic snarl would take a long time to unwind. We edged forward, taking turns with other drivers to get in the exit lane. I apologized for the delay and explained that this was one of the biggest crowds in the history of the stadium. Emil was clearly impressed and said so. "I just can't believe how polite and considerate you Americans are to each other. Every person that passed us when we were seated in the stands said, 'Excuse me.' You allow people to enter the traffic line ahead of you and they allow you to do the same without any yelling or threats. Back in Israel there would be hundreds of horns honking, people screaming at each other, and at least a dozen fist fights in a crowd like this."

The Israelis chose our Marine Corps schools, and AWS in particular, to educate selected officers because we taught tactics and the use of supporting arms at the brigade and division level, combat formations that were the same size as the ones they used. We also emphasized the coordination of air, artillery, and tanks with our infantry. They used our close air support doctrine as their own.

Early in our course we completed language questionnaires: our class was to become a test bed for a short language "rejuvenation" course. My two years of college Spanish qualified me to try out this "verbal enhancement technique." Our allied officers were the instructors, presiding over three classes per week in their native tongues. My group's instructor was a Navy lieutenant commander from Venezuela. His navy title hid the fact that he was serving in their Marine Corps as a major.

Our classes were quite simple. We held two-sided Spanish conversations, basic at first, but progressing quickly. We were not required to study, other than refreshing ourselves on fundamental vocabulary. It was awkward at first as we struggled to respond in class, but it soon became clear that we were indeed learning to converse in Spanish. It was painless and effective.

As we reached the end of the 90-day trial period, our Venezuelan professor told us he would deliver our graduation speech. He spoke deliberately and simply so that we could understand each word. What he told us seemed to be either a joke or a very serious announcement of revolution in Venezuela. He said that by this time tomorrow he would have led an assault on the Presidential Palace, and Venezuelan Marines would have completed a *coup d'etat* and seized control of the government. He recited all of the check points and objectives they would have taken, to include the newspapers and radio and television stations. He finished up without asking for the usual repartee from his students, and instead bid us farewell and good luck, "*Bueno suerte.*"

We were puzzled and not sure of the significance of what we had heard. The next morning he missed muster, and I went in to see the XO, LtCol "Frosty" LaHue. As I told him what we had heard, he held up a note that our Venezuelan rebel had left for the faculty. It said that he appreciated and respected the school, but he had a mission that called him home. We heard on the late evening news that his attack had failed. There had been only a few casualties, but he and his coterie of young officers were all in prison. During our morning coffee break, one member of our Spanish class noted that he had delayed his coup so that we could all get full credit for graduating from his language course.

During the year, we students intermingled in various exercises, so we got to know all of our classmates. One Marine aviator, Captain Ralph "Swede" Theusen, and I became especially good friends. He and his wife visited in our home and we in theirs on several occasions. One night about mid-year, Swede casually asked me what outfit I'd served with in Korea. I replied that I'd been in the First Battalion, Fifth Marines, Baker Company. We called ourselves "The Bandits." He looked shocked. "When?" he asked. I said my draft had arrived in late April and I had replaced Second Lieutenant Abel with the Third Platoon after he was killed. He stopped and thought for a minute, looked hard at me, and said, "I'll be damned! I think you sent me back to OCS. I was a machine gun squad leader attached to the Third Platoon. You look a lot like that 'new lieutenant' from the Naval Academy."

It was true. Swede had served a year in the Corps after WWII, then had left to finish college but stayed in the Reserve. He was called up in 1950 as a corporal. We sent him to OCS because he was a good trooper and he had a college degree. He had chosen flight training after Basic School and was now a photo/reconnaissance pilot.

The school gave me more than my share of demanding and interesting assignments. At the end of the year we took a condensed version of the Nuclear Weapons Employment Course. Some of us were selected to remain after graduation to undergo additional training for a month in what was then called NBC school (nuclear, biological, and chemical warfare). It was a sobering experience. I'm happy to report that that school is

114

no longer in existence. It was a product of the times. We had the weapons and had to have someone that knew how to use them.

There were few surprises when our orders arrived. Mine were to a year's tour, unaccompanied, with the Third Marine Division on Okinawa. We packed out again. This time the furniture would go into storage. Carol and the kids were going to spend most of the year with her parents in their winter home in West Palm Beach, Florida. Now, however, we would visit them briefly in North Carolina and then head on to Mississippi. I had another sad departure from Memphis ahead, but at least this time we didn't expect that I'd be going where anyone would be shooting at me. I was also happy that the kids were looking forward to living with their grandparents in Florida for a year. It was the summer of 1962.

Chapter 15

Landing Force, Seventh Fleet

The mid-summer flight in 1962 from Memphis to San Francisco was my first jet ride. My destination was Travis Air Force Base, where I boarded a plane chartered by the Military Airlift Command. It was no jet: a World Airlines Constellation, a four-engined prop plane. The flight was jammed with Air Force and Army dependents heading for Okinawa. There were little kids everywhere. The six Marines on board were leaving their families for 13 months. I thought about it all the way across, not bitterly, but reflecting on the different ways our services viewed the concept of "combat readiness" and deployed their forces.

The flight took 42 1/2 hours, including time on the ground in Hawaii and at Wake Island, where we changed an engine. Our bodies didn't have "jet lag," but we sure had "travel blahs." Lieutenant Colonel Bob Nichols from the division's G-1 shop met me. My assignment wouldn't be firm until I met the general the next day, but I was slated to become the Division Training Officer, in G-3, Operations.

The Commanding General was Major General H. W. Buse, who'd been Chief of Staff at FMFPAC during my Hawaii days. General Buse now commanded both the Third Division and Task Force 79, the combined Marine air wing, division, and logistic support team. All of the TF 79 ground units were on Okinawa, along with the wing's helicopters and a few support aircraft. All its fixed-wing jet aircraft were based at Atsugi and Iwakuni Air Stations in Japan. Although under the command of CG, FMFPAC in Hawaii, TF 79 reported operationally to the Seventh Fleet commander, hence our title of "Landing Force, Seventh Fleet."

Okinawa was still under total US control in 1962. Army Lieutenant General Lambert was the US High Commissioner or civil governor. He also commanded all Army troops in the Far East under a separate title. The Marines in their scattered bases and training areas controlled major portions of the island. We were the largest US military force in the Far East. The division was structured around its two infantry regiments, the Third and Ninth Marines. Battalion-sized units were constantly coming and going—for afloat duty on Navy amphibious ships, or to Japan, the Philippines, or Southeast Asia for exercises with allies or for training.

General Buse gave me a warm welcome. He invited me to play on his "noon league" basketball team. I thanked him and asked for a little time to get my feet on the ground. As expected, he assigned me to G-3 as the Division Training Officer. He wanted to improve the quality of training and had a number of personal goals for the division. He wanted to start testing all companies and battalions tactically as soon as possible, and he made that one of my top priorities.

My boss was Colonel Jack Williams, whom I had known as a staff officer at the Naval Academy. My section was small: I had an artillery captain, two sharp staff NCO's, and a clerk to help me. We controlled all of the ranges on the island and at Mount Fuji in Japan, and had a multitude of other responsibilities. We worked six days a week and checked our message traffic every Sunday morning. Work was our only compensation for being away from our families. We thrived on it. Someone remarked that the Corps squeezed two years out of you on a one-year unaccompanied tour—about right, I think.

116

The division headquarters was at Camp Hague, in the center of the island. It was expeditionary, but more than adequate. All of our buildings were Quonset huts. Four majors shared a hut, which was divided into tiny bunkrooms and a small central lounge..

We all ate messhall food, drinks were ridiculously inexpensive, and the officers' mess was our home. We went there to relax, play cards, see movies, attend Friday Happy Hour, or celebrate some special occasion. You might say we worked at being busy: we took trips all over the Far East in pursuit of our business.

Admiral Harry Felt was Commander in Chief, US Forces, Pacific. Normally called CINCPAC, this particular larger-than-life admiral was also known as CINCFELT. He had a way of putting his personal stamp on everything. I immensely enjoyed my opportunity to work directly for him. He brought together all of the senior allied military leaders of the Pacific each fall for the "CINCPAC Weapons Demonstration." These leaders gathered on our Seventh Fleet aircraft carrier off Okinawa, where they were briefed, cajoled, and educated on US military capabilities. The Navy put on a seaborne firepower display, then carried the VIPs ashore for a shorebased demonstration that involved everything we had in the Far East. Army, Air Force, Marine Corps, and Navy forces assembled from near and far to execute what I'd call a "capabilities show of force."

Admiral Felt orchestrated this firepower exercise personally, but did so only through his designated representative. All of the services received their guidance and orders from this CINCPAC representative. General Buse nominated me to be CINCPAC rep. Thereafter the messages streamed back and forth between me and Admiral Felt every day. It was quite an experience—a pleasant one, fortunately.

This demonstration illustrated the problems we had with the small firing ranges on Okinawa. It required B-29 bombers and other Air Force, Navy, and Marine aircraft to deliver every type of bomb and guided missile in our inventory. We fired Marine and Army artillery, had Army Special Forces and Marine reconnaissance parachute demonstrations, and showed off all of the anti-tank weapons, including the little Ontos— which almost stole the show with its rapid firing of 106mm recoilless rifles. The demonstration explained our infantry weapons, and fired them on specific targets.

We had some hairy moments when pilots made major errors during rehearsals. The good news is that we worked it all out, there were no injuries, and our bombs and missiles and bullets stayed within the narrow bounds of the firing ranges. Admiral Felt was pleased with the show and the response it elicited from our guests. General Buse was also very pleased. We had done what Admiral Felt wanted and we had done it well. He sent an especially complimentary message to General Buse later, commending our troops on the smoothness of the entire endeavor. I was the most relieved Marine in the Far East to have it over and done with!

In 1962, fighting was going on in Vietnam. At that time it was called guerrilla warfare, but Admiral Felt was attempting to brace up the Southeast Asian countries around Vietnam with this annual reunion and demonstration of US power. Late in 1962, after Admiral Felt's demonstration, we received a top secret message from CINCPAC. It concerned the Marine helicopter squadron that had been in Danang for some time supporting the Vietnamese Marines. The squadron's mission had started as a covert operation for medical evacuations only, but had grown into more open direct support. The squadron had deployed under strictly controlled and highly classified instructions from CINCPAC. It was code-named "Shoo Fly," and was beginning to receive threats and pressure from Viet Cong guerrillas. They had disabled two aircraft at night, and had stuck propaganda notes in the engine exhausts. The squadron commander was asking for additional security personnel.

Under the strict protocols of that time, only personnel from the air wing were allowed in Vietnam. Therefore, Task Force 79 was directed to organize, equip, and train covertly a special detachment of ground Marines to serve as security or rescue forces if a plane were forced down or crashed. The day the sensitive message arrived, Colonel Williams and I went over to see General Buse. They gave me the job of organizing this special detachment, but no one was to know what I was doing. I suggested that we create a special jungle warfare demonstration unit, ask for volunteers, screen them carefully, then take them all up into our northern jungle training area. The message activating this unit would imply that the volunteers would return to their parent units when the mission was completed.

Our activation message stated that the unit would train for several weeks and would travel around the Far East giving demonstrations. We had no shortage of volunteers, especially from non-infantry units that seldom got off of Okinawa. We needed 90, and 160 volunteered. I kept 120, because some would drop out in training, and we had to have some replacements ready. The regimental and battalion commanders were not happy with this requirement. Many suggested to me personally that I had dreamed this unit up so I that could take it all over the area on a boondoggle. Our counter-guerrilla training unit in the jungle infested Northern Training Area did an excellent job of training and conditioning these troops.

I interviewed each man before he was assigned to the final detachment. Every man that completed the course agreed to serve after he learned that the real mission was four months of duty in Danang. For an incentive, we shortened their overseas time in proportion to the time they served in Vietnam.

We flew the men to the wing headquarters at Iwakuni, Japan. There they became members of the First Marine Aircraft Wing and received bogus aviation specialties. Then a C-130 flew them into Vietnam. That's the way the buildup continued as President Kennedy raised the ante, bit by bit, to help the South Vietnamese. Within two months we were sending junior officers "in country" to be 30-day observers with the South Vietnamese Marines. The purpose of this gambit was to give them battle experience and a feel for this type of warfare.

As 1963 rolled around, our quota for security troops went up again. By then we were no longer going through the charade of transferring people to the air wing. Our pilots in the early days of Shoo Fly were unsung heroes, as were the troops we sent to protect them. It was dangerous duty. The Pacific command hadn't dreamed up these deployments: their orders came from the "head shed" as JFK decided he was going to finesse this communist insurgency with advisors and support personnel.

TF79 then received an additional requirement: we were to develop a sophisticated reinforced battalion raid plan as quickly as possible, rehearse it, and report when we had one or more units ready to carry it out. The top secret message described the likely employment areas as three different locations in North Vietnam. We had the units, the doctrine, the equipment, and the ships, but no suitable place to perform training at this level. I was tasked to find one pronto!

This requirement, as I learned later, was part of the National Security Staff's effort to increase the range of options available to the President. We didn't know where the order originated, but it did concern all of us that someone was thinking of throwing about 1200 Marines ashore in the heart of a hostile, militarily competent country to perform some destructive feat and then suddenly withdraw. The negative aspects of such an operation are too numerous to list, but we buckled down to deal with the requirement. The only isolated and acceptable area for rehearsing this maneuver I found was Corregidor Island, at the mouth of Manila Bay. Negotiations with the Philippine government were frustrating and slow, and the final approval came after I had been transferred to another job.

Preparation to carry out this battalion raid plan did become a requirement for each of the afloat battalion landing teams assigned to the Seventh Fleet. The ready unit was called the Special Landing Force, a reinforced infantry battalion of some 1400 Marines.

We finally put the finishing touches on the Division Order directing the tactical testing system General Buse had wanted. The regimental staffs would administer both the company and the battalion tests. The company tests were held on Okinawa, the battalion tests at Mount Fuji, Japan. The battalion tests involved the live firing of all weapons after a three-day maneuver exercise

Next I went to Taiwan to write up a joint exercise with the Chinese Marines. Because of demands on my time, I couldn't stay and execute the order. One reason I returned rather abruptly was my unexpected transfer. I was to become operations officer for the Ninth Marine Regiment, a prized assignment. This was the "Air-Go" regiment, the one prepared to fly out on Air Force transport aircraft and be landed in the middle of whatever was going on. Now I would have the opportunity to execute the order I had written and run a series of battalion-level tactical tests at the Fuji training area in Japan. It was a great job that let me get into many interesting things, and I had a super CO, Colonel George Stallings. Like my regimental commander in Korea, he had been a Parachute Marine in WWII. A Yale graduate, smart and somewhat unconventional, he gave me a loose rein and all the support I could ever need. I relieved Major Bob Lucy, who left me a good team: one of them was Captain Sam Fulton, a classmate at Amphibious Warfare School.

Meanwhile, the Third Division had received two new generals. Major General Jim Masters had relieved General Buse. His Assistant Division Commander was his younger brother, Brigadier General John Masters, my old CO from the Fourth Marines. General David M. Shoup, the Commandant, had assigned the two brothers to work together in the same command. It was our good fortune. My frequent assignments to serve under people I had served with before demonstrates one of the great strengths of our small Corps, a family, a Band of Brothers.

When the Secretary of the Navy paid TF 79 a visit late in the spring of 1963, the division held a formal reception in his honor. Field grade officers and commanders from all over the island were required to attend. The uniform was "dress whites." Six majors from Camp Hansen, myself included, piled into two of our "Mighty Mite" jeeps and drove the 25 miles down to the Army Officers' Club at Sukiran, the site of the reception. I was one of the designated drivers.

We did our official thing, went through the receiving line, visited, ate our share of hors d'oeuvres, and loaded up for the return trip home. We had agreed to stop by the officers' club at Kadena Air Force Base en route and take advantage of their Wednesday "two for one night" dinner. We entered the club and took seats in the main dining room. A large banner over the band stand proclaim this to be "Kadena Family Night." The place was filled with groups of parents with young children. It was a festive occasion.

The non-drivers had ordered a drink before we had a chance to realize what we were a part of. All of us were married and had children at home. These cute little pony-tailed girls and small boys in coats and bow ties just stopped our clocks. We all had tears in our eyes when Bill Hanlon, the father of five, said, "I think we better get out of here before I embarrass myself!" We all felt the same way. We paid our check quickly, then drove home in total silence.

We practiced our regimental headquarters air mount-out drills by flying to Japan for the tactical tests at Fuji. The life style at Fuji was indeed Spartan, but we enjoyed the change, the scenery was fantastic, and we did get weekend liberty in Tokyo. Our first visit to Mount Fuji lasted more than a week and gave me a chance to iron a few kinks out of our first tactical test. The second trip would last twice as long and would involve two battalions, back to back. General Jim Masters planned to observe our operations.

Meanwhile, my tour was winding down, and I didn't have any word about my new duty station. Just before I left for Camp Fuji, a letter arrived from my detailer, the officer in our Personnel Department that monitored my assignments. He told me I had been nominated to be the aide to Admiral Smith, CINCLANT/CINCLANTFLT in Norfolk, but Admiral Smith had unexpectedly decided to retire. I wouldn't be the aide to the new admiral, because someone else had taken that billet. The detailer asked me to "hang loose." It seemed that something else was in the wind, but he didn't say what.

General Jim Masters dropped in for a look at both of our tac test exercises, which were a week apart. Both units performed remarkably well under the stresses and strains we created to test them. At one point late in the second week, I was half dozing in my operations tent. It was after midnight, my coffee was stone cold, and not much was happening. Suddenly, a breathless young Marine from our communications center burst into the tent. "Major, you've got a personal message from the Commandant of the Marine Corps!" He handed me a sheet of teletype paper. Sure enough, it was addressed to me from CMC. But I was suspicious. In the past I had been a party to schemes that sent officers bogus orders to weird places as a practical joke. This was no joke, he assured me. It directed me "to immediately contact Commander Barney Martin, USN, c/o Sanno Hotel, Tokyo, Japan to arrange interview with CNO-designate, Admiral David L. McDonald, USN in conjunction with your assignment as OP-006." What was an OP-006? Then it dawned on me that Major Al Smith had told me something was in the mill. This OP-job must be for his personal staff. Why else would he be interviewing me?

I was right. The CNO-designate was replacing Admiral George Anderson, who had just been fired. (He had purposely gotten himself fired by making a public speech denouncing Secretary of Defense McNamara's TFX all-service aircraft.) Admiral McDonald had come from extended duty in Europe and was making a Pacific swing to get current on the many nuances of this huge theater. I happened to be along the route of his trip in Japan.

The next morning I contacted Commander Barney Martin at the hotel. He asked me how soon I could be in Tokyo. It would have to be the following day, I suggested. We agreed on a time. What to wear? I had field utilities, wash cotton khaki, rolled up in a bag, and a Hong Kong wash-and-wear ($24) suit that was standard officer liberty wear in the Far East. Martin said, "Wear the suit and call me when you check in at the Sanno."

120

I arrived late that night and left a message telling him that I was aboard. We met the next morning, and he briefed me a bit on the Admiral and on Mrs. McDonald. Barney Martin was the new Navy aide; I had been nominated as the Marine aide. The Admiral had asked for a ground officer with operations and command experience, though a Marine aviator usually filled the billet—a carryover from the old days when the Marine aide was the admiral's pilot. It was a lieutenant colonel's billet.

We went up to the top deck, where the VIP suite was, and knocked on the door. Admiral McDonald personally greeted us. He was my height, slim and handsome. "Mrs. Mac," as we later called her, was a beautiful, charming lady. I was sun-tanned and lean from my bachelor year of exercise and field time, but that $24 suit didn't do a thing for me. Nevertheless, they made me comfortable, and the interview started. He asked about my family and their health, about my education, and about my financial condition. I told him we were down to one more car payment, and we had $1000 in a Navy Federal Credit Union savings account. I owed no money and we were better off now than we'd been at any time since we married.

Then he asked me if I would like to work for him as his Marine aide. I had to be honest but I wasn't dumb. I told him that it didn't matter whether I wanted to work for him or not. The Commandant had ordered me to report for this interview: if the admiral saw fit to take me on I would promise to give him my very best shot. Then I paused briefly and said that I didn't play bridge or golf, but I supposed I could learn if I had to.

The Admiral seemed puzzled. "What do you mean it doesn't matter whether you want to or not? I asked you if you wanted to!" I repeated that I was ready to do whatever he would like for me to do. To be perfectly honest, I had never aspired to be an aide, but since CMC chose me for this interview I realized it was important. "It's entirely up to you, Admiral." He shook his head and said something about you Marines sure are different. On the other hand, he said, he appreciated my honesty. I told him I was honored to have been considered and pleased to have met both of them. He told me he would have to think it over but he would let me know shortly. Martin asked me to wait in the hall while he spoke with the McDonalds. He came out shortly and shook my hand, saying, "I think you got yourself a job, but he wants to sleep on it. I have a number of personnel matters he wants to include in a message I'm working on."

I received orders in a few days to report within ten days of detachment to the Chief of Naval Operations as OP-006, Marine Aide and Aviation Advisor. The CNO had hired himself a ground pounder: he wanted a field Marine. He told me later that one of my jobs was to make him a little smarter about the Marine Corps. He only knew the aviation side and realized he had a lot to learn. He said later that he chose me more because I told him honestly how I felt about being an aide than for any other reason. He had once been an aide himself. He hadn't wanted to be one either, but he learned from it and knew that I would too. He was right.

Chapter 16

E Ring

"Admirals, Generals, and Whiz Kids"

The Pentagon is a five-sided office structure made up of five concentric pentagonal rings, each five stories high, enclosing a central courtyard that has a small summer restaurant. At the height of the cold war, this restaurant was nicknamed the "Ground Zero Cafe" on the assumption that it would be the aiming point for the first nuclear weapon to be fired at the start of World War III.

The outside ring, the E Ring, has windows with an outside view. The other rings have windows that face other windows over a concrete drainage ditch. The most desirable rooms, the executive suites, are in the E Ring. They house the senior leadership of our nation's armed forces, both civilian and military—except for the Marine Corps, which had its principal offices in the nearby Navy Annex.

Before I began my three-year tour of duty with Admiral David L. McDonald, I had a great deal to do in a very short time. I flew in a Military Airlift Command charter jet from Tachikawa Air Base near Tokyo to Travis Air Force Base near San Francisco.

Flying standby, I managed to get on an American Airlines flight from San Francisco to Atlanta, with stops in Dallas and Memphis, where waiting passengers could bump me. The plane's several stewardesses took on a special project of keeping this Marine from being bumped. (They hid me in the john.) Since my arrival time was far from certain, I had told Carol, staying in an Atlanta hotel, not to worry about meeting me. I would call her at the hotel when I arrived. She didn't listen, I'm glad to say, and greeted me as I walked off the airplane at 3:30 in the morning—the prettiest dreamboat I could ever imagine! We called the kids and woke them up, then called my mother and woke her up. Then we had another honeymoon, and it couldn't have been sweeter. We used to say that the Corps always made you appreciate your family more by finding so many reasons to take you away from it.

Admiral McDonald had advised me strongly not to buy a house. He recommended renting. Primarily for that reason, we spent several days searching for a decent rental that we could afford in the Alexandria-Arlington area. There weren't any. Then we got lucky. I hadn't realized that we had resources for a down payment until a friend reminded me I could borrow against any of my several life insurance policies. In two days, I had a $3500 check and we found exactly what we were looking for at 2422 Taylor Avenue in Alexandria.

I was replacing a Marine lieutenant colonel aviator named George Knapp. He had worked for Admiral Anderson and was caretaking the job until I arrived. He outlined all of the duties he had performed, but we realized that these would change under the new CNO. From the very beginning the Navy Aide, Barney Martin, and I hit it off well. In two years, often working under severe stress, we never said a cross word to each other. He was four years senior to me and would serve as the admiral's personal aide. Both he and his wife Jinny were close to the McDonalds. I told him that I just wanted to be useful and part of the team. In keeping with a time-honored Navy tradition, we all stood in front of the admiral's desk for the "lineup" shortly after he arrived every morning. This was where I met Admiral McDonald for the second time.

The day before I reported to Admiral McDonald for work in the Pentagon, I checked in with my parent unit at Headquarters, Marine Corps. At that time, General David M. Shoup was Commandant of the Marine Corps. His Chief of Staff was Lieutenant General Wallace Greene, who had left instructions for me to report to him.

General Greene spent almost an hour with me and impressed me with the fact that I wasn't being sent over to some "fop" job in the Pentagon. First, in the strictest confidence, he explained to me that General Shoup had been totally at odds with the Navy senior leadership since early in his term, three and a half years ago, when he learned that Admiral Arleigh Burke had been recording a very personal, sensitive, private discussion they were having in his office. After Burke's departure, things had not gone much better with his successor, Admiral Anderson. Shoup was feisty anyway and difficult to work with, but General Greene told me that he personally hoped to improve this communication gap by working more closely with Admiral McDonald.

These are my observations. President Eisenhower had appointed General Shoup to be Commandant when he was a middle-grade major general, passing over all of the Corps' senior leadership. Ike was looking for an "independent thinker," and he found one in Shoup. Shoup also became close to John F. Kennedy while he was President. Shoup ran the Marine Corps with a handful of his generals, and treated the rest of the Corps' generals with contempt. He did not trust the Navy, and felt that the admirals in charge took his loyalty for granted.

General Greene wanted me to understand the undercurrents I'd be swimming in. He charged me with giving the CNO my very best, and added that whether things worked out with the CNO or not (some people fire aides almost on a whim), I had a good record and the Marine Corps would take care of me. His final remark was: "Your loyalty is to your boss, but you can serve the Corps well by being the best Marine aide he could ever have."

A few months later, General Greene, who had graduated from the Naval Academy a few years behind Admiral McDonald, became Commandant of the Marine Corps. Despite some disagreements, he and the CNO maintained an open and continuous dialog during my tour. I was happy to become a somewhat unusual conduit for this relationship.

The man I was now working for hadn't sought this pressure-cooker job. A southerner by birth and the son of a Presbyterian minister from Winder, Georgia, he was a gentleman—a very intelligent, personable officer who had blossomed in the aviation-dominated top hierarchy of the Navy. He was a tough-minded, disciplined man, but disliked confrontations: his reasoned approach was to talk things out.

He was an organized individual: he didn't need or want to have a large entourage with him. When he traveled, he traveled light and worked those of us who went with him hard. Personally, however, he was remarkably undemanding and thoughtful. We used to say that he didn't really need an aide—just someone to book the appointments and arrange his travel. I didn't want to be seen as eager or aggressive. In my judgment, that would be a sure way to negotiate a quick job change. My feeling was that if I performed every task offered as well as I could, more would come my way. It worked out that way.

At one of the morning lineups late in October, "Admiral Mac" was going through his pile of personal mail and distributing some of it to his staff for action. He came to an invitation to the Marine Corps Birthday Ball from General Shoup, and held it up. It got him started on an old pet peeve. When he was Commander of the Sixth Fleet in the Med, he had received invitations to these balls. He said it made him furious that young Marines

123

all had to kick in an enormous amount of their own money to host these parties for VIPs. It didn't have anything to do with a real celebration, and the way it was run had always made him especially mad. Then he stopped, smiled, and said, "What do you have to say about that, Charlie?"

I had been attending these lineups for more than two months without receiving any special recognition or assignment. They were usually brief. If he had special business with one of us, he would ask that person to remain afterwards. He didn't do that this time. Yet he wasn't trying to put me on the spot: this thing had just happened.

All eyes were on me: I didn't hesitate a second. "Admiral, I'll bet you never asked one of those young Marines you mentioned how he felt about that ball you attended. You would have been surprised. Sure, all of us have kicked in a lot of our own money at times to host important people at our annual balls. We're happy to do it, because it's our one day in the year to crow, to stop working and tell each other what being a Marine is all about. We do it in foxholes, in jungles, and in Naples. It sets us apart: we're proud, we're dedicated, and we want the world to know it. As a matter of fact, this one day each year makes all of the crap we have to put up with the other 364 days worthwhile. Sir, I wouldn't be here today if the Marine Corps didn't have a birthday ball each year. It's part of what we are. It's our annual rededication. We're the only service that feels this way!"

He nodded his head in assent, but changed the subject and shortly afterward dismissed us. When we got outside, Barney hit me on the back and said, "God, Charlie, you've sure got guts! The old man didn't know what to say." I responded that I hoped I hadn't blown it, but he'd asked me what I had to say! In a few minutes there was a buzz from the admiral. Barney went in. He returned with the invitation marked with the admiral's red pencil: "Accept with enthusiasm! DLMcD."

A week before the 10 November ball, I presented the CNO with a red Marine officer's cummerbund and a note recommending he might substitute it for his Navy gold one for the ball. He did just that. At the ball, when he was introduced to the 2,000 attendees, he stood up and opened up his dinner jacket to show the Marine cummerbund he was wearing. The house went wild!

Midshipman Second Class Roger Staubach and his band of brave football warriors took Navy football to great heights in 1963. The team ended the regular season with a 9-1 record and played Texas in the Cotton Bowl in what was called a national championship game. Both teams were being touted as number one. The CNO had been monitoring the season very closely, assisted by his Marine aide.

The season gave us an unusual opportunity to make some of the key games communication vehicles for both Congressional and Defense officials. The Admiral, although not a dyed-in-the-wool football enthusiast, accepted the invitations he received and attended all of the home games and several of the away games, mainly those at schools that had prestigious NROTC units—schools such as Michigan, Notre Dame, and Duke.

For the October 5th game against Michigan, he invited House Majority Leader Ford and his two young sons to travel with him. Gerald Ford, a former Michigan center, proved to be as amiable and low key as he has always been portrayed. The school and its NROTC authorities welcomed the visit. Navy impressed the nation with a resounding 26 – 13 triumph over a good Michigan team. Congressman Ford, who turned out to be a neighbor of mine in Alexandria, was a good sport over Michigan's loss.

One of my several responsibilities was to coordinate the Admiral's flight arrangements for away games and to coordinate things with the Naval Academy for the home games. I became known as "the football aide," a moniker Captain Ike Kidd hung on me. Ike was Adm. McDonald's Senior Aide and Administrative Assistant. He had been a Navy football player in his younger days. He recommended that we invite some of the Department of Defense "Whiz Kids" to attend the Notre Dame game on November second.

The Whiz Kids were giving us major headaches. The admiral thought the game might give them a chance to "ask some dumb questions" of his Marine aide and allow some cross-pollination to take place. It was an interesting day for me. Our guests were Alain Enthoven, the senior Whiz Kid, Assistant Secretary of Defense for System Analysis, Russell Murray, and one other associate. I learned, to my amazement, that Enthoven, the number three man in the Pentagon hierarchy, had never been to a football game. He had no understanding of what was going on, why people would cheer, what constituted a score. It worried me. This Ph.D. egghead wasn't a mainstream American if he couldn't spell "football."

I sat between him and Russ Murray, who was interested in learning what made the Marine Corps tick. We filled a yellow legal pad with sketches and notes on the way home. The good news was that Navy beat Notre Dame 35 – 14. It hasn't happened since.

On November 22, 1963 I was at work in the aides' office when the phone rang. Normally, one of the yeomen answered the phone, but I picked it up. It was word from Navy Flag Plot that President Kennedy had been shot in the head during a Dallas motorcade and probably would not survive the wound. He was presently in the emergency room of a Dallas hospital. The Admiral was informed and immediately departed for a meeting of the Joint Chiefs. I find it difficult to describe the shock and the sorrow we all felt over the loss of this young, charismatic leader. Soon we learned that he had indeed died, and the preparations for the state funeral got underway that evening.

Aides to members of the Joint Chiefs represented them at planning sessions held at the Military District of Washington Headquarters in nearby Fort McNair. There were daily meetings, and some working groups gathered more often. The planners produced and distributed much paper, but none was ever issued as a directive. The entire series of formal events in this national observance—the period of mourning, cathedral services, the funeral dirge, and interment—were executed flawlessly on oral orders and unofficial papers.

As the heads of state marched abreast down Rhode Island Avenue approaching St. Matthew Cathedral, Mrs. Kennedy had just been escorted inside the sanctuary. I can still see General De Gaulle and Emperor Haile Selassie striding abreast, the towering French giant and the diminutive Ethiopian side by side. Mrs. McDonald and I were standing next to the cathedral entrance waiting to enter. I noticed that the roofs of buildings across the street were all manned by police or military personnel. Suddenly we were startled by a very loud explosion immediately to my right. A huge pane of glass, at least six feet by six feet, had fallen onto the sidewalk, narrowly missing several police sentries. Nothing stopped, but radios all around were crackling with information. Apparently the glass had fallen from a construction site on the roof of the building adjacent to St. Matthew Cathedral.

Following the funeral Mass, the solemn procession proceeded to Arlington Cemetery. The gravesite portion was equally precise: a US Army Special Forces guard of honor, a funeral manual of arms by the Irish Guards, and a flyover of 44 Navy and Air Force aircraft that followed the 21-gun salute and the playing of taps. A chaplain blessed the eternal flame, and President Johnson escorted Mrs. Kennedy back to her car. It had been a long, tedious day, but everything had been executed perfectly, except for that loose pane of glass. Thank God no one had panicked. DeGaulle hadn't batted an eye.

Most Americans are familiar with the name Admiral Hyman G. Rickover. Some have called him "the father of the nuclear Navy." Others who knew him personally and had to deal with him called him a royal pain in the ass. A strongly opinionated, driving, and irascible figure, he was promoted to the rank of rear admiral by direction of Congress. He was promoted to full admiral, again by direction of Congress, at the age of 73 and remained on active duty until he was forcibly retired at age 82. With his congressional power base, he was beholden to no one but himself. Nevertheless, he did have to do business within the Navy. He dominated and controlled the entire nuclear construction program. He was 64 years old when the following incident took place.

Admiral McDonald felt that Rickover's personal management style was the opposite of what was generally accepted as leadership. He was also upset that the nuclear program's super high standards were "raping the rest of the Navy"—absorbing most of its top talent. He didn't like the man personally, but realized that he had to deal with him and at least try to tone down some of his wild demands on the personnel system.

One morning Admiral Mac asked me to stay after the lineup, and had me take a seat. He told me that he had given Ike Kidd instructions that whenever Admiral Rickover, who always dialed his own calls, called our office, his call was to be transferred to me, the Marine Aide. No one else was to talk with him. Absolutely no one! Then the Admiral looked a bit conspiratorial and said, "Charlie, you're well aware of how pushy, demanding, and unreasonable Hyman Rickover is with everyone. He expects to preempt God himself, to see me on demand. I'm tired of his impolite, abrasive style, and you're going to help me teach him a lesson." This was getting interesting. He continued, "You're the only member of my staff that I can rely on to carry out these explicit orders. Marines understand 'orders.' Whenever he calls and wants to see me, no matter what my schedule says, I want you to be extremely polite and invite him to come over right away. Then, after he arrives, I want you to make damn sure he waits at least one hour before you let him cross that entrance to my office. At least one hour! Do you understand?"

Yes, I understood this almost unbelievable order: I had become the "Rickover Aide," as my office mates dubbed me. Never once did I fail in this sacred mission. Mine was the unpleasant chore of having to stay with Admiral Rickover the first few times he went through this "humility drill," as we aides called it. He would storm about the reception room, telling me what a bunch of idiots the former CNO's had been, what screwed up outfits the Navy, the Naval Academy, the Navy Department, and the CNO staff all were. But he gradually learned that he was going to waste at least a full hour every time he came over. We saw a lot less of Admiral Rickover once he understood that.

Years later, after I had retired, I gave the keynote address at a three-day leadership symposium held in the Rickover Building at the Naval Academy. It took all the inner strength I could muster to avoid commenting on the irony of this symposium being held in a building named for a man who didn't know the first thing about leadership. He did a lot of good things for the Navy, I suppose, but the costs he levied on the system were hard to justify. He set up academic proficiency as the God of the Naval Academy, to the detriment of the art of molding and influencing others—the art commonly known as leadership.

One of our more pleasant chores in CNO's office was scheduling and hosting periodic luncheons and command briefings for the former Chiefs of Naval Operations. In the 60's, some half dozen were living in the D.C. area and were well enough to attend these gatherings. Their comments and questions to Admiral McDonald were priceless, often reflecting viewpoints they had held some 20 or more years earlier. From those who had served during the four-term Roosevelt era, we learned about their dealings with the President himself on a wide variety of matters. Roosevelt, who considered himself a knowledgeable "naval person," would frequently send them notes written in his own hand asking detailed questions about ship dispositions.

Their comments about these notes led us to look through the Operations Deputy's files. The OPDEP was the admiral charged with coordinating all Navy JCS matters for the CNO. In earlier years he had handled all operational matters. It was my honor and pleasure to go through this treasure trove and help sort it out for the Naval Archives. Mr. Roosevelt was quite a correspondent and stuck his nose into a wide variety of issues. His memos were priceless souvenirs of a simpler time. I wondered if anyone in the White House of that day knew of or kept account of the hundreds of notes signed "FDR" that had gone to offices all over Washington.

As I mentioned earlier, my boss liked to travel with a small staff. This meant that we all had to perform a variety of chores. At first I arranged the scheduling of aircraft for CNO, prepared detailed trip itineraries, paid the bills, handled official gifts, and served as an escort when the Navy Aide was otherwise occupied.

When traveling away from major Navy communications facilities, the admiral had to have a "secure and safe" means of communicating with Captain Kidd in Washington. That is how I became a cryptographer, albeit a limited one. It was interesting, at times critical, work, and I performed it when everyone else was sleeping.

I was trained in the Pentagon to use the personalized code established for CNO. I would use code rooms in US embassies or major military communications stations all over the world to transmit coded messages to Captain Kidd or receive them from him. I took dictation from Admiral Mac when he wanted to send a message, and entered it in a machine I had coded. I also decoded encrypted messages that had been sent to him and made only one copy. My typing had to be deliberate and completely accurate: the code machines didn't have a "spell checker" in those days!

The system was not very important when we started using it, but grew in significance as the Vietnam conflict got closer, commenced, and grew. Toward the end of my tour, I recommended that we take a junior officer communicator on the trips with us to perform my coding duties. The amount of traffic was keeping me up all night—and then I had to work all day. The Admiral agreed, and our travel staff grew by one—but only one!

We were struggling with the McNamara crowd: one idea that percolated out of a CNO-SecNav brainstorming session was that it might be wise to send a bright young naval officer, as smart as the Whiz Kids, to get some new blood into that closed shop that was causing so many headaches for all the services. At that time they were still pursuing the philosophy that one type of aircraft could be designed to do everything for everybody. While this is a small exaggeration, most of their initiatives led more toward the creation of military "Edsels" than the creation of operationally sound aircraft. "Cost effectiveness" was the OK phrase.

Vice Admiral B. J. Semmes, Chief of the Bureau of Naval Personnel, came up with an officer who was supposed to solve all of the problems with the systems analysts: he was one himself. He was Commander Stansfield Turner. A Naval Academy graduate, Rhodes Scholar, and certified smart guy, Stan Turner was supposed to convert the heathen civilian leadership. My best reading on Stan Turner was that he became one of them: they converted him. This is the same Turner who was President Jimmy Carter's CIA Director: I believe that the CIA never recovered from his reorganizing.

One of the major decisions made during the McDonald-Nitze years was the one to do away with the entire Navy bureau structure. Admiral McDonald and many of his predecessors had chafed at the independence of the Navy's bureau chiefs. The bureaus were enormous administrative structures that directed shipbuilding (BUSHIPS), shipyards and facilities (BUDOCKS), and aircraft (BUAIR)—the logistics backbone and lifeblood of the Navy. They were fiefdoms, each headed by a rear admiral, and they reported directly to the Secretary of the Navy. The top naval officer, the CNO, was not in their chain of command. The succession of civilian Secretaries of the Navy, men with political skills but little technical expertise, had left the running of the bureaus entirely in the hands of these "Bureau Barons," as they were sometimes called.

Admiral Mac wanted to change all that by putting them under a trusted four-star admiral in a new organization called the Navy Material Command. It would report directly to the CNO, not to the Secretary. Somewhat reluctantly, Nitze accepted this radical surgery— and whoever else had to bless it did. It happened. Every one of the bureau chiefs retired immediately under protest. The old structure was hard to bring down, and harder to keep down. In the mid 80's, a secretary with the zeal of an apostle reversed many of these changes in the interest of "restoring civilian control."

Admiral Mac had a bit of a devilish streak in him. In the fall of 1965, with the Vietnam War underway, we were planning a lengthy Far East trip for him, his top admirals, the Assistant Commandant of the Marine Corps, and the Deputy Commander of the Pacific Fleet. The itinerary included stops in Hawaii and the Philippines, time at sea with the Seventh Fleet, time with the Marines in Danang in the Republic of Vietnam and with MACV in Saigon, then another stop in Hawaii, and then on home. Captain Kidd didn't usually travel with the admiral, but he wanted very much to go on this pivotal trip, particularly for the Seventh Fleet portion. The admiral was sympathetic. Ike would accompany him from the Philippines to the Seventh Fleet while I went directly into Vietnam with Lieutenant General Mangrum and made the final arrangements for him and his admirals in that combat environment.

About a week before we left, our buzzer sounded twice: my call. I went into the admiral's office. He commented that Ike had a tendency to wear his trousers a bit short, and he needed my help to get this corrected before he took him out to the Seventh Fleet as his aide. Captain Kidd had a stocky build and fought a never-ending battle with his waistline. The admiral had decided what to do and simply wanted me to execute the plan. He told me to contact Angelique Kidd, Ike's attractive wife, and sign her on to the conspiracy. I was to abscond with all of Ike's white and khaki trousers, have them let out "two full inches," and return them, all within 24 hours. No problem.

128

With the full cooperation of Mrs. Kidd, the Admiral's driver, and a friendly Pentagon tailor, the deed had been done before the next afternoon had ended, and with little if any sign that the alterations had been made. As we walked out to board the aircraft at Andrews Air Force Base a few days later, the senior aide and executive assistant to the Chief of Naval Operations kept pulling up on his trousers. We all heard him say, "Damn. Guess I must be losing weight. Can't keep these trousers up!"

The author with CNO, Adm McDonald, visits 3rd Bn. Third Marines in Vietnam

Two and a half weeks later, I was ten pounds lighter myself after all that travel. We had returned to Hawaii for a day of rest and consultations with both CINCPAC and CINCPACFLT. I was in the Navy code room wrapping up my daily session with the personal messages when the door flew open. Standing in the doorway was Captain Isaac C. Kidd, pointing his finger at me. "You're the one. You're the one that had my trousers let out! I've finally figured out what's been going on!"

He wasn't angry, really. Our trip had been exhausting but fruitful. The only bit of levity on this entire journey had been the speculation over how long it would be before Ike would discover what ailed his trousers. I stood up, shut the door, and responded, "Sir, I was just carrying out my orders like a good Marine!" He didn't ask questions, but he slapped me on the back and shook my hand.

My E Ring years had their "interesting" moments, many of them during the trips we took to various NATO, European, and South American countries. One night, for example, I knocked down an entire wall of heavy pewter Viking shields in the ancient Norse home of the Swedish CNO in Stockholm. I was trying to squeeze past the many seated guests to reach the head of the long table with a gift. Later, I was somehow able to fix the gift clock when the Admiral inadvertently wound it backwards.

Then there was the call we made on General Franco in Madrid to consummate Navy base rights in Spain and our *quid pro* of older US ships. It was a formal affair, and I wore dress whites, but red ink from a cleaner's cellophane bag had stained the back of my white uniform. As an emergency solution, I had sprayed shaving cream all over the back, put talcum powder on it, and ironed it in to cover up the red ink. The Admiral wondered why I sat up so straight in the car and kept my back to the wall during the formal call.

129

This tour of duty gave me a lot to look back on and smile over, but it also taught me a great deal—about the Navy, the Marine Corps, the other services, the Department of Defense, the Congress, the Presidency, and this crazy, wonderful city we call our capitol.

I learned first hand about the inconsistencies and cruelties in national leadership. There was the absolute disdain that Lyndon Johnson, our commander in chief, showed for his top military leaders, the Joint Chiefs of Staff, when they appealed to him to use a decisive alternative to the buildup in Vietnam. He treated these highly respected military leaders like dirt and reveled in defaming them. I learned how little senior officers can do to change things in their major commands . . . and yet I also learned that there is a lot they can and should do to communicate positively with their people.

I watched the almost limitless variety of leadership styles used by people in high places. I watched and wondered where my "Band of Brothers" concept could ever fit in the Navy. I've never found the answer to that question. I saw many talented, superior leaders rise to the top to run the Navy, but I couldn't ignore the reality that too many ambitious, selfish, me-first officers got advanced to senior grades. It still worries me.

When I first came to this job I had the feeling that the Marine Aide was "a bastard at the family reunion": a member, but one not fully accepted or trusted. Now I am sure I was being overly sensitive, because I certainly became a full and valued member of this small but talented staff. Admiral Mac asked me to stay on a third year when my normal rotation date came up after two years. He wrote General Wally Greene, then Commandant, asking his advice about my staying. It was a beautiful letter that explained that he needed me because many members of his staff were leaving. General Greene responded positively, stating there was no better place for me than in a responsible position on his staff for another year. The deal was done. I made lieutenant colonel in December of 1965 and watched more history unfold. My third year was the best. When it was over, I received orders to the Second Marine Division at Camp Lejeune, N.C. I was detached on a Friday night and assumed command of an infantry battalion at Camp Lejeune at 10 a.m. on Monday the 6th of June. The Second Battalion, Eighth Marines didn't know it yet, but they were about to join my Band of Brothers.

Chapter 17

Second Marine Division
"Command, Deployment, and Saving the Cities"

In June of 1966, the Second Marine Division and its supporting elements at Camp Lejeune, N.C., formed the hub for all of the Western Hemisphere commitments of the Marine Corps. The USA maintained a sizable operational presence in the Caribbean because of our continuing troubles with Castro and instability in both the Dominican Republic and Haiti, but also staged rotating NATO contingents from this large coastal base. Fully one third of the division and its supporting Second Aircraft Wing were deployed continuously as 1800-man Marine amphibious units in the Caribbean and the Mediterranean. We maintained a defensive force of 1500 Marines at our naval base in Guantanamo Bay, Cuba. All of the troops in Fleet Marine Force, Atlantic, were either gone, going, or returning. Many were also being used to reinforce the Vietnam buildup. It was a very busy place.

Major General Ormond R. Simpson was the Commanding General of the Second Marine Division. He was the epitome of the warrior gentleman: an inspirational leader, an eloquent speaker. He projected his personality throughout the command, and he needed all of his considerable strengths to deal with his plateful of headaches.

The day after we drove down to Camp Lejeune, General Simpson approached me at a Sunday afternoon social affair. He asked me and my new regimental commander, Colonel Russell, to call on him at eight o'clock Monday morning. When we did, this larger-than-life leader gave us a candid rundown on the problems in his division, and explained why he had asked me to report immediately, without any leave. He didn't spare any punches.

The Second Battalion, Eighth Marines had just returned from a six-month deployment as the ground defense force for the naval base at Guantanamo Bay, Cuba. Post-deployment inspections had unearthed startling discrepancies. The battalion's weapons accounts were suspect, many personal weapons were missing, a large number of troops were "over the hill," and morale appeared to be at rock bottom. General Simpson directed that I send him within a week, via my regimental commander, my personal analysis of the situation. We were deploying to the Caribbean in late November as an amphibious ready force.

I thanked General Simpson for this opportunity to command, then went to the 10 a.m. change-of-command ceremony. The ceremony was a professional embarrassment. I had never seen any Marine unit look so ragged or march so poorly. After the short "koolade and cookies" reception, my wife told me that it was the worst thing she had ever seen, and she wasn't prone to make negative comments about things military.

My first action was to announce an officers' call, with swords, behind the headquarters at 6 a.m. the next morning. Then I ordered the entire battalion to assemble in the regimental gym with weapons at 9 a.m., when I'd talk to the troops. Following that talk, we were going to conduct battalion drill on the parade ground until they looked like Marines. All other schedules were canceled. There was a regimental change of command in five days and we were going to show the world that the Second Battalion, Eighth Marines could look and march like Marines.

The next morning I put the officers through a full hour of sword drill. The troops paid close attention when I addressed them in the gym at nine. After just one hour's battalion drill they looked sharp. In my short talk I had told them that their lack of professionalism had embarrassed me deeply. This was a brand new regime—no BS, just straight talk. You either give me 101% or you are in trouble. Looking sharp was wanting to look sharp, and giving a damn about your reputation as a unit. I promised them I would give them every reason to be proud of this battalion. Whether they were to serve under me for a week, a month, or a year, my goal was for them to look back when they departed and say, "Second Battalion, Eighth Marines was a damn good outfit! I helped make it that way!"

Things improved quickly. General Simpson called me after the Eighth Marines' change of command to say he was pleased with the battalion's performance. Colonel Russell, before departing, told me he had two majors on the way to serve as the XO and S-3. Colonel George Webster was to be our new regimental commander. There were no experienced supply officers available, but I did get the honor graduate from supply school, a bright-eyed young second lieutenant. He was smart and aggressive, and listened well.

I moved the former S-3, Captain Lang Forehand, to the logistics shop, S-4, and ordered him and my new supply officer to wade into the weapons problems. Things were bad, but not nearly as bad as we had thought. Still, 55 pistols had completely disappeared.

Major Harvey Harper reported in as my XO. Harv's expertise was in embarkation and amphibious matters. These skills were to prove invaluable. The new S-3, Major Joe Cody, had just come from Headquarters, Marine Corps, where he had been the Commandant's speech writer. Joe was imaginative and energetic, and had a golden pen. First Lieutenant Dean Aggers, solid and experienced, became my adjutant and personnel officer. A new team was coming together. Now to deal with our Marines who were absent without proper authority.

This was a new problem for me, but most units considered it a fact of life at Camp Lejeune. Calling in the adjutant, sergeant major, and the company first sergeants, I asked for their ideas and advice. First, how to prevent men from going UA; second, how to get the UA's back? I heard a lot of good ideas, and soon we came up with an aggressive plan. I gave unlimited telephone authorizations to our people so that they could call the absentees' homes of record and talk to the individual, his parents, family, or whatever. And the troops themselves began to volunteer information about where some of their buddies were salted away, usually on one of the nearby Carolina beaches. Teams went out to bring our troops back to the fold. Things improved slowly, but I would not be happy until the UA rate was zero.

My battalion was the nucleus of Landing Force, Carib 4-66. I would soon be wearing three hats: battalion CO, battalion landing team CO, and Commander, Landing Force. This landing force consisted of our battalion landing team (BLT); a reinforced helicopter squadron, HMM-162; and a logistics support unit. The BLT should have had about 1800 Marines, but we had to send one of our four rifle companies to Vietnam as an emergency reinforcement shortly before we deployed. We remained one rifle company short thereafter.

Ninety days before our November 28 departure date, we received top priority on supply requisitions, personnel transfers ceased, and we came under direct command of the commanding general. This was a time of intensive planning with our Navy counterparts in Amphibious Squadron Eight (PHIBRON 8). We were assigned five ships, one of which was *USS Guam*, a relatively new helicopter carrier.

LtCol. Cooper, Capt. Porter, RAdm. Bell, Capt. De La Mater CO,*USS Guam* at sea

Our commodore, the Navy captain commanding the amphibious squadron and the embarked Marines, was especially well qualified. Captain Ebenezer "Ben" Porter had headed up the Navy section at Marine Corps Schools in Quantico for the preceding three years. He understood Marines and amphibious doctrine better than any other Navy officer I've ever known. We had collaborated on Admiral McDonald's annual speeches to the students at Quantico and had established a comfortable rapport. He was to be my operational commander for seven months. He looked after "his Marines" and was concerned about their living accommodations in his ships. His favorite comment was that the Navy's ships of the line launched missiles, torpedoes, and airplanes, whereas his "amphibs" launched US Marines. We were configured to land by boat, helicopter, or a combination of both.

We were to become the floating US police force in the Caribbean. Haiti was restive, as always; Castro threatened Guantanamo almost daily; and there were still concerns about the stability of the Dominican Republic. The ships' home port was the naval base at San Juan, Puerto Rico, or occasionally the naval air station at Roosevelt Roads (also in Puerto Rico). Our training base ashore was on the island of Vieques, near Puerto Rico, which held Camp Garcia, a primitive base camp, and an expeditionary airfield. Vieques had wonderful landing beaches and a firing range where we could shoot all of our weapons.

The Cooper family, including Skipper Dog, the family pet, found a happy home at Camp Lejeune. The quarters were more spacious than our home in Alexandria, the kids' schools were on the base, and there were plenty of youngsters to make friends with. The beaches, inland waterways, and sports facilities were outstanding. Chip, a sophomore in high school, immediately became a surfer. Linda was in the eighth grade, wrestling with the "new math." The base had recently expanded the stables, and Carol enjoyed being both rider and children's instructor again. When it finally became obvious that our daughter preferred riding to piano lessons, we sold the piano and bought her a horse. All the mounts in the Marines stable had battle names: hers was named "Suribachi." These were busy, happy times for the entire family. Skipper Dog was in heaven, with rabbits, deer, and all sorts of wonderful scents to follow.

I could hardly wait to get my troops aboard those five ships and away from the distractions at Camp Lejeune. We had little time for battalion field work before

133

leaving, but half of the troops were combat veterans. What we had to develop was unit pride and identity.

Eighteen of our Marines were in the base brig serving court martial sentences. We needed people, and I remembered the replacement company I took to Korea, the brig rats of "Asshole Company." The sergeant major and I interviewed our troops in the brig. If each volunteered to rejoin the battalion, gave me his word to stay "squared away," and completed the deployment without further problems, I would clear his record of any misconduct. He could get out of jail, do what Marines do, and let life go on if he just played it straight. A seven months' cruise in the sunny Caribbean offered some positive incentives. Without a moment's hesitation each one accepted the challenge and returned to his company that same day. They all made it with flying colors, except for one bad actor who flew home in leg irons after a serious offense and was later discharged.

Lieutenant Colonel Dan Wilson, CO of our helicopter squadron, had a serious personnel problem. All of his pilots had had at least one tour in Vietnam and many were slated to return there after this cruise. They were gone so much that their wives were threatening to leave them. Most of the pilots loved the Corps, but they were bailing out in droves.

He had a plan and wanted to get my concurrence before he presented it to his CO and General Simpson. He wanted to leave about half of his most experienced pilots at home and have them flown down to join us for the major exercises. He would take all of his assigned aircraft, 14 UH-34's and 2 UH-1's, but not the two pilots per aircraft that were required for flying troops. He could carry out his crew training with one pilot per aircraft and double them up for limited lifts and emergencies. We could waive the two-pilot requirement if we suddenly had to move troops fast. I didn't like the idea, but I understood that we had to do something to help the pilots. After the Air Wing promised a dedicated transport to fly the pilots in on 24 hours' notice, I consented. Later, General Simpson and the Wing CG both blessed the scheme as a thoughtful initiative. When we left, we had all the pilots, because our initial exercise was an assault landing on Vieques in concert with the landing force we were relieving. Overall, the plan worked well.

Brigadier General Ed Wheeler, the Assistant Division Commander, was the commander for our initial exercise on Vieques. As it turned out, we actually performed as well as or better than the unit we were relieving. I was pleased and relieved when the final critique was over. We received favorable remarks and now could settle in on Vieques for some much-needed small-unit training.

We moved into our Quonset huts at Camp Garcia, where we were scheduled to remain until early January. The huts had running water, limited electricity, indoor plumbing of sorts, and cots. The squadron settled in at the small airfield and set up its maintenance shops. Our messhall served its first meal the night we moved in the first week in December. The weather was "resort" perfect. Then I received a call on the high-frequency radio net that we used to maintain 24-hour contact with the Commodore at sea. It ruined my day.

Commodore Porter told me there was a major problem in the Marine berthing compartments on *USS Guam*, our flagship. He put the commanding officer of the *Guam* on to explain it. Some persons, as yet unknown, had gone through about two-thirds of our troop compartments, broken open lockers, rifled the contents, taken valuables, tossed gear all over, and generally made one helluva mess. We still had one officer and about 30 Marines aboard ship serving as the ship's platoon. They had been assigned to the ship's laundry and mess facilities and were due to fly ashore the next day. Our officer had discovered the looting when he made his inspection of the compartments before leaving. The ship's CO was calm but obviously distressed and embarrassed. The last thing we both needed was a Navy-Marine confrontation at the beginning of the cruise.

He asked for ideas on how we should proceed. He stressed that he hoped to have the culprits in hand shortly. I needed some time to think it over. We had to convince our troops they wouldn't be short-changed. After a brain storming session with my staff, we came up with the answer. It was going to require help from a lot of people, including the Commandant of the Marine Corps, Congress, and some good Navy investigators, plus the outstanding administrative skills of my S-1 and the ship's platoon officer. I'm still amazed at how well it worked and how efficiently the paperwork was processed.

The staff worked all night getting ready, because I wanted to talk to all of the troops that had been embarked in *Guam* the first thing the next morning. Later I would talk to all of those not in *Guam* so that there wouldn't be any false rumors floating around. The skipper of *Guam* was delighted when I called to explain our approach and immediately set about helping us carry it out.

We told the troops what had happened, and gave each of them a printed claim form and asked them to list everything they could remember being in their lockers aboard ship. The statement would be the basis for their claim if gear was missing, but it would be checked carefully against the actual contents if their locker had not been rifled. They knew that only about half of the lockers had been rifled, but didn't know which. This was a good incentive for them to be absolutely honest. There were some 400 lockers involved, and the troops were not going back aboard ship for a month. This gave us time to get things working and for tempers to cool. From here on in, it worked like a well-oiled machine, a joint Navy-Marine Corps full-court press on a difficult problem.

The Navy caught the three culprits and recovered a large share of the valuables, but no cash. We submitted serious-incident reports up both the Navy and Marine Corps chains of command with recommendations that formal reimbursements be made after the investigation was completed. I received personal assurance that we could promise this to the troops. The Commandant, General Wallace Greene, called me to say that the Marine Corps was out of claim money for the year, but he had authority to request special legislation from Congress to get the necessary funds. The big Band of Brothers was working.

It all came together in the next few weeks. When we returned to the ship in January, both the ship's captain and I got on the PA system to talk to the sailors and the Marines about the remarkable efforts everyone had made. That set the stage for a close and warm camaraderie for the rest of the cruise. The troops received government checks for full reimbursement before they left the ship, and our paymaster cashed the checks for those who wanted greenbacks. A lot of hard-working, dedicated people brought this incident to a happy ending, but support at the very top is what made it work. Congress passed special legislation appropriating the necessary funds.

135

Our month ashore was a coming-together time for my new Band of Brothers. Unit identity is so important to troops. Soon each unit had its area marked by whitewashed rocks that identified it. We worked hard, but had time for sports, beach cookouts, and even a military field meet. We held a live fire exercise, during which we fired all of our crew-served weapons, including the Ontos, and invited the commodore, his staff, and the five ship captains ashore to observe it. Our Navy Underwater Demolition Team and reconnaissance Marines combined forces to catch a large quantity of spiny lobsters so that we could treat our guests to a special meal of charbroiled steaks and fresh lobster tails.

Christmas away from home and family is never pleasant, but we did what we could to keep our spirits up. Our battalion chaplain invited the local Catholic priest to join him for ecumenical services and Mass on Christmas Eve. We had a stand down from training and a special holiday meal. Some of the companies decided to do a little Christmas caroling. December 24th was my birthday, but I had a lot on my mind. Rather than sitting around getting lonesome, I went back to my office and resumed work on officer fitness reports.

About 11:45 that night I heard some muffled voices. Looking out the window, I saw my chaplain and about 50 troopers. Under his direction they sang a Marine version of "Silent Night," followed by "The Marines' Hymn" and a shouted "Happy birthday and merry Christmas, Colonel Cooper!" I stepped outside to thank them, and found my driver, the sergeant major, and XO standing there. My driver, a young black Marine corporal from Florida, was holding a small Christmas tree with blinking lights. His mother had sent the tree. I put the fitness reports aside for the rest of the evening: it was a touching moment.

We went back aboard ship early in January. It was time to resume shipboard life, enjoy some liberty in San Juan, and prepare for jungle training in Panama. The troops had not had liberty in more than a month. Both Commodore Porter and I were determined to prevent them from turning this first freedom into a bacchanal. We used the tried and true buddy system, backed up by a joint Navy-Marine shore patrol. In the meantime, the Navy had arranged to have a special USO-type show presented on *Guam*. All of the marquee entertainers in San Juan for the winter season agreed to participate and be our guests for a buffet luncheon afterward. We stacked C-ration cartons on the hangar deck to create a stage, rigged signal flags all over the place, and prepared for what turned out to be a memorable day.

Red Buttons was the enthusiastic emcee. Other performers were Jimmy Durante, Robert Goulet, Anna Maria Alberghetti, Paul Anka, and a cast of entertainers, all of whom were performing at the top hotels and casinos in San Juan. We squeezed the *Guam*'s crew, my embarked Marines, and about 400 Marines from the other ships onto that hangar deck, hanging some of them from rafters and girders. After the show and our luncheon, we invited all of the show biz entourage down on the dock, where our newly formed drill team performed a formal guard mount and pass in review for them. Jimmy Durante took the review with me, and actually wept afterwards, he was so overcome with emotion. What a great old gentleman!

During our two days in port, the weather had been gorgeous, we'd had the morale-boosting USO show, and most important, we had not had a single liberty incident reported. Ben Porter and I were relaxing over a morning cup of coffee in his mess when a worried messenger came in and handed me a piece of paper. It was from the

CO of the Marine Barracks in San Juan, Colonel "Bud" Jensen. He had received a call from the Chief of Police. Representative Carl Albert, Speaker of the US House of Representatives, was on vacation in San Juan, recovering from a recent heart attack. The previous day he had been assaulted on a street corner by a drunken uniformed Marine. Police had arrested the Marine, and Albert had been released from the San Juan General Hospital after being treated for a minor cut on his face.

The story emerged. We had assigned our engineer platoon of some 40 men to Marine Barracks, San Juan, to assist them in rebuilding their rifle range targets. One of their men, a Vietnam veteran, had previously received a month's restriction as punishment for drinking on duty. Our doctor had examined him, declared him a border line alcoholic and a liberty risk, and recommended he be returned to Camp Lejeune for a psychiatric workup. He should have remained on the ship awaiting transportation, but his officer decided to take him ashore. The Marine Barracks had somehow granted him liberty, not aware that he was under medical restriction with a major drinking problem.

He and a couple of buddies had gone to a bar, where he proceeded to drink zombies until he was almost blind. He had staggered out to a street corner, where he heard someone make a remark about "that disgusting drunken Marine!" He turned and lashed out in a besotted response and hit poor old Carl Albert, who just happened to be standing on the street corner waiting for a traffic light.

The Marine was now in the city jail. Carl Albert was in his apartment after receiving medical attention. Once I had learned these basic facts, it was imperative that I make a personal call on Mr. Albert immediately. Before I left, I determined that the Marine in question was a sergeant who had been home from Vietnam only a month before coming on this cruise, for which he had volunteered. He was a bachelor and had a good combat record.

Also before I left, I placed a personal call to the Commandant of the Marine Corps, because I would be dealing with the man who was next after the vice president in line for the presidency. General Greene took my call and asked that I call back after seeing Albert. He told me a Marine Corps logistics aircraft was due in Roosevelt Roads the next day. He strongly recommended I put our wayward sergeant on the flight with a "chaser" (escort) to return him to Camp Lejeune.

I called ahead to make an appointment with Albert. Soon I was talking with him face to face in his hotel room. He was a small, gentle man, much more concerned about the Marine than about himself. When he learned that the Marine was a recently returned combat veteran with some apparent problem, he stated that he would not prefer charges against the man. He himself had suffered no serious injury. I gave him the most sincere apology any person has ever received and told him we would fly the man back for medical evaluation the next day, if he had no objection. He had none, and reassured me that he bore no ill will, just concern for the young man's welfare.

That afternoon I drafted a Serious Incident Report (SIR) addressed to almost every important person in the US Department of Defense, including both my old boss, Admiral McDonald, and General Greene. The sergeant was later admitted as a psychiatric patient, found to be alcohol dependent, and placed in a treatment center in Portsmouth, Virginia. He was never tried for an offense. This was the only major liberty incident of the entire seven months' deployment.

After the much-needed break and liberty in San Juan, we set sail for Panama and jungle training at the Army's Fort Sherman in the Canal Zone. Our squadron left

Guam and operated from an Air Force base for the week. They left two of its "birds" at Fort Sherman to be used for search and rescue, if needed. About 100 of the squadron troops volunteered to go through jungle survival training with the ground Marines.

We used most of our Vietnam vets as assistant instructors to help the shorthanded Army instructors. The course taught survival, tactics, escape and evasion, and confidence building. We were the first unit in the history of the school that had no students refuse to execute some of the more harrowing "slides for life" on cliff-climbing obstacles. I was proud of my troops.

Brigadier General Wheeler flew to Panama to visit us for a few days and stayed for the graduation exercise. Our companies emerged from the jungle only an hour before the traditional graduation parade was to begin. We didn't rehearse or make any other special preparations for the formal review before General Wheeler and the Army lieutenant general commanding US forces in the Canal Zone. The troops ate a cold C-ration breakfast on the parade field, tucked in their filthy, sweat-stained utilities, and executed a flawless parade and review, dirty, grease-paint-smeared, and proud. Our squadron timed its fly-over to occur just as our troops passed the reviewing stand. They marched directly from the parade field to the docks 200 yards away, embarked in landing craft, and departed for our ships in the bay.

One helicopter returned from the fly-over to hover about 60 feet above the reviewing stand. A Marine sergeant dove out of the helicopter, fast-rappelled down a rope directly in front of the Army general, saluted, and presented him with our unit plaque. The helicopter returned to retrieve the sergeant and pick me up. In a blink of an eye, the last of the Marine Caribbean Landing Force was gone. We had planned it that way: quick, neat, and professional. CARIB 4-66 and its Second Battalion, 8th Marines had come a long way!

We had asked General Wheeler's assistance in having the Second Division Drum and Bugle Corps join us for a few weeks during the winter. We were planning a number of port calls, and the Drum and Bugle Corps would help with the ceremonies ashore. Several days later, a message informed us it would be waiting at the Marine Barracks in San Juan when we returned from Panama.

I was now able to report that all deployed units were fully combat ready in all categories. The only exception was the pilot shortage in HMM-162, and we could remedy that within 24 hours. We were ready for specialized advanced training, more liberty, and a much anticipated visit to Curaçao and Aruba in the Dutch Antilles Islands.

Our next visit to San Juan went smoothly. We began to make preparations for the visit to the Dutch Antilles. We were to compete against various Dutch teams in several sports. First, we had to create a soccer team out of whole cloth to play against an obviously skilled Dutch Navy/Marine team. This wasn't easy. As for the other sports: our basketball teams held a tournament to see who would represent us against the single Dutch team, and we pieced together rifle and pistol teams of experienced shooters. We expected to compete also in a military field meet, and we prepared tug-of-war and fieldball teams. Tug of war was pretty straightforward, but our fieldballers had to learn to push an eight-foot inflated sphere down the field and across a goal line.

Ceremonially, we had the Drum and Bugle Corps, and our Commodore had a lot of ideas. He had always wanted to have a joint Navy-Marine ceremonial parade with me serving as the commanding officer of troops and with a joint staff, leading three Navy platoons and three Marine platoons marching as two parade companies. He would serve as the reviewing official and host an honored guest. We would conduct the ceremonial parade every day on the docks at Willemstad, after which the ships would be open for visits by the public.

Three of the five ships visited Curaçao. Two smaller ships visited Aruba. These visits were the highlight of our deployment. The Dutch Antilles were small replicas of Rotterdam and the Hague: quaint, clean, and well constructed. The port of Willemstad was in the heart of Curaçao. A swinging bridge opened to allow our three ships to enter through a narrow canal. The Second Division Drum and Bugle Corps played on the flight deck while the sailors and Marines manned the rail as we entered the picturesque city.

The Dutch military and civilian communities just couldn't do enough for us. We won the basketball game by a large margin, but were wiped out in the soccer match 22 – 0. We won the fieldball and tug of war, and won the pistol match but were edged out in the rifle competition. The troops and sailors held a huge picnic for their Dutch counterparts under the sergeant majors' and leading chief petty officers' careful eyes. We had many beer-happy troops and sailors, but no problems.

The Navy and Marine officers hosted a formal reception at the beautiful hotel in an old converted fort. Everything seemed to be going well. The Commodore and I were sitting with the Dutch VIP's and their wives in the bar, watching swimmers through a picture window, when suddenly I saw a Marine lieutenant, fully clothed in his dress white uniform, dive past the window. He had taken a dare to dive off a balcony two stories above the pool. He turned out to be the battalion motor transport officer, who had been an Olympic-class diver in college. He went through some of the most artful agony I could arrange for him in the next few weeks. He learned a lot before he enjoyed liberty again.

Our final tattoo was memorable. The Dutch Navy band came down to give us a farewell serenade after the pass in review. I had to admit that "my sailors" looked just as good as the Marines, and they knew it. Ben Porter was a very proud commodore.

Toward the end of our Caribbean tour, a number of the men's wives came to San Juan to visit us while we were having a scheduled week's port stay there. My wife Carol was with the group, which arrived just as we received an unexpected order to deploy to St. Croix. We were to conduct a ceremonial parade and fly-over honoring the 50th anniversary of the Virgin Islands' becoming a part of the United States. We obtained permission to take the visiting wives aboard *Guam* for the short journey from San Juan to Christensted, St. Croix. We were able to get hotel accommodations for the women on short notice, and this unplanned diversion added an extra sparkle to the wives' short visit with their husbands.

We ended our cruise with a final brigade exercise. General Wheeler was again our commander. We held the exercise in the Salinas National Forest, a jungle-like training facility for the Puerto Rican National Guard. Task Group 45.9, or Carib 4-66, as we were known, reached its professional peak on this counter-guerrilla exercise. Carib 4-66 became history, but its Marines had become my largest and most potent Band of Brothers. We had improved consistently, and we set high standards for the units that followed. My greatest regret was that this superbly trained and motivated group of men must now disband. More than half of them would go to units in Vietnam: the rest of us would go a bit later.

My new regimental commander, Colonel Bill Mulvey, greeted me upon our return with the news that I would become his executive officer. The tour as regimental executive officer was interesting but brief. Early in the tour I received unexpected orders to attend a three-week IBM computer course at Poughkeepsie, N.Y. While at the school, which I enjoyed immensely, I learned that my next job would be on the division staff as the operations officer. This interesting and challenging staff billet fitted my background, training, and motivations to a tee. I relished carrying out my new responsibilities.

On April 4, 1968, in Memphis, Tennessee, Martin Luther King died of an assassin's bullet. This tragic event led to widespread rioting, burning, and looting in major cities all over the United States. The massive civil disturbance fed on itself, and went far beyond the ability of the National Guard to control it. Regular Army units went on immediate alert—and I received almost simultaneous phone calls from our superiors in Fleet Marine Force, Atlantic and Headquarters, Marine Corps. Later that day all military forces were placed on alert and messages from Washington began pouring into our communications center.

The instructions were confusing at first. Although one third of our division was deployed outside of the country, we were initially ordered to form some 40 battalions. Obviously, some non-expert had used simple arithmetic to arrive at this vastly excessive number. Numerous calls via several channels got the original numbers rescinded and set up a meeting in the Pentagon for 11 a.m. the next day. Major General Ed Wheeler, who had assumed command of the division, designated me, in my role as Division Operations Officer, to represent him at the working conference.

Our discussions the night before I departed for Washington reflected the doubts everyone had about what our nation was facing at the time. As Marines, we were reluctant to assume a Civil Disturbance role. Since our nation's beginning, the regular Army and the National Guard had dealt with civil disorders. It was in their charters, but this terrible backlash was obviously going to be more than they could handle.

Our people dug out long-forgotten field manuals on riot and civil disobedience control and dusted them off. They checked stocks of non-lethal chemical agents. They planned modifications to trucks. They investigated the location of stocks of helmet visors, shields, and batons for troops; special communications; and a crash training course. We chose the industrial area of our base as a site for training exercises.

When I finally arrived at home well after midnight, I had a briefcase and a head full of information. We could put our available five infantry battalions, four artillery battalions, and one shore party battalion in the field in five to seven days if the equipment was available. We could have two battalions ready on 48 hours' notice— again, if equipment was available. This was our realistic, pragmatic first offer. We could offer additional battalions if we had time to restructure and train other combat support battalions. We had no idea which direction we would have to go. We didn't want to mix Marine and Army troops in a city, and we wanted Marines to be commanded by Marines.

Even now, years later, it is difficult to describe the feelings of those of us representing Fleet Marine Forces, Atlantic as we flew into Washington early the next morning. The city was burning. Black smoke covered all of central Washington, and National Airport was closed to all but essential traffic. As soon as we had landed there,. cars and vans whisked us to the Pentagon. Our first choice was to defend Washington.

It was among the worst-hit cities. We had a good staging area at our base in nearby Quantico, Virginia, and already had first-class troops at the Marine Barracks in Washington. What's more, we had a reason for using Marines to guard the Capitol and the White House: part of our mission was to guard the Congress and the President "from all enemies, foreign or domestic."

Before this meeting could make any decisions, several of us not-so-senior officers had to almost shout down a couple of ill-informed young White House staffers who thought they were running the show. Then each of the major commands gave an assessment of its abilities and reaction times. Marine representatives from our Norfolk headquarters, Marine Base Quantico, and the Washington Marine Barracks supported me. My division was the largest Marine contingent, and it could react more quickly than any Army unit except the 82nd Airborne Division. The conference did assign the Marines to the DC area as our primary focus: the Army, with National Guard assistance, took Detroit, Chicago, LA, and the other major cities.

The meeting accomplished a great deal. It allocated forces to objectives, published schedules, established a command and control system, and set priorities on critical supplies and material. I reported to General Wheeler's Chief of Staff, Colonel Charlie Walker, by telephone: he would need every available minute to get the ball rolling. By the time I arrived home that night, we had received official confirmation for decisions announced earlier. It contained no meaningful changes and we went to work!

Our two-day training program, crash "hardening" of vehicles, and psychological preparation of the troops were largely successful. It was a sad and depressing mission, but all our Marines treated it with professionalism. A small number of black Marines asked for "request mast" with the Commanding General to avoid serving in the deploying units. General Wheeler talked to this group of about 20 Marines for almost an hour. Most of them opted to rejoin their units, while the remaining few elected to face disciplinary action for refusing to obey a lawful order.

It was a terrible chapter in our nation's history. But it demonstrated that, in order for the military to assist civil authorities during a national domestic crisis, we must have disciplined troops led by professional officers. We told our troops that their mission was to protect people and help local authorities restore law and order. I was proud to have been a part of this unwanted but well executed mission.

I received orders to attend the Army War College in Carlisle, Pennsylvania. School was to start in August of 1968. After a 10-month course, I would be headed for Vietnam. I was surprised to be among the first members of my class to attend a top-level school. Being an infantry officer, I had made the Army War College my first choice. The class of 215 students included eight Marines. Three of us were coming from the Second Marine Division.

We began planning for the move by discussing the most important things first: transporting Linda's horse Suribachi and the riding facilities available in Carlisle. Carol and I used a long weekend to visit Carlisle and talk to Marine students and school officials. We were duly impressed with this lovely little college town in the heart of Pennsylvania. For the horse we located a private stable at which Carol would also be able to teach youngsters riding. The stable owners had a beautiful thoroughbred that Linda could ride in numerous area shows.

Before we left Camp Lejeune, Chip surprised both Carol and me when he approached me and asked for my help in getting an appointment to the Naval Academy. I had encouraged him to seek an NROTC scholarship, and he had been leaning toward Georgia Tech, Chapel Hill, or Vanderbilt. When I asked him why he wanted to go to the Naval Academy, he responded, almost sheepishly, that he had decided that he wanted to become a regular officer. On his own merits and with some good hometown endorsements, he was able to obtain a 1969 congressional appointment from Congressman Jamie Whitten of Mississippi. (Whitten's predecessor, Will Whittington, had appointed me in 1946.)

Our departure from the Second Marine Division was a very happy one. Our many friends gave us a resounding sendoff with a round of parties and "sayonaras." Getting Suribachi into a horse carrier took six strong men about an hour, but we finally got him launched. Carlisle High School turned out to be an ideal college preparatory school for Chip. The school put him in college-level classes and pushed him hard. He was up to it, and it paid great dividends during that tough first year at Annapolis. Linda, too, learned to concentrate and use her study time wisely. She really got her act together while we were in Carlisle, and became a gifted rider as well as an excellent student. It was to be a memorable year for the entire family.

Chapter 18

Postgraduate Year at Carlisle Barracks
"Pondering the Big Picture"

The Army has its top-level school in Carlisle, Pennsylvania, at the site of the old Indian School. This school is a true postgraduate institution—a mind stretcher that puts its students through a year of concentrated reading, deep research, creative writing, reflection, study of national and international problems, and pondering the big picture. War fighting skills are not taught. Most students are middle-grade to senior lieutenant colonels or Navy commanders, along with a few colonels. These students are the cream of the crop in their services, and from their ranks come most of the admirals and generals selected later for senior leadership, especially in the Army and the Marine Corps. Less so in the other services.

The Class of 1969 convened in August of 1968 with slightly more than two hundred students. The eight Marines in the class included one aviator, one artillery officer, and six infantry officers. About half of the class had completed one tour in Vietnam and the rest of us were to go there when the course ended.

As we look back, Carol and I both feel that this was the most enjoyable and personally rewarding year of my entire career. One reason for this is the contrast between this year's pace and job pressures I had previously experienced. I had to look after no one but myself and my family. I could learn at my own pace. The workload was there, but any pressure was self generated. And worlds of activities—social, athletic, and professional—were also there. You might say we "worked hard, worked out hard, and played hard."

On most weekends during the horse show season, we towed the horse trailer to jumping and riding events throughout central Pennsylvania. Our daughter garnered more than her share of ribbons, along with an occasional bruise, in very competitive shows. Both of the youngsters became excellent skiers and visited the nearby resorts frequently with school-sponsored groups.

Carol enjoyed her teaching and riding. Her earnings largely offset whatever horse expenses we incurred. Linda's horse Suribachi had developed leg problems and couldn't jump anymore. Linda and Carol both had the use of a beautiful, well-trained thoroughbred jumper, so I had a local veterinarian take on Suribachi as a special project. He restored him to what appeared to be full health. After having thought that he was headed for a glue factory only three months before, we were pleased to be able to sell him to an experienced horse trader for considerably more than we had paid for him. I never looked back from that deal, my first and only attempt at horse trading.

At school the curriculum was an interesting mix of committee seminars, preparation of group reports, lectures by distinguished visitors, and personal research projects—all set within a series of one-month sub-courses. Each sub-course assigned us to committees for its duration. These small groups enabled us to rub elbows with a large number of people, and the leadership responsibilities rotated among the participants.

My research project, or thesis, was the focus of much of my interest and energy. I chose a difficult topic, one that no other student attempted alone. General William Westmoreland, the new Army Chief of Staff, while speaking to us early in the school year, had challenged us to study and write about "The Role of the Press in Vietnam." He

143

obviously had been terribly frustrated as Commander, MACV in trying to deal with the media. After giving it considerable thought and discussing my ideas with a faculty counselor, I chose the topic and had my outline approved. It was a difficult but enlightening project and was to prove more useful than I could ever have expected. An Army student team of five officers also chose that topic, but approached it in a much different way than I did. I learned later that General Westmoreland had asked for both of the papers to be delivered to his office immediately after they were turned in early in 1969. Later he wrote me a short note of appreciation, saying that he wished he had had the benefit of my reflections while he was serving in Vietnam. It was a gracious, thoughtful gesture, especially in view of the criticisms contained in my paper.

We graduated in June—as did my son Chip. The two proud grandmothers and my sister visited us so that they could attend the two ceremonies. Chip had passed all of the various physical and mental hurdles for the Naval Academy and would be sworn in just before I was to depart for duty in Vietnam. I had every reason to expect to command a battalion of Marines in combat.

As we drove out the main gate of Carlisle Barracks with Skipper Dog leaning out one of the back windows, I wasn't aware that someone was having my orders modified. When I checked in with my detailer at Headquarters, Marine Corps two days later, I learned of the modification. It floored me. I was being assigned to Headquarters, III MAF. This was the joint staff in DaNang that controlled all U.S. forces in the Northern Provinces, called I Corps. Someone wanted me to serve on his staff. A lieutenant colonel doesn't get a list of all the whys and wherefores of these assignment changes, nor does he have a lot of choice. Now I would have to figure out a way to work myself into a command billet.

The day before I was to leave, this proud father drove his 18-year-old son over to the Naval Academy and swore him in as a Midshipman, US Navy, after he had his blond locks shorn. He looked so young! As I drove back to Alexandria that day, I thanked the Good Lord again for the miraculous recovery that fine young man had made in his early years when a skilled board of physicians had forecast a short and handicapped life for him. I prayed that he would hold up to the physical challenges of the next four years. He was not the product of any preparatory school or college, but he had a good mind and would know how to use it after he adjusted to the confusing priorities of Plebe Year.

Linda would be attending a new high school, T. C. Williams, and was already making plans to do some riding at a farm in nearby northern Virginia horse country. It was a comforting thing to move back into our own home, a first for us. I expected that I would be assigned duty in Washington, either in the Pentagon or at Marine Headquarters, when I returned from Vietnam.

The job that lay immediately before me was to make the best of the year ahead. When I arrived in Vietnam in the summer of 1969, we were in our fifth year of this land war in Southeast Asia. No end was in sight.

144

Chapter 19

Vietnam, the Fifth Year, 1969 – 1970

In July of 1969 a chartered Continental Airlines Boeing 707 deposited me in Danang's heat and humidity. A small bus took me across the river to Camp Horn, home of the Third Marine Amphibious Force (III MAF) headquarters. Camp Horn had been a French army post, and the SeaBees had expanded it to accommodate this large joint service staff. Commanding it was a Marine lieutenant general, Herman Nickerson.

Upon reporting to the III MAF staff, I learned that my new job would be that of Secretary of the General Staff, replacing Lieutenant Colonel Jim Stemple. I spent a day or so trying to wriggle out of the job before Jim was detached, but my efforts were fruitless. Staff Secretary I would be.

It was a backbreaking job, one that had me working directly for both General Nickerson and his chief of staff, Brigadier General George Dooley. Every message, piece of paper, or person going to the commanding general had to have my approval. I learned to live on a few hours' sleep per night, along with an occasional short nap, and the new job became a challenge to be met and mastered.

Our offices were in old French barracks, designed in the 1930's to house a colonial regional headquarters. The SeaBees had constructed SEA-huts (Southeast Asia huts) for billeting and additional offices, and we used the familiar Quonset huts for a chapel, troop mess halls, and the officers' club and mess. Bomb shelters, trenches, and sandbagged machine-gun positions dotted the area, which was surrounded by barbed wire and a stout security fence.

Across the street from the main entrance, the Vietnamese Army maintained a huge ammunition depot. Most of it was open storage among revetments designed to lessen the effect of any blast. I asked if the fairly frequent rocket attacks had ever hit the ammunition dump and was told that the rockets were very inaccurate and had never hit anything vital in the area.

I was billeted in a BOQ (bachelor officers' quarters) about 100 yards from our one-story headquarters. The generals were billeted in house trailers drawn up in an area about 200 yards from the headquarters. A few trailers were reserved for VIP visitors. The generals' offices were air conditioned, a sheer delight for me when I sat in on a staff meeting or briefing.

Assisting me were an administrative officer, a gunnery sergeant steno/writer, several clerks, and a message center team of four Marine communicators, who processed all of the message traffic, in and out, under my supervision. Also, although he did not report to me, the MAF Protocol Officer, a lieutenant colonel aviator, worked under my supervision coordinating a full squadron of VIP helicopters that constantly ferried senior people into and out of our headquarters.

Flag and general officers used helicopters for all but local transportation. The weekly commanders' conference that General Nickerson conducted made our headquarters seem like a beehive, with the comings and goings of helicopters carrying key personnel from all over I Corps.

Coordinating all briefings and conferences was one of my main responsibilities. Principal commanders were expected to attend in person unless there was something approaching a total disaster occurring in their commands. Few were ever willing to admit they had a problem of that magnitude, although there were a couple of times when Major General W.K. Jones's Third Marine Division was embroiled in heavy fighting and he elected to send a representative.

Major General Ormond Simpson, who had been the commanding general of the Second Division when I served with it, commanded the First Marine Division, with headquarters across the river in Danang. He was always on a short leash with General Nickerson. First of all, he was nearby. More important, however, was the fact that earlier in the war General Nickerson had commanded the First Division himself. When he returned to Vietnam, he still seemed to regard it as his division. On a number of occasions, although he well knew it was contrary to all accepted practices, he relieved unit commanders in the division directly, without consulting General Simpson. Simpson, a strong commander, protested forcefully, but most of the removals were deserved and remained in effect.

My initial impressions of General Nickerson were not favorable. I thought him too protective of members of his own personal staff, especially his overly zealous aides, and intolerant and abrupt with his principal subordinate commanders—at times even insulting. These impressions changed with time, and I came to see his strengths. He was superb in performing the duties of the senior Marine in Vietnam. I learned a great deal from writing most of his sensitive personal messages as he communicated with General Abrams; the Commandant of the Marine Corps; the Commanding General, Fleet Marine Force, Pacific; the Commander of the Seventh Fleet; the Commanding General, XXIV Corps; and his senior Army and Navy commanders. Then too, I watched him deal with the never-ending stream of VIP visitors: top DOD and Navy Department civilian secretaries; journalists like Joseph Alsop; entertainers like Bob Hope and Martha Raye; and a good many Defense Department "experts." General Nickerson could charm any of these people, but only if he chose to do so.

I had to rise at 4:30 every morning to start putting together a message board for each of our three generals: General Nick, Brigadier General George Dooley, the Chief of Staff, and Major General George Bowman, Deputy Commanding General, III MAF. These boards dealt with every imaginable subject, some mundane and routine, some highly classified and very sensitive. Each was slightly different from the others. I had to decide who should see what and what would be processed for staff action without one of the general officers seeing it. It wasn't an easy call, but I soon established a system that had one officer and three Marines helping me. We could process the entire bag in about an hour. Each board usually wound up with about 100 messages on it.

I prepared the master board for General Nickerson. My assistants prepared the boards for the other two generals and a third for me to read more carefully later. When the Chief of Staff finished reading his board, it went to the Deputy Chief of Staff, Colonel Poggemeyer. We delivered General Nick's board to his "hootch" (trailer) early enough for him to get started on it during his breakfast. If the board contained something urgent, we highlighted it and put it on top.

On a few occasions, red hot messages received during the night needed his attention before morning. When this happened, I was alerted and approved the message for immediate delivery to the general by his aide. This same procedure applied to phone calls, which usually came in on the "scrambler," the secure classified information telephone line that General Abrams always used for talking with his principal commanders. I took all of these calls and decided whether or not to awaken the general.

I don't believe I ever got more than three hours of continuous sleep during the five or more months I spent at III MAF. I usually got around two. I managed to take 15- or 20-minute naps in the guest-VIP office during occasional lulls, and these kept me going.

Early in the fall of 1969, John Warner, the new Undersecretary of the Navy, visited III MAF, ostensibly to familiarize himself with what the Navy and Marine units were doing in Vietnam. Warner, an enlisted sailor in World War II and a Marine communications officer in the Korean War, also had something else in mind. His aide de camp, Lieutenant Colonel Bill Leftwich, an old friend of mine, told me what it was.

As a second lieutenant in the Marine Corps Reserve, Warner had served with a Marine aviation squadron in Korea in 1951, and had occasionally gone on combat missions, flying as a "back seater" in Marine night fighters. Now he wanted to fly back seat in an F-4 fighter-bomber on a strike over North Vietnam.

The secretary had finished his command briefing and was returning to pay a private visit to the commanding general. I had previously alerted General Nickerson to the coming request, and he smiled like the Cheshire Cat. Not long after Warner had entered the general's office, the buzzer summoned me and the Chief of Staff, George Dooley. General Nick turned to me and said, "Charlie, Mr. Warner wants to fly north on one of our strikes over Hanoi tonight." With a wink that only Dooley and I could see, he continued, "I want you to call General Gayle Thrash, over in the Wing, and tell him to lay on a seat for the Secretary tonight in an F-4. He's been through the pressure thing recently and brought his own flying togs and G-suit. He'll need a helmet. Tell him I'll have Mr. Warner over there by 1500 hours so he can eat dinner in their mess tonight. Also, tell him to call me back when it's all been arranged."

I carried out my orders. General Thrash didn't blink an eye. He said that he would use his group commanding officer as pilot and they would blow the hell out of some palm trees in Laos. He would call the commanding general to get "targeting instructions" on which type of enemy palm trees to blow away.

The new secretary flew on a rigged mission that took off with the big guys, rendezvoused with other aircraft, and formed up and then peeled off while talking a good game. He had a cover bird following him to ensure his safe return: there was no way CG III MAF would send this high-ranking civilian into harm's way over North Vietnam on his personal whim. But Mr. Secretary Warner was able to stand at the bar late that night and have a snort with the returning vets who had been "up North." Mission accomplished. Senator Warner, this is the real story! (He'll learn this for the first time when this book is published.)

The enemy forces in our vicinity were not equipped with long-range artillery, nor could they have concealed it for long if they had been. What they did have was 122mm Soviet rockets. Although they were inaccurate, they were simple to set and fire. The Vietcong used them effectively. They had enough range to threaten our entire Danang complex.

The First Marine Regiment patrolled the area from which these rockets were launched. It was, quite naturally, called the "rocket belt." In September of 1969, activity in the rocket belt reached a new high. Despite increased Marine patrols and contacts, the VC main force units would rush into the belt after diverting the Marines elsewhere, then would set up 10 or 12 rockets, fire them, and vanish into caves or prepared hiding places. Our patrols managed to intercept most of these attempts, but they missed one significant one.

On that occasion, the VC launched six rockets in the general direction of our III MAF headquarters. The first round landed in the open about 40 yards from my BOQ room at 3:30 in the morning. It made one helluva blast, and the alarm sirens went off almost at once, sending us all to our battle stations. Mine was in the command bunker, which was immediately behind our headquarters building. Grabbing flack jacket, helmet, boots, and my pistol, I flew out the door. One or two other rounds landed in our compound as I sprinted the 120 yards to the bunker.

When I reached the command center in the underground bunker, my first concern was to locate General Nickerson. He was up and was in his own small bunker, along with his two aides, waiting for the fire to lift before coming to the command center. Brigadier General Dulacki, the G-3, was in the command center and in communication with the CG and the Headquarters Commander in his bunker.

Our large bunker was eight or nine feet below ground level, and had a huge blast-proof door at its entrance. Marines guarded the stairwell and entrance outside to ensure that only authorized personnel entered. Within minutes of arriving, I found my niche, finished putting on my uniform, and looked for a cup of coffee. I noticed a major, the Intelligence Watch Officer, standing immediately in front of the five-inch-thick door.

Then the world seemed to explode. It was like being at ground zero when an atomic bomb went off. The huge door flew open and threw this large officer across the 40-foot room as if he were a beanbag. He hit the far wall with a splash of blood and slid to the ground. Dirt, dust, and smoke were everywhere. The three Marines who had been guarding the entrance came flying into the room like bowling balls, banging into tables, people, and walls. At the same time, there was the sound of a massive "Whoosh" overhead.

Our first thought was that we had taken several direct hits, but cooler heads noted that nothing the enemy had could have produced this effect, unless . . . Then the dawn began to break. Unless they had hit the ARVN ammunition depot and gotten a major detonation. And they had, as we soon learned. A lucky hit: a single rocket had fallen directly into almost 200 tons of antitank mines and set them off—at least 400,000 pounds of explosives. The result had been like a not-so-small nuclear explosion with its resulting shock wave.

Later inspection showed that about sixty percent of the III MAF compound had been leveled. Those structures still standing were severely damaged. There were many casualties, but we lost only two Marines. The injuries were mostly superficial: much ear damage and many cuts from rocks and flying glass. Even the major that flew so grotesquely across the room and up against a concrete wall survived. He had multiple fractures and internal injuries, but returned to duty after spending some time in a hospital in Japan. What saved him were his helmet and flack jacket and, I should say, a strong body and disposition.

There were no more explosions that evening, but it was a night to remember. I ventured out later and checked over our office building. It was probably the most durable in the camp and survived better than most, but it would need a new roof and internal reinforcement of the walls. All of the windows were gone, and shattered glass was everywhere. Much to my surprise, my typewriter and a pile of papers next to it

148

didn't seem at all disturbed. Most of our files survived, and the safes were all intact. The always-ready SeaBees arrived the next day and started rebuilding. It didn't take long. (Thank God it wasn't the rainy season.)

The ARVN ammo dump wasn't there any more. There was just a huge hole, and there were pieces of ordnance all over the area. The enemy had had a very successful night, but the very small number of fatalities was the good news for our side. Our people had reached their shelters before the big blast, and the system had worked. If we had been in our places of duty when the ammo dump went up, there would have been very few survivors.

On several occasions, when an infantry battalion commander in the First Division had been incapacitated by wounds, killed in action, or relieved for cause, I had presented myself to General Nickerson in full field gear and told him I could leave immediately to assume command of whatever unit it was. On my third try, he forcefully ordered me out—then recalled me immediately for a short conversation. Ole Herman the German finally showed his softer side. He told me not to give up trying. He needed me, but he would see what we could do after General Dooley left. The G-3, Leo Dulacki, would move up shortly to relieve Dooley, and Dooley didn't want to have to break in a new staff secretary just before he left.

General Simpson, who had tried on two occasions to get me freed to command a battalion, was about to be relieved by General Ed Wheeler, who was moving down after having been Deputy Commander of XXIV Corps. One of my most memorable evenings of this crummy war was one on which General Simpson got me sprung from my duties to join him as a guest at his mess, across the river. This was a brief but sentimental reunion of about 12 of us who had served under General Simpson in the Second Division. His remarks after dinner that evening were about the "Band of Brothers" and how its camaraderie perseveres through every conceivable adversity. He gave me a moving toast as his leading apostle, with my "Band of Brothers" leadership concept. I had two glasses of wine that evening, the first alcohol I'd had since arriving in July. Colonel Jim Harrell, the G-1 and an old friend from Hawaii days, escorted me home with two heavily armed jeeps of his Marines. It was a morale-boosting night— one I sorely needed.

Other senior visitors to III MAF occasionally brightened my hectic days. Admiral Bringle, Commander, Seventh Fleet, had been an acquaintance since he accompanied the football team on our summer cruise during my Naval Academy days. On one occasion, he invited General Nickerson, General Dooley, and me out to his cruiser flagship for a briefing and lunch. It was a brief respite and an opportunity to learn more about the Navy's operational problems.

Lieutenant General H. W. Buse, CG, FMFPAC, visited Vietnam each quarter. The most poignant visit by a senior visitor, however, came at Christmas, when Admiral John McCain, CINC PACIFIC, arrived at III MAF, as he did each year to "spend Christmas with his Marines." Admiral McCain arrived on December 23. He received the usual updates and staff briefings, then spent all of December 24 flying around I Corps, visiting Army, Navy, and Marine units in the field, where practicable. He then returned to HQ, dined with General Nickerson in his mess, and seemed thoroughly bushed after his travels. His aide checked him into his trailer and then secured for the night. It was about 11 p.m. on Christmas Eve, my 42nd birthday, and we were still working away in my office. I had dismissed all but two enlisted Marines, but General Dooley was at work, as always.

I was typing an action brief to attach to a large staff bundle when I looked up. There stood Admiral McCain. I jumped up and he waved me down. He knew me from my tour as aide to the Chief of Naval Operations, and he asked, "Got any decent hot coffee around here, Charlie?" I replied that we always had some hot coffee but it may not meet Navy standards. My sergeant had him a mug in no time.

He just wanted to talk. He recalled that I was from Mississippi and mentioned that his father, also an admiral, was born and raised in Mississippi, went to Ole Miss, and had been a founder of my fraternity, Phi Delta Theta. As he reminisced about his roots in the south and talked of his love for the people there, he never once mentioned his son, John, who was then a POW in North Vietnam. That son, at this writing Senator John McCain, was in both of our minds when the admiral asked me, "Son, do you all have a midnight communion service nearby? I have a special need to talk to the Lord about one of my children tonight." I told him I planned to attend the service at 11:30 and would be proud if I could take him with me.

As we walked slowly on down to the small chapel, I could see that my alert sergeant had preceded us and saved two seats near the left front. The small sanctuary was packed. The service was brief, as it had to be, and I know we both asked the Good Lord for some of the same favors, among them the safe return of his naval aviator son from the dungeons of the "Hanoi Hilton," as the prisoners called their special hellhole. Kneeling at the small altar next to this very special human being was a most moving experience. I truly felt that something unusual was happening to both of us.

When we returned to my office, that splendid, thoughtful man thanked me for taking the time to visit with a lonesome old man on one of his most difficult nights. I told him I just knew we got through to the Good Lord in great style tonight.

Years later, after Admiral McCain had retired, when his son had returned home but was still broken and suffering, we all met at a banquet in Washington, D. C. I was a new brigadier general then, serving as Congressional liaison. As we met briefly and the two McCains were introduced to my wife, Admiral McCain turned to his son and said, "Cooper is the officer who took me to Christmas Eve Midnight Mass in 1969 at Danang, the night the Good Lord told me he would make sure you got home safely."

Among our never-ending stream of visitors in late 1969, one individual was unique. Columnist Joseph Alsop, the better known of the two Alsop brothers, was a hawk on the Vietnam War. His widely read syndicated column consistently supported the US efforts to help the South Vietnamese. He was a strong proponent of "cutting the head off of the snake," meaning taking the war to Hanoi and Haiphong. He strongly supported blockading, mining the harbors, and using strategic air power to rain massive destruction on the enemy's cities. All of these things happened later under President Nixon, but they had not yet been authorized when Alsop visited us late in 1969. He always seemed to be extraordinarily well informed and decisive in his commentary on the tactical and strategic factors influencing the war. While serving as Secretary of the III MAF staff, I learned why.

His visit was the subject of a lengthy, extremely sensitive series of "back channel" messages from Washington, Hawaii, and Saigon. He was to be given access to and briefed on any and every bit of intelligence our command had available. Nothing was to be held back, if he requested access. No one individual other than Admiral McCain

150

and General Abrams had ever been offered so much closely held information. Alsop shared his insights with General Nickerson and our intelligence officer, Colonel John Canton, in my presence. He was an interesting individual and obviously had the ear and total approval of the nation's Commander in Chief. Hawkish columnists were not in great supply in late 1969! President Nixon valued him as an ally as he tried to find a way out of the morass he had inherited from the Johnson administration.

General Creighton Abrams visited us often and communicated with our CG by secure telephone several times a week. I answered the phone when he called, and we established some sort of relationship. Like many of the senior Marine generals I had grown up under, he addressed me by my last name, "Cooper." I liked his style and admired the way he operated. While some few senior officers seemed to delight in belittling a briefing officer when they received information that appeared to be faulty, Abrams was not so inclined. All of our principal commanders were usually present when he visited, and he would deal with them on an issue, not pick on the briefing officer. It may appear to be a small point, but it was an indicator of his style as a senior commander. He and General Nickerson seemed to get along well, and in this my opinion should be fairly accurate: my job kept me "close to the throne".

Lieutenant General Mel Zais, CG XXIV Corps, was to replace General Nickerson as the Marines drew down. On one occasion when General Nickerson was finally persuaded to take a few days to visit his wife in Hong Kong after more than a year on his second Vietnam tour, Zais moved up to assume his job temporarily at our headquarters. He called me into his temporary office and gave me my marching orders. He said, "I'm here just to keep this train on the track tactically. I don't want to get involved in any of your Marine Corps business or impede your paper flow on any subject. Unless it is a tactical matter, I don't want to see or hear about it. Understand?" I nodded and he continued. "My aide will get with you and lay out a visit schedule for me each day while I'm here. Weather permitting, I'll stay in the field with the tactical units until about 1800 each day. At that time I'd like a short office brief from the G-3 and G-2 on any significant matters I need to be aware of. Other matters that may need my attention will be at your discretion. I'd appreciate your filling the Deputy CG and Chief of Staff in on how I'll be operating."

He was a damn good soldier and a gentleman to boot. We moved a lot of paper while General Nickerson was gone, much of which Nickerson had sent back for rework! At the same time, General Dooley was finally relaxing a little and cleaning out his "Too Hard!" box before he was to leave us.

In monitoring the vast amount of information that came into our headquarters, I had a unique opportunity to observe the sophisticated tactics of the enemy and the way they eluded our forces. Our emphasis at this time was on searching out and destroying the enemy's base areas and supplies. This occasionally forced the enemy into open battle, where we had a huge advantage in firepower.

At this time, we were also evolving some new weapons. One of them was the Integrated Observation Device, commonly called the IOD. It was a laser rangefinder integrated with a massive pair of battleship binoculars. You could watch a man shave almost two miles away with these long-distance glasses from the World War II era. They had been the Navy's eyes before radar was developed.

An IOD working with an artillery unit on a commanding piece of terrain could give those guns first-round hits on anything within range. It was better than having a telescopic sight on a 105mm or 155mm cannon. We set up these artillery batteries on key mountain tops in enemy territory and protected them from ground attack, and they began to wreak havoc on the NVA and VC lines of supply and movement. We then added an infrared sight to the binoculars and made the IOD almost as effective at night, when the enemy forces did 95% of their moving. Our intelligence intercepts of the enemy's radio messages told us they were being badly hurt by this new system. Unfortunately, we were never able to produce these remarkable devices in any significant quantity.

The Marine Corps also developed a machine gun that fired 40mm grenades ordinarily used in the M-79 grenade launcher. Issued for test purposes, these guns were great area weapons, but proved to be too heavy for foot troops. Their reliability in bad weather was suspect, but we tested them and found them to be effective. They were especially helpful in a defensive position protecting the fire bases that contained our artillery and command units. They are now standard weapons in the Marine Corps arsenal.

The enemy continued to create a special hell for Marines and soldiers by using booby traps and self-detonating explosive devices. They had unusually sophisticated combat engineers, their most elite troops, called "sappers." Remarkable physical specimens, they were not only adept in the use of explosives, but were also trained to penetrate or breach obstacles such as barbed wire and mine fields. They had developed a technique for recovering dud US aerial bombs and artillery rounds and converting them into massive killing machines that were usually activated by a trip wire or a pressure device. They also had devices that they detonated by radio signal, some consisting of a series of 175mm artillery shells or even 500-pound bombs. These devices could wipe out most of a squad or a platoon and demoralize the survivors.

We countered these deadly devices by changing patrol patterns, spreading our people, using specially trained dogs, patrolling by helicopter, and using their own tactics against them on their routes. It was a never-ending chess match in which they usually avoided frontal contact and nibbled away at the edges until they found a weakness.

Our Chief of Staff George Dooley departed, and was replaced by Brigadier General Leo Dulacki, serving his second Vietnam tour. Having spent most of his tour as the G-3, he was thoroughly tuned in. Brigadier General Thomas Miller, a highly respected and experienced Marine aviator, moved into the G-3 slot. It looked as if, with these two experienced officers on the staff, I would become redundant, and my day of liberation from III MAF was drawing near. Finally, the powers that be agreed to have me relieve Lieutenant Colonel Frank Clark as CO of the First Battalion, Seventh Marines (1/7), then located in the heart of the Que Son Valley, operating out of Fire Support Base Ross. All concerned agreed on a tentative date of 10 January, a date that slipped a few days.

Major General Ed Wheeler, who had become CG of the First Division, welcomed my return to his command. About two weeks before the change, I visited the headquarters of the Seventh Marines at Landing Zone Baldy to meet with Colonel Codispoti, the commander of the Seventh Marines, and later spend a few hours on the ground with Frank Clark at FSB Ross. Clark had worked for General Dulacki before and would take over my job at III MAF. But I almost "bought the farm" en route to this pre-command visit.

The day I was to leave III MAF Headquarters for my brief visit to the Seventh Marines, I went out to the landing zone to catch the hourly MARLOG flight that ferried people and light equipment to the southern part of the division area. A Marine CH-46 helicopter landed, as scheduled, but it was loaded to the gills. I was the only passenger waiting. The pilot yelled for me to hop aboard: there was always room for one more. For some unexplained reason, I declined. I told him to go ahead, I would get a later flight. No need to overcrowd that helicopter, I thought.

The pilot shrugged his shoulders and waved as he pulled maximum power and lifted off. The plane was turning and gaining altitude when suddenly there was a sharp crack: the aircraft lost power and fell straight to the ground from about 500 feet. It hit in the nearby ARVN ammunition dump and immediately started burning. Several of us ran to the site and were able to pull a few of the injured out of the plane before it was totally engulfed in flames. As I recall, there were no more than a handful of survivors, all seriously injured. I caught an Army Huey flight about an hour later: we had an uneventful low-altitude flight into LZ Baldy, where the Seventh Marines had their command post.

It was late in the day by the time I had met with Colonel Codispoti and discussed the tactical situation in the Que Son area. I spent the night in the hootch of his regimental XO, classmate Bane McClintock, and the next morning drove up the dirt road to FSB Ross in a jeep. A helo was to pick me up there for my return in late afternoon.

Clark and his rifle companies had just returned from a bitter fight in the nearby mountains. His battalion rear, weapons units, and three batteries of artillery were in this old Vietnamese base that was now FSB Ross. Elements of a company of SeaBees had arrived to help construct facilities, and the base was crawling with Vietnamese laborers who were digging trenches and working on various projects on the congested hilltop that this small base occupied. The presence of the laborers highlighted the dilemma US commanders faced. We were forced to accept the "native labor" in order to pay them Vietnamese "public works" money we received from the South Vietnamese government. It was "make work" at its finest, but we couldn't turn it down. We knew beyond a doubt that the labor force was contaminated with spies and members of the communist infrastructure that maintained a shadow government and actually taxed the people in this area.

The battalion had moved to the base two or three weeks earlier, and the whole setup looked like an accident waiting to happen. The perimeter had only one thinly stretched roll of concertina wire around it. There were no continuous defensive positions or in-depth alternate defenses. Marines manned the old French-style blockhouses, sandbagged bunkers with roofs, at intervals around the base. They were above ground and offered ideal targets for enemy rocket-propelled grenades. Being inadequately defended, the base was a juicy target for the enemy. As Frank Clark and I made a hasty walk-around inspection, he volunteered that they had a lot of work to do, but he had decided to give priority to the offense rather than the defense. I didn't comment, except to say that I would tell Colonel Codispoti that he needed help in getting the barbed wire necessary for improving the defenses.

Ironically, neither of us knew that the enemy had already scouted the areas of weakness here and had planned for some time to mount a major attack to overrun and destroy this small base that was sitting astride their main supply route. They were waiting for fresh sapper battalions to arrive before undertaking this offensive action.

I didn't get to see Colonel Codispoti as I passed through his headquarters on my way back to III MAF, but I left word about the barbed wire problem with his XO before I picked up a helo that would take me back. When I got back to my office, I told both the new chief of staff and G-3 that I thought the position was perilous. They both showed interest, but it wasn't in the cards for them to be telling the regimental commander what he should be doing. They did remark that I'd have a chance to take care of it in a few days, anyhow.

But the die had been cast, as we later learned from captured sappers. No matter what had been or was being done, the enemy had decided to use everything he had to eliminate FSB Ross and punish the Marines. This led to a carefully planned attack on the night of January 6. Ironically, the battalion commander was absent, taking R&R in Hawaii. The attack involved the main elements of two sapper battalions—their finest assault troops, especially chosen for this task. The commander set up his command post about 200 yards outside the base and used wire communications to control four different penetration echelons. Under the cover of heavy monsoon rains, they were able to breach the wire undetected while Marine guard posts were destroyed by RPG fire. As the infiltrators started to carry out the planned destruction of selected areas, a heavy mortar barrage from their own guns blanketed the entire area for about five minutes. The mortars caught the sappers inside the base unawares, killed some of them outright, and confused and disoriented many of those who survived.

Other elements attacked later. Dozens of sappers got into the base, the artillery positions, and the supply area. At first, the enemy seemed to have people everywhere. Two things the enemy hadn't counted on turned the tide of battle and saved the day. First, his own barrage confused the infiltrators: second, elements of both Company A and Company B had for a variety of reasons entered the perimeter late that day after an extended period in the field. Company A was being reorganized as a Combined Unit Pacification (CUPP) unit, and Company B had come in to stage for a preemptive attack the next day. They were to undergo a very short respite that night. Some accounts suggest that 1/7 had some early warning of this attack from intelligence sources, but no one suggested that to me when I assumed command nine days later. These rifle companies, and particularly Company B, were in a central location, and made the key counterattack at the height of the battle to halt and eject the main enemy force. They killed all of the sappers who had penetrated and were running free inside our area. It was a bloody battle—one that produced many stories of face-to-face encounters.

As the fighting inside the area subsided, our troops swept the area outside of the wire, where they found 38 additional enemy dead and took three wounded prisoners. They also found large stocks of weapons, explosives, and grenades.

At the height of the battle, the assistant S-3, Captain Brian Fagan, pistol in hand, had confronted an almost naked sapper at the entrance to the command bunker. Staring down the barrel of an AK-47, Fagan aimed his pistol and pulled the trigger. The pistol misfired. The sapper shot him squarely in the face, but Fagan's pistol then fired and killed the sapper on the spot. Fagan returned to duty two weeks later! He had had his mouth open, screaming at the sapper. The sapper's round had entered the back of Fagan's throat and gone all the way through his neck without hitting any vitals.

The bad news was 13 Marines killed, 40 wounded and evacuated, and 23 slightly wounded and not evacuated. Although the enemy's initial penetrations were successful and carefully planned, his later confusion and the quick reaction of the defenders turned the tide before the enemy's large assault elements could get into the fight. Many of the men in these elements were killed outside the area by defensive artillery and mortar barrages that interrupted enemy forces massing for the main attack.

LZ Baldy, Memorial Service for C Company "... my most difficult job."

Colonel Codispoti had sent his XO, Lieutenant Colonel McClintock, to supervise the cleanup and assume command until Lieutenant Colonel Clark returned or I assumed command, which I did at FSB Ross 15 January. A heavy rain had enveloped the FSB, so the brief ceremony of passing the flag took place in one of the few huts left undamaged, the tiny base chapel. My tour as a combat commander had finally begun. I was ready.

Chapter 20

Back into the Field
"Combat Command"

My new command had an illustrious history as an aggressive and tenacious fighting unit. In the six months before I took over, its command philosophy had been "offense." These Marines were tough and courageous fighters, as they had shown by their response to the sapper penetration.

Seventh Marines Commanders

But despite the enemy's heavy losses, that night's action was no victory for our side. It showed up some glaring weaknesses that had to be corrected. We started by replacing the old executive officer, who had been in command the night of January 6, with a seasoned professional of my choosing, Major John Curnutt.

John was finishing up his tour as an intelligence officer at III MAF when I learned that I was to command First Battalion, Seventh Marines (1/7). I talked him into extending for three months so that he could complete his tour in the field with me. He was a Naval Academy graduate—organized, determined, smart, and well acquainted with the situation in the Que Son area. We would work well together.

The battalion S-3 was another competent and experienced officer. Major Dick Theer had been one of my students at the Basic School back in 1958. An Iowa University football player, he was finishing up his second Vietnam tour.

We would lose Company A under Captain Jim Van Riper when it became a CUPP unit, working with Popular Forces throughout the regimental area of operations—not under my operational control. This would leave me with three rifle companies. One of them would stay tied down protecting an artillery unit on top of a nearby mountain, where it used the new IOD (integrated observation device) to advantage to watch over the enemy's backyard in "Antenna Valley."

So I would have only two under-strength rifle companies, both commanded by first lieutenants. It wasn't a lot of punch, but help was on the way. Colonel Codispoti was to give me Company E, from 2/7, to help cover the large area west and north of FSB Ross.

Before I even unpacked my gear, I walked the perimeter of the base with the H&S company commander, Captain Clark, and the S-3 and S-4. I found that the command had made many defensive improvements, but we were still going to make a number of significant changes at FSB Ross that first night. In the pouring rain, Marine helicopters were bringing in load after load of barbed wire and the tools for installing it. A 40-foot observation tower I had requested was under construction back in Danang, and engineers were preparing a site for it. A heavy-lift helicopter would bring it here and install it as soon as weather permitted. Two other towers would follow later.

As we tromped the muddy base perimeter, I announced that base defense was no longer under the H&S company commander. My new executive officer, Major John Curnutt, would take command of defense when he arrived in a few days. He would use a secondary, fully operational, alternate command post for his headquarters. Until he arrived, all designated sector commanders would report to me. When we returned from the "recon," we scheduled a later meeting at which I would issue the new defense order. While my S-3 and S-4 worked out the details, I returned to my hootch to unpack.

Our problems weren't all tactical, however. The sergeant major informed me that he had four black Marines that wanted to see me at request mast. Sergeant Major Akins added that it had been some time since anyone had asked for request mast. I told him to get me some information on each of the men, their jobs, and their records, and I'd see them all the next day at 8 a.m. Tonight we had a new defense to set, and an enemy that, according to our intelligence reports, was anxious to finish what he had tried and failed to do on the sixth.

From that point on, the defense at FSB Ross was three deep. No defensive positions were above ground and vulnerable to RPG fire. No one was to sleep in his hut at night: all were deployed in mutually supporting tactical positions. It took a day or two to work the bugs out, but I felt much better about our alert system and our coverage of the gullies through which the sappers had gained access. A and B Companies had returned to the field, and finally, even if temporarily, the monsoon rains had let up.

That night I ate what would pass for a hot meal. The never-say-die mess sergeant, Staff Sergeant Potterf, working under a large tarpaulin, served all hands franks and beans with what appeared to be corn bread. It was delicious. We had a lot to talk about that night, but when I stretched out on a cot in the command bunker about 2:30 a.m., I felt we had done about all we could the first day.

The request mast at 8 a.m. was an eye opener, but not a surprise. Racial unrest had been disturbing the whole First Division. The four men that appeared before me were very nervous and spoke guardedly. They were all from H&S Company: one from 81mm mortars, one from the 106mm recoilless rifle platoon, and two from the motor pool. They were all wearing large afro hairdos, black-power bands on their wrists, and an assortment of beads around their necks. I had noted that many white Marines also wore these "peace beads" and some sort of distinctive band around their wrists. Haircuts were not exactly high on anyone's priority list, I observed. This would have to change, combat or not. To my dismay, I'd noticed that even my otherwise totally competent and brave battalion surgeon, Lieutenant (Dr.) Urban, was wearing the peace beads. I thought, all of these outward symbols would have to go . . . but first things first.

My office and hootch was next to the command bunker. I sat behind my field desk and had folding camp stools brought in for the Marines to sit on while we talked. I opened the dialogue after they had all reported and taken seats. I stressed that there was nothing routine about my having request mast at a combat outpost on my first full day as the new CO. I had elected to see them as soon as possible because I expected they had something important to tell me. They all nodded. They were all privates or PFCs. Their message, which poured out of them, was that I should know that there was a lot of prejudice in 1/7, that the white staff NCO's hated black Marines, and the officers didn't care. They offered no specifics, though they did complain about not being able to schedule black discussion groups, attend classes on black history, and form black clubs. They saw any refusal of these requests as resulting from racial prejudice. They seemed not to recognize that we were a combat infantry unit in the middle of daily battle with the enemy.

I listened patiently until they had aired all of their requests and complaints. Then I asked them a few questions. Where had each of them been during the sapper attack? How long had they been in 1/7? What led them to believe that an infantry battalion fighting an enemy 24 hours a day had time to let some of its Marines off duty to take school courses and socialize? Their responses convinced me that their goals totally ignored our primary combat mission. Their concerns were about individual "rights": any denial of these rights resulted from racial prejudice. They were naive, carefully rehearsed, and dead serious. I assured them that I took what they had to say quite seriously, but they had to understand that my first job was to fight the enemy and win. My second job was to look after my Marines, but not to grant special privileges to any group.

I promised them that if there was any bigotry or even a symptom of racial unfairness in 1/7 I would seek it out and deal with it. I asked them to help me and not to be part of the problem. They could come see me at request mast, but they also had to obey lawful orders. Before I dismissed them, I told them that I had a lot of urgent matters before me, but they had my promise that I would remember every word they told me. They would have to trust me to do what was right and fair for all Marines, not just my black Marines.

The discontent these Marines had expressed ran deep: it would take me more than two months to get to the bottom of it. Two of these black Marines were later to help me understand the problem; the other two, it turned out, were a major part of it. This issue turned out to be the most vexing aspect of my entire command tour. I tended to be more concerned over it than fighting the enemy, and I had to allocate a large share of my time and effort to coping with it.

I intended to use my "Band of Brothers" leadership creed as a positive remedy for this serious negative challenge. Marines must all be members of the same family and take care of each other. The hard question for me was how to make it happen while fighting a skillful and determined enemy. It wasn't going to be easy.

The Seventh Marines had moved into the Que Son Valley and its adjacent mountains in mid-1969 because the Army's Americal Division, south of the First Division, on the western side of the valley, could not prevent the enemy from sneaking through the valley into the I Corps area. We had to establish a stronger, permanent military presence that would disrupt and destroy the NVA and VC units attempting to use this avenue as their main access route.

The South Vietnamese had undertaken a massive relocation of families from the western portion of the valley. They had resettled most of the families in new villages near US or ARVN compounds. This is where Company A was doing its CUPP duty—increasing our presence throughout our regimental area and giving these new settlements added protection. It kept Company A very busy.

FSB Ross was in what I later called "Indian Territory." A "free-fire zone" bounded it on three sides: no known "friendlies" were in that zone, and we could fire at anything that moved in it. The few families remaining had avoided relocation and harbored the enemy. The valley terrain was uncultivated rice paddies, tree lines, deserted hamlets, countless trails and paths, and some well-worn dirt roads. There were few good observation points, FSB Ross being one of them: a rock pile that protruded thirty or forty feet above the valley floor. Our towers would later add another 40 feet. The entire area was a maze of hidden positions, trenchlines, camouflaged foxholes, booby-trapped paths, and deserted villages that sometimes came to life at night.

Our troops had night observation devices, a portable sensor device called a PSID, and claymore anti-personnel mines that we used extensively at night. We used the claymore mines both defensively and offensively, rigged with a trip wire or detonated by hand as part of an ambush. They were exceptionally lethal, and both sides used them in a deadly sort of cat-and-mouse game.

Most of our casualties were from mines or booby traps. Many of the latter were dud American mortar shells, artillery rounds, or aviation bombs, expertly rigged in a connected series and buried under likely trails or bivouac sites.

The enemy studied our habits just as we did his. He used small children to lure our patrols into ambushes. He used women and children as combatants, having them pose as refugees and ask for medical assistance, then spring into cover as the enemy opened fire.

During the day at FSB Ross we received infrequent but unusually accurate fire from long-range machine guns and occasionally from 82mm mortars. Our counterfire with mortars and artillery was so quick and accurate that the enemy had pretty much discontinued this practice by late February. Our companies were assigned areas in which to operate and in these areas were allowed unrestricted use of supporting fire, to include air strikes when appropriate. Artillery fire was always immediately available to them.

They conducted various kinds of operations. During the daytime, they often established an observation point and from there called down fire on suspected targets. They had to do some patrolling, but this was not a normal daytime activity unless they sighted the enemy. When possible, daytime was a resting time for the troops—a time to clean weapons, heat rations, and relax in covered positions in preparation for extensive night activities. These "night acts" were multiple ambushes along probable enemy access routes.

When I arrived, the rifle companies didn't move much at night. They hunkered down and tried to intercept the enemy in their night "poses," as the troops called them. Company B was an exception. This aggressive unit under First Lieutenant Ron Ambort used small roving combat patrols they called "killer teams." A team would set up and wait for about an hour. If this led to no action, the team would move to another pre-determined location and try again. If the team saw lights or smelled smoke, it would investigate. This method of operating proved effective: on several occasions it interrupted VC cell meetings being held in deserted hamlets. We increased our night ambushes tenfold over the next six months.

The life of the individual Marine rifleman was physically tough and always dangerous. These Marines lived by their wits and weapons, using only what they could carry. They rarely had fixed, prepared defensive positions. They were seldom in a group larger than a twelve-man squad when they got into a fight. For them night was especially harrowing: this was when the enemy forces came out in strength. This was also when our Marines' chances of being blown up by a misstep on a mine or booby trap were greatest: these devices cost us casualties almost every day. During rainy season the troops were always wet, cold at night, and fighting "immersion foot," the Vietnam version of the trench foot of World Wars I and II—and they rarely got to eat anything better than C-rations.

Who were the enemy to these brave young troopers in the field? They were faceless and always threatening. During the day, any male of military age that the trooper spotted was a target. And he had to suspect even the women and children he came across. Every trooper had heard tales of the 8- or 10-year-old girl that got one of our troopers to approach her by pointing to a body on the ground, then pulled a wire that activated a claymore mine, killing the Marine. I marveled that the Marines and their Navy corpsmen could show compassion to wounded civilians or even the relatively rare captured enemy soldier when treating their injuries. The necessary suspicion was a battlefield nightmare that U.S. forces had never had to contend with to this extent. We taught all incoming troops the "rules of engagement," but concern for everyday survival soon muddied these waters.

I thought about the skill levels of these young troops and their almost-as-young officers, and started giving them training that would increase some of their basic skills, such as firing at night and setting up an ambush after dark. It helped. We also started to improve their combat meals by supplementing their rations with some of the tried and true goodies I had always craved when I was fighting in Korea. We sent them cans of cheese, bacon, peanut butter, and jelly, along with fresh bread, apples, oranges, and loads of chocolate bars. Later we started sending out long-range-patrol rations (dehydrated food) every fourth day to relieve some of the monotony of the C-rats. I was also able to get thousands of small bottles of Tabasco sauce, part of a large gift from the McIlhenny Company, whose founder had been a general in the Marine Corps Reserve. The troops' favorite supplement turned out to be hard-boiled eggs, which they could store away and eat while on the march. It was a start, and the troops appreciated these things much more than having hot food delivered by helicopter in the field— which was a tactical and logistics nightmare for all concerned. I soon ended the helicopter hot-meal program.

During the last two weeks of January I was preoccupied with improving the defenses at FSB Ross, getting my new XO on top of the problems in our supply and communications platoons, and establishing a relationship with the officers and men in my new command. I made a list of things to do in the first few days, and one of the first things on the list was to get the Vietnamese civilians off the base. We'd have no more concessionaires' stands selling to the troops, and no more Vietnamese barbers. We ordered barber kits for the entire battalion and required the artillery units to do likewise. Each company would have two designated barbers, both NCO's, one black and one white. Experience was not a prerequisite. No one would be allowed to wear power bands or beads. They could wear religious symbols around their necks, under their skivvy shirts.

We started a small weekly bulletin, which was also a mail-home newspaper. It gave me a chance to talk to the troops and to name people who'd been promoted or nominated for an award. It was also something on which Private Smith could jot a note, then send it home to his family. I used it to introduce the "Band of Brothers" philosophy and the idea of the 1/7 "Family." This paper didn't contain anything that would in any way give aid or comfort to the enemy if he were to find a loose copy.

We started a blitz meritorious promotion program to get the Marines commanding squads and fire teams up to the authorized grades. And we instituted an organized "rehab" program for the rifle companies that included clean uniforms, showers, and hot food when they came back into the base area for a 48-hour stand-down. This also was a time to retrain them, to inspect their equipment, and for me to talk to them. I put John Curnutt in charge of these and many other projects. I didn't intend to spend much time at FSB Ross after the first few weeks.

One of the problems I found at FSB Ross was its electrical supply: jury-rigged and unreliable electric generators, a problem that plagued Marine expeditionary bases throughout Vietnam. We just didn't have the right type or number of field generators to meet our needs, and the ones we had made an enormous racket. In 1/7 we were using a number of begged, borrowed, and stolen small generators to meet minimal power requirements for our command and communications installations. Every heavy rainstorm short-circuited the wiring and caused power failures. We had to do something about this, but the Marine Corps didn't have any generators for us.

Then an unusual-looking angel landed on my doorstep: a Marine gunnery sergeant, the Battalion Communications Chief, came to see me about a possible solution. His brother-in-law was an Air Force lieutenant colonel in command of an air base squadron in Danang. That squadron seemed to have many of the things we needed, including industrial generators of formidable wattage, a single one of which would solve all of our electrical supply problems.

The brother-in-law was apparently a great admirer of Marines. I suggested that the gunny contact him and invite him up for an overnight visit to our position. We would give him the full VIP treatment and let him have a feel for the front-line combat situation. I hoped that all this would play to his sympathy and generosity and incline him to "lend" us one of his generators until we could obtain Marine replacements.

What happened was even better than that. When the gunny and the colonel talked, they made a deal before they put down their phones. The colonel would personally deliver the generator in an Air Force low-bed truck, complete with a crane for unloading it. His only request was for a Marine security escort from LZ Baldy, which was more than an hour's drive away along the frequently mined or ambushed road that served as our main supply route. He would remain overnight, but the truck would return immediately after delivering the generator.

We quickly made all the arrangements, and two days later the shiny brand-new generator, still in its packing case, arrived as promised. It was like greeting a foreign head of state. My entire staff and half of the troops at FSB Ross turned out to watch it being unloaded.

My radio operator was a draftee corporal who had an advanced degree in electrical engineering from Virginia Tech. When he heard me say that we didn't have anyone qualified to wire this new power behemoth, he volunteered to do it. It turned out that he had run a small generating station for Virginia Power before entering the Marine Corps. We now had an electrical engineer of our own, but I kept him as my radio operator!

All our Air Force benefactor wanted was to have my name on a requisition form as certification of need. Nevertheless, we and our enemy gave him an exciting show that evening when two of our units made contact with VC forces, and FSB Ryder, our IOD artillery base, acquired numerous targets in Antenna Valley. The next morning we dubbed him an "honorary Marine" and celebrated with a hot breakfast of black coffee, "shit on a shingle" (creamed beef on toast), and canned peaches. An early helo logistics flight took him home. He'd have a few good stories to tell his buddies back in Danang.

This marvelous new machine allowed us to add a perimeter lighting system that covered several of our more vulnerable positions. Our electrical engineer supervised the men of the communications platoon as they climbed the new poles and installed the floodlights that some other USAF unit apparently had had in excess of its needs.

About a week after finishing all this work, we had a visit from our regimental and division commanders, Colonel Codispoti and Major General Wheeler. Our little base had been transformed, but General Wheeler seemed none too happy over my going to the Air Force for assistance. He stated that he would look into getting us a proper USMC rig so that I could return this "blue thing" to the Air Force. It never happened, and I'm sure that fine gentleman learned something about the state of his own generators when he looked into replacing the blue thing. As a combat Marine who was always short of something, I had known and used the generosity of our more affluent sister services in both peace and war.

During my first few weeks with this battalion, I was very much concerned that the enemy would attempt to complete what he had started on January 6. Radio intercepts and intelligence reports indicated that this was his intention. Within days after my arrival we found evidence of sapper activity in the newly reinforced wire obstacles we had rushed to completion. Our troops sighted small enemy units frequently, and occasionally had a chance to engage them. We rushed to install a series of sensor beds around the base. Major Dick Theer had been the Division Sensor Officer before joining 1/7, so he had a great deal of experience. The sensors became effective immediately: we executed numerous fire missions as a result of their alerting us to enemy activity. Follow-up patrols invariably found blood trails, clothing, and signs of activity. It didn't take the enemy long to begin searching for and cutting our buried cables. Ploy followed counter-ploy: it was a frenzied period. There was much activity but no attacks.

Our people sighted small enemy units to our north, west, and south every day. Engineers sweeping the road from LZ Baldy had a truck destroyed by a command-detonated land mine just a mile from our base. We put Company B near the entrance to Antenna Valley to intercept a VC main force battalion reportedly proceeding our way. On February 12, after several days of scattered contacts, Company B set out to chase enemy elements moving south along the Song Ly Ly River, our border with the Americal Division. The second platoon, under Second Lieutenant Robert Carney, was

162

pursuing enemy units aggressively when it fell into a skillfully laid ambush. It suffered heavy casualties, and the conversation I had with the normally calm Lieutenant Ambort, the Company Commander, led me to call for the immediate deployment of our "Jump CP," my command group. His company seemed in extremis.

What followed was a two-day battle. After arriving by helicopter in a hail of enemy fire, I asked immediately for regimental assistance in moving C Company to my vicinity and in determining whether the Army could send a company or two from its side to help encircle the enemy forces located in a hill complex. I had no idea how strong the enemy was, but I could see that he was organized and well armed, and had set a classic ambush. This was no small-unit maneuver.

My request got an immediate response. C Company arrived within the hour. Two Army companies reported in via radio and received my orders. The Army battalion commander arrived in his helo to accompany me on a reconnaissance of the area. The hill mass was much more extensive than I had realized from studying the map.

Before we had stabilized the situation, a helo carrying our commanding general and regimental commander arrived and came under heavy enemy fire. I was not too happy that they would come in after I had reported our rather dangerous situation. Without using much tact, I'm afraid, I finally convinced Major General Wheeler and Colonel Codispoti to leave our very exposed position. They were both "fire horses," but the middle of a fire fight was not the place for senior guests.

The first day ended with C Company attempting to flank the enemy from the rear, but they demonstrated their inexperience by crossing the river without having properly secured the far bank. This brought about their own battle and cost them several men.

We couldn't bring in artillery because our positions were too close to the enemy, but we used air all evening to strafe, napalm, and rocket the positions from which we were receiving fire. Late that night we recovered the body of a C Company Marine hero killed trying to knock out a machine gun on the river bank. It had not been a good day. We had 13 Marines killed and 13 wounded in action. B Company's second platoon had lost its platoon sergeant and had been decimated.

The Army companies arrived the next morning as we moved cautiously through the previous day's battle sites. I was sure we had located a major installation, and wanted to check out the hill complex thoroughly. The enemy had wisely used the boundary areas between our major units as staging areas, because these were normally no-fire zones.

What we discovered that morning were positions prepared as two classic ambushes. We also found six enemy dead and evidence of many more. It was the main force battalion we had been looking for, but there were other units too. The hill mass was part of a hospital or recovery area. It had dozens of small wards under the trees, and medical supplies were all about. There was also evidence of a very hasty withdrawal, and we found and destroyed tons of rice that they had left behind. The enemy had obviously pulled out with most of his dead and wounded in the night. Now we and the Army units could return to our other missions. C Company was flown back to its previous area of operations.

I decided to take the half-day walk back to FSB Ross with B Company. It was an opportunity to observe them after this traumatic experience and gauge their effectiveness, and to take a look at the situation in the more-populated area south of our base. The villagers were able and willing to give us information. Through our interpreters we learned that many villagers had been drafted to carry the enemy's wounded and dead the night before. They estimated that the enemy force was more than a hundred men, and it had lost at least a third of their strength, dead or wounded.

In my oral report to regiment I asked for permission to return to this area soon with a larger force to give it a good hard look. The area in which we'd fought had been a rest camp and rehab center. There had to be a hospital nearby.

I told regiment that the flexible boundary agreement with the Army had proved effective. The Army companies had been very helpful, even though they had arrived too late for the battle. We'd seen a cooperative effort between the Army and Marine Corps on a relatively low level. Such short-notice mutual support had not been a common practice before.

Recovered documents indicated that we had unearthed and disrupted the operations center for a field headquarters, a rear service staff, a finance section, and the regional supply section for MR-5. We would indeed have to return. The enemy worked almost entirely underground and usually had a vast maze of tunnels in a complex of this type. I learned early that Marines were not good searchers. We had to teach them how to unearth the ingeniously hidden tunnel entrances, which were usually near a source of flowing water, either a streambed or a river. Learning this skill would take time, but we were to become very good at it.

As we walked through the gate of the 1/7 compound, I reflected on the status of my available fighting forces. B Company would stay "inside the wire" tonight, the 13th of February, and take over the close-in responsibility for the area due west of FSB Ross the next day. Ron Ambort and I had a long talk that evening. He seemed optimistic about his troops morale and anxious to get back into action to put "some hurt" on the enemy.

I radioed C Company's CO, First Lieutenant Jim Deare, a slow-talking southerner and a law graduate from Ole Miss. He assured me that they had been resupplied, had talked over their battle mistakes, and were "back in battery," implying that they were ready for whatever mission they were assigned. First Lieutenant Bill Campbell's D Company was still atop FSB Ryder, defending the artillery battery that was using IOD so effectively for firing into Antenna Valley. I cautioned him to remain especially alert. The enemy usually took time to plan his actions, but he always acted decisively against something that was putting pressure on him. FSB Ryder was well defended, but no position is impregnable, especially against the sappers. My warnings were justified: an attack was imminent.

The first word we received of the attack was a report from D Company that dozens of grenades were being tossed into their perimeter from positions down the hill. They reciprocated with their own grenades and 60mm mortars. The attack ebbed and flowed until we decided to use Marine air to make an illuminated attack and drop napalm on the forward slopes, which were heavily wooded. We would burn them out.

Dropping napalm only a few yards from friendly troops at night is ticklish. Nevertheless, the first few strikes, flown under aircraft flares that lit up the whole valley, were spectacular. My Air Officer and I watched the entire operation through binoculars as we monitored the air control radio net. Enemy action had ceased after the fourth bombing run: the upper slopes of the mountain were covered with fire. Now a plane was to make one more run before the three aircraft returned to base.

We could see the aircraft turn in on its run. I had just commented to my Air Officer that the pilot seemed to be cutting it pretty thin when the aircraft flew into the mountainside and exploded into a million pieces. We were all stunned. The flight leader came up on the net to say he would monitor the SAR (rescue) net and asked that we do the same. He had enough fuel to stick around for a while.

For a few minutes it looked as if we lost two fliers in that burst of flame. Then, only moments later, we heard a beeper on the SAR net. Simultaneously, Lt. Campbell, up on the mountain, reported spotting at least one parachute descending on the far side of the mountain, out of our view.

As it turned out, both fliers had ejected a split second before impact, and had landed somewhere on the lower slopes that had been burning a few minutes before. Using a coded system, they were able to tell us roughly where they were. D Company immediately sent out a squad-sized rescue party under command of the company XO. Within half an hour, they had found the two survivors, reported them able to walk, and headed back, taking them up the steep mountain to their defensive positions. The night attack was over.

I flew out early the next morning to visit Ryder and pick up the two tired but greatly relieved Marine airmen. They had escaped death by a microsecond. The air-ground team had done its job in spades: Ryder was safe. The enemy never penetrated the perimeter, but we did suffer some non-medevac casualties from the grenades.

That short battle after the ambush, which occurred less than a month after I'd assumed command, brought out some key points. One concerned my company commanders. Although personally courageous and physically tough, they were not broadly capable leaders: they had severe limitations due to their youth and inexperience. They all did a few things very well, but their failure to follow basic tactical procedures on several occasions leading up to and during the Song Ly Ly River battle prompted me to get much more involved in company operations.

B Company was the most aggressive and successful of my units. It was almost like a wolf pack, with Lieutenant Ambort being its "alpha male" leader. It suffered more casualties by far than the other companies did and seemed to have a penchant for making avoidable errors, the ambush at Song Ly Ly being a key one. It also reported almost twice as much enemy activity as the other units. I began to wonder if all the reports were valid, or if the author of their situation reports might be using a little imagination. I would have to follow them more closely.

C Company, under Lieutenant Jim Deare, had caused the fewest problems during the time I had observed it. He was tactically sound, but he and all of his officers were products of the repetitious type of small-unit warfare they had been conducting. The company seemed to have no list of standard equipment for the troops. Very few of the troops had entrenching tools, and almost no one had a gas mask.

C Company's squad leaders had all been chosen according to their time in combat rather than their rank. When capable corporals and sergeants reported in, they served under PFC squad leaders who'd had ten months in Vietnam. I remembered doing some of this in Korea myself, but 1/7 had overdone it, and now I had to deal with it.

The river crossing errors during the battle occurred after I had pointedly reminded Jim Deare of the procedures to secure the opposite bank before exposing his men. He had issued the right order, but had failed to supervise it properly. It happens in the best of circumstances, but we had to do better.

165

I hadn't seen a lot of D Company, except in its defensive role on Ryder. Lieutenant Bill Campbell seemed solid, capable, and totally dedicated to his men. I planned to rotate the company off the mountain soon, but when it repulsed the night attack so successfully, I was glad he was there to handle the matter so coolly and effectively.

All of the rifle company commanders reported that they had no race problems in their units. That problem was in the rear exclusively. My sergeant major was apparently a good field Marine, but his bitter references to "black militants in the rear" gave me my first cause to pause as I continued to feel out this troubling issue.

E Company, 2/7, attached for this period, did yeoman work, had numerous small enemy contacts, and suffered a sizable number of booby trap casualties during its patrolling activities. These frustrating and deadly devices were the enemy's best weapon, and they caused steady attrition.

During this period I started monitoring radio nets at night, particularly if something was happening or about to happen. For the remainder of my tour of duty, I dozed at night with a radio earphone in each ear, and awakened instantly if I heard something of interest. I was determined not to let my young commanders know of my concern and not to threaten their command function, but I wanted to be there if needed. I seldom was, but on a few occasions the need was critical. We were improving, but the more I learned about my young troops and their leaders, the more concerned I became.

If one of these units was attacked by a larger force at night, could it repel the attack? How could it if its troops never dug in? Suppose the enemy used CS on one of the companies and our troops panicked. CS was a form of "super tear gas" delivered via hand grenades and 82mm mortar shells that could temporarily disable and panic the strongest unprotected individual. I was familiar with the properties of the gas, having used it extensively in training during my Caribbean deployment from the Second Division.

One of my immediate goals was to ensure that every member of the battalion and our supporting artillery units had a serviceable gas mask. We worked night and day to get the new masks issued to the troops. Intelligence reported that the enemy now had CS gas comparable to the CS we had.

Once the troops had the masks, we conducted all inspections during rehab periods with the troops wearing them. If the filter wasn't clean and functioning, the individual would just pass out. After we'd carried out our crash plan to get everyone fitted, equipped, and tested, I decided to find out personally about my troops at the base camp. My method was a bit drastic and very painful for some, but it worked a small miracle in finding out who did and who didn't have a serviceable gas mask.

I called in the S-3, the H&S company commander, the sergeant major, and the battalion surgeon to tell them what I was going to do. One of the recent additions to our defensive perimeter was a number of rocket-propelled CS gas grenade launchers. Each launcher held about six rockets that would go 40 or 50 yards into the air before bursting to spread the gas over an elliptical area the size of a football field. The gas would settle and permeate the soil for a considerable time. As it descended, it looked like a "greasy fog bank." I decided to set one off at high noon, aimed straight up. That's how we would find out who had a gas mask and who didn't!

The battalion mess sergeant did not serve a noon meal, so most troops would be eating a C-ration lunch in their work places. Every man was supposed to have his mask either on his belt or within easy reach. We had stressed this point for several weeks.

At 12:15, I walked out to the nearest canister, rotated it skyward, and launched it with a pull of the lanyard. Simultaneously, the sergeant major rang the gas alarm siren and shouted "Gas attack!" Suddenly our battalion looked like an ant colony dispersing to avoid bug spray. We learned quickly that almost 90% of the troops had masks and used them immediately. The usual 10% that didn't get the word were at first miserable, then sick as dogs, and finally lined up at the supply hooch to draw either a mask or a serviceable filter. The fumes lingered for hours. I wasn't sure that these devices would be useful in an enemy attack: the wind could make them work against us. But they sure worked like a charm for my purpose that day.

Ironically, the enemy pulled the same trick on us a few weeks later, attacking B Company in its night defensive positions. The enemy sprayed the positions with gas, then followed it up with an attack—expecting little or no resistance. Our troops clobbered them. So our crash efforts proved to have been most effective and timely.

The enemy never used gas on us again. We never used gas offensively, but did use it to deny the enemy the use of caves, tunnels, and underground storage sites. We exploded CS crystals with primer cord, impregnating the soil for periods as long as four months.

As my special projects for 1/7 continued to bear fruit, I felt better about our logistics, communications, defensive positions, watch towers, and structured rehab program for the rifle companies. I was still uneasy about our tactics and techniques for fighting the enemy. But we couldn't stand down and retrain, so we had to retrain on the run, so to speak.

I watched with concern as B Company again reported both successes and failures. One of its small night combat patrols had interrupted a VC cell meeting, killed four or five VC, and captured a couple of enemy weapons. This gutsy use of reconnaissance Marine techniques for patrolling seemed to bear fruit, but it was risky.

On February 19, one of B Company's day patrols responded to a signal from a young boy who was pointing at a body on the ground. As the patrol approached him, he detonated a claymore mine, then picked up an AK-47 automatic rifle and fired at them. One Marine was killed and two were wounded. This not unusual use of a small child had occurred near a VC hamlet called Son Thang. It led to a brief but fierce fire fight that almost seemed like the straw that was about to break the back of embattled B Company. They had been ambushed again, this time by a small boy and an unseen enemy.

Late that afternoon, Lieutenant Ron Ambort made an unusual request of my S-3. Could he have permission to minimize his night activities that night? He sounded depressed, and he said he thought his troops needed some rest. I got on the radio and discussed the matter further with him. He suggested that they put out only one "night activity," a killer-team, as they called the roving combat patrol. The rest of the company would "hunker down" in a sound defensive position. I approved the request.

That night I stayed tuned to both the battalion tactical net and B Company's tactical net. They used the keyed signals as a radio code for their patrols. No voice communications were allowed except in an emergency. These company-level radio nets were not "covered" (encrypted). The enemy could intercept their transmissions— even as I could.

Early in the evening a message from B Company reported that their patrol had established a hasty ambush and encountered a column of fifteen or twenty VC. The patrol reported killing six male soldiers and one female. The details were very sketchy and immediately aroused my concern. I told the S-3 to ask for more information and to ask specifically about enemy weapons. Lieutenant Ambort said he would get more info when the patrol returned. He called later to say they had one captured weapon, an SKS rifle. I was not convinced that the report was an accurate one, and asked for the serial number of the rifle. In a few minutes a response came in with a number. I told Ron Ambort we would be at his position early the next morning, and that I'd want to see the rifle and talk to the members of the patrol.

This was the beginning of an investigation into what I've termed a tragic "incident." It is a good example of both the irony and the heartbreak produced by this strange war we were fighting. I am describing it carefully, because some dedicated Marine historians have become so mesmerized by the "laws of war" that their historical accounts of what a handful of young, bitter, frightened Marines were facing became more idealistic than realistic, in my opinion.

The next morning, Major Theer and I proceeded to the B Company position by helicopter. As they produced a rifle, I remembered that they had reported a captured rifle earlier that week. I asked if this was the same one. The answer was a less-than-convincing "negative." I remained skeptical but didn't press the point further.

Then I was surprised to learn that this had been an all-volunteer patrol. The commander of the second platoon, Lieutenant Carney, had asked for volunteers. Here in front of me were the five very junior Marines who had stepped forward. The patrol leader was a machine gunner, Lance Corporal Herrod, who had arrived recently from the Third Division. Machine gunners do not normally lead patrols of this type. The five did not know each other well and had never worked closely together. None of the experienced NCO's had gone out with them.

One of the five had just joined our battalion from the Third Reconnaissance Battalion. His rifle had a shortened barrel, a folding stock, and a recon-style silencer on the muzzle. Another member, a black Marine, had joined the battalion less than two weeks earlier. To me, this tossed-together patrol appeared to represent a breakdown in professionalism.

Either on the way back to FSB Ross or shortly after we got there, Major Theer and I got on the radio and talked with Lieutenant Grant, my Intelligence Officer, while he was out on patrol, checking our sensor beds. I was convinced that B Company's patrol report was false, and I wanted him to check out the area in question. Soon after that, his small patrol visited the hamlet of Son Thang and made a startling discovery. Only 500 yards from B Company's position they found the bodies of 16 women and children. There were spent shell casings all over the place. Although it looked awfully bad initially, I did remember that B Company had had a fire fight in this area the previous day and had lost a Marine in the ambush. These people could be victims of that battle—but my instincts told me that wasn't the case. After discussing it briefly with Dick Theer, I told him to have B Company return to the base area. And I ordered Lieutenant Grant to collect all the available information, take pictures of the remains, and then bury them in the hamlet before returning. He was also to identify and describe the location of each of the bodies.

168

Late that afternoon the patrol returned after carrying out its grisly orders. I had John Curnutt join us as Dick Theer and I debriefed the entire patrol and viewed the photos. Lieutenant Grant was a thorough and responsible officer. He had a topnotch SNCO assistant, and they both gave us a complete account of what they had discovered. After dismissing them, I picked up the land line telephone to talk to Colonel Codispoti, my regimental commander, at LZ Baldy. I told him there'd been a very significant happening, something that required me to fly to his headquarters that night to report it. Without being specific, I strongly suggested he call General Wheeler and ask him to send his Assistant Division Commander, Brigadier General Bill Doehler, to Baldy to receive my brief also. I simply stated it was that important.

Colonel Codispoti accepted my recommendations. He offered to request a helo for me, and we set a time. I asked that only he, his XO, and General Doehler attend my brief. Again, he acquiesced. Then, as later, in this most difficult situation for a battlefield commander, my superiors at all levels were supportive and cooperative.

I spent about an hour briefing them on the situation, the battlefield circumstances, B Company's background, and a bit on the five very inexperienced Marines that had been sent out. There were few questions. I gave the polaroid photos to General Doehler and spent about half an hour writing out in longhand what I had briefed them on.

Later that evening, after returning to FSB Ross, I received a phone call from General Wheeler. He had all the facts currently available and didn't press me for more information. He told me he was going to report the incident up the line and he wanted my thoughts about sending the media up to my location. What we agreed to was a daytime visit, for a group of 25 or 30. I would brief them, orient them on the area, and not give them any of the names or details of the incident, since an investigation was underway. They were to be given complete access to me and no one else; they would not be allowed to wander around the fire base. I asked that they understand that before coming. Also, they should be told we may come under fire during their visit. As it happened, we did.

B Company came in early the next morning. I called for Ron Ambort and his five Marines to report to me personally in my hootch. I wanted to see them as a group: to tell them what we knew about their actions, and that we knew they had submitted false official reports. They all started to blurt out their stories, but I stopped them and warned them of their rights. I told them that this was very serious business, and that there would undoubtedly be trials to sort out what had happened. I added that I would ask the Commanding General to have them tried before combat-experienced Marine officers, and that I intended to offer my own testimony about the battlefield environment we were facing in Que Son Valley. I told them that my S-3, Major Theer, would be the initial investigating officer, and he would be the next person to talk to them. This was the last occasion on which I talked to the five Marines as a group. In the next day or so, they were sent to pretrial confinement in the III MAF brig.

After the enlisted men left, I informed Ron Ambort that I was deeply disappointed in him, and that he would be relieved of his command the following day. He had not realized the full extent of the tragedy until I laid out what the S-2 patrol had unearthed. He had been protecting his troops, but now he was crushed to realize the gravity of what occurred. The facts weren't all in by any means, but the picture was filling in rapidly.

I hadn't yet figured out who would take over B Company. The press would be arriving at the landing zone in just one hour. Damn, things couldn't get much worse, I thought. The media arrived exactly on schedule. There were about 20 of them, one was a woman from a European news service. All were carrying cameras, including several of the bulky TV shoulder cameras. The III MAF press officer with them handed me a list. It seemed to me that except for one TV network every major news gathering agency was present, including international wire services and radio. We escorted them into our one underground briefing bunker, where I had a large area map displayed. We were able to squeeze all of them and their equipment into the tiny room. I introduced myself and asked each of them to briefly stand up and do the same. Some of the top US correspondents were present.

I told them that we had discovered the bodies of 16 women and children in a hamlet near the fire base. We had reason to believe that a patrol of five Marines from B Company that was in that vicinity the previous evening could be responsible. The matter was under investigation, so the names of the individuals would not be available. I continued with a description of the type of warfare we were conducting in this hotly contested area. I depicted the area as "Indian country," a free-fire zone from which all friendly families had been removed by the South Vietnamese government, and noted that many of the hostiles we encountered daily were women and even children. I cited the several recent incidents involving B Company.

I told them that B Company was a proud, aggressive, and tough fighting unit that had suffered heavy casualties in recent fighting. Then I spent some time discussing the "fog of war" that had prevailed in this valley since I had assumed command slightly over a month ago.

The briefing went well. There were good questions to which I responded calmly— until one reporter really raised my hackles. He referred to the incident as a "mini My Lai" and I exploded. I asked him to stand up. I noted that we had some civilian deaths that concerned me deeply as they always did. These men could not be labeled guilty until all the facts were in and they had undergone a trial, if that were to become necessary. "To equate this with My Lai burns a hole in my britches! We called you in two days after the incident. We're trying to get on top of a situation that we discovered just hours after it occurred. We're being honest, frank, and professional about the entire matter. Mr.____, this is no My Lai, and you'd better find a better synonym if you want to write or talk about the proud Marines of this fighting battalion. We've got problems aplenty, but we deal with them! We don't hide them or cover them up. This is a nasty war. It isn't neat and tidy, but we are responsible for what we do or don't do. I don't shrink from that." He apologized.

After the briefing and the question-and-answer session, I took them all up to the highest point near our 81mm mortar positions to point out the direction and distance to the hamlet. Without warning, we began to receive long-range, scattered machine gun fire from the general direction of the hamlet. The 81mm mortars returned fire immediately. They placed 20 or 25 rounds in the target area and the hostile firing ceased. The reporters had all scrambled for cover, but peered over the rocks as our mortars returned fire. It was ironical to have pointed out that this was a free-fire zone and then have the enemy show them why.

We returned to the relative safety of the area around the briefing bunker. The TV network reporters wanted to do one-on-one interviews with me outside the bunker.

170

They conducted two separate, comprehensive interviews. Each covered most of the major points from my briefing. After the interviews and a few more questions, we gave them all a cup of mess hall coffee and a chance to visit a designated "two holer" before returning to the landing zone for the return flight.

Within 24 hours the story and my face were on the front pages of newspapers all over our country and abroad. Clippings that my family and friends saved showed me that the reporting had been accurate and free of innuendo. The media did not render any judgment in advance, but 1/7 wasn't to escape media scrutiny for the rest of my tour. The ordeal just beginning would not be pleasant, but the much-maligned press always treated us fairly and factually, as we had them. Extensive coverage was to last for more than six months.

Colonel Bob Lucy, the First Division Legal Officer, visited us and promised to send me two captain attorneys immediately to assist Major Dick Theer in his preliminary investigation. They were very helpful as Theer examined the hamlet and collected evidence. The case then moved through the many wickets of the Marine Corps judicial system. Dick Theer did a thorough job of sorting out the facts as we had them. I forwarded his report and requested that a formal pretrial investigation be commenced as soon as possible. A very competent staff judge advocate, Major Robert J. Blum, was assigned to perform the investigation, the military equivalent of a grand jury investigation.

There were six principals involved: First Lieutenant Ron Ambort, Lance Corporal (later Private) Randell D. Herrod, PFC Thomas R. Boyd, Lance Corporal Michael S. Krichten, PFC Samuel G. Green, and Private Michael A. Schwartz. Major Blum had to deal with six different attorneys and with me—not an easy task. We differed on what charges should be preferred against the troops, and I wasn't convinced that the company commander should be tried by a court martial. Ron Ambort was a brave and loyal officer who had served the Corps extremely well under trying conditions. He had not been aware of all the circumstances when he sent his initial report. However, he had sent me information that he knew was false. That was wrong and totally unacceptable, but I recommended to the Commanding General that he receive nonjudicial punishment in lieu of a court martial. General Widdecke, who had relieved General Wheeler after he was injured in a helicopter accident, approved my recommendation. Ambort was fined and reprimanded. His career, had he chosen to make one of the Marine Corps, was ended, but he was not to face a court martial.

A different court tried each of the men. I testified in the first and last trials. For the others my testimony was used as a deposition on the vagaries of the battlefield and the fog of war these young men were subjected to. One Marine, Lance Corporal Krichten, testified under a grant of immunity. Herrod was tried last.

Major Blum, who later retired as a senior judge advocate colonel after a brilliant career, was quoted as saying, "Lieutenant Colonel Cooper could never quite accept the fact that his Marines were guilty of murder." While I don't agree with what he said, he did correctly point out my dedication to the young men who were caught up in this tragic incident, an incident that turned out to be one of the defining moments of this long and confusing conflict.

I had watched their trauma from close up. On the one hand, they had seen artillery and air strikes destroy hamlets from which they had received fire and where Marines had died. Artillery and air strikes are impersonal weapons and are not directed at

171

individuals. Troops use personal weapons to disable individual enemies. They are expected to be discerning and they must be responsible. But who is the enemy when a child has just helped spring an ambush on your platoon—an ambush that killed your platoon sergeant, who was also your good friend? This was a very tough call. The four trials showed how tough it was: they convicted two of the men and acquitted two others.

Private Michael A. Schwartz was 21 years old and a high school dropout. He had already accumulated a substantial disciplinary record in the Marine Corps. He was the first to be tried, on a charge of premeditated murder as a noncapital offense. He was convicted on 12 of the 16 counts and sentenced to life imprisonment and a dishonorable discharge. His sentence was later remitted to one year's confinement, but the discharge remained unchanged.

Private First Class Thomas R. Boyd was tried second and was acquitted of all charges. He had been offered an entirely new court panel, but he and his attorneys elected to be tried by the judge alone. That strategy proved to be fruitful.

Private First Class Samuel G. Green, Jr. was tried shortly after Boyd. He faced a panel of three officers and two enlisted men, which convicted him on 15 counts of unpremeditated murder. He was sentenced to 5 years at hard labor, forfeiture of all pay, and a dishonorable discharge. The Commanding General later reduced this to one year's confinement, but retained the discharge. His discharge was later upgraded to "General," after intervention by James H. Webb, a former Marine infantry commander who had himself fought over this same area, and who was later to become Secretary of the Navy. Green, however, took his own life in July of 1975, before this action was completed.

Private Randell D. Herrod was tried last, one week after Green's trial ended. The military judge was Commander Keith B. Lawrence, JAGC, USN. A team of four civilian attorneys and Captain Robert C. Williams, his military counsel, defended him. Two of his attorneys were members of the Oklahoma Legislature. Months earlier, I had agreed to his defense's request to give the same testimony about the battlefield environment that I had given in previous depositions or trials.

Just four days after I'd come home from Vietnam, I was summoned to return for this trial. Herrod was acquitted of all charges and released from confinement. In a brief office ceremony immediately after the trial, he was awarded a Silver Star medal he'd earned while serving with the Third Division.

Chapter 21

Winding Down Our War

Our war didn't pause while we were dealing with the aftermath of the Son Thang incident. Now B Company needed a new commander, and no one in the company was suitable. I chose an officer about to make first lieutenant who had already established a reputation as a responsible leader. He was Lieutenant Joe Doss, a mature and serious-minded young officer then serving in H&S Company. We talked about his new assignment only briefly. I told him B Company would return to the field immediately, but it would replace D Company atop FSB Ryder. He would have a few days, maybe weeks, to get acquainted with his company, but he wouldn't have the command long, since I expected a captain in soon. But his role would be a very important one: the company needed a strong leader, and right now! I encouraged him to call me personally, any time, day or night, if there was anything he wanted to discuss. He left after assuring me that he would take good care of B Company. The next day we rotated the company up to Ryder and brought D Company down to spend a night in the base before returning to the field.

Busy times were ahead for 1/7. First, we were going to become the division's "swing battalion," meaning that we would operate under direct operational control of the commanding general to hit targets of opportunity anywhere in the division's area of operations, often on very short notice. We would usually be reinforced by other units, and we would have priority on air support, particularly assault helicopters.

Second, in the near future we would be moving our battalion headquarters and rear elements from FSB Ross to Landing Zone Baldy, where we'd be co-located with the regimental headquarters. Ross was now in good shape defensively, and I looked forward to performing offensive missions that would allow me to lead my troops in the field.

In early March, General Wheeler summoned me to his headquarters in Danang. Something big was in the mill. The intelligence community had reliable information from a key source that the Viet Cong infrastructure for the I Corps area, made up of five Vietnamese provinces, was to have a rendezvous in an area north of the ROK Marine Brigade, near the beach. Some 200 people were expected to attend, and NVA regular soldiers were infiltrating in to protect this important meeting. General Wheeler had me briefed on this information and asked me for my approach to isolating and capturing this elusive enemy group, which was the enemy's shadow government for our operational area.

After studying the map for a few moments, I told him that I would need about eight rifle companies in order to cordon off the area. We should land that night in an illuminated night assault. I reminded him that I had only two rifle companies of my own available. B Company was still defending FSB Ryder. I suggested that his Assistant Division Commander and I visit the ROK Marines to feel them out about participating. They were difficult to work with and were very sensitive about having someone else command their troops. But I thought we might convince them to set up blocking positions on their flank with three companies. We would then assault with five Marine companies and tie in with them.

The ADC, Brigadier General Bill Doehler, and I flew immediately to the ROK Marine Headquarters to talk with Brigadier General Lee. After some posturing, he agreed to my request, subject to message confirmation. I was to send him a liaison officer as soon as our plans were firm. In very short order, Dick Theer and I worked up a general plan. It would involve the first night assault ever conducted with CH-53 helicopters. Our forces normally used these huge aircraft only for logistics or administrative lifts. But we had to get five Marine companies on the ground almost simultaneously, and these big helos were the only way we could do it. Three other rifle companies would join us: their CO's all reported to me at the Division Headquarters within the hour.

I proposed a massive cordon operation. We would stage all of the US Marines at LZ Baldy, only six miles from the objective. We would put about 90 Marines in each heavy lift helo, standing up, with safety lines extending across the aisles of the aircraft as supports. Each company would be divided between two helicopters, which would land in sequence in a carefully laid out series of landing zones. The entire operation. would be executed with "the lights turned on"—illuminated by aircraft flares. The Navy would position SEAL teams in small boats off the beach to ensure that the enemy did not attempt to escape by sea. Members of my "jump command post" staff would remain airborne in a CH-46 helo until I called them in. I would fly in the command helo with Lieutenant Colonel Andy Andrus, who would control the air assault. Andy was a real pro, and we worked out the air details in short order. The landing zones would be prepped with a set number of artillery rounds, the last round being smoke or white phosphorus, marking the LZ itself.

General Wheeler and General Gale Thrash, CG of the Third Marine Air Wing, approved the concept before I briefed the wing and division staffs. Minutes later, the wing and division staffs assembled in the briefing theater, where I issued the final oral order. Andy Andrus briefed the air portion of the helo lift and assault.

It was about 5 p.m. when we left the theater. H-hour, touchdown in the objective area, was to be at 4 a.m. Preparatory fire would commence 15 minutes before that. A large contingent of intelligence specialists and MP's would join us in the objective area when we called them in. We expected to take a number of prisoners and needed on-the-spot assistance in controlling and interrogating them.

Despite the short-fused nature of this operation, the dangers inherent in a night helicopter assault, the difficulty of coordinating supporting fire, and landing right on top of a suspected enemy, the operation worked like a charm, with only a few minor glitches. One company landed out of position, but hurriedly moved to its proper location. Our C Company actually landed right on top of an entire squad of NVA soldiers who were running away. They killed three of them and captured five before I even landed. When dawn broke, I was on the ground and in communication with all of my companies and the ROK Marines, and our units were linked up. On this day I learned again what poor searchers Marines are. We commenced sweeps of the entire area at dawn. By late afternoon we had had zero enemy contact except for the squad we caught in a landing zone.

We knew well the enemy's skill at tunneling, but how to find the tunnels? Marines marching along abreast and looking down at the ground almost never discover anything. I called in all of my commanders late in the afternoon to discuss search techniques. After discussing why we seemed to have missed the whole thing, I asked for suggestions. We decided to divide the entire area into grid squares and assign each to a small unit. Once a squad or platoon knew this was "their ground," it would locate anything in it that was suspicious.

We completed deploying to the grids before dark. I was concerned about friendly fire incidents during the night, but we had none. At first light, the tunnels started opening up, and we captured about 90 people. All had been concealed in deep tunnels, some of which had large, multiple chambers. We also captured a number of files, many documents, and a few weapons. Several young children were among our captives. All of these people had been out of sight underground, right under our noses.

I was disappointed. It looked as if we had caught a lot of elderly civilians, mostly women. But our interrogators were ecstatic. They explained that the children were "runners," there to be cover for the women. These were indeed VCI, Viet Cong Infrastructure operators, they claimed. The second morning, the troops improved their search techniques to unearth a number of caches of weapons and ammunition, but no more troops or people. We had suffered no casualties.

In the meantime, I had gone back to division headquarters to make arrangements for our next operation, a return to the Song Ly Ly River complex where we had had our short battle early in February. Our battalion rear, under the ever-efficient John Curnutt, had relocated to LZ Baldy. B Company had been relieved at Ryder and would be waiting for me at our new base of operations. In two days we would return to the Song Ly Ly River valley to check out the entire area. This time I would be reinforced with an RF (South Vietnamese Regional Forces) company to help screen the civilian population, and all three of my rifle companies would be available. We could take as much as a week to ensure that the area was no longer being used as a hospital, rest camp, and headquarters. The operation would commence on 9 March.

The first thing I asked for at our new command post was a watch tower like the ones we had installed at Ross. The engineers and Seabees had it installed within the week, right next to my operations center. My S-2 intelligence scouts manned it day and night, using 20-power binoculars and night observation devices. They were able to uncover a great deal of enemy activity close to our base at LZ Baldy that we would never have discovered without this productive observation post.

The Song Ly Ly operation lasted from 9 March to 16 March, but never produced the results I had hoped for. We had to teach our troops how to search all over again. We went three days without any action, except for scattered night contacts and a few productive ambushes that netted some VC transients. My original command post site was directly on top of a sophisticated underground operating room and medical storehouse. General Wheeler visited us and inspected our captured stocks of nurses' uniforms, antibiotics, and surgical tools. We took him back to the site of the original ambush of B Company, where he had landed in a hail of gunfire some weeks earlier. Their ambush positions were truly impressive.

The RF company proved much better than our Marines at searching villages in the area. They verified that this had indeed been what we suspected, but that the enemy had moved away after the battle a month earlier. It was still an alternate personnel infiltration route, but not a main supply route anymore.

My command group was a small unit, but I never used any troops from a rifle company for security. What I started doing on this operation was to become standard procedure: I took a section (2 tubes) of my 81mm mortars with me to furnish immediate short-range indirect fire support to the companies. Whenever we were to be where we'd have direct observation and fields of fire, I also took a 106mm recoilless rifle. Except for the 106, we could move by foot, and we often did so.

A command group that stays in one place more than a night or two is asking for trouble. We stayed light, moved often, and never underwent any enemy attacks. I used the mortarmen and off-duty radio operators along with my intelligence troops for night security and to conduct short local patrols. I accompanied them frequently. My search techniques bore fruit on a number of occasions, revealing tunnels under wells, under fireplaces, and in other unlikely spots.

Shortly after he had been relieved as company commander, Lieutenant Ron Ambort came to see me. We were still at Ross, but he knew that we would soon be operating under the division's control. He said that despite what had happened, he was still a Marine and he wanted to help me fight the battalion. He just couldn't stand not being assigned to some useful task. He asked if he could accompany me as part of my "jump CP" to coordinate night security, conduct ambushes and patrols, or do anything else I wanted him to do. In other words he was offering to be my "headquarters commandant" in the field. I accepted his offer immediately. He accompanied me on several of our subsequent operations. Skilled in field craft, he was able to make our command post setup much more effective and secure in the field. It helped his morale a great deal, I believe, to have this useful bit of responsibility.

During the spring months, we spent most of our time in the field on short operations for the division. On March 20 we were airlifted into the heart of Antenna Valley, the enemy's home base six months before. We were under the protective guns of FSB Ryder. While we scouted the entire valley, a team from the division installed a series of large sensor beds. Our rifle companies made no contact with the enemy, but one of Ron Ambort's ambushes near my command post scored a major hit on an NVA column moving through the valley at night. It was a short, violent, and effective fight. We suffered no casualties, but punished the enemy severely. Ron was especially proud of his communicators and mortarmen, who manned the ambush position. He had been with them during the entire episode. Score one for the headquarters "pogues," as the rifle companies called them.

As I approached the midpoint of my tour as CO of 1/7, I could see that a number of factors were influencing the evolution of this fighting battalion. For one thing, we were receiving practically all of our new members from Third Division units that were being rotated back to Okinawa. Many of them were top-notch, experienced people, but we also got a number of junior troops who were substandard. At this stage of the war, we had an unusual number of marginal people, both draftees and enlistees. The former Third Division troops had been fighting the war in a WWI environment in the barren northern provinces. We, of course, were in the middle of a densely populated area. Reorienting these people to our rules of engagement would take more than a simple two-hour briefing.

There were unquestionable racial tensions in the battalion when I took command, but that was true throughout Vietnam at the time. There had been precious little opportunity to deal with them until we left Ross and moved to Baldy. Our replacements from the Third Division were from the same cross section as the troops we already had. There were a few bigoted white rednecks, as I viewed them, and an equally small group of malcontent black Marines carrying chips on their shoulders. My challenge was to find common ground for all of them within our Marine family, the "Band of Brothers."

Because of "closet drinking" I had discovered at Ross shortly after taking over in January, I closed all sources of alcohol to everyone. At that time and place, I had no use for clubs or off-duty hangouts. It was ridiculous even to consider drinking in the face of the enemy. And if there were tensions of any kind, drinking in confined quarters would tend to exacerbate them. The no-alcohol edict applied to everyone: our duties required all hands to be ready for action 24 hours a day.

Although I spent most of my time operating in the field, I flew back to our base for short periods to meet with the XO and "home staff." Now was the time to deal aggressively with improving military smartness in the rear, get the "Band of Brothers" up and running, and get a handle on the race issue. We had some top-notch white and black senior NCO's that both the XO and I talked to at length about the issue. When we were in from the field, I spent a lot of my late evening time talking to some of the black Marines who had originally come to see me at request mast. This was to pay off in a big way.

More good news. The Marine Corps issued us six of the new 40mm grenade machine guns to test. And the booby-trap dogs we had long been promised began to arrive. They were immediately effective.

A new Catholic chaplain reported to us for duty and instantly became one of my most prized assets. He picked up on the "Band of Brothers" theme as if it had been his own or, as he used to say, "one of God's better ideas." Lieutenant J.J. Pierce, USNR, "Fatha" Pierce, an imposing figure of a man, had played college football at Holy Cross. He had earlier served with Marines as a Navy hospital corpsman and later joined a monastic order of the Catholic Church. There he had been trained as a physician's assistant and emergency medical specialist. As the war droned on, he volunteered to return as a chaplain with the Marine Corps. Having him with us was like having another doctor, a psychiatrist, another sergeant major, and an inspirational priest. This hard-nosed, dedicated apostle carried a sidearm because he was "trained to protect the wounded." He also carried a B-2 medical kit, the same kit that field corpsmen used. I could easily tell him my concerns and thoughts on any issue and get back honest and thoughtful responses.

Other new people arrived to relieve people whose tours were up. Captain John C. Wilson, an experienced infantry officer and former enlisted Marine, took command of the volatile B Company. He was just what they needed. As I later wrote on his fitness report, "He combined courage with competence," a priceless combination in our complicated scheme of fighting. Captain Tom Stouffer, a linguist and former interrogator, assumed command of C Company. Lieutenant Jim Deare moved up to my Operations Section. In mid-spring, Major Dick Theer departed and Major T. G. McFarland replaced him as my S-3.

We were evolving into a tight-knit, skilled fighting unit. Our retraining of the companies was paying dividends in combat efficiency. I asked my XO and adjutant to take a very hard look at all of the people and billets in the battalion rear. Were we allowing some people to "hide" from active field duty? How were they performing in their jobs? We needed more troops in the field, and I had an idea about where to find them.

All our malcontents seemed to be in rear area cubbyholes, and now that we were in a larger base, the subject of drug use surfaced. These issues were part of the kaleidoscope of command challenges we had to deal with, whether or not I was gone 80% of the time on field operations. In 1970, dealing with subcaliber or malcontent Marines was almost as big a commander's headache as was his NVA counterpart. Our Commandant in Washington, General Leonard Chapman, was aware of that fact and was soon to come to our aid.

During our busy spring months, our commanding general and his operations officer almost "bought the farm," as the troops say. While lifting off from a tiny clearing, their helicopter's rotor blade struck a tree and the plane crash-landed, out of control. There was no fire, and the crew and the two passengers survived, but General Ed Wheeler suffered a double compound fracture of his leg and Colonel Cy Waldrop had extensive rib and shoulder damage and multiple bruises.

Shortly after the accident, General Wheeler was flown back to the States for treatment, and General Charles F. Widdecke relieved him. Like General Wheeler, General Widdecke had been a regimental commander earlier in the war. He was an experienced war horse. Cy Waldrop would stay on as his G-3.

My regimental commander, Colonel Codispoti, was relieved by another experienced officer, a World War II Raider and former CO of 1/7, Colonel Ed Derning. I had known Colonel Derning at III MAF and had great confidence in him. Our regiment would "stand down" under his control, later in the summer, as major elements of the First Division rotated home.

Our role as division swing battalion became much less demanding after General Wheeler's accident, but we still conducted quick-reaction operations when targets presented themselves. One day we made a short two-company assault on another possible VC base area on our northern boundary with the ROK Marines. The enemy was again using the peripheral areas, marked by streams or rivers, because they made up a buffer zone, almost a "no man's land," that our forces were not monitoring adequately. When we got there, we found another extensive hospital and rest camp site, and unearthed considerable quantities of rice, but the people had just departed. The fires were still warm.

We felt unquestionably that the enemy had received advance warning of our search operation. It had taken several days of negotiation with the ROK Marines to get permission to move into their area. Apparently, information about the impending operation had again leaked out. This problem was a fact of life we had to live with. They had better intelligence than we did.

All of the rice we unearthed had the American handclasp insignia on the bags, which meant that originally USAID had issued it to the South Vietnamese government. We kept finding tremendous amounts of this rice being used to feed enemy troops, right under our noses. It was frustrating to turn this rice back over to local village chiefs who probably were in cahoots with the enemy.

As we assumed responsibility for a large area north of LZ Baldy and ventured into the much-fought-over Phu Loc valley north of the Que Son mountains, Colonel Derning from time to time reinforced us with another rifle company. The enemy was moving right through this area in large numbers, and we needed all the troops we could get in order to try to do something about it. We could often see the enemy from our observation posts in the early morning and shortly before dusk in the evening. We kept increasing the number and sophistication of our night ambushes to intercept and punish him.

We had an average company strength of about 150 "effectives" deployed in as many as ten separate positions at night: covering avenues, trails, and paths was no simple chore. We had worked for months on developing the necessary night skills, improving our ambush night firing techniques, teaching our troops noise and light discipline and night movement, and instilling confidence in the leaders of the small units. It became a chess game that I was playing with my VC or NVA counterpart. As we got better, we won a few. B Company, sitting astride the principal avenue, scored the big hits.

One evening Captain John Wilson called in to report a change to one of his previously reported "night acts," our term for a classic V-shaped ambush. One of his lance corporals, with eight men, had asked to move about 100 meters due south to cover what he perceived to be a trail. Our technique was to move into a position at dusk, listen and observe, then relocate after dark to the primary position. This tricky bit of maneuvering involved putting out claymore mines in the dark, having everyone oriented in the proper direction, and maintaining absolute silence thereafter. The men were usually armed with a combination of M-79 grenade launchers, M-16 rifles, hand grenades, and a large number of anti-personnel mines—the directional, lethal claymore.

About midnight this particular ambush, only a mile from LZ Baldy, heard its outer mines explode as an enemy force stepped into the trip-wire trap. A violent fight ensued and we heard numerous explosions. I picked up a radio tuned into the B Company tactical net and heard the squad leader asking for illumination over his position. He used the Marine vernacular to say, "We just got a whole shitpot full of gooners. I've got one man wounded in the leg, but he's OK. Ask for medevac helo after we police up what we've got here."

John Wilson had monitored the same call. He called me on the battalion net to say he had a helo request working. He was sending an officer and another squad, located nearby, to help sort out the situation.

Meanwhile, several other companies had contact that night. The enemy was out in force, using four different routes to bypass us. After the medevac mission was completed and I was told the wounded Marine had been stabilized, I decided to pull my cap over my face in our Operations Center, stretch out on an empty table, and catch a short nap. In just a few minutes, the landline telephone rang. A chief hospital corpsman back at "Charlie Med," the field hospital at Danang, wanted to talk to me. He said that our wounded PFC was in the operating room and doing fine. He had a leg wound, but it wasn't too serious after the bleeding was stopped. What he was calling about was that when he went through the man's pockets to collect all of his personal effects, he found more than $20,000 in American $10, $20, and $50 bills. He thought I ought to know about this. I thanked him and asked that he put it in a guard-mail envelope and send it to me personally so I could sort it all out.

By this time Lieutenant Pete Kammerer and his squad had reached the ambush site. He found 18 fully uniformed dead NVA officers, five of whom were women. It was obviously a paymaster unit. Their heavy packs were loaded with Vietnamese piasters and US greenbacks, and two packs were loaded with hundreds of brand new Seiko watches. Apparently one of our wounded man's buddies discovered the money before the medevac and gave the wounded PFC a large handful of "change" to help pay off his folks' farm in Missouri!

The total of our haul was more than a million US dollars and twice that much in Vietnamese currency. The documents we recovered showed that this was the I Corps paymaster, a lieutenant colonel, NVA. All of the officers were captains or higher.

Our young squad leader received a well deserved meritorious promotion, but the money had to go back to Division as U.S. property. I made a feeble effort to ask for $10,000 for our recreation fund, but my request was denied—for proper legal reasons, I presume. General Widdecke did hear of our request and saw that the Seventh Marines augmented our rehab kitty with an additional $5,000. Our wounded Marine was returned to duty within a few weeks. I welcomed him back and carefully explained to him why he had to forfeit his "mortgage money." I think there are still some staff pogues from our division intelligence section who are saying "Charlie Cooper's troops probably kept as much as they turned in." We didn't.

Our intelligence sources began to be more effective in alerting us to special enemy activities. Scarcely a week after the paymaster episode, we had word of a heavy mortar company and a sapper battalion operating in our area. When B Company submitted its proposed night acts for the evening, all via covered radio, of course, I noticed that one key trail was not covered. I talked to John Wilson and asked that he adjust to cover this route. He pointed out that he had already deployed all of his units, but he did have about 12 Marines in his command post with him. He would slide over about 80 yards to cover the trail with his communicators and supply people. He added that he had plenty of claymores to cover a 30-yard segment of the trail.

His command post hadn't been in its new spot more than half an hour when all hell seemed to break loose at the new ambush site. He called for illumination and reported a major contact. The artillery lit up the area with flares, and the firing continued for another 15 minutes.

First reports were sketchy, as always. We had no wounded, strangely enough, but two Marines were unaccounted for. He said that they had to be careful because some of the mines may not have exploded. He would hunker down, try to locate the Marines, and police up the area at first light. Then he called to say one Marine had been located and was fine, just out of position. One was still missing. Before I departed to fly to his position the next morning, he reported that one Marine, a brand new replacement, had been killed.

What we discovered as we examined the battle site was amazing. There were more than 25 enemy dead, all sappers in their high-top black tennis shoes, black shorts with black headband, and bare chests. Many more must have been wounded. It was strange that the enemy had left their dead. They almost never did this.

The sappers had been carrying a large number of heavy mortars and ammunition for them, and this was scattered all over the area. The dead sappers were remarkable physical specimens, very large men for Vietnamese, built like college wrestlers, muscular and well nourished. I estimated that most of them were five-foot-ten to six feet tall.

John Wilson's ambush had been very effective. The Marines had received very little return fire. Our new man apparently got excited and stood up to fire on the enemy and this had been his downfall. It looked as if the enemy had left all of his mortars with us, and most of the ammunition.

The only "racial incident" to occur during my tenure almost became a bloody scene, but two courageous Marines, one black and one white, saved the day. Despite my

180

trepidations about allowing beer sales in our enlisted club at LZ Baldy, I finally allowed the club to open for a few hours in the early evenings. About the second or third night it was open, a fight started in the club and spread outside, and the participants raced back to their huts to get their weapons. Within minutes, the area immediately below and in front of my hootch had two lines of Marines facing each other. There were about five armed white Marines, with weapons at the ready. They faced about 12 black Marines, also armed, weapons at the ready. Just as I learned of the situation and stepped out to deal with it, the Battalion Officer of the Day, our motor transport officer, First Lieutenant R. F. Marye, dashed into the small enclosure. He had five members of the guard force with him, three black and two white Marines, all with M-16 rifles at the ready. The three forces now formed a "U," with the guard at the bottom, between the two adversaries.

Firing could start at any moment, I thought. I jumped as Lieutenant Marye pulled out his .45 pistol and fired it in the air. He kept his pistol at the ready and walked between the two groups. He spoke calmly and coolly. "I don't know what's happened to cause this, but I'll find out and Colonel Cooper will deal with it. We are all Marines and I'm issuing you an order, right now, as Marines! If you don't obey it immediately, I'll place you under arrest for attempted murder, inciting a riot, and disobeying a lawful order. Do you all understand?" He paused and glanced around as they all slowly nodded their heads. Then he said, "When I tell you to, slowly remove the magazines from your weapons, clear them, and lay them on the ground in front of you. Do you all understand?" Again, slow nods by everyone. Then he said, "Now, do it!"

The first person to move was the six-foot-four black Marine that had become my confidant. As he laid down his rifle he said, "We don't need this. The CO will do what's right." At that moment, all the others, black and white, followed. The guard collected the weapons, frisked each Marine for weapons, and had them sit down in place, under guard.

The standoff was over. My XO had arrived and watched the happenings until this point, when he descended into the small area. He told the men there would be a thorough investigation into the matter. Each of them would be asked to make an official written statement about what had happened. After this statement was completed, their weapons would be returned when they gave their word that they would go to their hootches and remain there unless ordered out.

The five white Marines on one side of the standoff had included a staff sergeant, a sergeant, and three PFC's. Most were from the communications platoon. SNCO's were not even supposed to have been in this small club for the junior troops. Our short investigation concluded that the staff sergeant had used vicious racial slurs, started a fight, and, in effect, incited the standoff. He would probably have been killed in the initial melee if the big black Marine I referred to hadn't intervened during the fight to save him. Later, this same Marine was instrumental in reducing the tension when he said what he did and laid down his weapon. He was only a PFC, but he was a leader. He and a brave lieutenant had saved the day. It had been a near thing.

A special court martial tried the staff sergeant and convicted him of inciting a riot, assault, and threat with a deadly weapon. He received a bad conduct discharge in addition to fines and several months' incarceration. All of the others involved appeared before me at office hours. The blame had been pointedly focused on one individual. I reduced some of the men and fined some of them, but privately praised the tall black

Marine who had become a full member of the "Band of Brothers" without "black" in front of the "Brothers." I recommended Lieutenant Marye for a Navy Commendation Medal and made him the commander of a provisional rifle company I activated later.

Within a week of this incident we received a very timely ALMAR, a message from the Commandant of the Marine Corps addressed to all battalion and squadron commanders in combat. Its subject was "Operation Clean House." This single sheet of paper improved morale and efficiency in 1/7 at least 100%.

In a few words General Leonard Chapman noted that our administrative discharge system had failed to serve the people who needed it most, the front-line combat commanders. He added that unfortunately the Marine Corps was handicapped and ill served by a large number of substandard individuals who did not contribute to their units' missions. He noted that in many cases they had an adverse effect on the combat readiness of the units that most needed well-disciplined and close-knit troops. The Marine Corps was going to reduce its strength by 50,000 men in the next year. The right place to start was in Vietnam. "Hereafter, battalion and squadron commanders are authorized to discharge any individual up to and including the rank of Sgt who they feel is not positively contributing to the success of their unit. No justification is required other than the aforementioned statement. Men so identified are to be detached and dispatched out of country no later than 48 hours after being so identified." This is not an exact quote, but it's the way I remember it. I called for the sergeant major.

My sergeant major had gone home on emergency leave. His replacement was a very special Marine, one I had known since he reenlisted in my company as a corporal back in 1952. First Sergeant R. G. Neeley, soon to be Sergeant Major Neeley, had been the company first sergeant of A Company, under Captain Jim Van Riper. He was great with the troops. He came running into my hooch expecting the worst, but I was smiling. I asked him, "How many men do we have in your little black book?" These were the disruptive individuals, suspected druggies, borderline bigots, black militants, and generally undesirable characters. I explained why I had asked the question. Without opening his black book, he responded "Thirty-one, sir!" I continued, "How soon can you have them out of here?" He smiled and said, "Colonel, they're all in H&S Company. I can have them out tomorrow!"

My trustworthy sergeant major was as good as his word. I'm sure they were happy to return home: I was overjoyed to send them there. I did not have another disciplinary problem or request mast for the remainder of my tour. Incidentally, the black Marine I referred to earlier was recommended for a meritorious promotion by Lieutenant Marye in the motor pool. He later became a squad leader in a new unit we formed up called "Zulu Company." ("Zulu" is the phonetic alphabet's name for the letter Z.)

As April turned into May, some of my key personnel changed. My new S-2/S-3 was a mercurial and controversial officer, Major Alex Lee. Alex and I had become acquainted earlier when he was CO of the III Force Reconnaissance Company, working directly under Lieutenant General Nickerson, CG III MAF. Alex was brave, resourceful, and resolute to an extreme, but he antagonized a number of senior Marine commanders while in this special-operations-oriented reconnaissance command. The First Division and Third Air Wing staffs did not care much for Alex because of the demands he made on their resources to support his ambitious tactical concepts.

When his command was deactivated, no one wanted him for a meaningful assignment. He was reassigned to the division logistics staff as about the fourth assistant to the G-4, a tragic waste of his leadership and tactical skills. When I was called and asked if I would accept him as my operations officer, I put off a decision until I had talked to him personally. His style would have to change, and I wanted to assure myself that it could. He arrived, supposedly seeking my approval, and almost blew it immediately.

He was so confident, so sure that I would accept him before he had even appeared before me, that he visited the operations center, where he proposed a number of significant changes and mouthed off a great deal about the leadership of the division in front of the young officers and troops.

He was still wearing his "you need me" personality when he came to see me. He apparently thought he had a job already and had set about reorienting my battalion. In less than five minutes of conversation, I became convinced that 1/7 would be better off without him, no matter how competent he was. I told him so and ordered him to catch the next flight back to Danang. If he could come off his high horse, I was prepared to have him "help me fight the battalion." As I told him, I really didn't need a senior S-3, and certainly didn't need one that would add to my headaches rather than helping me. He had failed his interview for the very reason I had insisted on having one.

In about ten minutes he returned, calmed down, a completely different person. He asked to work for me. He promised no repeat of what had just happened and made a most acceptable apology. Alex stayed and prospered. After that one short conflict, we worked well together under a wide variety of circumstances. I was to say a lot of very good things about him on his later fitness reports. He knew his career was in jeopardy—he had earlier conflicts while in Recon Company and didn't need any more. Now he was "back with the troops" and doing what he did best.

He took over both the S-2 and S-3 jobs, since Lieutenant Grant had departed. He served 1/7 well and gained my complete confidence. Later, after Vietnam, he was promoted to lieutenant colonel, but, unfortunately, failed selection to colonel in subsequent years.

Another one of my junior officers told me he wanted to do more to help his Corps and country. This infantry officer, a first lieutenant serving as the 81mm mortar platoon commander, had been with us for several months. This large platoon, which was supposed to have two officers, had earlier been the source of some of our racial problems. The lieutenant had been assigned there because of his experience, and he had made a big difference.

After "Operation Clean House," he came to see me. He told me that he felt he could contribute more by serving in a rifle company, and asked to be assigned to B Company, our battalion lightning rod. After a few moments' reflection, I told him I would talk to Captain John Wilson, B Company's CO, and then get back to him. John said he'd be happy to get another experienced officer. We were getting into some very sophisticated night work and John welcomed additional officer leadership. For some reason, though, I worried about him. He was older than most lieutenants, having had considerable enlisted service. It had impressed me that he had followed the Marine tradition of asking for a troop-leading job closer to the "sound of the guns."

He went out to B Company with me by helicopter the next morning. While we visited with John Wilson, we discussed some special tactics for that evening. The platoon that the new officer would be commanding would be moving to a problem area at dusk. As we flew away en route to the other companies' positions, I thought about

183

how far we had come with our tactical skills, and also how the officer experience level had improved.

Back at LZ Baldy, I grabbed a quick sandwich for supper and climbed up into our 40-foot observation tower to watch the troops of B Company deploy into night positions. John Wilson had told me by radio that the platoon I was watching was his new officer's. As dusk began to descend, I could vaguely make out a group of about five Marines moving along, carrying several radios. It came up on the company radio net to give a coded report that it was nearing its assigned position. Seconds later, I witnessed a huge detonation—one great enough to create a mushroom cloud. The enemy had guessed right and had booby trapped that site with what was later determined to be at least a 500-pound bomb. We never found a recognizable shred of the remains of these five Marines: all that was left was a huge hole in the ground.

It was a tough war. Watching five men go up in smoke was particularly agonizing. You ask yourself: For what purpose? It breaks your heart. No amount of toughness or experience teaches you to deal with these things. I can still see this bright young officer with his pencil-line mustache sitting in front of my desk, asking for duty "closer to the guns." God rest his soul and those of all the other fine young men who gave their lives in this crummy war.

Shortly after that terrible experience, I was told that my regimental commander, Colonel Ed Derning, was en route to my command post. The Seventh Regiment was only about a half mile from my headquarters, so I crawled down from the tower to meet him. The explosion and the resultant casualties had been reported earlier by land line, with a message to follow with the details. I was depressed, to say the least, and I'm sure my CO knew that. He brought me some interesting news—good news, it turned out.

Both sides in this war had the wherewithal to intercept the other side's radio messages. We called the results of this reading of the enemy's mail, so to speak, "signals intelligence" or "special intelligence": SI for short. Our gathering techniques were quite sophisticated and broadly successful, but the information they produced rarely got down to us in the field.

What Colonel Ed Derning had in his pocket when he called on me that evening was a message the NVA area commander had sent. This area commander was the man with whom I'd been fighting head-to-head for more than three months—a brigadier or senior colonel. I knew his name and he knew mine, and what he had to say about me was very interesting. As Ed Derning put it to me, "Charlie, the best fitness report you'll ever receive was just filed by the NVA commander you've been facing."

The message, intercepted and translated in its entirety, was directed to his senior commander, our equivalent of a corps commander. He was requesting reinforcements and additional resources. He commented on me by name, saying that I was completely unpredictable, didn't use conventional tactics, and had reduced his combat effectiveness and personnel strength to the point where he was no longer able to execute his assigned missions. He asked that two sapper battalions be made available at once so that he could crush and severely punish this reactionary, unorthodox commander.

He described my tactics, saying that I had created hundreds of small offensive night attack units. Then he described his large losses over the last three months and closed with an urgent plea for prompt assistance.

184

I would have liked a souvenir copy of that message, but Ed Derning had already stretched the regulations just to allow me to read it. He added, a bit tongue-in-cheek, "He was obviously exaggerating your effectiveness just to get some more troops!" However complimentary the message was to me, it was a warning for both of us. In the coming weeks, the enemy did step up his offensive activities. One or possibly two sapper battalions attacked the regional forces headquarters between Baldy and Ross within the month. It was a hand-to-hand donnybrook that completely destroyed the headquarters compound. We figured this night attack cost them more than a hundred killed and many more wounded. Wounded prisoners confirmed they were new sapper units and had just arrived.

The intercepted message, though merely interesting to us, had done its job for my enemy counterpart. He had gotten his additional troops. They weren't through trying to even the score with 1/7, but we would be ready.

Although companies from other units reinforced 1/7 from time to time, I had to operate most of the time with three maneuver units. As I mentioned earlier, our review of the battalion's rear echelon had shown that we could pull enough people from it to form a provisional infantry platoon or even a small company. We did muster enough troops to form Zulu Company.

I made First Lieutenant Marye, my Motor Transport Officer, the Zulu Company commander. His gunnery sergeant was a former rifle company gunnery sergeant who had two months left on his tour. We pulled out about half of the 81mm mortar and 106mm recoilless rifle platoons to form the nucleus. Others came from all across H&S Company, many from the motor transport section. The company's final strength was about 95 Marines. We borrowed two hospital corpsmen from the battalion aid station to work with them in the field. We set up a training program that lasted about four days. For its graduation exercise, the company conducted daylight patrols north of LZ Baldy. From those, it progressed to night activities farther out, using our mobile ambush techniques.

Some of our marginal Marines became very productive and creative troops in the newly formed unit. We didn't give them more than they could handle, and I was quite aware of their initial vulnerability. We didn't leave them out in the field for long, usually returning them after two days. A lot of interesting chemistry took place. There was instant bonding among the troops. Shared dangers and mutual support do that to Marines. The Band of Brothers found some new siblings. The skin color division was about half and half, with a good mix of NCO's. They designed and created their own "guidon," or company flag, and immediately asked to be billeted together as a tactical unit when back "inside the wire."

During the first week after Zulu assumed tactical responsibilities, one of its ambushes scored a hit on a small VC patrol trying to skirt the perimeter of LZ Baldy. They killed five of the enemy and captured five automatic weapons and a brand new Chinese field radio. Morale soared. The following week I took them out on a small operation with me.

While not assigned the most difficult missions, they performed creditably, and proved again that our experiment was working. They continued to operate as a separate tactical unit until the battalion "stood down" later in the summer and was rotated out of Vietnam. Two of its men were wounded in action, though not seriously, and none were killed. My guess is that these motor transport drivers, mortarmen, clerks, and supply

185

pogues have told their buddies and kids a few sea stories about their time in a very special company of Marines, Zulu Company, in the First Battalion, Seventh Marines. Fortunately, the experience brought out the best in all of them. To my knowledge, they never had one disciplinary problem or a request for transfer. They were serving with me deep in the jungle of the enemy's Base Area 112 the day in late July that I was relieved as CO.

We were fortunate to have three different types of specially trained war dogs operate with us. Most of them were German shepherds, but we also had several dobermans. The sentry or patrol dogs were the ones we used in the field to help detect the enemy or alert us if they were near. The drug dogs worked exclusively in the rear areas in the never-ending war against illegal drugs.

The third kind of dog was the last to arrive and the one most appreciated by all of us. It was the booby-trap dog. On at least two occasions, the alertness and skills of these sensitive animals saved my life and the lives of those with me. They weren't fed unless they detected a booby trap, which meant that they had a maximum field time of about two days if they made no detections. They pointed much as a bird dog would, or they sat down next to the booby trap. On a few occasions, this sitting down proved disastrous for the dog when it sat right on an explosive device.

The booby-trap-dog handler usually led a patrol and always checked out a possible bivouac site before the patrol used it. The handler had the dog on an extendable leash that could stretch out to 50 feet.

Our first booby-trap dog went to B Company. We had intelligence reports of a new anti-personnel mine designed to bring down helicopters. It was called a "butterfly bomb." The bomblets, up to 20 in number, resembled large butterflies. The enemy put them among tree limbs around clearings that might be used as helicopter landing sites. Air pressure from rotor wash would set them off and destroy the helo while it was still in the air. Our first encounter with this device occurred the day after our first booby-trap dog started his field duty. As we approached the B Company position in a CH-46 helicopter and started our descent into the clearly marked landing zone, we saw a red smoke grenade explode on the ground. Responding to this emergency signal, we immediately turned away.

John Wilson came up on my radio net to explain. The dog had gone on the alert, and his men were now carefully trying to determine why. He would select an alternate site where we could set down. We landed a short time later and learned that there were indeed two strings of butterfly bomblets in the trees around the zone, rigged to fire simultaneously. Before I left the area, an engineer working with B Company fired a remote explosive charge near one of the bomblets. The resulting explosions of butterfly bombs took the tops off the trees, clean as a whistle.

Before I left I had to meet that very special dog. Duke was his name. He got a special Alpo meal that day. Duke stayed with us for about a month, but died leading a patrol. He detonated a mine as he was sniffing it. Fortunately, his handler and the Marines following were not injured.

Although a few malcontents gave the command some headaches, the great majority of the Marines and Navy men serving in 1/7 consistently went above and beyond what was expected of them. As I had in the Korean War, I witnessed frequent attempts by wounded troops to return to their units in the field before they had been discharged from medical treatment. When we brought companies in for a 48 or 72-hour rehab period, I had our surgeon and hospital corpsmen check each man for wounds as he emerged from that long-awaited shower. They found many "purple heart" wounds that had not been reported or treated. This powerful loyalty among the men in the small units took me back to my days as a platoon commander with Baker Company in Korea. It was the most reassuring and heartwarming experience I had as a commander. These combat Marines were indeed a family, and the strength of their bonding defies description. However, we had to temper this overwhelming drive with good medical judgment.

I used to ask myself, *"What manner of men are these young, gaunt, and weary looking Marines with their huge packs, rifles, ammunition belts, and canteens? Thousands upon thousands of men in the States are dodging the draft, fleeing the country, struggling to get into graduate school, feigning homosexuality, all to avoid serving in combat. Here, in the middle of a hell on earth, almost daily several more of these youngsters are trying to sneak a ride aboard my helicopter to return to their units, hoping the sergeant major or I won't recognize them. They're deserting, but in reverse, as they escape from medical treatment and return to their parent units. They try to lose themselves in the groups of replacements we are flying out to the companies. There's the drive, the calling, the need to return, return to your buddies because they need you and you need them. The Band of Brothers, that's what it's all about."*

With the single exception of a young assistant surgeon who refused to go into the field, I never had a Marine or sailor attempt to avoid field duty. On the other hand, we awarded a large number of Purple Heart medals to men after discovering unreported wounds, usually from shell or grenade fragments.

Not all the members of our Band of Brothers were Americans. Canadian volunteers served with distinction in my battalion—and in others. In the normal course of events, I would not have known that some Marine who had acquitted himself with great distinction in a fight was a Canadian citizen, but it did surface so often that I asked my personnel officer to do some research. It turned out that 27 Canadians served in 1/7 during my tour. Every one of them had received a battlefield promotion, been decorated for bravery, or been wounded at least once, or, in many cases, all of the above. None of them had caused any disciplinary problems or had ever come to my attention except in positive ways. Several had extended to serve a second tour.

Why were Canadians serving in the US Marine Corps—and in Vietnam, yet? I believe there are a number of reasons. First, the Corps has always had an attraction somewhat analogous to that of the French Foreign Legion for young men from other countries looking for adventure and combat experience. Second, honorable service and a combat tour would guarantee immediate US citizenship and a continuing career in the Marine Corps, if desired. Third, Canadians are an adventurous lot. They have fought with us or against us in all of our wars.

Later, I was proud to be able to recognize the Canadians who had served in 1/7 in a very special way. A few months after returning from Vietnam, while serving on the Joint Staff in Washington as a new colonel, I received a call from the Division of Information at Headquarters, Marine Corps. A Canadian Scottish Militia Regiment, the Stormont, Dundas, and Glengarry Highlanders, was to have its anniversary dinner in Kingston, Ontario. They wanted a recently returned combat field commander to be the dinner's guest speaker. This reserve regiment had served with the Marines in Korea and had maintained professional ties with the Corps over the years. I was pleased to be able to speak to them.

Some weeks later, in their cavernous armory, I joined these Scot-Canadians, who attended in all their kilted, tartan regalia. It was indeed a gathering of the clan, young and old, even including some kilt-clad veterans of the Boer War. After considerable libation, a memorable roast beef dinner, and a colorful introduction, I commenced my short speech. I opened by noting that whereas during the Vietnam War my country had sent Canada its draft dodgers and cowards, Canada had sent us its heroes. I mentioned the number of Canadians serving in my battalion and asked them to join me in saluting each of them. I went down the list prepared by my former adjutant, Captain Lada, still serving with 1/7, now at Camp Pendleton. I read, for example, "Corporal William T. Hightower, Kingston, Ontario: two meritorious battlefield promotions, Bronze Star medal for heroism, the Navy Commendation Medal, two Purple Hearts." When I finished reading each name and the honors that went with it, the room erupted in applause. The officers, young and old, jumped up on the huge mess tables, stomped their feet, and toasted each Marine. By the time I had finished the list of 27 names, the room was a shambles, but all the shouting and cheering stopped and the room fell silent when I finished. All but two had been wounded, three had been killed in action, and all had performed exceptional service. I asked those present to join me in a moment of prayer for those three deceased Marines and their families, then I sat down. No speech was necessary. The room erupted again. Our Canadian brothers, and that's what they were, finally halted and gave me a regimental cheer of appreciation. It was a very special night for me, one I'll never forget.

By 1970, the US Air Force had developed very sophisticated night-flying gunships—transport aircraft that could deliver extremely accurate supporting gunfire from a relatively high altitude. The C-130, C-123, and even C-117 aircraft became slow-flying, high-endurance fire bases that used computer-controlled-and-directed fires more accurately than did any other weapon we had in the inventory. The aircraft were especially useful to my battalion because of the large number of small units we had operating independently. There was no other way to give them timely, accurate fire support when they got in trouble. We gave these planes a lot of business.

Our small units were able to talk directly to the pilot or controller in the aircraft. The flight crews would place tracer fire from a variety of guns on a spot, and have the man on the ground adjust their aim. Sometimes these trusty and reliable "birds," some known as "Puff, the Magic Dragon" or "Snuffer Man," would stay on station, giving powerful fire support, for hours, until our unit was in control of the tactical situation. Circling slowly in the dark sky, they would call in additional aircraft when they were getting low on ammunition. I always marveled at the reassuring tone of voice and almost fatherly manner of those aircraft commanders when they were communicating with an excited and badly frightened young Marine. Many were the times I sent a message of praise back to this very special squadron after one of its planes had spent a long, tedious night nursing back into the fold a small Marine unit that had been surrounded by the enemy. I take my hat off to these superb airmen, who still maintain this ability, operating with our nation's special operations forces against America's enemies worldwide.

The variety of skin diseases, foot infections, boils, and intestinal ailments my battalion surgeon dealt with would equate to about 15 years of private practice—as he

188

used to say. Up until late spring, I hadn't been one of his patients, but I had a large boil on my left shoulder that persisted and continued to grow. As we neared the date for an extended field operation, I reached the point where my body armor rubbing on that boil produced unbearable pain. Finally realizing that I had to deal with it, I called Dr. Urban in for a "consultation." I told him of my boil and of our impending raid into the enemy's base area, and asked him to operate on me "tonight." It was thirty minutes before midnight. I did not want to leave the battalion area to go to better facilities: I wanted him to do the necessary surgery in his little sickbay hut. He examined the golf-ball-sized lump and agreed that it needed immediate attention.

Within the hour, the surgeon and his staff performed minor surgery on that damn lump. It was indeed ready for lancing, but a surprise was in store for my young doctor—and for me! As he opened me up and started cleaning the incision, he asked for tweezers. He used them to remove a small silver-colored metal spring, about 1 1/2 inches long. He said, "I didn't know you'd been wounded, Colonel. When did this happen?" I told him he was a small child when I was wounded, back in 1951. This was obviously a detonator spring from that Chinese concussion grenade that had blown me down the hill on the 28th of May, 1951. I'd been carrying it around all these years, and it had finally worked its way out. Fortunately, it was accessible. After receiving an antibiotic shot to suppress any infection, I was discharged from sick bay and "returned to duty." It healed "in jig time."

John Curnutt—loyal, efficient, and solid to the end—was to be rotated home in late June. We got a second-tour major, John Sheridan, as his replacement. We started planning for one more major tactical effort before 1/7 was to stand down in late July. I had always wanted to enter the enemy's bread basket, so to speak, in Base Area 112. We made elaborate plans and coordinated them with an operation that the South Vietnamese Marines would be conducting nearby.

Meanwhile, my son Chip had completed his Plebe Year at the Naval Academy. After some initial problems getting his priorities sorted out between Plebe duties and academic duties, he had switched his major and was making excellent grades. During the spring he had written to ask my advice about where he should go on his summer cruise. He could choose a ship in the Atlantic, with an opportunity to visit Europe, or any one of many options in the Pacific, including riding an amphibious ship coming to Danang to start pulling out Marine heavy artillery and engineer equipment. I told him that he should check out the blond-haired, blue-eyed Scandinavians, if at all possible, and leave the war to me. He would have plenty of the Pacific later.

Naturally, he ignored my advice. Late in June I received a post card from Hong Kong saying he was en route to Danang on an LPD. Since I expected to be in the "bush" when he arrived, I asked Colonel Cy Waldrop, who knew Chip from our Camp Lejeune days, to keep an eye out for his ship. I asked him to at least get him off the ship for a meal, if he had the time. I expected to be up to my neck operationally, and didn't think I'd be able to see him when he arrived. He said he'd take care of it.

Two days before we jumped out into BA 112, we found a sizable NVA force moving in daylight about a mile north of LZ Baldy. This was uncharacteristic of the NVA, and we jumped on them with everything we could muster. It almost looked as if they were trying to move into hidden positions near Baldy, possibly for a later attack. At any rate, with the battle joined and two of my companies engaged while the other was being picked up by helo, I received a strange message. "Sir, Scatterbox 23 is inbound!"

Scatterbox 23 was the call sign for the commanding general. My God, why does this have to happen when I've found more enemy than we've seen in three months? I asked the operator who was aboard the helo. He checked and said, "Iron Mike's dependent." I was Iron Mike, so this could only be my son! What was going on? Within a few minutes the helo landed and out jumped Midshipman Third Class Chip Cooper, wearing Marine utilities, helmet, flak jacket, and a .45 caliber pistol. The helo lifted off, and I waved him over to my bunker. We had received some long-range machine gun fire during the battle that was going on not far from here.

Cy Waldrop had been as good as his word. He had found Chip scrubbing the deck in the crew's head and brought him out to the CG's mess for lunch. As he entered the mess wearing his navy dungarees, General Widdecke saw him. "Aren't you Charlie Cooper's son?" he asked. When Chip said he was, the general said, "Your old man has a small war going on up near LZ Baldy right now. Would you like to go up and see him for about an hour? I'm not going to be using my helo for a while, so you can have a short visit if you'd like. But I can't have you running around in those Navy clothes. Cy, get him in cammies, a flak jacket, helmet, and a pistol. Son, you know how to use a pistol?" Chip said he had fired expert on the .45. And so it came to be. A thoughtful CG, an old friend, and a young son who got to spend about an hour with his old man while he was doing his Marine thing.

We didn't have much private time together, but the battle ended while he was there. I ordered one of the companies nearest Baldy to return through the wire. He joined me as I greeted each of the troops individually as they crossed back inside the perimeter, dirty faced, soaking wet, but smiling as I shook hands with each of them. We had suffered only one minor wound, and the wounded man walked back with this company. Chip, 19 years old at the time, said, "They all look younger than me!" I responded, "That's because they are." He left shortly after that: the general needed his aircraft.

From July 1 to 15 we had worked the eastern portion of the regimental area of operations. On July 16 we were to assault the Song Thu Bon River Valley and the An Chau Dao Mountain Range. We were so far away from friendly artillery that I took my fire base with me—an 81mm mortar section and a 4-gun platoon of 4.2-inch mortars sited at my command post. The operation was scheduled to last until July 25. I had asked to be relieved of command while in the field, still fighting the enemy on the 24th, rather than upon our return to the rear the next day. Colonel Ed Derning agreed to my request.

It was an ambitious undertaking, but we knew that any operation planned this far in advance had a way of being leaked to the enemy. We maneuvered for three days without any more than occasional contact with small NVA patrols. On the fourth day, I called for two helicopters for a personal air and ground reconnaissance of the river basin. As we were circling the widest point of the river to commence the ground search, I noticed an unusual pattern of gentle mounds on the river banks. They were invisible from the ground, grown over with grass and weeds. We landed next to them, put out local security, and started digging. Mounds indeed! They were dozens of buried warehouses, filled with rice, weapons, ammunition, and assorted medical supplies. Some of these mounds were as long as football fields. After two days of unearthing these huge buried storehouses, we turned the follow-up recovery or destruction of their contents over to the Army Special Forces units that had been operating on the periphery of BA 112.

190

My closest call of the war came not from the enemy but from ARVN artillery. They had recently been reequipped with Marine 175mm guns. Their airborne spotter aircraft mistook my CP and firebase for an enemy redoubt. Huge shells bracketed us—over, under, left, and right of us. We knew the enemy didn't have these weapons, and the direction suggested they were coming from An Hoa, a joint ARVN/USMC fire base. Using every available means of communication, including airborne observers and screaming voices, we were able to turn off the ARVN cannon cockers before they made one final correction and blew us to smithereens.

The good news was that there were no US casualties and that we discovered much enemy gear. The bad news was that we had no meaningful enemy contact. We did, on this our "graduation exercise," as the troops called it, function perfectly.

There were no speeches at my change of command. Only the CP troops were present, and most of those were out on security duty, but I did bring in one squad from Zulu Company. It was commanded by a six-foot-four black Marine corporal who wore a huge smile on his face. We had been through a lot together. It started at my first request mast and ended, appropriately, with him commanding the one squad of troops in ranks for the brief ceremony. The whole battalion had profited from our relationship. Lieutenant Marye had sent him over to be the "honor guard" as I transferred the battalion colors to Lieutenant Colonel Paul Riegert on July 24, 1970, the day before the battalion was to stand down from field duty.

My war was over. This battalion had become as good as I could make it. Its men were proud and they were good, but my heart still aches when I remember those memorial services.

> *His bayoneted rifle stuck in the ground, his helmet mounted upon it, a Marine has gone to his final place. We who remain behind can only remember, thank God for his friendship, weep, and pray for his loved ones.*

From my last memorial service, for Alpha and Bravo Companies in July 1970:

> *Whenever we lose a true friend, it is natural to ask why, but the answer never comes. Our friendship with these departed comrades has already made our lives better. The true measure of a man's worth in this world is not how long he lived, but the quality of what he left behind. We are the product of the people we associated and served with. These Marines, honored here today, will live on in our memories of courage, hardships, and heartaches shared on the field of battle.*
>
> *They will never be forgotten. I ask God to comfort their families and help them find peace. We who remain thank God for the honor of serving with such brave and selfless men. Amen.*

Chapter 22

Return to the "Puzzle Palace"
Duty with the Joint Staff

During my last months in Vietnam, two significant personal things happened in Marine Headquarters in Washington. First, the Marine Corps selected me for promotion to the grade of colonel, and second, it assigned me to the Logistics Directorate of the Joint Staff in the Pentagon for my next tour of duty. As I headed home in September after testifying in the Herrod court martial, I relished this homecoming. For the first time ever, I was to return home to find my civilian clothes, uniforms, and all family effects just as they were when I left more than a year earlier, comfortably ensconced in our little brick home on Taylor Avenue in Alexandria, Virginia. Son Chip was now a "Youngster" (sophomore) at the Naval Academy, and Linda was starting her senior year at T.C. Williams High School. Their sweet mother was lovelier than ever.

The Volkswagen "fastback" I had ordered from Germany arrived in Baltimore the day I was promoted to colonel. It would be my commuting car: we had again become a two-car family. Our family beagle, Skipper McDonald Cooper, was not too happy to see me back: I apparently infringed on his "space." In my year's absence he had enjoyed sleeping on my side of the bed and using my pillow. My first order for him to remove his carcass brought a bared-teeth snarl, which lasted until I picked him up and gave him a big hug before putting him back on his rug. Our daughter helped by inviting Skipper Dog, as we called him, to share her four-poster bed.

It took me most of my remaining leave period to learn to sleep through an entire night, but it was a nice problem to have to solve! Carol and I celebrated our twentieth anniversary on the 23rd with a very special dinner and evening in Washington. I reported into the Pentagon the next day, September 24, 1970. The Joint Staff paper mill would be a drastic change of pace. As I told myself while driving to work that sultry September morning, "No matter what happens in this new job, at least no one is shooting at me!" That philosophy was to be a crutch to lean on whenever the frustrations of staff work and red tape ruled (or ruined) the day.

I was assigned to the Operations Branch of the European Division of the Logistics Directorate, known in Pentagonese as "J-4." We handled current operational matters of a logistics nature for the entire western European area, NATO, Africa, and the Middle East. There were eight of us, lieutenant colonels and colonels, all sharing one large room and one busy secretary. I was the only Marine.

I spent my first few days learning how to get around the building, visiting our counterparts in the other directorates of the Joint Staff, and learning the ABC's of the staff paper system: the "flimsy, buff, green, red stripe" sequence. Since all the business we handled was classified, we were not able to discuss any of it on the telephone. We had to do a lot of walking to coordinate staff papers with other concerned agencies.

The staff, greatly expanded at the height of the Vietnam War, was grossly over-manned. A few people stayed very busy, and constructively so, but the vast majority of the assigned officers were underused except during short periods of crisis. There were a number of ways to deal with this situation. Some sought additional work and responsibility and got it. Others accepted the minimal work level as an opportunity to do other things: earn advanced degrees, prepare for employment after military retirement, or become almost-professional jocks by spending half of the working day in the athletic club or following the new fad of jogging or distance running.

I looked for work and found it aplenty. When international crises arose, I usually found myself leading a response team for J-4. My first experience, just days after reporting in, involved giving medical assistance to the Jordanian government in response to a Presidential order. We chose US field hospitals and deployed them from NATO units in Europe to treat the large numbers of casualties in Jordan after King Hussein's Legion crushed an abortive Palestinian attempt to seize power. We selected two Army and Air Force fly-away medical hospitals, MASH units, for immediate deployment. It wasn't a difficult staff task, but it was an interesting experience and taught me the essentials of working a "paper and a problem" with all four military services. My boss seemed to be pleased with what I had done: until I left almost three years later, whenever we had a major crisis my phone was the first to ring.

After spending a year on the operations side of the house, I moved into the Plans Branch as Branch Head. Plans was a more interesting assignment and gave me the opportunity to travel in Europe. We dealt with huge problems that involved many agencies. One of the many interesting long-range negotiations we dealt with was the US-FRG (Federal Republic of Germany) Off-Set Agreement, which established the amount of money that West Germany paid the US for maintaining American forces in that country. It was a sizable sum—more than $2 billion per year. The State, Treasury, and Defense Departments all played parts in these negotiations, with Defense being the dominant player.

This was not an unpleasant tour. I learned a lot and did a lot of "missionary work," teaching the other services who the Marines are and what we can do. In turn, I got a new appreciation for what a relatively small piece of the pie the Marine Corps was. Especially in the area of logistics, we required massive support from all three of the other services, and this tour brought that home to me. Another good thing about the tour was that, with some judicious planning, it was possible for me to take all my authorized leave. This was a novelty: I had had to throw away earned leave in all but two of my more than 20 years of Marine Corps service.

The director's billet called for a three-star general or a vice admiral, and there were two deputy billets that called for two-star officers. My first director was Air Force Lieutenant General O'Keefe, a very decent man, who was rebuffed by higher authority when he tried to reduce his officer strength by 25 percent.

The next director was a tall, aggressive three-star general from the army, Walter Woolwine, an interesting man. Early in his tour I had to brief him on a subject I had been shepherding for more than six months. I had prepared a message dealing with the matter for him to release, and it was on his desk before I entered his office. We had not met before. When I knocked and entered General Woolwine's office, he started his conversation with me by asking, "Are you the idiot that wrote this stupid message?"

While it would be impossible to remember the exact words that followed, that day is still very clear in my mind. I took a deep breath, looked him directly in the eye, and responded. "General Woolwine, we have never met before. I'm Colonel C. G. Cooper, US Marine Corps, but you already know that. I am not an idiot and don't accept being called one, and that message is a product of about six months of hard work by a lot of competent people. Your predecessor and I worked on the draft together about a month ago. It has been fully staffed in the Joint arena and has both State and Treasury concurrence. If you want to discuss any specific portion of the message, I'll be glad to answer you, but first I demand that you apologize for what you called me when I entered your office!" At the time I never gave a second's thought to the consequences of my response. Even now, I still feel that it was the correct one. Apparently General Woolwine did, too.

His reaction was to pour a cup of coffee, point to a nearby chair, and ask me to sit down. He offered me the coffee, apologized, and said that he deserved what I had said. He did have a question or rather a comment on the message, which I answered quickly. There was a pause in the conversation while he signed the message and handed it to me. I rose, stood in front of his desk and said, "Is that all, Sir?" He nodded his head and I about-faced. We were to work together for another year and a half and become rather close professionally. He was a good man and a friend to this day but his proclivity to bully, to test the mettle of an action officer, had given us a most uncertain start.

In my second year I learned that the Marine Corps would welcome my request for a "split tour" in Washington. I submitted the necessary request to have a two-and-two tour, two years in the JCS billet and two years at Headquarters, Marine Corps, instead of spending three years in the JCS billet. My old boss, General Ed Wheeler, was chief Manpower Planner for the Marine Corps. He promised to give me a responsible management position if I were available. My request sailed along smoothly until, as a part of the final colonels' slate for next year, it reached the desk of the Commandant of the Marine Corps for approval. He approved the entire list, with one exception. He lined through my name and initialed it, deleting me from the list without comment. I saw General Wheeler at a reception in Quantico that weekend. He told me he had no idea what prompted the Commandant to remove my name. I didn't know General Robert Cushman, the Commandant, personally and had no idea why he had denied my request.

In my last few months with J-4 I earned my spurs, so to speak. I wore two hats, being assigned to work full time in the Pacific Division and still maintain my job in the European Division. In 1973, as the South Vietnamese armed forces slowly disintegrated under increasing pressure from the NVA forces, the US was trying frantically to stem the tide by pouring in more arms and supplies and giving the South Vietnamese more air support. This final, emergency-stoked effort to pull chestnuts out of the fire was code named "Project Enhance." It involved a forced-draft infusion of more than $2 billion worth of arms, equipment, supplies, and tools of war. We had to get all this into South Vietnam within an unbelievable 30 days! The Pacific Division of J-4 did not have the manpower, talent, or experience to supervise such a huge project.

Major General William G. Johnson, USMC, General Woolwine's senior deputy, called me at home at 6:30 one Friday evening. He told me to put my drink down and grab a toilet kit because there were big things waiting for me—that it might be a while before I got home again. He added, "Hurry up! General Woolwine, General Pattillo, and I are all waiting to see you!"

I knew that things in Vietnam were nearing total disarray and correctly surmised that somehow I was about to get involved. The three generals had decided that they had to bring in some new blood to help pull off this massive, unprecedented attempt to save a dying country. The decision to do this had been made at the top, and it was up to J-4 to convert a two-paragraph order into action. When I entered General Woolwine's office, he seated me and forced a cup of coffee on me. Calmly and logically, he and his two deputies walked me through the problem they faced. They wanted me to take a few of my own people and superimpose our small task force over the hardworking and conscientious Navy Supply Corps' Pacific Division chief and his staff. I had until eight the next morning to take stock of my assets and problems, and work out a plan of attack. He would hear it at that time. At nine, we had to brief the Chairman of the Joint Chiefs of Staff, who in turn would take our recommendations up the line to the Secretary of Defense and the White House.

I worked through the night, and by seven o'clock Saturday morning I had a handwritten plan, a few acetate transparencies for briefing, and a fair appreciation of the obstacles to be overcome. My first step had been to ensure that I'd be at peace with the leaders of the Pacific Division. That wasn't difficult. They all welcomed our help. I later surmised that they had requested assistance in the first place. They had been overwhelmed by the immensity of the project and would cooperate, "salute smartly," and do whatever they could to make my plan happen. This was a good start.

I brought in three of the best officers from the European Division—two Army lieutenant colonels and one Navy commander. I chose the call sign or nickname of "Enhance 6." My officers were "Enhance 1, 2, and 3." In three weeks we managed to locate, identify, and deliver the goods of war, as directed.

The most interesting of many telephone confrontations I experienced occurred as I tried to convince the Air Force that it had to fly an entire tank battalion from Okinawa and Japan into either Danang or Hue City. The Air Force had for many years touted the C-5 Globemaster heavy-lift aircraft as capable of lifting any tank in the US inventory. The truth was that this aircraft's wings had proven to be weaker than expected: the Air Force routinely avoided loading the planes to their design maximum gross weight so as to avoid overstressing them. Some future modification would have to correct this embarrassing shortcoming.

The powers that be in the Pentagon were well aware of this when I located one company of Marine medium tanks on Okinawa and two companies of Army light tanks in a supply depot in Japan. The order came to me to "Do it!" After a heated conversation between me and an Air Force general on Okinawa, the Air Force reluctantly accepted the mission to airlift one composite tank battalion of 45 tanks (15 medium, 30 light), trucks, jeeps, ammunition, and technical personnel to Vietnam. A brigadier general was aircraft commander on the first mission, a sort of test flight, carrying a medium tank into Danang. The wings didn't fall off, and within 96 hours the tank airlift was completed. The tanks were instrumental in halting an NVA tank attack some days later, but I've yet to figure out who the South Vietnamese found to drive these vehicles, maintain them, or fire their guns. Our tech reps and advisors couldn't have done it all.

As I reminisce about those arduous days, I remember the awful meals from the "automat," the short naps on the rug, the showers in the athletic club, and meeting Carol at the mall entrance to receive clean clothes. The Pentagon has never had adequate facilities for people who must work around the clock or remain on board for days at a time.

This gargantuan effort was the last major logistics "flail" before we finally realized that the Vietnamization Project would not succeed. We couldn't prop up the South Vietnamese much longer, but we spent an awful lot of money and effort trying.

It was both a sad and a happy day when I left the Pacific Division to return to my old desk. We had worked our tails off to carry out a mandate that few of us ever believed had any chance of succeeding. We all knew that we in J-4, from top to bottom, had done our best. General Woolwine was sad as he thanked all of us involved.

At about 10:30 one morning early in 1973, not long after my name had been deleted from the colonels' list, I received a phone call from Colonel Bob Howard, the Military Secretary for the Commandant of the Marine Corps. He asked me whether I had my uniform with me in the office. I replied that I did not, but that I could correct that situation in less than an hour if necessary. He said that it would indeed be necessary, because General Cushman wanted to see me in his Pentagon office at exactly one o'clock, and I should be in service greens. I was surprised at this, and asked if I might inquire why General Cushman wanted to see me. He laughed and said, "He wants to talk to you about your next assignment." Needless to say, I made the round trip home and back in short order and was in the prescribed uniform waiting in General Cushman's outer office when he arrived shortly before one 'clock.

We shook hands and he invited me in as he started to unpack a huge briefcase. He seemed to be in good humor and had me take a seat as he went through the papers he'd unpacked as if searching for a specific paper, which he soon found. He sat down, peered over his glasses at me for a few seconds, and said, " I guess you've been wondering why I scratched you off of the colonels' slate." I nodded and said that I had been curious but figured he must have had a good reason. He smiled and said that indeed he did. He commented on my record, stressed the considerable command experience, and finished by saying he had selected me to become the next Commanding Officer of Marine Barracks, Washington. What a relief and what a wonderful bit of news!

This was one of the most prestigious colonel assignments in the Corps. I would be working directly for General Cushman. "The 'oldest post of the Corps,'" he reminded me, "is the heart and soul of the Marine Corps, and we have to be very careful who we assign to take custody of it. Mrs. Cushman and I will look forward to having you and your wife as our neighbors. We'll have you relieve Colonel Twomey some time in May of this year." He stood and extended his hand. The meeting was over, but it had given my morale a shot in the arm. Within the hour Colonel Dave Twomey, a classmate of mine and CO of the Marine Barracks, called to congratulate me. As I told Carol that night, the Corps hadn't forgotten me after all. As some wise old Marine was supposed to have said: Do your best, show a little patience, and things will work themselves out!

Chapter 23

The Palace Guards, Marine Barracks, Washington

Marine Barracks, Washington houses the official battle colors of the US Marine Corps. It is home for the Commandant, the Assistant Commandant, two senior lieutenant generals, the Marine Band, the Marine Drum and Bugle Corps, the Marine Corps Institute, and a small battalion of hand-picked troops. These troops, in addition to performing the ceremonial functions that have brought them national and international acclaim, also function as the President's "Palace Guard." Located "within easy marching distance of the Capitol," where President Thomas Jefferson positioned them when the city of Washington was being planned, they are responsible for the security of the presidential retreat at Camp David, serve individually as directed in the White House, and become a combat-ready military escort for the President should he have to leave Washington in a national emergency. The command is inexorably tied to the Presidency, making it a unique, demanding, and at times frustrating assignment for the commanding officer.

Vice President Ford takes a review at Marine Barracks just before becoming President.

The commanding officer lives in the center one of six sets of spacious old senior officers' quarters. He is, among other things, the landlord, innkeeper, and host for the thousands of guests that visit this tiny bastion of tradition and military perfection each year. The summer evening parades at the Barracks and at the Iwo Jima Memorial in Arlington Cemetery are impressive examples of perfectly executed traditional military ceremonies. Setting the pace for similarly impressive events by other military services, these patriotic parades play to packed stands from early May until late September of each year. In 1974, *Reader's Digest* published an article entitled "An Evening to Remember," which noted that this parade was an occasion to savor and remember for the rest of your life. No one who has attended would disagree.

My tenure as commanding officer started in May of 1973. It was a busy time for the Cooper family. Son Chip was to graduate from the Naval Academy early in June, as was our daughter's boyfriend, Steve Thompson. My son's best friend, Steve had joined our family as an "adopted" son some two years earlier. He and Linda were very much in love. Linda, who had finished two years at Mary Washington College, would continue her physical therapy studies in Richmond at the Medical College of Virginia. We no longer needed our home in Alexandria, so we sold it to a young army major.

After an impressive and extremely warm afternoon change-of-command ceremony, General Leonard Chapman, our distinguished former Commandant and former CO of the Marine Barracks, congratulated me and added: "Charlie, every Marine officer in his own heart should strive for perfection, particularly in command. But this is the only place in the Corps where you not only can achieve it, but it's expected of you! Good luck!"

Later, in General Cushman's office, I received the only direct oral orders of my tour. They were short and explicit. I had inherited an embarrassing and surprising drug problem among the select troops at Camp David. Some 12 Marines had just been summarily transferred. His remarks dealt with that subject. "Charlie, I don't want to ever hear of another problem about Camp David—drugs or anything else. I want you or your XO to visit that unit once a week, reorganize it if necessary, and keep an eye on it. You understand?" I understood, and Camp David did indeed remain a focal point during my tour of duty as CO Marine Barracks.

In this "zero defect" environment, Carol and I lived our lives pretty much in a fishbowl. Quarters 3 was like Grand Central Station. Maintenance and security personnel treated the house as public domain. We learned to deal with it, enjoyed many aspects of it, and were blessed with the finest group of officers and senior NCO's I had ever seen in the Corps. We especially enjoyed the warm camaraderie our general officer neighbors and their wives established with us.

Early on, I discovered that the manpower quality problems I had escaped while in the Pentagon were still present in all of the services, even in our beloved Corps, even at the "Oldest Post of the Corps." All of our Marines, including the Marine bandsmen, had to be cleared for "White House Access." This was required by the Secret Service for all personnel who may be in the vicinity of or have physical access to the President. It includes extensive background checks, some taking as long as six months to complete. More than half of our carefully screened applicants could not meet the high security standards set by the White House. A few Marines who had joined us recently after having passed their interviews and physical and ceremonial tests were wanted by police

198

for serious crimes. In one bizarre case, we found that a member of the barracks guard force was wanted for murder. He was later convicted and received a life sentence. We had great difficulty in finding Marines who could meet all the requirements: over 6 feet tall, lean, fit, intelligent, with an impeccably clean record, and motivated for duty in Washington—but as in all else at Marine Barracks, we persevered!

The heralded Marine Band came under a temporary shadow that led to some long-needed restructuring. The director was retired prematurely after some of his illegal practices and indiscretions came to light. Charged to investigate the situation and take corrective action, my Executive Officer, Lieutenant Colonel Bill Duncan, and I formulated a far-reaching plan to bring the band into the official administrative and legal fold of the Corps. We uncovered long-overlooked administrative, legal, supply, and morale problems and dealt with them speedily. After the old director departed, I called the band together, told them that Major Jack Kline was their new director and I was now the "Godfather of the Band," an apt term in view of the many reforms we had to institute. The reforms were well received, and the "President's Own" prospered as never before. Colonel John R. Bourgeois, who became the director in 1979, was commissioned from the enlisted grade of master gunnery sergeant and became a junior director during this reorganization phase.

The band took in its first female members during my tenure. The necessary adjustments were more difficult than they should have been, because the male band members resented special treatment the former director had given the first women recruited for the band. We dealt with these problems—and had new uniforms designed and authorized for women in both the marching band and the concert unit. The numerous changes, long overdue, let the band concentrate on what it did best, perform magnificently in the John Phillip Sousa tradition as representative of the finest in military music. One of my most treasured possessions is the small plaque I received from the band. Having once been a high school cornet player of "some distinction," I was designated an *Honorary 3d Cornet Player in the Marine Band.*

During this same period, the Drum and Bugle Corps came under the dynamic leadership of newly commissioned Master Gunnery Sergeant Truman Crawford. More than twenty years later, Colonel Truman Crawford was still leading this colorful and spectacular group to even higher levels of excellence. It still steals the show at Friday night parade concerts.

Even such a prestigious post was not without financial difficulties. I learned, however, that there are a lot of creative ways to stretch the taxpayers' dollars. For example, during one period of belt tightening, my bright young supply officer, Major Carmen Pastino, informed me that we were running short of 40mm shells for our saluting battery. The fixed guns were on the end of the parade "deck," as we nautically called our parade ground, facing toward the Commandant's house. As part of the ceremonial honoring of distinguished senior guests, we fired the prescribed number of rounds from the saluting battery. The Marine Barracks were in the heart of southeast Washington, so our salutes rattled windows in that part of the community, but the police and neighbors accepted the ceremonial fireworks as traditional and without too much complaint. We did a minimum of practicing, however.

When Carmen Pastino told me how low our stock of shells was, I asked him to seek out his Navy supply buddies and see if he couldn't appeal to their sense of largesse for the poor Marines. He returned shortly to announce a bonanza. A small base in Maryland was being closed, and we could have all of their 40mm shells—a large number, it seems. Since we planned to use the shells the following Friday, I decided to test fire the guns at a dress rehearsal earlier in the week. It was a good thing!

As the saluting battery fired the first shells on that beautiful, clear summer morning, I knew immediately that something was wrong. They were about twice as loud as normal and the blast effect in our small quadrangle was staggering. I immediately raised my hand and shouted "Cease Fire!" By this time the battery had fired at least six shots. In the midst of the deafening silence that followed I could hear the clink of broken glass falling from the windows of the Commandant's house, 100 yards away. We had blown out at least four of the huge windows facing the parade field. I thanked my lucky stars that General and Mrs. Cushman were out of town, no one was injured by the flying glass, and my supply officer was calling a glass company before I could get all of the facts straight. By midafternoon the windows were as good as new.

The Cushmans either never learned of this weird accident or elected not to mention it. Major Pastino, a bit wiser about looking Navy gift horses in the mouth, disposed of the "overcharged munitions" posthaste. If I hadn't rehearsed the guns and this had happened in front of 2500 guests and the Commandant on Friday night, I probably would not be writing this account right now. As Mom used to say after some unusually significant fiasco, "All's well that ends well."

During my first year at "8th and I," the nation suffered economic woes; the Vice President resigned and was replaced by Congressman Gerald R. Ford; and the OPEC-inspired gasoline shortage slowed Washington and the nation as a whole. Then in 1974, investigations into the Watergate affair built to a climax. It became apparent by mid-summer that President Nixon's days as President were numbered. Those of us involved in his support and personal safety were aware of impending major changes. It was an unsettling time, and the Secret Service was in a constant snit about presidential security.

And not to be ignored was the real-life effect of this unusual change of presidents on the young Marines who had been especially trained to give their lives, if necessary, to protect the holder of that office. Suddenly the elected president is removed from office and replaced. The King is gone. Protect the new King. I tried to discuss this with every Marine under my command in the week following the change of presidents. I talked to them all in small groups. My message was simple and straightforward. "We have just witnessed an historical event and helped to make it happen: the orderly transfer of national leadership other than by an election. Only in this great country could such a normally disruptive event take place without a trace of violence or unrest. That is partly because you and others like you were at the ready, guarding and protecting the President until it was no longer required. Then you shifted gears without a hitch and dedicated yourselves to serving his legal successor. You can tell your grandchildren that you were at 8th and I in 1974, and you can be proud of it!"

The Marine Barracks had a few household pets living on board, and of course had its own mascot. Ole Henry, the world's meanest tomcat, lived next door to us in the quarters of Lieutenant General and Mrs. Herb Beckington. He was *king of the block*, dominating every dog and cat anywhere in his vicinity—the only cat I've ever seen that routinely caught and devoured squirrels.

200

Our Barracks' mascot was Chesty, a magnificent young English bulldog. He was not the smartest dog in town, but he was a handsome dude and had learned to do his walk, sit, and prance routine for our evening parades. We tried to teach him to salute, but it was above "his pay grade and IQ," as the troops said. Handsome and pugnacious-looking as he was, however, and despite all we did to train and encourage him, he fell apart and cringed whenever Henry threatened him.

Henry knew this and delighted in scaring the wits out of him. It had been this way ever since an occurrence in June of 1973, while the Corporal of the Guard was taking Chesty around the compound on a leash for his morning exercise routine. Old Henry was waiting in ambush on the Beckingtons' side porch. As Chesty came abreast of the porch, Henry leapt on his back like a feline jockey, dug in his claws, and bit Chesty on the back of his neck. I think he almost scared the young dog to death. After separating the animals, the corporal reported to the Officer of the Day, who in turn reported to me. All I could do was arrange for Chesty to make a trip to the vet. This did nothing to restore the courage of the Barracks mascot, a featured attraction for thousands of visitors.

Chesty's situation had serious ramifications. If Henry appeared anywhere in the area of the parade field during a parade rehearsal, Chesty would refuse to perform. The pet situation had to be dealt with quickly. Using great tact and diplomacy, I convinced General and Mrs. Beckington that Henry's conduct was such that he had to be securely locked inside of the house on parade nights, and that we further would appreciate the same during scheduled rehearsals.

Chesty, on the other hand, was treated as if he were a Marine. We maintained a record book for him, gave him periodic physicals, and graded him in conduct and professional proficiency. He received a number of accolades and was always honored in front of the troops. However, he wet on my office rug and stole cookies from a plate during one visit to my office. For this we brought him to "Office Hours" before the commanding officer, where he received reduction in rank to private as his punishment. His outstanding performance in subsequent weeks, however, earned him a meritorious promotion to PFC. He never repeated his indiscretions in my office and retired from active service as Sergeant, USMC (Dog).

In 1974, General Cushman invited President Ford to be the honored guest at the November tenth Marine Corps Birthday Memorial Service in Arlington Cemetery. Again, the Secret Service went into high gear. The reviewing stand and small amphitheater at the Iwo Jima memorial is a particularly vulnerable and open area, because high-rise apartment buildings surround it. A sniper in any one of them could easily sight in on a person seated or standing in the front row of the reviewing area. Hundreds of agents and troops were positioned in and around the area and in all the surrounding buildings. We war-gamed and discussed every conceivable option, we thought.

As the ceremony proceeded on that cold November morning, the time came for us to escort the President to the reviewing area. He was wearing a special protective vest under his overcoat as General Cushman and I ushered him to a position between the two parade guidons. At that moment there was a sharp crack of multiple rifle shots. President Ford reacted by ducking, I pushed him to the ground and fell on top of him. General Cushman joined the pile-up, and three Secret Service agents protected the lot of us by piling on top of the general. Within a second, I heard a second volley and then a third. The one thing no one had even considered "taking precautions against" was the salute of blanks from a nearby military funeral.

I told the President that I thought we had just heard the third and final volley from a nearby funeral. He laughed as he was getting out from under the pile and said, "I'm just glad it wasn't mine!" We all dusted ourselves off, and that genial gentleman, the President of the United States, stuck out his hand to me and said, "Thank you, Colonel Cooper. That could have been the real thing!" Gerry Ford was one nice guy!

In January of 1975, the Marine Corps convened a selection board to choose eight colonels for promotion to brigadier general. My name was in the pot, as they say, and lightning did strike. I've always said that "making general" was a lot more pleasant than being one, but that the accompanying feeling of relief, satisfaction, and pride is almost impossible to describe. At the time I was in my 24th year of commissioned service. The assignment slate published in the weeks that followed had me scheduled to leave Washington and assume command of the Marine Corps desert base at 29 Palms, California. This was an artillery and combined arms training base about 30 miles from Palm Springs. It was a plum assignment for a new brigadier and earned me the nickname of "King Hussein" from my fellow selectees, referring to my desert kingdom.

Colonel Duff Rice was chosen as my successor at the Barracks, and the date for the change of command was set for late May or early June. Our last spring at the Barracks was an especially pleasant time, as we prepared for the parade season, brought in new officers and troops, and began looking for a new car for our cross-country drive. Our daughter Linda was to graduate from the Medical College of Virginia in June. She and Steve Thompson were to be married the next day in our old Alexandria church, Emmanuel Episcopal. It was an exciting time, but we were both concerned about the timing for the graduation, wedding, and the cross-country trip. But things were in the mill that would take all of that right out of our hands.

The civilian powers that be, the Secretary of Defense and the Secretary of the Navy, determined that a new Commandant of the Marine Corps would be appointed in July, following a period of unusual turbulence in the General Officers ranks. The officer eventually chosen was Lieutenant General Louis H. Wilson, who was then serving in Hawaii as Commanding General, Fleet Marine Force, Pacific. General Wilson had been a company commander in General Cushman's battalion during the battle for Guam in WWII. Cushman, a major at the time, had received a Navy Cross and Wilson, a captain, had received our nation's highest award, the Congressional Medal of Honor. A Mississippian and my former CO at the Basic School, he arrived in Washington several weeks before the June 30 turnover and made some significant plans for the future.

His first step toward putting those plans into effect was to cancel the entire assignment slate for brigadiers. We all received word that General Wilson would personally call each of us about our new assignments.

General Wilson did call, informed me I was not going to 29 Palms, and told me he was keeping me in Washington to serve as his Assistant for Congressional Liaison. He added, "What do you think about that, Charlie?" I was momentarily speechless. He asked, "Charlie, you still there?" I responded that I was. I just didn't know what to say. He laughed and said, "Well, if you're worried, that was my first job as a new Brigadier and it didn't hurt my career too much! You are the best I have available to handle our special relationship with the Congress. You know Washington, have a great record and a good southern accent. Besides, I believe you and Carol own a home in Alexandria." I said, "General, I appreciate your confidence. You know I'll do my best . . . but we sold the house in Alexandria." He concluded by saying, "Better get yourself another, then, 'cause you're starting work the afternoon after your change of command on 2 June."

That day in June was a wonderful conclusion to an unforgettable two years. It was exactly 25 years after my commissioning at the Naval Academy. My emotions almost overcame me as I said farewell to my spit-shined, ceremonial, but tough-as-nails "Band of Brothers." They too believed in each other and our family concept of brotherhood in arms. General Cushman officiated at the formal parade and promoted me to brigadier general during the ceremony.

I had found another house, in Lake Barcroft, near Falls Church, Virginia. It was in a lovely area and an easy drive from Headquarters, Marine Corps. As usual, Carol supervised the moving crew that came in to pack our effects. Our new home would be a tight squeeze: our huge quarters at the Barracks had allowed us to accumulate too much family furniture.

Our daughter graduated from college and married on schedule. Both the rehearsal dinner and wedding reception were in historical John Phillip Sousa Bandhall at the Barracks. Lieutenant (jg) Stephen C. Thompson became an official member of the Cooper family, then he and Lieutenant (jg) Chip Cooper returned to their destroyers in San Diego. Chip's marriage to a beautiful Maria Luna would follow six months later in San Diego.

So ended an unforgettable chapter in our lives. I put the shiny new stars on my uniform and went to work the next afternoon.

Chapter 24

"Working the Hill," USMC Congressional Liaison

I was to have only a two-day turnover with my predecessor, Brigadier General Ernie Reid, who had orders to take command of the base at 29 Palms, California, my original assignment. We spent those two days touring Capitol Hill, talking while we walked about, and meeting as many key people as possible. My clients would be the 535 congressmen and senators, but the key Armed Services and Appropriations Committee members and their staffs were the objects of our hurried calls on those two days. As we raced from office to office, I was both exhilarated and awed by the scope of my future responsibilities.

I soon learned that the old business principle of "getting to know the territory" was more than half of my new job. In later months, after having met and established good professional ties with all of the key people, I could get as much done with a phone call as I could have earlier with several days of effort and much anxiety.

Secretary of the Navy William Middendorf had me attend his office briefing every Monday morning to give him a short oral report on the progress of any Marine Corps business with Congress. My Navy counterpart, Rear Admiral Gus Kinnear, met with the Secretary every day, and accompanied him on his visits to or appearances at hearings on the Hill.

General Wilson had inherited a Marine Corps that was struggling mightily with the "all-volunteer" concept. A proud and traditionally all-volunteer service—except in time of war when all services used the draft—the Marines hadn't anticipated the many headaches of recruiting without the impetus of a draft. None of the services had. By mid-1975, the attempts to meet recruiting quotas by accepting recruits of less-than-desirable quality was producing some serious and potentially explosive problems. Unfortunately, these problems surfaced before our new senior leadership had an opportunity to get a handle on the issues and deal with them. "Big Lou" Wilson wasn't happy with the news that he began receiving, but his leadership and courage in dealing with these problems became legendary.

The bad news subjects were (1) recruit abuse in boot camp, and (2) reports of cheating and malfeasance in recruiting practices. These two issues were to dominate General Wilson's agenda during his first year as Commandant. Fortunately, he had excellent assistance in his Director of Manpower, Lieutenant General Robert Barrow. A former Commanding General of the Marine Corps Recruit Depot, Parris Island, he had first-hand knowledge of how far down into the manpower barrel our recruiters had been reaching.

These issues surfaced when a recruit died at the Marine Corps Recruit Depot, San Diego after a pugil stick battle. The ensuing investigation revealed a series of breakdowns in our well-established training system. It also revealed that quality control measures had failed, and turned up evidence of the manipulation of recruiting tests. The media seized on the particulars of the recruit's tragic death and published the life story of this hapless individual nationwide. It seemed as if more bad news was appearing every day, and this led, as it had to, to hearings on Capitol Hill.

Congressman Lucien Nedzi, chairman of the military personnel subcommittee, House Armed Services Committee, presided over the hearings. He was a patient, fair, and thorough man. General Wilson persuaded Senator Sam Nunn not to hold Senate hearings until after the House had acted. Additional hearings in the Senate were later deemed unnecessary.

House Armed Services Committee staff members insisted that recruits and recruiters be chosen randomly to testify before the committee. They went to great lengths to preclude any possibility of command preparation or influence. The testimony was therefore unpredictable, and proved to be fascinating for those present: candid, instructive, and more convincing than anything we could have imagined. The poised and enthusiastic comments of our 18-year-old recruits about their pride and love for the Marine Corps turned the hearings into testimonials. The professionalism of the recruiters and their comments on the caliber of young high-school-aged Americans were especially enlightening. The statements of both groups were well received and supported the Marine Corps in the fundamental issues involved.

General Wilson told the committee that he would reduce the numerical strength of the Marine Corps to whatever level was necessary in order to restore our traditional quality. He promised swift, decisive action.

The importance to the Marine Corps of this period in 1975 could be equated to the importance of the victory at Guadalcanal in WWII. It turned the Corps around by establishing clear goals and objectives pertaining to its most treasured asset, its troops, and the unique way we train them. General Wilson saved the institution of Marine recruit training and bought time for us to rid the Corps of substandard people.

In 1975, the Commandant of the Marine Corps, while fully active as a member of the Joint Chiefs of Staff, was still somewhat like "the bastard at the family reunion." He was a respected part of the family, but not quite the same as the other service chiefs—in effect, not a "full member." He voted on issues only when they were deemed to be of "direct concern to the Marine Corps." General Wilson, like his predecessors, did not accept the premise that Marines were second-class citizens whose representative could vote only under special circumstances.

Early in his term of office, he told me that he wanted me to study two key problem areas and propose legislative solutions. The first was full JCS membership for our Commandant, to include eligibility to become the Chairman of the JCS. Second, he wanted the Assistant Commandant to be given permanent four-star rank, not rank tied to a Marine Corps strength of more than 200,000 troops. (All the other services had permanent four-star deputies.)

During the first year we were able to correct the four-star-rank issue. With full support from Senator Stennis of Mississippi, a valuable ally, Congress fixed the matter with a one-line "legislative rider" on the authorization bill. It deleted the numerical caveat to four-star rank from the legislation: a simple "pen change" that became law without anyone's noticing it until Lieutenant General Sam Jaskilka was promoted to general and later attended a JCS meeting in General Wilson's absence. It was like painless dentistry. No one dared to oppose it openly, and no one had an opportunity to do so if they had chosen to. It was a proper, well deserved, legislative finesse.

The other issue wasn't as simple, but it too yielded to the legislative wizardry of General Wilson. In brainstorming the issue with General Wilson and his top generals, I pointed out that we could use the legislative rider technique again, but only under the most discrete circumstances. This would increase the Commandant's status significantly, and both the Army and Air Force would undoubtedly oppose it if they became aware of the impending change. General Wilson pointed out that if he attempted to do this early in his four-year tour as Commandant, his efforts would unquestionably appear to be self serving. On the other hand, if he prepared a succinct legislative change, carefully solicited key supporters in the Senate and House, then waited until near the end of his tenure, it could again be a *"fait accompli"* without any personal overtones. Following that guidance, my office prepared the legislative draft more than two years in advance. A quarter of a page long, it was to be attached to an authorization, appropriation, or other defense bill. I put it in a plain white envelope and handed it to General Wilson. He read it, smiled, placed it in his center desk drawer, and kept his own counsel on the matter thereafter. Shortly before General Bob Barrow relieved him in 1979, the Commandant became a full member of the JCS, as we had planned.

In January of 1977, the Marine Corps saw fit to select me for promotion to the grade of major general. When he congratulated me, General Wilson also took the occasion to say that he planned to give me command of the next Marine division that became available. At the time we had three active divisions and one reserve division. As we moved into 1977, it appeared that my promotion would occur during the summer months when vacancies resulted from expected retirements.

By late spring there was no word on my assignment to a division. During a ride over to Capitol Hill one day, General Wilson noted that I probably would stay on in my current assignment for a third year. It had been a busy, exciting, and challenging two years. We had kept the AV-8 Harrier VSTOL aircraft alive on the Hill. We had won the fight not to have the F-14 fighter aircraft foisted on the Marine Corps as an F-4 replacement. We wanted the newer, less expensive, broadly capable F-18 for many reasons. It was a close vote in both the House and Senate. The aircraft company lobbyists were everywhere, but we persevered. The investigation of recruit abuse and followups on the Hill had gone very well. Our stock seemed to be high. Navy and Department of Defense legislative relations were sound and cordial. There was never a dull moment, but I really felt good about the way our small staff and Hill representatives were functioning.

As is so often the case, General Wilson, a most capable leader when he became Commandant, had still managed to grow with his job. We spent a lot of time together, and I learned to read his body language and moods as well as anyone on the staff. Most notable among these was the staff proposal to commence "unit rotation" overseas with infantry battalions and aircraft squadrons. He had rejected this as being impractical, but had it instituted later, and with great success. He wisely noted that the complicated plan would take much longer to implement than the staff had allowed. He was correct, but the readjusted plan itself became one of his most important and successful legacies. It paid handsome dividends in morale, efficiency, and improved retention.

Early in the summer of 1977, a much respected and admired general officer, Major General Ed Wilcox, Commanding General of the First Marine Division at Camp Pendleton, died of a heart attack while in his quarters during the noon hour. He was an active athlete and exceptionally fit, so his death came unexpectedly. Two days later, I was summoned to the Commandant's office, where I found out that Carol and I were to make a speed run across the country. The Corps was sending me back to command, back to the First Marine Division for the third time, and this time we weren't at war.

Within three days of my notification, I had been promoted to major general, Carol had us packed, and we departed on that somewhat delayed trip across this great country.

Brigadier General Marc Moore, the Assistant Division Commander, who had assumed command of the Division, was awaiting my arrival. I was to be double-hatted as commander of both the division and the First Marine Amphibious Force, a field command that included the division, the air wing, and the Force Service Support Group. Major General J. K. Davis, the Wing Commander, had assumed the MAF billet pending my arrival. We had agreed in advance that there would be no formal change of command ceremony in deference to Ed Wilcox's passing. After a short visit with daughter Linda, son-in-law Steve, and their six-month-old son Craig, in Oregon, we raced down the Pacific Coast highway. We arrived at Camp Pendleton on August 7, and I assumed command the next morning in the First Division CG's office. J.K. Davis had flown down from El Toro for the brief ceremony and a short visit.

My "Band of Brothers" had grown again—from a platoon to a reinforced division—but I was back home, where it had all started twenty-six years before. That first day I called in Colonel Bill Masterpool, my chief of staff, to discuss a special letter I wanted to publish to the Division. It was to announce my "Band of Brothers" leadership concept. His immediate enthusiasm and support were most encouraging. We prepared and published it that day.

UNITED STATES MARINE CORPS
1ST MARINE DIVISION (REIN). FMF
CAMP PENDLETON. CALIFORNIA. 92055

IN REPLY REFER TO:
7/AJAL/ajal
5390
AUG 1977

From: Commanding General
To: Distribution List

Subj: Band of Brothers Leadership Concept

1. The term BAND OF BROTHERS has been used by historians to describe the immensely close comradeship and mutual respect existing among combat Marines during the most difficult early days of the Korean War. In essence, it describes the total effect of a military brotherhood where each man is the same, never lets a comrade down, and would give his life to protect a fellow Marine, if the need arose. This all for one, and one for all approach has made us unique among the world's military services.

2. Throughout our history we have survived as a service because in the heat of battle we have consistently produced a cohesive fighting team, essentially unselfish in its approach to duty. I have personally experienced the effect of this unique Marine brotherhood in two Wars - have participated in it - and am alive today only because my men followed the basic idea of "never letting a comrade down". Several Marines died rescuing a severely wounded Lieutenant Cooper in 1951. I can never forget it.

3. Since my early days in the Marine Corps, I have made every effort to foster in all of my commands this close knit feeling of pride in organization, mission, and mutual respect among men that leads to success in combat. Many of our non-combat difficulties can also be resolved by a better understanding of the attached basic principles. See Enclosure (1).

4. In summary, this concept is a broad approach towards better communications, problem solving within the chain of command, but most of all, a more tightly knit, proficient, and motivated BAND OF BROTHERS here with the "Old Breed". I consider it an implicit mission to show the entire Marine Corps that if there is a better way for men to live and work and, if needed, fight side by side - we are capable of developing it. With your interest and help, I'm sure we can.

C. G. COOPER

DISTRIBUTION: B & C

BAND OF BROTHERS

1. ALL MARINES ARE ENTITLED TO DIGNITY AND RESPECT AS INDIVIDUALS, BUT MUST ABIDE BY COMMON STANDARDS ESTABLISHED BY PROPER AUTHORITY.

2. A MARINE SHOULD NEVER LIE, CHEAT, OR STEAL FROM A FELLOW MARINE OR FAIL TO COME TO HIS AID IN TIME OF NEED.

3. ALL MARINES SHOULD CONTRIBUTE 100% OF THEIR ABILITIES TO THE UNIT'S MISSION. ANY LESS EFFORT BY AN INDIVIDUAL PASSES THE BUCK TO SOMEONE ELSE.

4. A UNIT, REGARDLESS OF SIZE, IS A DISCIPLINED FAMILY STRUCTURE, WITH SIMILAR RELATIONSHIPS BASED ON MUTUAL RESPECT AMONG MEMBERS.

5. IT IS ESSENTIAL THAT ISSUES AND PROBLEMS WHICH TEND TO LESSEN A UNIT'S EFFECTIVENESS BE ADDRESSED AND RESOLVED.

6. A BLENDING OF SEPARATE CULTURES, VARYING EDUCATIONAL LEVELS, AND DIFFERENT SOCIAL BACKGROUNDS IS POSSIBLE IN AN UNSELFISH ATMOSPHERE OF COMMON GOALS, ASPIRATIONS, AND MUTUAL UNDERSTANDING.

7. BEING THE BEST REQUIRES COMMON EFFORT, HARD WORK, AND TEAMWORK. NOTHING WORTHWHILE COMES EASY.

8. EVERY MARINE DESERVES JOB SATISFACTION, EQUAL CONSIDERATION AND RECOGNITION OF HIS ACCOMPLISHMENTS.

9. KNOWING YOUR FELLOW MARINE WELL ENABLES YOU TO LEARN TO LOOK AT THINGS "THROUGH HIS EYES", AS WELL AS YOUR OWN.

10. ISSUES DETRACTING FROM THE EFFICIENCY AND SENSE OF WELL-BEING OF AN INDIVIDUAL SHOULD BE SURFACED AND WEIGHED AGAINST THE IMPACT ON THE UNIT AS A WHOLE.

11. IT MUST BE RECOGNIZED THAT A BROTHERHOOD CONCEPT DEPENDS ON ALL MEMBERS "BELONGING" - - BEING FULLY ACCEPTED BY OTHERS WITHIN.

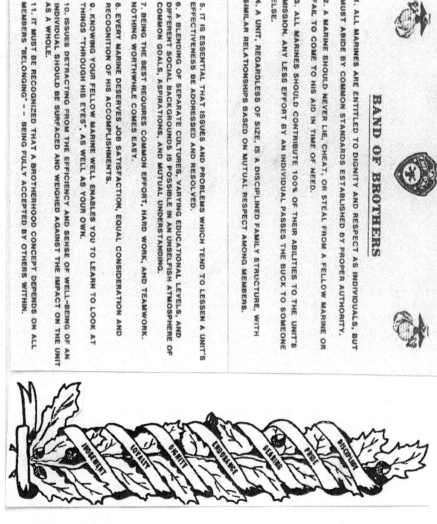

Chapter 25

Return to the "Band of Brothers":
CG, First Marine Division

This was my third tour in the First Marine Division: the first as a platoon commander, the second as a battalion commander, and now as the division commander. In the summer of 1977, the Corps faced a number of thorny problems. The first and most pressing, in my opinion, was that of improving the quality of the force: recruiting and retaining good men and women and ridding the Corps of those not meeting the higher standards established by General Wilson. The second was the massive materiel and supply problem—our aging weapons and equipment—and a funding problem that affected our training and left us with inadequate supplies and ammunition. Third, we were now required to start integrating women Marines into our battle-ready Fleet Marine Forces for the first time in our history, and pregnancy was no longer justification for a discharge.

The First Marine Division was facing these problems as I arrived to assume command. There were a lot of questions and not nearly enough answers, but this post-war trauma was not unusual. We historically entered a post-war period with worn-out weapons and equipment and with many units either in cadre status or greatly undermanned. I learned about one aspect of these problems immediately, and in a very personal way.

The afternoon of my first day I called in Captain Jim Rigoulot, my senior aide de camp, and told him that I wanted to draw a full issue of "782 gear," a Marine expression for the pack, helmet, suspenders, pistol belt, canteens, and essential field gear every Marine carries on his back. I had planned to stow my fully loaded pack in my office to demonstrate my personal readiness and the readiness of the division I commanded—as I had done whenever I'd commanded before. Captain Rigoulot departed and returned shortly with a wry look on his face. He reported, "Sir, Headquarters Battalion does not have any 782 gear. I understand it was transferred to the regiments last year when they were preparing for the CG's inspection."

I could hardly believe him, but he was actually telling me that our supply shortages were still critical. My chief of staff explained that my predecessor had taken this unusual step to maintain the readiness of lower units. The equipment had not yet been replaced because of funding shortfalls. I was pleased to learn soon after this that the regiments and separate battalions of the Division were adequately equipped—and that they were by and large commanded by combat-experienced and dedicated professional officers. I would have to deal with an elusive drug problem, some scattered racial unrest, mostly in the Force Service Support Group, and an increasing number of women arriving each month to be fitted into division slots. First, I had to locate the additional resources needed for this major upgrading of readiness.

We would use a two-pronged approach. First, we would try to do much better with the resources we already had. We would teach old-fashioned supply discipline techniques--- and I intended to commence this reorientation immediately. Then I discovered that our division was lowest in priority of funding, far behind the other two Marine divisions, one on the east coast and one in Okinawa. Getting our priority modified would take some high-powered selling to my boss in Hawaii, Lieutenant General Les Brown, and our Commandant, General Wilson. General Brown controlled the money and General Wilson

210

controlled the people. What I wanted would be major reallocations. I expected that both generals would agree with me when I made our case to them. But first we had to convince them that we had our self-help act together.

The decision to retain rather than discharge pregnant women had added a whole new page to the book. This wasn't what I wanted in my Marine Corps, but "the cow was out of the barn," as General Wilson said. "Don't fight it, deal with it, and see what you can do to make it work."

As usual, I was blessed with good people to help me. Colonel Bill Masterpool, my first chief of staff, was a one-of-a-kind old-line Marine who proved invaluable during my first few months. He welcomed my initiatives and was of great assistance in telling the "Band of Brothers" story. (My Band of Brothers concept was something he had always felt but had not been able to articulate until we joined forces in 1977.) As his retirement approached, I gave him command of the Fifth Marine Regiment. He led it during a mechanized brigade exercise we conducted in the desert shortly before he retired.

When he left my headquarters to assume command, I brought in an unusual replacement, Colonel Bill Tiernan, my staff judge advocate, a lawyer and former infantry officer. It proved to be the best move I made in my two years of command. (He was later promoted to brigadier general and served as the Corps' top legal officer, heading the Judge Advocate Division at HQMC.) As we shifted a few key staff billets around and received some new talent, the division staff's performance seemed to reach a new, higher level.

In the meanwhile, I was not neglecting my other command assignment: Commanding General of the First Marine Amphibious Force (I MEF). The I MEF staff was principally a planning, non-operational staff group. I did not have operational command of the division, wing, and Force Service Support Group, except when ordered to take command for a specific operation. I was charged with planning, training, and preparing for deployment without operational control. It was a hard nut to crack if you took your job seriously, but I always had great support and cooperation from both the Wing and FSSG commanders. The Navy's amphibious commander at the time was especially supportive of our training initiatives.

The few times we activated the MAF staff for training operations, I passed command of the division to my Assistant Commander, Brigadier General D'Wayne Gray, and served as the MAF CG for the exercises. We "went to the field," went to sea, and loaded all of our troops and many of our supporting supplies aboard ship, albeit we did it in column formation. (While one regiment was making an amphibious landing, another embarked for a day or two at sea before landing.) Using a relatively small fleet of amphibious ships and having the air wing operate from imaginary carriers and expeditionary fields, we executed very useful and productive MAF-level exercises on the West Coast for the first time ever. The cost was peanuts, and we learned a great deal.

For the first year, while I was commanding, directly or indirectly, some 56,000 officers and troops, my wife and I did not have the services of an enlisted aide or steward. A few years earlier, Senator William Proxmire had led the effort to destroy the steward corps of all the services because a few senior officers had abused the privilege of having stewards. In 1975, the entire Marine Corps had only 13 enlisted aides. At that time we had 65 general officers, almost half of them serving in command billets, living in government quarters, and having many social obligations. The Commandant had to ration the few remaining stewards carefully. Carol and I finally received one during our second year, but we hadn't waited for his arrival before starting to carry out our social obligations. As always, my sweet wife and I worked as a team to solve the problem.

Two Sundays a month became "Black Bean Sundays," as the officers of I MAF called them. On these Sunday afternoons my wife and I held "at homes" for 40 to 50 people, field grade officers (majors and above) and their wives from the division, wing, and FSSG, in our quarters. There was no supplemental funding for this: we served basic cocktails and a simple but hearty supper of black bean soup, spinach salad, cheese toast, and white wine. My two aides and their wives helped serve and clean up. I cooked the soup and served it. Carol did everything else and was the world's greatest hostess during what we tried to make a relaxed and pleasant visit to the commanding general's quarters. It worked. In our second year we followed the same plan after I taught our new steward, Gunnery Sergeant Beard, how to make black bean soup.

My assignment as Commanding General, First Marine Division gave me an opportunity to teach the "Band of Brothers Leadership Concept" on a very large scale. My practical definition of leadership describes it as the art of motivating people to carry out their assigned duties in an unselfish and, if possible, enthusiastic manner.

In my many years of teaching this subject, I have always encouraged troops or students to take stock of their personal resources and use them in the most effective ways for their particular situations. These can range from physical bravery and example in battle to giving the troops better ideas for governing their individual performance and personal lives in peacetime. Physical bravery in itself isn't always a smart approach. It might even be dumb: might get you and others killed. And when bullets are flying, it's no time to philosophize with the troops. They want a strong, professional, competent leader. In peacetime or when not facing daily tactical dangers, a leader can manufacture the glue that holds men together in battle and apply it to increase individual and unit proficiency. This is what my "Band of Brothers Leadership Concept" was intended to foster. *It is a better idea.* Few would disagree, but how to sell it on this large a scale?

My approach was to offer the concept as the Commanding General's standards of conduct. I had the principles printed up on wallet cards and handed out to the troops. Standards of conduct: I didn't intend them to be any more than that, though one sergeant said, when he distributed the wallet cards: "These are the 11 commandments according to General Cooper. Follow these and you'll stay out of trouble, help make our platoon the best, and become a better Marine in the process."

I encouraged my commanders to use the principles as counseling tools, to establish unit goals, and to foster positive initiatives in small-unit seminars. And I wasn't reluctant to take the message personally to the troops at every opportunity. They were always responsive. The set of principles was a vehicle that I could use to enforce zero tolerance for bigotry in any form, eliminate malcontents or malingerers, and encourage grass-roots feedback on better ways of solving problems.

Soon the small cards were in every wallet. We gave larger, parchment-like scrolls listing the principles as awards at meritorious masts. These became prized possessions. Once we had published these "rules of engagement," we had to emphasize them at every opportunity. An important occasion for doing so was the welcoming address to newly arrived troops.

An organization of approximately 20,000 Marines and sailors has a lot of new arrivals every day. Normally, the largest group would accumulate over the weekend, so I chose to speak to new arrivals in the reception center every Monday morning. My staff officers rotated the duty of giving the welcome address on the other four working days of the week.

On my first Monday I faced more than 100 new arrivals—officers, staff NCOs, and troops. My welcoming address was the story of my joining the First Division as a second lieutenant in combat and some of the experiences I had that led up to the formulation of the "Band of Brothers" concept. It was an adaptation of a leadership theme I had used since Korea—an approach that challenged the new arrivals and welcomed them into our family.

I hadn't realized that my aide, my chief of staff, and the Division Public Affairs Officer had been in the back of the room listening to this, my first welcome address. I learned later that they all found my talk inspiring. Colonel Bill Masterpool approached me a bit later and requested that I consider videotaping this same message for distribution throughout the division.

The taping had to be done in a studio, but I wouldn't agree to it unless I could have at least 50 troops in the studio to talk to. They got the troops and then taped me talking to them. As we edited the tape, I added a recitation of the principles while battle film clips were shown as background with the printed principles superimposed in the foreground. The staff played the finished tape to new arrivals every day that I didn't appear at the reception center, and we distributed copies to every battalion-sized unit.

Whenever a unit invited me to speak to the troops, I made every possible effort to accept. What resulted were countless breakfasts with companies, batteries, and even squadrons. I usually concluded my remarks with the candle metaphor I had learned so many years earlier. I challenged my troops to light their own candles in the unselfish pursuit of excellence.

I didn't talk to every Marine in the command, but they all heard about the candle, either from me or from someone who'd attended one of the meetings at which I'd described it. One day a guard really caught my attention as I entered the gate of the Fifth Marines encampment. He saluted and said, "Good morning, General Cooper. Sir, my candle is still lit!" This simple yet powerful pledge of commitment follows me to this day and never fails to give a tug at these old heart strings. It's still a better idea: idealistic, yes, but inspirational and logical to young men and women interested in doing their best and being a part of the best. It was motivation for better racial understanding, the rejection of bigotry, and the self-policing of drug abusers.

My second year was a particularly uplifting time. As we watched our readiness improve significantly, my pride soared. Reenlistments blossomed. General Les Brown, my boss at FMFPAC, pushed a number of rapid-response readiness issues and kept us on our toes with surprise inspections and mount-out drills. We welcomed these tests. Although he did have a quick temper, this former enlisted ground Marine, who had ascended to the rank of lieutenant general after commanding at every level of Marine Corps aviation, proved to be a fair, generous, and wise commander. I learned a great deal from him, and used it to good advantage when I assumed his position a few years later.

As my second year was winding down, I received a phone call from our Assistant Commandant, General Robert Barrow, who had been slated to replace General Wilson in mid-summer. He told me that in a few months I would be moving a few miles south to relieve Major General Dick Schultz as CG of the Marine Recruit Depot in San Diego. That was wonderful news! We had come to love Southern California—and this would give me another opportunity to command. Also, this new job now entailed responsibility for the Western Recruiting Command, extending all the way from Indiana to American Samoa. I thanked him for his confidence in me and told him how difficult it would be to leave the First Division.

He reminded me of a conversation we had once had about the question: "What makes the bloom fall off the rose?" This was an analogy to what happens to some of our Marines after they leave boot camp, having come out shiny bright, motivated, and eager to serve. All too many of them lose that edge, motivation, or sense of pride. He asked me to do some serious thinking about the process before I left the division. I did, and I got some help.

I invited all of my CO's to bring their sergeant majors to my next weekly commander's conference, so the conferees included all of the regimental and battalion commanders, their senior enlisted advisors, and my senior staff officers. At the conference, I told them about General Barrow's question. I cited the attrition rate among Marines during their first enlistment, and pointed out that it was too high. I wanted each person present to give this issue serious thought and give me the benefit of his observations and reflections. What could we do better? I told them to keep their responses informal, and gave them a week to mull over all sides of the issue.

Several days later, my division chaplain, Captain (Father) Tom Kelly, a Catholic priest who had served all of his time with Marines, had served two tours at Parris Island, and was recovering from cancer surgery, appeared at my door. When I invited him in, he said he had been trying to write something down for my "roses" request, but he felt he had to talk to me. And so he did, simply and profoundly. "General, the bloom falls off of every rose. It's God's way. Some fall off sooner than others. We all have our down times, discouragements, failures. At times everyone thinks of cashing it in, or loses his drive. The Corps should not focus on merely extending the temporary miracle of boot camp. That has been and always will remain a model of conversion, one that we must maintain at the present level. But my point is just this. We've got to go out and find the 'right kind of rose bushes to plant': the right kind of young people; high-quality, special young people that we can plant, feed, train, nurture, and watch as they blossom. Sure, our roses will lose their blossoms, but with follow-up leadership, care, and encouragement, like your 'Band of Brothers,' these roses will continue to bloom, over and over again. Any rose that is neglected will die away. Our Marines are the same way. Boot camp doesn't guarantee a lifetime of selfless service, but strong roses, properly planted and nurtured thereafter will consistently produce beautiful flowers. Remember, roses aren't easy to raise. They need a lot of attention!" Father Kelly said it more effectively than that, but it was clear and straightforward: a simple statement counseling against taking our troops for granted.

The contributions from the other men who'd been at the conference were all well thought out and useful, but his short commentary won the day. It still applies. The "Band of Brothers" is the follow-through he was recommending, but top-quality recruits are also a must.

On August 8, 1979, in a ceremony that lasted exactly one hour, I turned over my dual commands to a combat-experienced officer of high repute, Major General Frank Quinn. It was two years to the day since I had assumed command.

Chapter 26

Making Marines: Boot Camp and Recruiting
MCRD, San Diego

Shortly before leaving the First Division, I learned that three drill instructors at San Diego were being charged with recruit abuse. Something had failed again: I would inherit three courts martial dealing with a problem we thought we had solved.

And yet, though these latest charges were unfortunate, the system had surfaced the abuse immediately and corrected it, and no serious harm had resulted. The situation did show, however, that a few drill instructors, no matter what they had been taught or told, still hadn't accepted the limits on their authority over recruits—couldn't accept that degrading acts and the laying on of hands were absolutely forbidden in the still physically rugged regimen and pressurized atmosphere of boot camp.

San Diego was where the death of a recruit three years earlier had precipitated congressional hearings and the revamping of the entire system. Hadn't we learned anything from that? The three courts martial were in the forefront of my thoughts during my early weeks at the Recruit Depot.

The local and national media were even-handed and accurate in their reporting of the trials. We gave them full access: the trials were open. A reporter for the *San Diego Union*, Kip Cooper, a former Navy chief petty officer, took background information we gave him and wrote a number of accurate articles about the cases. We had met previously when he interviewed me at Camp Pendleton early in my tour there. I had familiarized him with the Band of Brothers concept. He showed understanding in his commentary on the trials and their results.

When the trials finally ended, the three individuals were separated from the Marine Corps after having been reduced in grade to private and having spent short periods in confinement. The training program was sound, but the "seventh troop-leading step: supervision," had not been implemented properly. The system, however, had surfaced the matter within hours. With this as a background, I promised General Barrow that we would not "throw the baby out with the bath water" during my tour. We would maintain the high standards and let our drill instructors carry out their mandate, but would not let this situation recur. It didn't.

The U.S. Marine Recruit Depot, San Diego is certainly one of the most aesthetically pleasing bases in the Marine Corps. Built on reclaimed tidal swamps in the early 1920's, the depot, with its Spanish architecture and sweeping parade and drill field (called the "grinder"), is adjacent to the San Diego International Airport, next to the Naval Training Center, right in the heart of San Diego. Over the years the city and the airport have whittled down its acreage. During the Carter administration, some White House wag actually proposed selling the entire base to get money to build new facilities at Camp Pendleton. The future of the base had been somewhat in question after this odd proposal surfaced, but my marching orders led us in quite the opposite direction: "Plan and request funding to modernize, consolidate, and reestablish the viability of this historic place." As local pundits talked of building a road through the base to ease airport traffic, I circled the wagons and warded off back-door efforts of the San Diego Port Authority to enlarge its fiefdom. We

215

withstood the pressures, both in San Diego and in Washington, and proceeded with plans for long-overdue maintenance and modernization.

MCRD, usually referred to as the Recruit Depot, was like any other Marine Corps base, except for its small size. We had five sets of senior officers' quarters, officer and enlisted clubs, a post exchange, barracks, a theater and auditorium, medical and dental clinics, mess halls, processing centers, obstacle and confidence courses, a massive headquarters building, one of the world's largest drill and parade fields, and extensive athletic facilities. The Corps recruited some 25,000 young men per year from the Western Recruiting Region, and trained them all here. (The women Marines we enlisted trained at Parris Island, SC.)

It was during my first year at San Diego that the Corps finally reached its twin goals of quality and quantity under its new standards. As some recruiters would say, "we probably left some blood along the trail" in the process. The intensity, competitiveness, and frustration of meeting monthly quotas did result in some unwanted attrition among our field recruiters, but this decreased as we became more careful in selecting those we sent out to recruit, and trained them better. Recruiting will always be the most demanding professional challenge in the Marine Corps short of combat. We had to find "the right kind of rose bushes to plant." It wasn't easy.

One of the obvious advantages of having one general in charge of both the recruiting and the training of the recruits was the quality control that could result. It gave drill instructors and recruiters, often antagonists, the same master. Interaction improved. Each depot also received a second general officer to assist in covering the span of control.

I spent almost a third of my time visiting district headquarters in San Francisco, New Orleans, and Kansas City, and many of their stations and substations. I often made these trips in a turboprop executive aircraft that could land at the airports of small towns.

The community of San Diego supported its Marine Recruit Depot. The mayor at the time was Pete Wilson, whom I had known as a Marine lieutenant in my Hawaii days. Retired Lieutenant General "Brute" Krulak, a San Diego resident and prominent civic leader, was most helpful in introducing the Coopers around the city. Later we hosted General Krulak at my headquarters while he wrote a book, *First to Fight*, a significant contribution to post-WWII history. (He donated its proceeds to Marine Corps family charities.)

The community was full of distinguished retired Marine and Navy officers. General Lemuel Shepherd was in this group and brightened my day every time he paid my office a visit. (He had pinned a Purple Heart medal on me in 1951 when my medical evacuation plane stopped in Hawaii on the way home.) And what a thrill it was to enjoy the company and listen to the ruminations of men such as Shepherd, Krulak, Admiral U.S.G. Sharp, General Edward A. Craig, and many others I had served under and admired.

Early in the tour, my depot sergeant major turned out to have a serious problem. This once proud and capable senior NCO had become an alcoholic. After two counseling sessions proved fruitless, I gave him the option of committing himself voluntarily to rehabilitation or being ordered in by me. His future would depend on the results of his rehab. He wisely chose to commit himself and returned a changed man about two months later.

His departure allowed me to bring in a former associate from Marine Barracks, Washington, Sergeant Major Lee Bradley, who was currently serving as sergeant major of my Headquarters Battalion. Lee Bradley was one of the finest people or Marines I had ever known. Barrel-chested, handsome, articulate, and commanding, he was a black Marine who personified the tenets of the Band of Brothers. As I told General Barrow, if Lee Bradley had one more year of college, he would probably be a regimental commander or higher. He was that good, and a dedicated family man to boot.

He had an immediate effect on the S/NCO's at the depot. He instinctively smelled out problems and dealt with them as his office allowed. A man for all seasons, he was another of the many individuals who contributed so meaningfully to my professional successes. I couldn't admire or respect anyone more.

One of the practices that I found interesting and useful was that of meeting with the depot's honor graduates two days before their graduation. There were usually about ten of them, one from each graduating platoon. Many were sons of Marines. Most were outstanding athletes. One was a former Army captain, a West Point graduate, who wanted to earn a Marine Corps commission via OCS. Whatever their backgrounds, they were uniformly outstanding young men. For ten weeks they had not been allowed to speak except when spoken to by their drill instructor. Once I seated them in my office and relaxed them a bit, they became more than voluble.

Each carried a Band of Brothers card in his pocket, and each had seen my video presentations instructing him on the concept, its genesis and purpose. After viewing the video presentation, they had received follow-up instruction from their officers and drill instructors. I asked them questions about the 11 principles to open our dialogue. Then I asked them for recommendations for improving boot camp. Their responses were uniformly positive. I asked to meet their parents, if they were attending the Friday graduation, after the final parade and review.

On one occasion, a tall, lean honor graduate, resplendent in his brand new dress blues, approached the reviewing stand after the troops had been dismissed. He was accompanied by his father, whom he introduced as a former Marine. The father had tears in his eyes as he greeted me. He said that this was the proudest moment in his life. Then he reached for his wallet and pulled out a small, dog-eared sheet of paper that listed the 11 Band of Brothers principles. At the bottom was the signature, "Semper Fi, C. G. Cooper, 1st Lt. USMC, Nov. 1952." His son produced a card that I had signed just two days before, 28 years later. It was a touching moment for all three of us. This proud father had served under me at Camp Lejeune, and had carried that message all these years.

It was a challenging and rewarding tour—and passed all too quickly. Things improved markedly for the Marine Corps during those two years. The country elected a new President, who announced immediately that he wanted to revitalize the military services. He also wanted to see more of them around Washington. General Barrow told us that after the Inaugural Parade Ronald Reagan asked the Joint Chiefs why the military wore civilian clothes in Washington most of the time. General Barrow responded that a previous President had wanted to minimize the military presence in Washington and chose this means of doing so. President Reagan said, "Well, I'd like to change that. I'm proud of my troops. How do I do it?" General Barrow replied, "Sir, you just did!"

Carol and I had fallen in love with San Diego, and the high quality of people assigned to the command made my work there more than enjoyable. And we loved our comfortable quarters at MCRD, made all the more comfortable by Master Sergeant Beard, still with us as my enlisted aide and steward. I began to wonder what was next in store. After two super command jobs back to back, what could I expect?

The phone call came in late spring of 1981. I was to be Commanding General of the Marine Corps Base, Camp Lejeune, North Carolina. I was pleased to have yet another

217

command, but wasn't too sure what this particular assignment was signaling. But my always wise and supportive wife reminded me that this was the best place General Barrow could put me: he couldn't promote me, because all of the new three-star billets had been filled.

OK. This could be my twilight tour in the Corps, but I would be the best base commander I could be. It is a huge base, the largest in the Corps, and the home for most of our enlisted schools. The Second Division and Second Force Service Support Group were home-based there. The Marine Corps Air Station at New River was adjacent and was soon to be added to my jurisdiction—my big jurisdiction.

We had enjoyed two earlier tours there, one when I was a young lieutenant and the other when I was a lieutenant colonel. Now we would live in the big house at the end of the street, the one with a boat dock on the river. I remembered our earlier experiences and immediately began to think of improving base services in a variety of ways after looking over the situation. Carol and I would hit the ground running, as usual, and we would accept whatever happened after that.

Headquarters Battalion, under the watchful eye of Sergeant Major Bradley, put on a memorable short ceremony, reminiscent of Marine Barracks, Washington, as Major General Duff Rice relieved me in early summer of 1981.

We headed our Audi east. This would be another short break, so we planned to skip family visits and saved our precious days for a leisure drive across country. Another adventure was about to begin.

Chapter 27

A Different Challenge
"The Top Cop"

Carol and I had 20 days to travel, reflect, and enjoy being together. These were very special commodities for a general officer of Marines and his wife.

We were familiar with Camp Lejeune, having been stationed there twice before, but some of the things we heard while traveling were disconcerting. The national news reported that two Marines in the Second Division had been ambushed and murdered on the base. Two other Marines had been arrested and charged with the murders. The implication was that drugs were involved. That got my attention and accelerated my thinking about ideas I had been considering since learning of my new assignment.

If the Marine Corps was going to give me command of its largest base, I was going to treat the job like a combat command. I'd make this an exciting place to live, work, or just watch— whether it was by fixing pot holes promptly, running a first class commissary (grocery), using the post exchange to make shopping convenient, or attacking the crime and drug problem with every resource at my disposal. The Band of Brothers family concept would set the stage.

As we traveled, Carol and I discussed things we remembered about the base that could stand improvement. We hoped that most of them had already been improved, but my determination to inject an operational flavor into the often stodgy, routine base environment grew as we neared North Carolina.

It was good to see Spanish moss again, hanging from the towering oak trees amidst the pine forests, inlets, and swamps. But it was hot as blazes when we arrived in June, two days before the change of command. The air conditioning in the VIP guest quarters worked, thank goodness, but not much else did! That was an early warning.

Camp Lejeune, in a thinly populated coastal area 50 miles north of Wilmington, North Carolina, was constructed during the WW II buildup, and was designed to be self-contained, much like a city. The base was to serve primarily as a training and home base for a Marine division and its reinforcing ground elements, with air facilities nearby to support aviation commands. It became a major school center as well: its broad white-sand beaches were ideal for amphibious training.

The camp's own school system taught children in grades from kindergarten through high school. The teachers and support staff were Department of Defense employees. Although the system was relatively small, the quality of the education it offered its students was generally higher than it was in the neighboring communities.

The city of Jacksonville was adjacent to the base. It had grown from a sleepy "Tobacco Road" town in the 40's to a thriving community of more than 35,000 people by 1981. The base, with its large civilian work force and payroll, was its principle industry. One of my key responsibilities would be to deal with the local authorities, both the elected officials and the police forces. In view of our large size and large effect on the entire area, the dealings would involve city, county, and even state authorities. I had a few unpleasant memories of Marine-city relations from my earlier tours, but on this tour my first visits, inspections, and official calls were very positive. The police forces of the city and the county appeared to be professional, well staffed, and very cooperative —a far cry from the situation in the early 50's. The city and county fathers promised to support my efforts to deal with crime, both on and off the base. I noted, however, that the "robber's row" of sleazy strip joints, pawn shops, "massage parlors," and "movie mates" was much bigger than it had been in the 60's. A quick tour of this area with the chief of police reinforced my interest in doing something about these lecherous businesses.

First, however, I had to get my thoughts organized. I wanted to have an overall concept of operations to discuss with General Barrow when he paid us a short visit about a week after I assumed command. One thing was certain: the VIP guest suite would no longer be ignored and ill equipped. The more-than-20-year-old mattress on the bed had been replaced the day I took over.

With the Band of Brothers creed at the forefront, my plan was designed to get everyone's attention focused on problems that had to be solved. It was not enough to reduce crime in all of its aspects and deal with the growing drug problem, though we certainly had to do that. We had to improve the quality of life for everyone living at Camp Lejeune: troops, dependents, and civilian employees. In order to be effective, we would have to get as many people as possible involved in the process. I planned to start off by holding a press conference as soon as we had worked out most of the details.

I had to get my boss's approval before starting this program, because drug testing was a key ingredient and that would take money and major medical support from the Navy. Some of my proposals would be controversial and would draw a lot of attention. I needed an assurance of support from the very top. Knowing General Robert Barrow as I did, I believed it would be forthcoming.

My private discussions with General Barrow could not have been more satisfying or motivating. As I outlined the problems, the resources available, the political realities in the civilian community, and my aggressive, somewhat unorthodox approach, I could see him getting excited. He noted that the Marine Corps badly needed a drug program, but he was having trouble getting the Navy's attention on the matter of laboratory support for widespread drug testing. He concluded our discussions by saying, "I almost wish I could change jobs with you for a while. What you're proposing has not only interested me, it has excited me. Let's get on with it. I'll stand with you all the way. Give me a monthly written update with all of the particulars. Maybe you will become our test bed."

Those comments were my marching orders. The base inspector became my operations officer. The chaplain was in charge of community relations programs in all of the government housing areas. We opened a fraud-and-abuse hot line. The calls were surprisingly reliable and useful. My Naval Investigative Service (NIS) commenced undercover activities in the base schools (drugs), the post exchange (reported kickbacks), and the commissary (suspected kickbacks). All were very successful. We started conducting random car searches and portable drug tests at all the gates and in organizations. With the assistance of state highway police we conducted random searches of civilian traffic entering and leaving the base. We installed additional lighting and set up more security patrols throughout the base, especially in quarters areas. MP's from the Second Division had been augmenting our base MP's, and we increased that augmentation. We reestablished the services of "courtesy paddy wagons" in Jacksonville. These were Marine Corps vans with MP's that would pick up Marines on liberty who appeared to have had too much alcohol and return them to their command without incident, before they got into serious trouble.

Our Armed Forces Disciplinary Control Board reviewed the status of all questionable Jacksonville establishments, invited their proprietors to appear and defend themselves, then recommended that some be placed off limits for military personnel. I had the final decision after my staff attorneys had reviewed the board's recommendations.

For the first time since WW II, we started having armed Marine MP's walking foot patrol with the Jacksonville police. This was a touchy, somewhat risky course of action, but the symbolism was powerful and we made it work. Business in the bordellos went down, as did our disciplinary incident rate.

We kicked this program off with a press conference that was videotaped and shown on regional TV and on the base several times. Area TV and radio stations and newspapers asked for interviews, and I accommodated them willingly. These appearances became sort of a continual speaking tour. I welcomed the opportunity to make use of the "bully pulpit," and announced that I would welcome speaking invitations. From Rotary Clubs to chambers of commerce to schools to church groups to the annual Methodist Convocation, I spoke and urged the citizens to join us in reducing crime, improving their neighborhoods, arresting or running off the criminal element, and making our entire area a better place in which to live and work.

Over and over I told the good citizens of Onslow County about our Band of Brothers and encouraged them to form their own. I gave each listener one of my imaginary candles and urged him or her to light it and let its flame reflect the holder's unselfish pursuit of excellence. I always concluded my talk with the comment "what this base and county need most is more candles, held high, reflecting a determination to make things better for all of those around you. . . and when our paths cross again, tomorrow, next year, or later, I hope when we exchange salutes or greetings that you will say to me, 'General Cooper, my candle is still lit!'"

While the community at large was becoming more active in support of its law enforcement and elected officials, the agencies themselves showed new zeal and energy. Although the many law enforcement agencies had come together routinely in the past at periodic luncheon-type meetings on the base, these occasions now became operational conferences of great importance. They included the FBI, the North Carolina Bureau of Investigation, the Drug Enforcement Agency, sheriffs from two counties, the Jacksonville Chief of Police, our Provost Marshall, the senior NIS agent, and often a representative from the state Attorney General's office. Our tenant units, the Second Division, the Second FSSG, and the Second Air Wing, all sent representatives as well. The governor visited us on two occasions to encourage our efforts. Early tension between these law enforcement agencies melted away as we moved aggressively to support their agendas while they participated in ours.

As for quality of life, my fine logistics chief, Colonel Dick Shigley, had picked up on my demand for better service at the commissary, better maintenance of barracks and quarters, and the establishment of a farmer's market on the base for the sale of local produce. Our family service center expanded and our counselors left their home nest and went into the field, principally to the enlisted quarters areas, to become more accessible.

It was an exciting time, indeed. I was sued twice. One surplus store owner that we knew was dealing in stolen government property challenged my not allowing him to advertise in our base newspaper. I ended up in Superior Court in Raleigh, where I told the judge that "when you go to war, you have to be prepared when someone starts shooting at you." There was no judgment against me personally, but we did have to allow that crook to advertise in the paper for a few months.

Our operations in the base dependents' school were remarkably effective. A young Navy hospital corpsman volunteered to assist the Naval Investigative Service by serving under cover as a new student. In two months he confirmed what we had feared. We had drug pushers among the students, the chief of which was the daughter of a highly respected colonel. She had helpers. A chaplain's son was implicated, and the train of drugs ran into a stylish women's dress shop in Jacksonville.

Those families living on the base with children involved as pushers we kicked out of base housing. All users' parents were required to attend drug counseling with their children or also move off the base. I talked to all of the school's teachers immediately after the bust was announced. I told them to wake up and report problems. No more living with them. If parents tried to interfere, they would answer to me. My message to them was that they must motivate, teach, and counsel, but never tolerate this climate in the school again.

Later, I addressed the entire student body. You could have heard the proverbial pin drop. They were still in shock, it appeared. I discussed why we had done what we had done, and reminded them that using or selling drugs is very serious business. I promised them that some day they would remember this day and thank the good Lord that they had been a part of a system that didn't coddle drug pushers or users . . . that they would learn from it. Much to my surprise, the seniors voted to invite me to be their commencement speaker a few months later. Someone had listened.

Many years later, when my wife checked into the naval hospital in Bethesda, Maryland, for cancer surgery, a young nurse attending her asked me if I had ever been CG at Camp Lejeune. I replied that I had and told her when. She said, "General, I was a senior that year. I'll never forget what you did for us at the high school or what you told us that very special day. Thank you again!"

Not everything we attempted worked the first time, but it was a wonderfully rewarding year. Shortly before we left, in the summer of 1982, the Methodist bishop asked me to address the Methodists' annual convocation. I spoke of my roots in the Methodist Church, my goal of making our area a better place for everyone, and, most of all, the satisfaction I got from addressing people who really cared about others. Of course, I gave each of them one of my imaginary candles, complete with instructions on how to use it. Carol's mother, Vesta Edgerton, was visiting us and attended the service with Carol. Afterwards, she told me that I had missed my calling, that I should have been a minister. But then she hesitated and said, "I guess you really didn't miss your calling. Only a Marine could have given the message that you gave today." She's gone now, God bless her, but she helped me realize that all our efforts and the expenditure of energy that went into them were indeed worthwhile.

Robber's Row didn't disappear while I was there, but now a county hospital has replaced those businesses. General Barrow published my final report on the War on Crime and the drug testing system in a letter to all general officers. Late in the spring of 1982, I made a presentation at the joint Navy-Marine Corps conference on drugs in Norfolk. Shortly thereafter, the CNO and CMC both formally announced that a zero-tolerance drug policy would start within a few months. It wasn't going to be easy. There were many legal and logistical hurdles to be gotten over in that first year, but the war was launched Corps-and Navy-wide.

When it was announced that I would leave after a year and get my third star as Director of Manpower at Headquarters, Marine Corps, my provost marshal invited me to a farewell dinner with "the troops," my military policemen. Those troops turned out to be a who's who of law enforcement in eastern North Carolina. Each organization got up and made a short talk about what we had accomplished and thanked me for my support, but the crowning blow was the plaque they presented to me. It hangs right behind me today, one of my most treasured possessions. Suitably engraved with the logos of all the law-enforcement organizations, it also has a legend: "Camp Lejeune's Top Cop."

Then a group of NCO's from my Headquarters Battalion asked to call on me. They walked into my office with a large wooden replica of a K-bar Marine fighting knife. When talking to them some months earlier at a leadership breakfast I had told them how I was wounded in Korea, and how my weapon had been shot out of my hand. I had commented that the enemy started a counterattack and the only weapon I had left was my fighting knife. I mused that I really needed one about three times as long. Here, beautifully hand crafted, was a Marine K-bar, mounted on a stand, exactly three times the size of the original. My Band of Brothers had again left me speechless. This unusual gift is ensconced on a shelf to my immediate right, and will always remind me of that very busy, special year in our lives, when we were able to make things work a little better with the help of an awful lot of good Marines, sailors, and citizens of North Carolina.

I could summarize this brief chapter with the word *synergy*. The generous people of Onslow County were just waiting for some guidance to direct their constructive juices in the right direction. Marines always respond to positive, strong leadership. In this case, it came mostly from the lower levels, with good and better ideas working upward and with encouragement from the top. The law enforcement rivalries may have returned by now. They'll always be there, but at least the various agencies did see the results of cooperation and team effort. And most important, a few long-lived seeds were planted and are prospering. A young boy, aged 9 or 10, came over to our table at a restaurant one night shortly before we left in 1982. He said, "Sir, I heard you speak at the Methodist Convocation and my Mom said it would be okay for me to tell you that my candle is still lit, Sir. God bless you!"

Chapter 28

Director of Manpower for the Corps
"Top Quality and Quantity, Finally"

General Robert H. Barrow was beginning his fourth and final year as Commandant of the US Marine Corps when I arrived to assume my duties at Headquarters. He had chosen me to head the department that managed the Corps' most precious asset and over half of the Corps' annual appropriation. After passing an interview with the Secretary of Defense and gaining approval from both the Reagan White House and the US Senate, I became the junior of seven three-star generals in the Marine Corps. I relieved Lieutenant General Ed Bronars and inherited his superb group of general officer subordinates, all of whom were to reach three- or four-star rank in later years.

I had to testify before the Senate Armed Services Committee in support of our multi-billion dollar account two days after I arrived. The four services' Manpower Chiefs would be the principal witnesses. Many of these annual hearings are largely ceremonial. This, my first, amounted to a very warm "welcome back" from the committee members, who remembered me from my days in congressional liaison. I delivered a brief statement without notes. "I'm pleased and extremely proud to report to this distinguished committee that we have kept all of the promises and commitments we made to you in 1975 when our Corps was undergoing very difficult times . . . both in quantity and quality. We have devoted talent, resources, and imagination to turning the all-volunteer concept into a reality. And we intend to keep it that way." Senator Stennis, Chairman, and Senator Nunn, the Manpower Subcommittee Chairman, responded by holding the Corps up as an example for the other services. I received no further questions or comments. The groundwork laid by General Barrow, Ed Bronars, and countless others had made the hearing a pleasant experience. It was a great start, but things weren't necessarily going to be that easy thereafter.

General Barrow's heir apparent was his Assistant Commandant and Chief of Staff, General P.X. Kelly. They worked well together and fostered an almost family-like atmosphere among the senior officers helping them run the Corps. We had an awful lot of things going on, but my goals were clear and straightforward: first, keep the quality and quantity constant in our primary resource, our people; second, continue the unit rotation program, improve it, and increase the number of overseas billets in the Pacific in which our Marines could be accompanied by their dependents; third, deal positively with the problems accompanying the increasing numbers of women in the Corps; fourth, get the "War on Drugs" fully operational. The Secretary of the Navy, John Lehman, supported us fully in all these matters, and enjoyed an unusually high rank in the pecking order among the political appointees in the Reagan hierarchy.

We had learned the hard way the importance of "the recruiter on the street." If you want a first-class aviation metalsmith, you had better send one out to find a clone. The same applies to officer procurement. Top-quality officer candidates require your very best officer recruiters. This logic dictated that, outside of war, we had to give the recruiting service our top quality people. Some of them were not too happy to draw this type of duty, but their professionalism made the difference. Many of those hand picked colonels were to become general officers later. Recruiting continues to be our top focus, even when we're "down-sizing."

I was designated head of a special task force examining the issue of increasing the number of dependents accompanying Marines overseas to Okinawa and Japan. It involved a rather complex, and really unnecessary, battle with the Air Force over turf, funding, and priorities. As a new Brigadier, General Barrow had been CG of the Marine Corps base, Camp Butler, on Okinawa in the early 1970's. He had long been concerned that Marines had to live more austerely and spend more time away from their families than soldiers and airmen serving alongside them in the Far East. He also was unhappy with the relatively low funding levels the Corps received for overseas bases. He proposed taking several initiatives to end this disparity, and our task force was examining what steps were required.

When the Army relinquished control of its major complex of facilities, closed down its major headquarters, and removed all of its tactical units from Okinawa, the Marine Corps became the American armed service with the largest number of units and people on the island. Therefore, the Army handed the majority of those facilities over to us. However, cooperative control over dependents' housing and support facilities such as schools, commissaries, post exchanges, and clubs was a sore point with the Air Force. When it came to working out who controlled what, what was joint or exclusive, who funded maintenance, and so forth, the Air Force put up a protective wall. They were totally uncooperative.

General Barrow's response was typical for him. He went to the Secretary of the Navy and convinced him that we had an issue of fairness, and then went with him to call on the Secretary of Defense, "Cap" Weinberger. The fallout from this meeting was a SecDef letter to the Navy, Marine Corps, and Air Force clearly delineating future Okinawa relationships. The Marine Corps logically received the senior management responsibility on Okinawa, but the Air Force and Navy prerogatives were properly protected. At least it seemed so to us.

But the Air Force fought us tooth and nail at the three-star level on the key issues. Lieutenant General Larry Welch, later Chief of Staff of the Air Force, was the principal protagonist for the blue suiters. I was his Marine Corps opponent. The squabble lasted several months, with little progress at our level. When I could clearly establish that there was obstructionism, I took it to General Barrow, who launched SecNav Lehman at the Air Force Secretary. SecDef's letter was explicit and Lehman loved to get into a fight he knew he could win.

As a result of this reasonably short bureaucratic struggle, our manpower department could begin the increased accompanied-tour program for Okinawa and Japan immediately. It has been successful and has greatly improved the operational readiness of our forces. It stabilized the regimental, air group, division, wing, and logistics staffs by giving their personnel two- and three-year tours—with family—just as the other services had done for decades. Our squadrons and infantry battalions continued to rotate overseas and back to their families and home bases every six months. This is a complex procedure, but we have learned how to make it work even with the high tempo of operations that we maintain. Our Marine Far East forces have been reduced since 1983, but the system still works. The difference is that now we live as well as our sister services do, thanks to the boldness and imagination of General Bob Barrow. "Fair's fair!" he used to say.

225

Women in the Corps: God bless 'em! These were the early days of the feminists' campaign to increase the numbers of women and the billets for them in all the services. At this point, we had been directed to place women in the Fleet Marine Forces, but had learned the hard way that we had to have a thorough analysis of which billets women could and should serve in. Simply opening staff billets for women didn't deal with the issue properly. The combat exclusion law in effect at that time created major questions about women, and we also had yet to deal with the surprisingly high pregnancy rate among our female Marines.

This was the topic of my first call on Assistant Secretary of Defense Frank Carlucci. He noted that our combat orientation was definitely a matter to be appreciated, but he suggested that we should be able to double the percentage of women in the Corps from five percent to somewhere in the neighborhood of ten percent. He asked for my comment. I told him I had received a lot of very fine women Marines when I commanded the First Division. We were the Corps' test bed for integrating women in combat units. They were loyal, well trained, and eager, but we had more questions than answers when they started arriving in 1977. Most of them went into fields such as intelligence, administration, and communications. Soon they made up almost 80% of my headquarters staff sections in those disciplines, but they couldn't even ride in a ship of war, much less go into a combat area. The order to recruit more women had not been thought out properly, and lifting the pregnancy ban had opened a Pandora's box. I noted that 14 percent of the 159 women I had in the division were pregnant at one point. Of these, half were not married and some had had two or more children by different men. Combat readiness? I admitted that we had come a long way since 1977, but we had to learn from these initial mistakes and prepare a meaningful plan to use women in a wider variety of billets. You can't just push a button to do this—or issue an order. I assured him I would give it my closest attention and we would do a thorough analysis. I promised to keep him posted on our progress. He accepted my assurances, and we did indeed study the matter very carefully. Brigadier General Tony Lukeman's study team beat the issue almost to death. We made some progress but no breakthroughs.

DACOWITS (Defense Advisory Committee on Women in the Service) is a blue ribbon panel sponsored by DOD that uses college presidents, judges, prominent feminists of all ilks, and non-military women of distinction to advise SecDef on policy for women in the military. These patriotic ladies are sincere and well intended, but generally they are not service wise, have never heard a shot fired in anger or fired one, and largely follow the feminists' agenda. Their premise has been: "The military is suppressing opportunities for women. Anything a man can do I can do better, or at least as well." As a somewhat old-fashioned southern-gentleman type of guy, I have never subscribed to the proposition that we must have women defend this nation by killing its enemies. Nor do I believe that they should serve in the combat arms of our military organizations simply to ensure that they could be promoted to the highest military ranks.

This panel invited me, as the Director of Marine Corps Manpower, to address it on several occasions. I told them a lot of war stories, thanked them for their interest, and pointed out what I honestly considered to be the limits of and major problems in the mixing of the sexes. They always gave me rousing applause and invited me back, but called me "the bloody general." I suppose I was and still am.

In 1982–83, we held the line on the number of women, but we opened up many meaningful billets to them. A year or so later, I was president of the first brigadier general selection board to select a woman Marine, Colonel Gail Reals. Gail was a remarkably competent lady. Unfortunately, she left the Corps embittered that she had not been promoted to the grade of major general a few years later.

Subsequently, a lady Marine, Lieutenant General Carol Mutter, another remarkable individual, served in my old job as Director of Manpower for two years starting in July of 1996.

The Director of Manpower makes a point

As for the war on drugs, we first had to solve the Navy's technical problems to ensure quality control and reliability of drug tests. These tests would be challenged in court, and we wanted them to be challenge-proof.

Then we got our zero-tolerance program under way. Its fundamental principle is that drug use is unacceptable and will not be tolerated. If you want to lose your rank and your job, maybe serve time in prison, and destroy your family, just use drugs. The Marine Corps will not tolerate anyone who attempts to destroy our "Band of Brothers." For officers, it's one strike and you're out; for senior NCO'S, the same. Younger troops, depending on their past record, may get a second chance. We're not in the rehab business. If you have a problem, you're gone. This may sound cruel, but we had to clean the boards and move on. We ran random surveys to determine the level of use before the program began, and continued these later to weigh our effectiveness. While these surveys all had their plus and minus factors, they were extremely useful. Our troops clearly wanted a

227

hard-nosed, consistent, aggressive drug program. We gave them one, and it's been a much better Corps since then.

I had been told my job was a two-year stint, after which I could expect to retire. It was late spring and I was one year into this final tour of duty when the not-very-surprising word leaked out that P.X. Kelly had been approved by the White House to relieve General Barrow as Commandant on July 1, 1983. Shortly after that, General Barrow buzzed me and asked me to step into his office.

Bob Barrow had a low-key sense of humor, and he hated to suppress good news. So when I entered his office he had a broad grin on his face, and had P.X. Kelley standing beside him. He said he had a proposition for me—but he wanted me to consult my wife before I gave him my decision. He knew very well that he had told me I'd stay in my job for two years, but something had come up. He didn't know whether or not I would want to accept it. He droned on and on about it, trying to string out this mystery as long as he could. By this time I had correctly surmised that I wasn't going to be Director of Manpower much longer. Finally, he said it. "I'd like to send you and Carol out to Hawaii early in June to relieve J.K. Davis and Jane. Do you think Carol will go along with this?" I was going to become Commanding General, Fleet Marine Force, Pacific, and Commander of Marine Corps Bases, Pacific. I'd be commanding two thirds of the fighting Marine Corps! He added, "This would be for another two years, of course. P.X. wants to bring J.K. in as his Assistant Commandant so as to have an aviator in that job, and you're my first choice to relieve him. What do you think? Want to talk it over with Carol first?" After assuring him my bride would not have any problem packing out for Hawaii, I gave my least impressive response ever, just "Thanks again, Sir, for your confidence. I'm speechless!"

Before we departed, Bob Barrow bestowed on me one of the greatest honors of my career. He sent me in his place to speak at the Naval Academy graduation and to commission the 150-plus new Marine officers in the graduating class. Carol and I flew over to Annapolis with Secretary Lehman, Chief of Naval Operations Admiral Jim Watkins, and their wives in a Navy helicopter. I spoke briefly but emotionally on a brilliant sunny day in late May 1983, 33 years after I had graduated. Then I had a grip contest with the entire graduating class, including the women, whose grips were almost as firm as those of the men.

Two days later, we flew to Seattle to enjoy a short visit with my daughter's family before heading to Honolulu. My headquarters would be at Camp Smith, a WWII Naval hospital converted into a joint headquarters for my command and that of the Commander in Chief, Pacific, who at that time was Admiral Robert Long. Admiral Bob Foley was the Pacific Fleet Commander and would be my immediate operational commander. I would have the Marine Corps' top field command, spread throughout the Pacific and the West Coast. One final tour with my "Band of Brothers"!

Chapter 29

CG, Fleet Marine Forces, Pacific
"A Dream Come True . . . 'When Do You Make Admiral, Son?'"

As we flew out of Seattle headed for Honolulu, thoughts about the next two years raced through my mind. This was indeed my magic moment. I'd aspired to reach the upper tiers of command in the Corps so that I could make good things happen and here I was.

My principal command goal, throughout my career, at every level, had been to encourage the bonding of Marines in the unselfish pursuit of excellence. I aimed to create the glue in peacetime that would hold units together under the most adverse circumstances in combat. This bonding is certainly not unique to the Marine Corps, but we have taken both personal and unit pride to a higher level than our sister services. To be a Marine, no matter what specialty, was and always will be something special. Encouraging this bonding under the "Band of Brothers" philosophy was to become my top priority. It was the culmination of my career—with its Korean War genesis in which I first experienced so vividly the brotherhood of men in battle.

In 1983, a major goal of the Reagan administration's cold war strategy was to ensure that our Department of Defense had whatever resources it needed to establish absolute superiority over the Soviets. This meant new weapons, greater readiness, increased strategic mobility, and top-quality people for the all-volunteer force. It was a good time to be serving our nation. Ronald Reagan was good for morale: he made us proud to be Americans.

One of my pleasant chores would be to oversee the introduction of new aircraft such as the F-18 fighter-bomber and the CH-53E heavy-lift helicopter, as well as the operational development of the new Maritime Prepositioning Concept. To improve strategic mobility and shorten response times in the most likely areas (Korea and the Middle East), we would now use huge air-conditioned cargo ships as mobile warehouses that contained a full brigade's set of weapons, heavy equipment, and all the supplies 16,000 Marines would need to fight for 60 days. Marrying up these ships and their stores with airlifted troops from the US at a protected port or airfield was an ability we had to perfect in short order. We worked hard and learned a lot. The concept later proved itself in the Persian Gulf War. It has now been expanded to include major Army units as well as Marines.

General Barrow's program to increase the number and types of accompanied tours in the Far East was also of major importance. We ironed out the last of our differences with our Air Force brethren. A Marine family tour in the Far East in comfortable circumstances was no longer an idle dream. The principal commanders and staffs could now serve multi-year tours with their families. Our infantry battalions and aircraft squadrons would rotate every six months, markedly improving efficiency and continuity of command.

I was fortunate to have extremely able people assisting me, from top to bottom. My first deputy commander was Major General Joseph Went, an aviator, logistician, fiscal manager, and all-around problem solver. He was as smart as he was personable. He later rose to four-star rank and served as Assistant Commandant of the Marine Corps.

My Force Sergeant Major, Lee Bradley, had served with me twice before. He was an impressive, intelligent, articulate man, and proved to be of inestimable value to the entire command. A black Marine who looked as if he had just stepped out of a recruiting poster, he was my constant companion, at home and on the road.

Sergeant Major Lee Bradley

A third indispensable player was my chief of staff, Colonel Jarvis Lynch, whom I had known since his second lieutenant days. Quick, decisive, and cerebral, he was to become my alter ego. He was selected for promotion to brigadier general just before I retired, a tribute to his talent and sterling record.

Because I commanded units from the Indian Ocean to our West Coast, I spent at least a third of my time traveling to visit these forces. One of our major commitments was to reinforce US forces in Korea. The South Koreans needed continued assurances that we were ready and willing to act. Admiral Crowe, the new CINCPAC, encouraged me to make frequent visits to assure them of the readiness of Marine air and ground forces to come to their aid. Our major bases were in Japan, of course, and the subject of flying combat missions from Japan was a very delicate matter. He also urged us to maintain close professional relationships with all of the services of the Japanese Self-Defense Force. They greatly respected the US Marine Corps and chose to emulate our combined arms training techniques. The improvement of their operational abilities was very much in our national interest.

I was impressed by the high state of readiness of both American and South Korean forces on my first visit to that country. The South Koreans knew of my service as an infantry lieutenant in our Fifth Marines during the Korean War, and always acknowledged it most respectfully when I visited. During my first visit, when I was inspecting our US front-line forces along the demilitarized zone, I landed, briefly, on the hill where I was seriously wounded in 1951. Hill 907 overlooks the "Punchbowl," the scene of much heavy fighting later in the Korean War. From atop Hill 907 you look directly across the DMZ into North Korea.

South Korea has become a major industrialized nation, but it will always have the same constant national nervousness that the Israelis have—a result of being right next to heavily armed neighbors who are dedicated to their demise. This omnipresent threat from an unstable North Korea means that the South Koreans must struggle to balance a fledgling western-style democracy with constant wartime military readiness.

Both the Army and Air Force had three-star headquarters on the island of Oahu. The Navy, of course, with its fleet commander, Admiral Bob Foley, and the CINC, Admiral Bill Crowe, was the dominant service. I worked directly for both Admirals. It may have

230

confused them at times, but it never bothered me. This dual role has now been clarified in both the Atlantic and Pacific. Marines will always be closely tied to the Navy, but now the Commander of Marine Forces reports directly to the Commander in Chief, Pacific, an important difference.

Admiral Bill Crowe was an interesting man to work for. He understood and functioned well in the game of international geopolitics. President Reagan eventually appointed him Chairman of the Joint Chiefs of Staff, principally because of these skills. He came to the President's attention when he presided over a series of special briefings all of the services gave to the President and his party during their stopover en route to China. Erudite and politically astute, he was a key actor in the unseating and subsequent removal from office of Philippine President Ferdinand Marcos.

He and I shared a love of tennis and often played doubles when our two schedules allowed. It rained so often at our Camp Smith joint headquarters that the tennis courts were constructed of crushed lava rock, complete with tiny drainage holes. We laughed about our "all-weather tennis courts," and we often played in the rain. He had a Marine officer son and I had a Navy officer son: we consoled and counseled each other.

Life in Hawaii can be very pleasant. We enjoyed nostalgic memories of our younger days when I was a captain in the Fourth Marines from 1956 to 1958. The First Marine Brigade was still at the Marine Corps Air Station, Kaneohe, on the other side of the island of Oahu.

Family visited to help us celebrate both of our Hawaiian Christmases during this tour. For the last Christmas, 1984, both of our widowed mothers and our two children and their families were with us. It was a special, once-in-a-lifetime occasion. We invited my mother to come early, so that we could have some private time with her. She was 83 years old and, although generally alert mentally, had been slipping somewhat after several mini-strokes. Despite my 39 years' service in the military, my dear Mom never made any pretense of understanding what it was all about.

The night before the rest of our family was due to arrive, my wife and I took Mom out to dinner at the Outrigger Canoe Club, a delightful establishment on Waikiki Beach where we enjoyed honorary membership. It was a storybook evening, with roving musicians, wonderful seafood, sea breezes, and a beautiful moon. After dinner, Mom reached over and placed her hand on mine. She said, "Son, I'm so proud of you. You've been so successful in your Marine career. You've survived so much danger. You and Carol raised two wonderful kids and they're both doing so well with their families. I have so much to be thankful for, but I have just one question." I said, "Sure, Mom, what is it?" She looked me right in the eye and said, "When are you going to make admiral?"

I usually tell that story only to my Naval Academy Classmates. For some reason, they seem to get a special kick out of it. God bless her! She's gone now, but she just thought that admiral had to be the highest thing in the world, next to President.

We finished our Marine Corps careers, my wonderful wife and I, on July 31, 1985. It was 39 years to the day after I had taken the oath as a Midshipman in 1946. My successor was a close friend and associate, Lieutenant General D'Wayne Gray. We stood on the tarmac at the Marine Corps Air Station that day for the ceremony that ended my career. It ran exactly 60 minutes, consisted only of marching units, and was perfectly orchestrated by a young lieutenant colonel operations officer for the First Marine Brigade. His name was

Charles Krulak. He later was to become Commandant of the Marine Corps. We all said he had promise.

Many people have asked me over the years since I retired if I miss the Corps, miss being in charge, miss the responsibility. I always answer that of course I do, but I have refused to look back, to express any regrets, until this book. I ran that train to the end of the line—until it wouldn't go any farther—then I got off to let someone else back it up. Being a U.S. Marine for more than 35 years was the greatest experience a kid from Clarksdale, Mississippi, could possibly have had.

Many of my friends and associates have encouraged me to conclude this book with some pointed judgments, about combat experiences in two wars or significant trends in the Corps during my 35+ years. Although I appreciate that advice, I will decline. My goal has been to tell the story of a young Southerner who chose to serve his country in the US Marine Corps, his adventures, problems, and successes in an exciting and rewarding life, possibly to motivate young officers to choose a similar path themselves. Hence, Cheers and Tears. Just an old Marine's story. I hope you have enjoyed it. Semper Fi!

"Cheers without tears!" Carol and Charlie

232